IT WAS A raucous time of duels with words and swords, the fifty-year period between the War of 1812 and the Civil War called the Age of Jackson. It was, in its own special way, a time of revolution. People weren't killing each other, and mobs didn't riot in the streets. But enormous changes were shaking and transforming America. And a generation of political geniuses appeared, to wrestle with the nation's prospects and with each other. The men? Andrew Jackson. Daniel Webster. Henry Clay. John C. Calhoun. Martin Van Buren. And the issues? How to make America truly democratic. How to hold the Union together, when slavery was threatening to tear it apart. What to do with the Indians, who seemed to many to stand in the way of America's westward "destiny." And—probably most important to us today—how to solve the fierce power struggle between the President and the Congress.

The revolutionary Age of Andrew Jackson changed much of America's way of life. It established the nation's basic political practices and patterns. It stands at the beginning of the modern America we have inherited.

THE
REVOLUTIONARY

COLLECTION OF THE BOATMEN'S NATIONAL BANK OF ST. LOUIS.

AGE OF
ANDREW JACKSON

Robert V. Remini

 PERENNIAL LIBRARY

Harper & Row, Publishers
New York, Cambridge, Philadelphia, San Francisco
London, Mexico City, São Paulo, Singapore, Sydney

(title page) The Verdict of the People, by George Caleb Bingham, shows how the American people, in ever-increasing numbers, were creating a democracy during the Jacksonian period. Here they express their will via the ballot box on election day in a little Missouri town. The clerk, left, reads the results from the courthouse steps.

Photo credits appear following page 202.

A hardcover edition of this book was published by Harper & Row, Publishers, Inc.

THE REVOLUTIONARY AGE OF ANDREW JACKSON. Copyright © 1976 by Robert V. Remini. All rights reserved. Printed in the United States of America. No part of this book may be used or reproduced in any manner whatsoever without written permission except in the case of brief quotations embodied in critical articles and reviews. For information address Harper & Row, Publishers, Inc., 10 East 53rd Street, New York, N.Y. 10022. Published simultaneously in Canada by Fitzhenry & Whiteside Limited, Toronto.

First PERENNIAL LIBRARY edition published 1985.

Designer: Joyce Hopkins

Library of Congress Cataloging in Publication Data

Remini, Robert Vincent, 1921–
    The revolutionary age of Andrew Jackson.

    Reprint. Originally published: New York : Harper & Row, c1976.
    Bibliography: p.
    Includes index.
    1. United States—Politics and government—1829–1837. 2. Jackson, Andrew,
1767–1845. I. Title. [E381.R42 1985]   973.5′6′0924 [B]   85-42588
ISBN 0-06-091290-1 (pbk.)

85 86 87 88 89 MPC 10 9 8 7 6 5 4 3 2 1

For Joan

CONTENTS

BOOK III
THE GROWTH OF PRESIDENTIAL POWER

List of Illustrations

Acknowledgments

THIS BOOK IS based on extensive reading of manuscripts and other documents of the Age of Jackson, particularly private letters by the major figures, speeches in Congress, presidential papers and messages, and other official and unofficial sources. Many conversations reproduced here, especially those involving Jackson, are taken from James Parton, *The Life of Andrew Jackson* (New York, 1860). Others come from Martin Van Buren's *Autobiography* (Washington, 1920) and Thomas Hart Benton's memoir of his career in the Senate, *Thirty Years' View* (New York, 1865). The description of Jackson's inauguration is largely based on the letters of Margaret Bayard Smith, the wife of a Maryland Senator: *The First Forty Years of Washington Society Portrayed by the Family Letters of Mrs. Samuel Harrison Smith,* edited by Gaillard Hunt (New York, 1906).

Contemporary narratives by travelers and foreign visitors have been quoted extensively since many of them met the principal figures of the period and described their impressions. They also traveled around the country and talked with Americans from every social and economic class. Two Englishwomen, in particular, provide extraordinary insights into American life and character. Sometimes they are devastatingly critical. Harriet Martineau, who wrote *Society in America* (New York, 1837) and dined in the White House, rather liked Henry Clay but thought John C. Calhoun a "cast-iron man." Frances Trollope, who wrote *Domestic Manners of the Americans* (London, 1832), thought rather poorly of American manners.

Other colorful descriptions of American life in the 1830s from which I have quoted are: Michel Chevalier, *Society, Manners, and Politics in the United States* (Boston, 1839); Captain Frederick Marryat, *A Diary in America* (London, 1839); J.S. Buckingham, *America* (London, 1841); Thomas Hamilton, *Men and Manners in America* (Philadelphia, 1833); and Alexis de Tocqueville, *Democracy in America* (New York, 1835).

Now that I've duly acknowledged my obligations to Jackson, his friends and enemies, and other writers of the period for supplying many of the ideas and words that form the core of this book, I should like to express a more immediate and personal obligation to several people who share whatever merit this book contains. First, Sam B. Smith and Harriet C. Owsley, editor and associate editor of "The Papers of Andrew Jackson," a project located at the Hermitage in Tennessee to publish all the important documents relating to Jackson's life. Over the years they have provided me enormous personal and professional support as we strove together to uncover every last scrap of Jackson material, wherever it might be, both here and abroad. The Ladies' Hermitage Association, charged with the responsibility of maintaining the Hermitage mansion and grounds, has shown extraordinary wisdom and imagination in recognizing their charge not only to preserve the physical remains of Jackson's life but his place and importance in American history. Both directly and indirectly the Association has advanced Jacksonian scholarship in countless ways, the latest being its unstinting support of the publication of the Jackson papers.

I owe a special and deep debt of gratitude to Elaine Edelman, a truly great editor, who originally invited me to write this book and then prodded me to make it worthy of the people who crowd these pages. In this final version of the manuscript there are deep traces of her editorial skill and personal commitment, and I am proud to acknowledge her unique and valuable contributions.

Finally, my daughter Joan also wanted me to write this book, and for all kinds of good reasons it is now hers.

Robert V. Remini
April 1975
Wilmette, Illinois

THE REVOLUTIONARY
AGE OF
ANDREW JACKSON

BOOK I
A NEW AGE

1

A Changing Society

THE NATION WAS in the midst of a profound revolution when Andrew Jackson entered the White House on March 4, 1829, as the seventh President of the United States. It was not a violent revolution. People weren't killing one another. No mobs rioted through the streets to vent their rage. Nevertheless, momentous changes were occurring throughout the country, changes that transformed American society and government. Indeed it is not an exaggeration to say that many of the characteristics commonly thought of today as being typically American developed during this "revolutionary" era.

Historians call it the Age of Jackson and think of it as the period in American history roughly bridging the years from the end of the War of 1812 to the coming of the Civil War. But whatever the title and however it is called, it was an age of change, an age of innovation, an age of reform.

The United States was only forty years old at the time of Jackson's election to the presidency. When the nation began in 1789 as a republic under the Constitution, it had a small population of a few million people occupying thirteen states strung along the Atlantic seaboard. Its society had been confined, huddled along the coastline for more than a hundred and fifty years, since colonization first began. The Appalachian Mountains served as a barrier to the west, but also provided protection against the terrors of the vast wilderness that stretched beyond. During the entire colonial period of American history, settlers had hardly moved more than a few hundred miles inland from the Atlantic shore. Most colonists were farmers and lived in small communities in which there was close contact. The ties of family, church, and community were strong and produced a sense of security and belonging. It was a closely knit society and relatively stable. Some even thought there was overcrowding!

With the conclusion of the American Revolution, a genuine westward movement began. Then, starting early in the nineteenth century, the country burst its narrow confines. Within a few decades the nation was converted from an insulated, agrarian society squeezed between ocean and mountains into a dynamic, industrial society sprawled across a three-thousand-mile continent. Gone were the old ties of family, church, and community; gone, too, was the security they provided. A people so long hemmed in by a mountain chain scrambled over it and raced across the fertile valleys on the other side, reaching the Mississippi and fording it, clearing the land and creating new states in the process. It had taken nearly two centuries for Americans to occupy a ribbon of land hardly more than a hundred miles in width. During the next sixty years, they would go the rest of the distance across the continent to the Pacific Ocean, nearly three thousand miles. A tiny rural nation struggling to maintain its existence became a continental power whose future greatness was now assured.

In the forty years from the adoption of the Constitution to the inauguration of President Jackson, the thirteen states had grown to twenty-four. In the South and Southwest, Alabama, Mississippi, Louisiana, Tennessee, Kentucky, and Missouri had been added to the Union. Farther north, Maine, Ohio, Indiana, and Illinois had achieved statehood. The admission of Missouri during the 1820s was particularly significant. Not only did it provoke an open controversy over slavery (which was resolved by the Missouri Compromise that retained a balance in the Union between free and slave states), but Missouri was the first state that lay totally west of the Mississippi River to enter the Union. It marked a great stride in westward expansion.

But geographical expansion was not the only change produced in this "revolutionary" age. There were social, psychological, economic, and political changes that influenced the history not only of the United States but of the entire western world.

American society itself had changed. It was different. Everyone could see that. "Our age is wholey [*sic*] of a different character from the past," said Senator Daniel Webster of Massachusetts. "Society is full of excitement." Foreign visitors instantly noticed this excitement when they talked with people. The spirit was contagious. It was a spirit of "Go ahead." "The whole continent presents a scene of *scrambling* and roars with greedy hurry," observed an Englishman. "Go ahead! is the order of the day."

More than that. "*Go ahead* is the real motto of the country," commented most foreigners who analyzed the mood of America during the Jacksonian age. But precisely what did that mean?—"Go ahead." For individuals it meant the consuming need to make money. There was a restless, driving desire to be better off, and this was the ambition of all classes of society, none excepted. "No man in America is contented to be poor, or expects to continue so," stated one magazine of the time. Americans believed that in Europe children were lucky if they could maintain the station and income of their parents. Lucky if they did not slide to a lower social and financial condition. Not so in America. In America it was expected that children would improve their station, make more money than their parents, get a higher-paying job, find a better life. That's what "go ahead" was all about.

So the sons took off. They vaulted over the mountains seeking to satisfy their ambitious yearning in the west. They wanted something better than a slice of a small inheritance, and they believed they could find it away from home. Some were hardly into their teenage years when they bid farewell to their families to search for that better life. There was only one way to describe them. Restless, searching, driving. By the time of Jackson's inauguration in 1828 it was the prevailing mood of the country.

For instance, way out "west," Chicago—a tiny settlement just getting started on the high prairie above the shore of Lake Michigan—crawled with people. And the buying and selling! the land speculation! the agitation and activity! It stunned every person who visited the town. The land speculation was especially amazing. The times and places of land sales were announced by a black man, dressed all in scarlet and carrying an enormous scarlet flag, sitting astride a snow-white horse: Lord, they said, he was beautiful to see. At every street corner where he stopped to sing out his announcement, a crowd of people flocked around him.

This land mania infected everyone. New arrivals to Chicago were propositioned constantly. As they walked down the streets, storekeepers hailed them from their doors. "Hey! You want to buy a farm?" they shouted.

One young lawyer in Chicago claimed he realized five hundred dollars a day by merely making out titles to land. Another said he realized within two years—two years, mind you—"*ten times* as much money as he had before fixed upon as a competence for life."

But there was a price—a high price—Americans paid for "go ahead." They no longer had the security of a tightly integrated society in which all persons had a place and knew their responsibilities and what was expected of them. In the past everybody had belonged; all were important to each other and to society as a whole. Individuals, no matter what they did for a living or what their social position, had the comforting knowledge that they were needed and wanted. And this strong sense of belonging and participation was buttressed by powerful links of family, of community responsibility, and of church membership. But "go ahead" changed all that. With men and women on the move, scrambling to achieve material success, they had no time for the needs of others. Their responsibility was to themselves and their own goals. Never mind the neighbors. Let neighbors keep their distance and mind their own business. The needs of the community in maintaining a stable society were problems for "others" to bother about—whoever those others might be. Besides, in what now became a constant moving from place to place, few people had a real attachment to any one community. Not like the old days, when families lived for generations in a particular town. Now one was almost expected to keep moving geographically if he hoped to "go ahead" financially. And with sons breaking free from the family at an early age to seek their futures and fortunes, and girls marrying in their teens and taking off with their ambitious husbands, the strong ties of family as an important component in American society were gravely weakened. Families dispersed so quickly that the sense of belonging that characterized colonial life vanished.

This left a terrible void. And to some extent the social history of Americans during the first half of the nineteenth century is the history of the search for something to fill that void. If they no longer had family or community or membership in a particular church to give them security, they needed something else to fill their lives and give them meaning and purpose. In time most of them found it in work—the hard, persistent application of their talents and strengths to achieve their ambitions. Americans had always believed in work. It was part of their Puritan past, but now it had an urgency that foreigners instantly detected the moment they set foot on this continent. It pulsed throughout society. One foreigner claimed that the first command of American society was to "Work!" And no excuses. "Work," he wrote, and "at eighteen you shall get . . . more than a captain in Europe. You shall live in plenty, be well clothed, well housed, and able to save." Everything else followed from this command. "Be attentive to your work, be sober and religious, and you will find a devoted and submissive wife; you will have a more comfortable home than many of the higher classes in Europe. . . . Work, and if the fortunes of business should be against you and you fail, you shall soon be able to rise again, for a failure is nothing but a wound in battle."

Thus the first article of the American faith was simply this: Keep your nose to the grindstone, lead a clean and sober life, and you cannot fail. And what was the reward? Money. Money and those creature comforts that make life more bearable. It also brought social standing, recognition that one was engaged in useful pursuits, a judgment from society that one's life was a "success."

Following this Puritan work ethic, a young man of the Age of Jackson began earning a living by the time he was fifteen. By twenty-one he was expected to be established, to have his own office or workshop or farm or whatever it was that constituted his "living." And by twenty-one a man was expected to be married. Indeed, if he was not established and not married by twenty-one, society judged him peculiar and no-account. "He who is an active and useful member of society," wrote one visitor, "who contributes his share to augment the national wealth and increase the numbers of the population, he only is looked upon with respect and favor."

Women's duties were rigidly fixed from the moment of their birth. They were expected to be wives and mothers. They were expected to be submissive—first to father, then husband—loving, gentle, and domestic. Interestingly, at the very moment the family condition was weakened, Americans exalted marriage and regarded the tie between husband and wife as the central moral bulwark of society. At the same

7

time women enjoyed precious few "rights," they were placed on a pedestal and revered for their "piety" and "purity"—in short, they were commissioned the moral guardians of the human race. It was in the Jacksonian era that the exaggerated, if not distorted, views of women as to their gentleness, frailty, piety, morality, and purity developed. During this period the pronounced male affection for his mother— "Momism"—is first observed. And the higher woman rose on her pedestal, the more she lost ground in attempting to gain equality with males.

But whether one was male or female, the habits and tone of American life as established in the early nineteenth century were those of an "exclusively working people." From the moment Americans got up in the morning they were hard at work and continued at it until bedtime. Rarely did they permit pleasure to distract them. Only public affairs or politics had the right to claim their time for a few minutes. And only on Sunday did Americans refrain from business, not only because of the strictures of organized religion but because it supposedly proved them God-fearing and therefore sober and clean-living. "The American of the North and Northwest," wrote one observer, "whose character now sets the tone in the United States is permanently a man of business."

According to Europeans, American men even looked as if they were built for work, as if work were God's intended objective "when He fashioned the American." Tall, slender, lithe, he had "no equal" in promptly responding to the demands of business, whatever those demands might be. This Yankee type had a hawkish look about him that bespoke shrewdness and cunning. Though gangling, rawboned, and sinewy, he was a clear-eyed, sharp-witted, practical man of affairs with educated instincts to search out the sources of wealth.

As Americans succeeded in improving their own individual economic lot, they necessarily advanced the well-being of the country. They fanned out across the continent, clearing land, planting, harvesting, searching all the avenues leading to personal prosperity. They galvanized the economy and raised the standard of living.

There was a noticeable jump in the standard of living during the first half of the nineteenth century. During the long colonial period the standard of living had remained relatively stable and relatively low. Then, with the building of a free, independent domestic economy, the standard of living for most white Americans rose sharply.

Building a free, independent economy was important in the

8

revolutionary changes that occurred in America during the Age of Jackson. But it took time. When the nation first won its independence its economy was based almost exclusively on international trade. But during the final years of the War of 1812 much of the nation's coastline was blockaded. Its ships could not get in or out of its harbors. Consequently the country had to look to its own resources and not rely on trade with Europe. It was forced to build its own internal economy. So capital investments went into industry and manufactures, instead of shipping. Manufactures, especially textile products, multiplied rapidly. Although industrial expansion was the most dramatic, agriculture—the main preoccupation of most Americans—also increased its productivity.

Thus, the War of 1812 compelled the United States to take a new direction into rapid industrial development. The factory system, which had already begun in Great Britain, was introduced when plans of a newly invented textile machine were secreted into the United States. And because of the great natural resources in the country, like coal, iron and water power, and because of the increasing labor supply provided through immigration, the Industrial Revolution quickly established itself in America.

What happened in Lowell, Massachusetts, is a good example. Lowell was a quiet, pleasant little New England town situated at the confluence of the Concord and Merrimack Rivers. Most of its inhabitants were farmers. But with the coming of the Industrial Revolution to Lowell in 1820, because of the easy access to water power, the town became a booming manufacturing center. By the late 1820s there were a variety of factories in Lowell: flour mills, glass works and machine manufacturers, iron and copper works, foundries and shoe factories. But the principal industry in the town was its textile mills. Once it was fully mechanized Lowell manufactured upwards of fifty-two million yards of cotton cloth a year. By the use of man-made canals the waterpower generated was sufficient to operate 286,000 spindles.

But the industrialization of America was not simply the product of hundreds of factories turning out useful manufactures. There was also a "Transportation Revolution." Again it was the War of 1812 that set the revolution in motion. For the war reminded Americans of the perpetual danger of invasion by British troops from Canada. The need to move troops rapidly to repel invasion produced a demand for improved transportation and soon the nation engaged in a gigantic program of building roads, bridges, highways, turnpikes and canals. Improved transportation and communication were first seen as essential to the nation's safety, but they also stimulated commerce and industry.

The individual states led the way in this feverish rush to construct public works. The Pennsylvania Turnpike stretched from Philadelphia to Lancaster and the Wilderness Road cut across Virginia into Kentucky. The great National Road, begun in 1811 from Cumberland, Maryland, steadily inched its way westward nine hundred miles to Vandalia, Illinois, in 1838. New York began the mighty Erie Canal in 1817; completed eight years later, it linked the Hudson River to Lake Erie in a 363-mile stretch that permitted water transportation from the Atlantic Ocean to the Great Lakes. This canal made Ohio, Michigan, Indiana, and Illinois accessible to the thousands of European immigrants who soon came flooding through the port of New York. The value of land and of personal property in New York City rose sixty percent in five years and the Canal itself earned nearly a million dollars annually. The activity generated by the Canal enormously enhanced the wealth, population, and power of New York. It became the Empire State. Its immediate and visible success prompted other states to imitate this colossal feat, and during the 1820s a mania of canal building swept the country. In Pennsylvania a canal system linked Philadelphia with Pittsburgh. Cleveland on Lake Erie was joined to Portsmouth on the Ohio River by canal. And the building of the Illinois and Michigan Canal in the late 1830s and 1840s made it possible to travel by water from Lake Michigan to the Illinois River and from there to the Mississippi River. When the War of 1812 had ended there had been less than a hundred miles of canals in the United States. Twenty-five years later there were well over three thousand miles.

Better and quicker transportation aided this generation of hustling Americans to drive faster and deeper into the continent. Moving goods, supplies, manufactured articles, and agricultural staples from one section of the country to another was important in developing a free, independent domestic economy.

Still, canals and roads and bridges and turnpikes paled in significance when compared to the railroads. The railroads, which began to be built late in the 1820s, were absolutely central to industrializing America. Not only did they quicken travel and westward expansion across the continent—burrowing through, around, and over mountains—but they created new communities and, with them, additional markets. Wher-

10

ever the railroad stopped, or changed direction, or intersected with other forms of transportation, a town or city sprang up. Railroads became lifelines stringing communities of people together over thousands of miles, from the Atlantic coast to the Great Plains beyond the Mississippi River and eventually reaching the Pacific coast. They were the nation's arteries, providing a constant flow of people and commodities from city to town to remote rural community and pumping economic life to all the areas they served. Furthermore, the railroads attracted financial capital in the form of investments from foreigners as well as Americans who sensed the opportunity to make an economic killing. Investors found railroads irresistible. They were drawn by the prospect of enormous profits, particularly after the federal government lavished the roads with land grants and other subsidies to encourage their growth. Within a few decades a stupendous amount of money was generated, much of it squandered, much of it badly used, much of it siphoned off by swindlers. But enough remained to build a nation. It was the coming of the railroad to Chicago, for example, that catapulted that hustling lakeside community of land jobbers into a roaring metropolis of merchant princes, the hub city of the entire West.

The first railroad in the United States was built in Massachusetts in 1828. But the important history of railroading really began the next year with the construction of the Baltimore and Ohio Railroad. Symbolically, the man who lifted the first spadeful of dirt to start that construction was Charles Carroll of Carrollton, the last surviving signer of the Declaration of Independence. To some observers it seemed appropriate that a man who had signed the document that brought forth an independent nation should also, by the action of a shovel, signal the beginning of a modern, industrial society for that nation. Within two years the B & O consisted of thirteen miles of road; but within another six years over one thousand miles of track stretched across eleven states.

The speed and ease with which Americans accepted and adopted modern industrial tools won the admiration of foreign visitors. It explained how a society was revolutionized. The American, said one foreigner, was remarkable in his ability to adjust himself—and anything else for that matter—to the demands of business. "No one else can conform so easily to new situations and circumstances; he is always ready to adopt new processes and implements or to change his occupation. Where in Europe young men write poems or novels, in America,

The "Transportation Revolution" began symbolically with the opening of the Erie Canal in 1825. New York's Governor DeWitt Clinton poured a barrel of Lake Erie water into the Atlantic Ocean, in what was called the "marriage of waters." The Canal cut the cost of transporting a ton of goods from Buffalo to New York from $100 to $15.

especially Massachusetts and Connecticut, they invent machines and tools." The American "is a mechanic by nature." He prizes gadgets and tools which make life more agreeable.

It was extraordinary how many important tools and gadgets were invented during this Jacksonian age! Many raised the standard of living. Some changed society and the economy. Even so-called minor inventions altered social life. For example, the invention of a special bit permitted cutting ice so that large chunks could be shipped without melting and then brought into city homes. Having ice for refrigeration meant that people could congregate in cities where, unable to produce their own food, they could still enjoy fresh food almost anytime they wanted. This ability to store food was vital to the growth of American cities.

At this time, too, the process of canning foods was developed, an invention that had a most profound impact on the eating habits of the American family. "Opening a can" to prepare lunch or dinner became a way of life for some. Americans, by and large, are not gourmets and never were—we are a nation of hamburger and hot-dog eaters—so the can made it very easy to dispense with all the preparation needed for fixing meals. It left more time for work.

Americans proved how inventive and adaptable they were in other ways. For instance, when oil was discovered in Pennsylvania, there seemed to be no apparent use for it except as a base for "snake oil" in medicine shows. But some "go-ahead" Americans used their ingenuity to create a market for it by developing a special lamp—a kerosene lamp—to burn the oil, and then trumpeted it around the country as an inexpensive and efficient source of illumination for the home. With that, a new business—indeed several new businesses—were off and running. But what was so "typically American" about all this was the way the opportunity was handled. Here was a product of little apparent use and with no market. Americans created the market. They came up with a gadget to burn the oil and then successfully peddled it with a massive advertising campaign.

Also during this age there were some spectacular inventions: the mechanical reaper for harvesting grain, invented by Cyrus H. McCormick in 1831; Charles Goodyear's process of vulcanizing rubber in 1839; Samuel F.B. Morse's telegraph in 1844; Samuel Colt's revolver in 1835; and Elias Howe's sewing machine in 1846. These were only the most important. Anaesthesia, discovered by a dentist named William T.G. Morton in 1842—the discovery was also claimed by at least three other men—was one of the most valuable and important discoveries in the entire history of medicine.

What made these inventions so spectacular was that they revolutionized entire industries, created new industries, or developed new processes which advanced the industrialization of the nation. The new companies resulting from these inventions attracted additional capital into the country. New jobs were created. New markets found. By 1840 the country—especially the North and Northwest—was hurrying toward rapid industrialization. The country had begun converting from a rural and agricultural society to an urban and industrial one. There was a long way yet to go, but it was the beginning.

In the South the push toward industrialization was not so obvious, although some industrialization could be found. But even in that section there was enormous economic energy. The principal business was cotton, and eventually—that is, just prior to the Civil War—the South was growing two-thirds of the total world supply of cotton. The plantation system widely utilized in the South was based on black slavery. However morally indefensible, the system—in the opinion of some recent historians—was far more efficient and economical than the methods of farming pursued in the Northwest.

But whether North or South, East or West, the nation during the Age of Jackson throbbed and pulsed with energy. "Life consists in motion," wrote one visitor, and in the relentless need to be better off—to make it. When foreigners chided Americans about their pursuit of wealth, they were promptly corrected. Americans hotly denied that they valued wealth more than other people. They simply insisted that the pursuit of money in other countries, especially in Europe, was necessarily confined to a very small group of people—the privileged few, the upper class, the aristocracy—while in America it was open to all. Everyone should have the right to make money if he had the drive and desire to go after it. That's what freedom was all about. "In this country," wrote one commentator, "there are no established limits within which the hopes of any class of society must be confined as in other countries." Here children are expected to do better than their parents because here there is "equality of opportunity," which in turn has produced "universal ambition and restless activity."

When Jacksonians talked about equality they were not thinking in literal terms of everyone being equal. They realized that everyone was not equal—and maybe there was some advantage to that. Talents varied,

14

abilities differed. What they did believe and were committed to was the notion of equality of *opportunity*. Everyone should have the opportunity to make it, to get ahead, to achieve financial success. No one should have special privileges that work to the disadvantage of others. Thus, one of the functions of government was to see to it that the race for success was a fair contest. Government must serve as a referee among all classes in society and prevent any one from gaining an advantage over the others.

Privileges, or what Jacksonians called "artificial distinctions," that blocked equality of opportunity had to be removed by governmental action. And Americans were particularly conscious of political and economic privileges. Political privileges included the right to vote or hold office because of wealth or social standing. Restricting the right to vote to persons owning at least one hundred dollars worth of property had been the classic form of political privilege during the colonial era. But this practice started to fade rapidly as Americans dissolved their political ties to Great Britain and geographical ties to the Atlantic shoreline. As they moved westward Americans established local governments that did away with property qualifications, giving every white man over the age of twenty-one the right to vote and hold office. Consequently, when Western states such as Ohio, Indiana, Illinois, and Missouri applied for admission into the Union, their constitutions specifically guaranteed white manhood suffrage. In no time the influence of the West was felt in the East. Several of the older states whose constitutions had been written in the eighteenth century called new constitutional conventions in the 1820s and not only liberalized the franchise but democratized the entire political process. For example, though several state constitutions had originally provided that presidential electors be chosen by the state legislatures, the constitutional conventions of the 1820s abolished this practice and provided *popular* election of presidential electors.*

Economic privilege, on the other hand, took the form of monopolies or exclusive rights and franchises which granted advantages to some but denied them to others. These privileges were particularly hated because,

---

*The electoral system written into the Constitution provides for what is in fact indirect election of the President. Each state is allotted a number of electors equal to its number of representatives and senators in Congress. These electors are appointed as the states direct. In the beginning they were chosen by state legislatures, later by popular vote. Yet as late as 1860 electors in South Carolina were still chosen by the legislature.

granted by the government, whether state or national, they institutionalized inequality. When the Massachusetts legislature, for example, gave a charter to the Charles River Bridge Company to build the one and only bridge across the Charles River to connect Boston with Cambridge, and to charge a fee to anyone using the bridge, the people in the area protested. They wanted a free bridge. When a second company was proposed to satisfy the public clamor, the Charles River Bridge Company pointed to the clause in its charter which implied *exclusive* rights to the bridge business over the Charles. Eventually the entire matter landed in the United States Supreme Court, where the right of a state to grant exclusive privileges at the expense of community need and desire was struck down. Monopolies were so despised in this age committed to equality of opportunity that one writer went so far as to define liberty "as nothing more than the total absence of all MONOPOLIES of all kinds, whether of rank, wealth or privilege."

To most Americans, therefore, the elimination of privilege necessarily provided equality of opportunity. They regarded privilege as synonymous with "aristocracy," a term held in the highest contempt since the Revolution. Conversely, "democracy" was defined as the removal of every political and economic barrier blocking the progress of all citizens in their quest for personal freedom and material happiness. If this nation was to be truly democratic, editorialized the New York *Evening Post*, then there must come the end "of all privilege." Indeed, the writer continued, every democratic advance achieved in this country in the past had come as a result of "breaking down the privileges of a few."

The job of the government was clearly understood as assisting this process. Not that Americans wanted a government that constantly intruded on their lives and private affairs. Far from it. As a matter of fact one Washington newspaper published a brief motto over its masthead: "The World Is Governed Too Much." And this conviction was shared by many Americans. Most people seemed to feel the proper function of government was in the role of referee or honest broker. The government should see to it that no one group or class in society gained advantages over others, particularly government-granted advantages. Thus, monopolies had to be abolished and voting rights equalized. In the contest for the pursuit of happiness, the government had to make certain that the contest was a fair one. No one must have a head start as the result of government-granted preference.

When all is said and done, two basic qualities tell the most about Americans in this Jacksonian era. First, they were materialists. They were out to make it. They wanted money, and they wanted the security and social position it provided. "At the bottom of all that an American does," said a shrewd foreign commentator, "is money; beneath every word, money." Perhaps this was the substitute they found for all that had been lost from that earlier and simpler time when men were content to stay close to the place where they were born.

The second basic quality about these Americans was that they were champions of equality—that is, of course, for those who were white and male. Women did not need equality. They were up there on their pedestals shining forth beauty and goodness. To give them equality would demean their status in society. So the poor unfortunate female had no rights. She was chattel. She could not vote or hold office; her "right" to property was limited; she could not enter most professions; she could not make a will, sign a contract, or witness a deed without her father's or husband's consent; and her children could be taken from her if her husband so directed. Nor was there any concerted drive for equality for blacks or Indians on the part of most Americans. Women, blacks, and Indians just didn't enter the thinking of these people when they argued for equality.

To fault Americans of this period for failing to understand what the modern world means by equality is a pointless and futile exercise. But if they are examined on their own terms, with all their faults and limitations, they make an exciting bunch to watch as they changed their world and shaped so many things that became basic to the American system. Not all they attempted can be described here. The list is much too long. The efforts to achieve women's rights; the temperance and peace movements; the reforms of education, penal institutions, and insane asylums; the religious innovations; the search for perfection in communal living—all these are far too complex and involved to discuss in a short book. Besides, these reform movements expressed the thinking and activity of a relatively small number of Americans. They were not typical. What will be attempted here is a discussion of the *political* issues of the Jacksonian age—those which had a major impact on the history of the country or still maintain their relevance today. These issues include the problem of keeping the relatively new Union in one piece despite sectional arguments, especially over slavery; the push toward a more democratic society; the problem of the Indian presence in the midst of a white society; the growth of the power of the presidency; and the changing structure and operation of the federal government as controlled by the emergent two-party system.

And central to all these issues—the one person around whom much of the controversy of this era raged—was Andrew Jackson.

Jackson's name still clangs with the sound of battle. Disagreement over his accomplishments and contributions persists to this day. Here was the man whose election to the presidency his contemporaries considered the mark of a new era in American politics. That era was later termed "the rise of the common man." For with the widespread removal of restrictions to the suffrage, the electorate trooped to the polls and chose this westerner as their President, a man who had not only risen from poverty to fortune on the frontier but also gained undying fame in the War of 1812 as the conqueror of the British invaders.

Jackson was both a product and shaper of his age. He was the living embodiment of the changes and improvements that had occurred in the country since the Revolution. He was the symbol of the aspirations and expectations of Americans committed to "go ahead" and the creation of a more equal and democratic society. He was simply "the Hero," the man whose military victories restored the nation's confidence in its ability to face a hostile world and proudly—defiantly—proclaim its liberty and independence.

Andrew Jackson was the nation's image of itself.

2

Andrew Jackson

THE LIFE OF Andrew Jackson spanned the years in which the nation moved from colonial status to an independent, bustling, thriving republic, just emerging as an industrial society, sure of itself and its future, and chewing up a continent as fast as Americans could clear it of Indians, Mexicans, Spaniards, Englishmen, and any others in their way. Jackson's life began in poverty and ended in unparalleled success and triumph. It was a life that epitomized what would later be called the "American dream." He was a "self-made man"—to use a term invented at this time—who through his own efforts and talents climbed from obscurity to the rank of first citizen in the nation.

Andrew Jackson was born on March 15, 1767, in the Waxhaw settlement on the northern South Carolina frontier, a remote community on the rim of civilized life. His father had migrated with his wife from Carrickfergus in northern Ireland, and died shortly before Andrew was born. During the American Revolution his mother died of cholera while nursing patriot soldiers held captive aboard British prison ships in Charleston harbor, and his two older brothers also died during the Revolution, their deaths indirectly connected to the war. Orphaned at the age of fourteen, Andrew drifted from place to place and one occupation to another, including schoolteaching and saddlemaking. In these early years he gained a reputation for a fiery temper, easily ignited by a thoughtless word or hostile glance. Frequently he was sullen, depressed, and angry—no doubt because he felt alone in the world. For a time he led a wild life, drinking, gambling, mischief-making. When he was seventeen he decided that he would become a lawyer, since that occupation offered the best opportunity for a young man anxious to make his fortune and place his mark on the world.

So off Jackson went to North Carolina, to a town seventy-five miles from the Waxhaw settlement called Salisbury, where he entered the law office of Spruce McCay. For two years he prepared himself for admission to the bar by "reading law" with McCay and making himself generally useful around the office by copying papers, running errands, and cleaning the rooms. Not that his serious purpose tamed his wild spirits. "Andrew Jackson," said one man, "was the most roaring, rollicking, game-cocking, horse-racing, card-playing, mischievous fellow, that ever lived in Salisbury." Years later when the sober-minded people of Salisbury heard that Jackson was running for the presidency, they were appalled. "What?" cried one woman. "Jackson up for the President? *Jackson? Andrew* Jackson? The Jackson that used to live in Salisbury? Why, when he was here, he was such a rake that my husband would not bring him into the house! It is true, he *might* have taken him out to the stable to weigh horses for a race, and might drink a glass of whiskey with him *there*. Well, if Andrew Jackson can be President, anybody can!"

Nevertheless, he learned the law, enough of it at any rate to be certified by two judges on September 26, 1787. The judges said Jackson was a man of "unblemished" moral character and in their judgment would not dishonor the profession. Reckoning that his best opportunity and hope for future success lay west of the Alleghenies, Jackson packed a few belongings, a gun, and a wallet containing letters of introduction, and headed west. He did not get very far when he ran into trouble. At Jonesboro he fought his first known duel. Apparently the other man made some sarcastic remark about Jackson's legal ability. In any event no one was hurt in the duel and Jackson's honor was restored.

All his life Jackson suffered from a violent temper, although after he married, his wife helped him to bring it under control. But when it exploded, it terrified everyone within the sound of his voice. He could flood a room with the sounds of God's wrath, roaring and lashing at those who had triggered the explosion. During these convulsions his deep blue eyes blazed with such passion that observers feared he would burst a blood vessel and bring on a stroke. Yet those who really knew him later claimed that most of these tantrums were faked in order to intimidate people and get what he wanted, that even during the height of a great passion when he was screaming and threatening, he was in absolute control of himself. "No man knew better than Andrew Jackson," wrote one man, "when to get into a passion and when not." Because he was so good at these performances, he found they were useful in dealing with men and bending them to his will, especially politicians.

In 1788, when he was twenty-one, Jackson arrived in Nashville, where he met Rachel Donelson Robards. Her family had been among the first settlers of Tennessee. Unfortunately, when Jackson met Rachel she was already married to Lewis Robards, a man pathologically suspicious of every move his wife made. Eventually, when she could stand the suspicion and quarrels no longer, she ran away from him. And Jackson went with her—for protection, he later said. Then Rachel, after waiting several months to give Robards enough time to obtain a divorce, married Jackson.

It was a mistake. There had been no divorce, although Rachel and Andrew thought there had, and for two years she was technically a bigamist. Later, on January 17, 1794, after Robards had in fact obtained a divorce on grounds of desertion and adultery, she "remarried" Jackson. These unfortunate circumstances caused much sorrow and trouble for the couple, particularly in later years when Jackson emerged as a presidential candidate and his political enemies thought they could injure him by splattering the details of the marriage in the public prints.

Sensitive to the point of violence about the circumstances of his marriage, Jackson fought several duels with men who let slip some stupid or vicious remark. He fought his most famous duel in 1806 with Charles Dickinson, a young neighbor who had a reputation as the "best shot in Tennessee." The immediate cause of the gunfight was a disagreement over a horse-race wager, but Dickinson had made some derogatory comment about the marriage while drinking in a tavern. He had taken Rachel's "sacred name" into his "polluted mouth," and Jackson demanded satisfaction.

The two men met with their seconds and surgeons on a lovely late

21

May day in 1806 in a poplar forest near a river bottom not far from Nashville. "How do you feel about it now?" Jackson was asked by one member of his party.

"Oh, all right," came the reply. "I shall wing him, never fear."

Eight paces were measured off and the two men took their places facing one another. "Are you ready?" asked John Overton, Jackson's second and his oldest friend in Tennessee.

"I am ready," replied Dickinson.

"I am ready," responded Jackson.

"Fire!" cried Overton.

Dickinson quickly raised his pistol and fired. The ball struck Jackson directly in the chest, causing a puff of dust to rise from Jackson's coat.

"He is surely hit," thought Overton, "and in a bad place, too." But Jackson did not fall. In fact he hardly moved. He stood perfectly still, then slowly raised his left arm and pressed it tightly against his throbbing chest. "Erect and grim as Fate he stood," wrote an observer, "his teeth clenched, raising his pistol."

Aghast to see his enemy still standing, Dickinson cried out, "Great God! have I missed him?" As he spoke Dickinson stepped back two paces, leaving the mark and thereby violating the dueling code since it was tantamount to running away.

"Back to the MARK, sir!" called Overton, his hand on his own pistol ready to shoot Dickinson, as the code directed, if he failed to respond.

Dickinson realized what he had unconsciously done and immediately returned to his proper position. He had to stand there and wait, sweating out each moment until Jackson returned the fire.

Raising his gun and taking careful aim, Jackson squeezed the trigger. With a *click* the hammer sprang forward but stopped at the half-cocked position. Jackson drew the hammer back again and aimed a second time; all the while Dickinson just stood there, his entire body tensed to receive the shot.

Jackson fired. The bullet tore through Dickinson's body a trifle below the rib cage. Dickinson's face paled, he swayed slightly and then slumped forward. His friends rushed to his aid and gently seated him on the ground. They stripped away some of his clothes. His trousers reddened. Blood gushed from his side. There was nothing anyone could do, and Dickinson slowly bled to death.

Overton walked over to Jackson and told him what had happened. As the two men walked away the surgeon joined them and noticed that one of Jackson's shoes was full of blood. A quick examination showed that Jackson had suffered a broken rib, possibly two. Dickinson had aimed well, but Jackson's loose-fitting coat, buttoned over the chest, had saved his life. Because of it Dickinson had misjudged his target. He aimed for the heart but struck a rib instead.

"But I should have hit him if he had shot me through the brain," was Jackson's final comment.

That last remark says something about Jackson's character—how fierce his resolution when he had set his mind on a particular object. He willed himself to stay alive and kill Dickinson. In the future, even though his body throbbed with pain because of his several wounds and ailments picked up fighting Indians and British soldiers, he willed himself to keep going, to fight on, to pursue his goals. Later, as President, he repeatedly faced political enemies who maneuvered to thwart his intentions or cripple his legislative goals. Even when he lay prostrated in his bed, his lungs bleeding because of his ancient wounds, his eyes glowed with determination to "go ahead" and fight through to political victory.

Despite his marriage problem, Jackson prospered as a lawyer and planter. Indeed, his marriage was very advantageous to him, for he had allied himself with one of the leading families of Tennessee.

When Jackson had first arrived in Nashville he had been appointed public prosecutor, and he established his reputation for law enforcement almost overnight. He enforced seventy writs against delinquent debtors in his first month on the job. Naturally his conscientious performance of duty infuriated some of the debtors. One of them walked up to Jackson one day and to show his anger deliberately stepped on the young man's foot. Calmly, Jackson turned around, picked up a piece of wood, and knocked the man out cold. There was no fooling around with Andrew Jackson.

His career moved steadily ahead. He was elected to the convention that wrote Tennessee's constitution. He was the state's first representative to the United States Congress, and in 1797 was elected to the U.S. Senate. Later he was appointed a judge of the Superior Court of Tennessee.

When the War of 1812 broke out Jackson happened to be Major General of the Tennessee militia. It was sheer luck. He was the General by virtue of nothing more than his election by the militiamen. Despite his lack of military training or experience, he quickly proved himself an excellent general because of his natural qualities of leadership. Soldiers respected him. They knew he was tough and brave, and they trusted him.

Ordered to subdue the Creek Indians who had attacked settlers along the Alabama frontier, Jackson crushed them in a series of splendidly executed military engagements and then imposed a treaty that forever destroyed their power to menace the United States. In admiration and affection his soldiers began calling him "Old Hickory," because hickory was the toughest wood they knew.

Still, it was not his reputation for killing Indians that launched Jackson's national career and reputation; it was his phenomenal victory over the British at New Orleans during the War of 1812. The nation had gone to war with England, not simply to redress such grievances as British seizure of American ships and impressment of American sailors, but to prove to itself that it could safeguard its independence and freedom against all European hostility, especially England's. But the war turned out to be one unmitigated military disaster after another for Americans. It brought into question the United States' capacity to defend its independence. The war seemed to nullify the fruits of the American Revolution. Profound despair gripped the nation.

Then came the Battle of New Orleans. On January 8, 1815, Jackson, with an army of volunteers from most of the Western states plus blacks and pirates, smashed a British army attempting to invade the country from the Gulf of Mexico. Over two thousand invading soldiers were killed or wounded, while less than a dozen Americans fell before British guns. It was a fantastic victory. Britain, the conqueror of Napoleon, the colossus of western Europe, had sustained a crushing military defeat at the hands of American sharpshooters and cannoneers. This single battle confirmed to the world—or so Americans claimed—that the United States could defend and protect the freedom it had won just a few decades earlier. Europe might sneer at American independence and Britain assault it, but Jackson—"by God"—taught them to respect it.

From the moment they heard about the victory, and its dimensions in terms of men killed and wounded, Americans idolized Andrew Jackson. He had restored their pride in themselves and in their nation. He had renewed their self-confidence. So, said one writer, you can talk about Columbus, Benjamin Franklin, Washington, and Jefferson and all they had accomplished; you can talk about fifty years of democratic government, a free press, and free schools, about a country whose population had quadrupled and its resources multiplied tenfold—but what did it all add up to? The "result of all was," he said, "that the people of the United States had arrived at the capacity of honoring Andrew Jackson before all other living men."

Now nothing was too good for him. No praise too extravagant. No honor too lavish. He was the Hero.

Jackson added to his fame and the nation's further glory when, in 1818, he invaded eastern Florida, which was still held by the Spanish, in order to stop frontier attacks by Seminole Indians. He defeated the Indians, drove out the Spanish, and seized control of Florida. Again it was a stunning performance, and although his actions provoked an international furor and almost precipitated a war with Spain, they ultimately led to the formal and legal acquisition of Florida by the United States. The treaty that arranged the transfer of ownership also provided that Spain surrender its claims in the extreme Northwest called the Oregon country, thus catapulting the United States into a trans-continental power. What had begun as a series of settlements along the Atlantic shore in the seventeenth century now in the nineteenth century stretched three thousand miles from ocean to ocean.

The American people could never do enough for Andrew Jackson. He had their devotion, their trust, their love. So, a few years later, they raised him to the presidency, accepting his leadership in 1828 as testament to their profound faith in his capacity to govern and guide the nation. Of course there were some who questioned military prowess as a qualification for the presidency. They supported the reelection of the incumbent, John Quincy Adams. Senators Henry Clay of Kentucky and Daniel Webster of Massachusetts were two such men. They agreed the Hero could kill Indians and invading foreigners rather handsomely but doubted he was presidential material. Clay called him a "military chieftain" and worried for the safety of the country under his direction. After all, Jackson had a very limited education, and nothing in his civilian career, according to Clay, indicated a capacity or ability to administer the government.

But Jackson was different from ordinary men, protested his supporters. It wasn't his military career alone that made him stand apart. Not any one thing, really. "One must not separate his talents . . ." wrote a contemporary, "but take the tout ensemble of the man, and I venture to say there is not such another in the United States. . . . History is sure to preserve the name of any man who has had the strength and

25

Andrew Jackson

This engraving of Andrew Jackson was made from a portrait painted in New Orleans in 1815, at the time of Jackson's military triumph. A reasonably good likeness, except for the Napoleonic hair swirls.

genius to stamp his own character on the people over whose destinies he presided.'' By his election as President of the United States in 1828, Andrew Jackson seemed a living symbol of the advance of American democracy.

Jackson's election, expressed by more than half a million of his fellow citizens, was his greatest triumph. But it came at the very moment of his greatest personal tragedy. He had not yet taken office. He was home in Tennessee, living at his plantation—Jackson had no pretensions, and called it his farm—just outside Nashville. It was a December day and all were going about their business in the usual way. Jackson was in the fields overseeing the work of his slaves. His wife Rachel—whom he had idolized probably from the moment he laid eyes on her—scurried about the large house, which Jackson called the Hermitage, supervising the duties of her servants. Rachel was a heavyset and dark-complexioned woman, pious and charitable, who loved to sit in her rocker and smoke her pipe and listen to her husband recount his many adventures. Everyone called her ''Aunt Rachel.'' That's how affectionate they felt toward her.

On this particular day Old Hannah, one of the house slaves, asked Rachel to come into the kitchen to give advice about the preparation of the evening meal. Rachel explained what she wanted to the cook and then returned to the sitting room. Suddenly, she stopped in her tracks. She clutched her heart and let out a scream. Sinking into a chair, she struggled for breath, falling forward into Hannah's arms. Servants came running when they heard the scream and lifted Rachel gently onto her bed. Hannah tried to apply the only remedy she knew. She vigorously rubbed her mistress's side ''till it was black and blue.''

Still no relief. The stricken woman writhed in agony. She gasped for breath. She twisted and turned, clutching the bed sheets as she groped for release from the pain.

When Jackson heard what was happening he came running from the fields, ''his face lined with alarm beyond description.'' A niece hurried in from her house nearby. Soon the Hermitage was filled with relatives, friends, and servants, all trying to be helpful but all incapable of doing anything useful. The doctor finally arrived and did what he could to make her comfortable. For the next few days Rachel suffered great pain. During this time Jackson left her side for only ten minutes.

Rachel survived the first onslaught of a massive heart attack. Within two days she was feeling a trifle better; the intense pain had subsided and she could breathe with less difficulty. She begged her husband to leave her and get some sleep himself. But Jackson refused; he distrusted her reassuring words.

Over the next several days Rachel continued to improve. She was now free from pain, although she was weak and listless. Jackson stayed with her, watching, praying. By Monday, December 23, Rachel appeared so much better that she finally talked the General into lying on a sofa in the adjoining room to get a few hours' sleep. The doctor remained in the house and there were servants watching Rachel's every move. It seemed at last that Jackson could safely leave her.

It was nine P.M. Jackson kissed his wife and retired to the next room, removing his coat. He was gone only five minutes. The servants lifted Rachel from her bed so that the sheets could be arranged and smoothed for the night. While sitting in the chair, supported by Hannah, Rachel suffered a second attack. She let out a long, loud cry. There was a "rattling sound in her throat." Her head fell forward and she never spoke or breathed again.

Jackson raced into the room when he heard the cry. The doctor, relatives, and servants rushed in, too. Rachel was quickly returned to her bed. The doctor listened for life.

Jackson, almost beside himself with fear, searched the doctor's face to catch some knowledge of his wife's condition.

"Bleed her," he commanded.

The doctor opened her arm, but no blood flowed.

Jackson froze.

"Try the temple, Doctor," he pleaded.

Again the doctor cut into her flesh. Two drops oozed from the incision and stained her cap. That was all.

Her husband refused to believe that Rachel Jackson was dead. For hours he stared intently into her face, hoping to see signs of returning life. Not until she grew cold did he accept the truth that his beloved was gone.

The servants then prepared a table "for laying her out." His voice choking, Jackson said to them, "Spread four blankets upon it. If she comes to, she will not lie so hard upon the table."

The body was arranged and Jackson spent the night by Rachel's side, his face in his hands, grieving. Once in a while he would look into the face and feel the heart and pulse of the one person to whom he was totally and utterly devoted.

A friend arrived the next day and found Jackson still sitting there. He was wholly inconsolable. He had quite lost his voice. He sat in the room nearly all the next day, only stirring a little to sip some coffee which was pressed on him by his friend.

On Christmas Eve, 1828, Rachel Jackson was buried in her garden just a few hundred yards from the Hermitage mansion. Ten thousand people came for the funeral, double the population of Nashville. In part it was a tribute to a woman known for her charity and gentleness; in larger part it was a salute to her husband, to whom they wished to demonstrate their affection.

Jackson, bowed down with grief, was helped to the graveside by two army friends. "I never pitied any person more in my life," wrote one man. "I shall never forget his look of grief."

Jackson never fully recovered from the shock of Rachel's death. As far as he was concerned, she had been murdered by those vile "pander heads," as he called them, who had slandered her as a bigamist and adultress during the election. They drove her to her grave, he said. "May God Almighty forgive her murderers as I know she forgave them," he wrote. "I never can."

Jackson's friends urged him to think about his responsibilities as President. There was the inauguration ahead; there were plans to be formulated for the commencement of his administration. But he remained inconsolable, just sitting in the Hermitage, hardly stirring himself to acknowledge the presence or questions of his friends. "My heart is nearly broke," he wrote as he finally summoned the strength and will to pack and leave for Washington.

On January 18, 1829—almost a month to the day after Rachel's initial attack—Jackson boarded a steamboat to begin the long journey to the nation's capital to assume his presidency. As his boat ascended the river, other vessels, crowded with people, circled around, serving as a kind of escort. People standing on the decks called to Jackson, shouting their cheers. Each time he heard the salute the President-elect came out on deck and returned the greeting by tipping his hat. What a democrat, the crowd agreed, truly a man of the people. What previous President would have responded so instinctively and so graciously? Clearly, Jackson's election marked a new beginning in the relationship between the government and the people.

The Hero arrived in Washington early in February to begin arranging some of the details required by his imminent inauguration. For the most

29

Jackson en route to his Washington inauguration, suggesting the easy and natural rapport he had with the immense crowds who greeted him.

part Jackson kept out of sight for the next few weeks, trying to avoid a popular demonstration to acknowledge his presence. But that did not keep the people and his party from standing witness to his inauguration as President on March 4, 1829.

By the thousands they came, mobbing the capital "like the inundation of the northern barbarians into Rome," sniffed Senator Daniel Webster. And they came from every part of the country and represented every walk of life—farmers, mechanics, merchants, frontiersmen, city dwellers. "I never saw such a crowd here before," said Webster. "Persons have come five hundred miles to see General Jackson, *and they really seem to think that the country is rescued from some danger!*"

Twenty thousand people swarmed through the streets and avenues of Washington on inauguration day. They headed for the Capitol, where on the east portico Jackson would recite the oath of office and read his inaugural address. The day was bright and balmy, one of those magnificent spring days that Washington sometimes enjoys in early March. Around the Capitol building and into the square in front of the east portico people gathered "like a great agitated sea," moving, jumping up and down, shoving and pushing, anxious for the ceremonies to begin. Some of them swept up the long portico stairs to get a better position but were stopped by a ship's cable that was stretched across the stairs, two-thirds of the way from the bottom. After what seemed like an interminable delay the doors of the rotunda finally opened. Marshals marched out looking dignified and solemn, followed by the judges of the Supreme Court of the United States.

Then the people saw Jackson emerging from between the columns of the portico. They started shouting, waving, and clapping their hands. "Hurray! Hurray! Hurray!" they cried.

"Never can I forget the spectacle," said one man, "nor the electrifying moment when the eager, expectant eyes of that vast and motley multitude caught sight . . . of their adored leader." In an instant, as if by "magic," the color of the whole mass changed—"all hats were off at once, and the dark tint which usually pervades a mixed map of men was turned . . . into the bright hue of ten thousand upturned and exultant human faces, radiant with sudden joy." Jackson stared for a moment at this ecstatic mass of humanity, and then in a gesture that thrilled the crowd, he bowed low before them. He bowed to the "majesty of the people."

Jackson looked very dignified, very impressive. In fact Mrs. Daniel Webster, who was no great admirer of the Hero, had to admit that he was

31

the most "presidential looking" of all the recent candidates for chief executive, and that included men like incumbent President John Quincy Adams, Henry Clay of Kentucky, John C. Calhoun of South Carolina, and William H. Crawford of Georgia. At the time of his inauguration Jackson was nearly sixty-two years old. Tall and cadaverously thin, he carried himself with military stiffness. His face was long, with a sharp jaw, and lighted by clear blue eyes. His short gray-white hair bristled and stood almost as erect as the President-elect himself.

As Jackson stared down on the sea of faces before him cannons began booming from Alexandria and Fort Warburton to punctuate the solemnity of the moment. He then turned to read his inaugural speech and the crowd hushed to hear his words. As Margaret Bayard Smith, the very intelligent and aristocratic wife of the Senator from Maryland, said: "It was an almost breathless silence." Francis Scott Key, author of "The Star Spangled Banner," gaped at this singular spectacle unfolding before his eyes. "It is beautiful," he gasped, "it is sublime!"

Jackson began to speak. "Fellow-citizens," he said in a near whisper. "About to undertake the arduous duties that I have been appointed to perform by the choice of a free people, I avail of this . . . solemn occasion to express [my] gratitude." But Jackson's voice did not carry very well in this outdoor arena and so only those nearest to him heard his words. Fortunately, the speech was short, lasting hardly ten minutes. Among a number of things, he said he hoped to extinguish the national debt as well as safeguard the rights of the states. But what was most important to him, he declared, was "the task of *reform*, which will require particularly the correction of those abuses that have brought the patronage of the Federal Government into conflict with the freedom of elections . . . [or] have placed or continued power in unfaithful or incompetent hands."

When Jackson finished his prepared speech Chief Justice John Marshall stepped forward and administered the oath of office. That done, Jackson took the Bible from the marshal who held it during the oath taking, pressed it to his lips, laid it down reverently and then bowed again to the people. "Yes," said the haughty Mrs. Smith, "to the people in all their majesty."

The crowd could no longer restrain itself. The people charged forward, broke the chain barring their way, and swarmed around the President, reaching out and clutching his hand to shake it. Only with difficulty did Jackson escape back through the Capitol and down the hill to the gateway that opened to the long avenue leading to the White

House. Here again the new President was stopped by a "living mass" that was "impenetrable." After a time some friends forced an opening through the crowd so that Jackson could reach the horse which had been provided for his journey to the executive mansion. As the Hero mounted, the crowd let out a shout. Everything he did seemed to please them. Then, slowly, he headed for the White House, and oh, said Mrs. Smith, "such a cortege as followed him! Country men, farmers, gentlemen, mounted and dismounted, boys, women and children, black and white. Carriages, wagons and carts all pursuing him to the President's house." People standing at the upper windows of their homes cheered the President as he rode by. As usual, Jackson responded by tipping his hat.

Never had there been such an inauguration of a President. Never before had the ordinary citizen—the common man—so spontaneously expressed his enthusiasm for a new administration. When Thomas Jefferson was inaugurated chief executive twenty-eight years earlier he simply walked from his boardinghouse to the Capitol, was sworn in, and then walked back and joined his messmates at the boardinghouse for lunch. But here was Jackson riding toward the White House with an enormous mob in tow. It suddenly occurred to a number of gentlemen and ladies who were watching the procession from the safety of their homes that this motley crew of farmers, workers, boys, women, children, and lord-knows-what-else were intending to enter the "President's palace," as they grandly termed the White House. The "palace" was about to be invaded by the masses, the rabble. People from "the highest and most polished," said Joseph Story, the learned jurist, now an Associate Justice of the Supreme Court, "down to the most vulgar and gross in the nation" poured into the executive mansion. Hundreds of them by the minute jammed their way through every door of the building. "I never saw such a mixture," moaned Story. Most of them were common, ordinary people. "The reign of KING MOB seemed triumphant," he said. "I was glad to escape from the scene as soon as possible."

When Mrs. Smith and her family arrived at the White House they were aghast at the spectacle taking place in the "palace." "What a scene did we witness!" she wrote. "*The Majesty of the People* had disappeared, and a rabble, a mob, of boys, negros [*sic*], women, children, scrambling, fighting, romping. What a pity what a pity."

A modest reception in the White House had been planned; what occurred was shocking to those used to "elitist" republicanism. Barrels of orange punch had been prepared, but as the waiters opened the doors to carry them out, the mob rushed forward to seize them. The punch splashed on the carpets as waiters and guests collided. Glasses fell to the floor and were stepped on; pails of liquor were overturned; "and the most painful confusion prevailed." It was mortifying, said one observer, to see men "with boots heavy with mud, standing on the damask satin covered chairs," just to catch sight of the President.

And poor Jackson. They nearly killed him. He was, said Mrs. Smith, "*literally* nearly pressed to death and almost suffocated and torn to pieces in their eagerness to shake hands with Old Hickory." Finally the pressure got so bad and the danger of actually injuring the President became so real that a number of men formed a ring around him and led him to a back entrance so he could escape the dangerous exuberance of the people and return to his temporary lodgings at Gatsby's Hotel.

But the President's disappearance did not dampen the mood of the celebrants. The mayhem, if anything, got worse. Cut glass and china worth several thousand dollars was smashed in the struggle to find refreshments. Ladies fainted. Men were seen with bloody noses. At last someone got the bright idea of removing the liquor and ice cream into the garden. As the refreshments disappeared outside, men and boys jumped through the windows to get to them.

Just in time, breathed Mrs. Smith with relief. The house could not have survived the pressure much longer—to say nothing of the furnishings. "We had a regular Saturnalia," laughed one Congressman who witnessed the rampage and described it to a friend. The mob, he wrote, was "one uninterrupted stream of mud and filth."

Ladies like Mrs. Smith and gentlemen like Justice Story had come to the White House expecting a levee, such as those calm, slightly aristocratic receptions that had honored the presidencies of George Washington, John and John Quincy Adams, James Madison, and James Monroe. But instead they found people gathered *en masse*, joyously, raucously, destructively celebrating the inauguration of their Hero.

"It was the People's day, and the People's President, and the People shall rule." That was the sum and substance of it, according to most contemporaries. It was the end of limited republicanism, established under the Constitution, restricting government to the few—the educated, the wellborn, the property owners. Here was the beginning of truly popular government in America—at least in spirit. And for the next eight years, under the administration of President Andrew Jackson, that spirit, in several particulars, was translated into political reality.

3

The Democratic Party

THE EMERGENCE OF a truly democratic, popular government did not happen just because the people willed it. Nor was it a simple process of evolution going back to colonial times and stimulated by the doctrines of the Declaration of Independence, the Revolution, or the genius of the Constitution. To a large extent, popular government emerged because a relatively small group of men engineered it. These men were gifted politicians. They were outstanding public officials, and the most prominent included men of varying political opinions such as Martin Van Buren of New York, Henry Clay of Kentucky, Daniel Webster of Massachusetts, Thomas Hart Benton of Missouri and John C. Calhoun of South Carolina.

To understand the contribution made to democratic government during the Jacksonian era it is necessary to look back prior to Jackson's election, back to the beginning of the nineteenth century, back to the early days of the Republic. Two developments triggered the democratic changes that occurred during the Jacksonian years. The first was the broadening of the franchise. In the preceding three decades the states had steadily eliminated restrictions on voting, so that by 1828 a great many white males over twenty-one enjoyed the right of the ballot.

Because they enjoyed this right did not necessarily mean they would exercise it. Frequently—more times than not—they had to be urged and courted and cajoled into exercising it. "Our old way of conducting elections," wrote one politician in Illinois, "required each aspirant for office to announce himself as a candidate." Then he traveled around the state, making speeches, conversing with the electorate, soliciting votes, and "whispering slanders" against his opponents. Now, with a greater number of people enfranchised, it was necessary to devise "new modes" of soliciting and concentrating and controlling voter participation. This new situation encouraged skillful, ambitious, and intelligent politicians to invent ways to involve and manage the mass electorate. Eventually they succeeded, and their success constituted a radically transformed electoral process. The process was democratized.

The second development was the emergence of political parties in America. From the beginning the leaders of the new American nation had expressed a deep horror of political parties, calling them cabals of willful men devoted to their own selfish purposes and not the good of the general public. George Washington said parties were instruments of dissention and discord, and John Adams declared that the "division of the republic into two great parties . . . is to be dreaded as the greatest political evil under our Constitution."

Despite these fears and warnings, a two-party system developed within a few years of Washington's inauguration as first President. Washington had brought into his Cabinet two highly intelligent, individual, and opinionated men who fundamentally disagreed on the direction the government should take and set about competing with one another to gain a commitment from Washington to their point of view. Thomas Jefferson as Secretary of State and Alexander Hamilton as Secretary of the Treasury represented two conflicting philosophies of government. Hamilton insisted on wide powers for the federal government in order to inaugurate an economic program that, by uniting private interest to public duty, would produce a strong and efficient national economy. He understood that only a government which guaranteed the financial interests of its constituency was likely to succeed. Jefferson, on the other hand, took exception to Hamilton's concept of expanding federal power. He emphasized the need and value of local autonomy in order to preserve individual freedom.

The two-party system which began to emerge was the best thing that could have happened to the country. Most Americans were (and still are) essentially conservative in their politics. As a matter of fact no genuinely radical ideas or parties have ever taken deep root in the nation. Even so, Americans demand change, although they abhor revolution. Thus, with a two-party system as it developed, change could be achieved through normal shifts in government administration from one party to another, all obtained in regular elections through nonviolent party contest.

The fears of Washington and other Founding Fathers about parties slowly changed during the first decades of the nineteenth century. But the really big change came during the Jacksonian age with the appearance of a new breed of professional politician. Men like Van Buren, Clay, and others lacked the accomplishments of the statesmen of the Revolutionary generation. They could not match their careers against those of statesmen such as Washington, Jefferson, Hamilton, Madison, and dozens of others who had won the Revolution, written or signed the Declaration, framed the Constitution, or adopted constitutions for their states. When the politicians of this second generation came before the American people and asked for votes, they could not offer the kind of distinction and accomplishment that the first generation had provided. So, lacking extraordinary credentials, they were forced to rely on the party system to advance their ideas and careers. Ambitious for the offices once occupied by the Founding Fathers, who were dead or fast dying off by this time, they shrewdly recognized party organization as the best means of gaining their objectives. Not surprisingly, they praised the party system as the surest safeguard for a free and representative government. Modern government, they contended, demanded well-functioning political parties openly arrayed against each other. Parties preserved liberty by allowing for organized opposition. They would inhibit governmental corruption by providing periodic reexamination of the conduct of public business at election time. In sum, these men argued, democratic principles in government were impossible without party politics.

Thus, within a forty-year period, from the founding of the republic under the Constitution to the Age of Jackson, political thinking had shifted from viewing parties as destructive instruments to seeing them as essential to democratic government.

These second-generation politicians—the Van Burens, Clays, Websters, and hundreds of others—quickly became professional in the art of politics. It was their business to win elections; they had to depend on their skill as organizers, as speakers, and as managers to capture the support of the American voter. They were men of uncommon ability in one or another endeavor. A few of them were outstanding public speakers; others, intrepid organizers or managers. One was a profound political theoretician. Many were outstanding statesmen, men of high principle, committed to popular government and individual freedom. They supported either the Jeffersonian doctrine, which urged limiting governmental power, or the Hamiltonian position of expanding the central government to assist the progress and prosperity of the entire nation. But in these early Jacksonian years all of them actively engaged in restructuring the two major parties to modernize their operation. Their activities in party politics will be emphasized here, rather than their individual philosophies or principles of government, because these activities had much to do with advancing democracy within the American nation.

Perhaps Martin Van Buren was the most typical and most successful of this new breed of politician. Known as the "Little Magician" or "Red Fox of Kinderhook" because of his extraordinary skill as a political manager, Van Buren, over the years, built a political organization in New York known as the "Albany Regency" to run the political business of the state while he was absent in Washington. This was one of the first statewide political machines in the United States. It had a governing council set up in Albany consisting of some of the state's best political talents, including William L. Marcy, Silas Wright, Jr., Azariah C. Flagg, Benjamin F. Butler, and Edwin Croswell, editor of the *Albany Argus*, the party's newspaper mouthpiece.

Two of these men became United States Senators, two became Governors of the state, one might have become President of the United States except that he died before the convention could nominate him, another won appointment as United States Attorney General, and still another became Secretary of State. All obviously men of talent. With control of the state legislature, the Regency directed the political affairs of New York, encouraging young lawyers and newspapermen in the state to accept Regency leadership and seek advancement in elective office through its sponsorship and support. It devised and invented means for keeping the electorate loyal to the party and regular in its voting. Through the *Albany Argus* it informed the faithful of the party line.

Van Buren was born in Kinderhook, New York, on December 5, 1782—just a year after the nation had won its independence. He was the

38

son of a tavern keeper, and through hard work and native intelligence he learned enough law as a clerk in several law offices to be licensed to practice within the state. Thereafter his rise to political prominence was swift. He had learned his politics in his father's tavern. He had learned how to influence men, how to talk with them, how to win their confidence. First he was appointed fence-viewer, then Surrogate of Columbia County; subsequently he was elected state senator, state attorney general, and then United States Senator.

Van Buren was a short man, probably no taller than five feet four and a half inches, which explains why it was not enough to call him a "Magician." It had to be "Little Magician." (And it says something about the new style of politics during this Jacksonian age that all the Presidents of both parties, beginning with the Hero in 1828, had nicknames: Jackson was the Hero or Old Hickory; Van Buren, elected in 1836, was the Little Magician; then came Tippecanoe and Tyler, Too, otherwise known as William Henry Harrison and John Tyler; James Knox Polk was Young Hickory, elected in 1844; and finally, in 1848, Zachary Taylor was called Old Rough and Ready. The six Presidents who preceded Jackson never had such nicknames. The democratization of the presidency obviously included some inelegant side effects.)

Van Buren was fair-complexioned with light, sandy-colored hair and "small brilliant eyes" under a bulging forehead. Most people, except of course his enemies, thought he was one of the most charming men of his age. Men and women vied for his company because he was friendly, urbane, and gracious, and his conversation "rich in information." He was courteous to all, perhaps overly so. He never showed what he was really thinking. He was very discreet, very guarded, very careful in everything he said and did. Consequently, he was frequently accused of being "non-committal" on most important political issues. There was a story repeatedly told about him that illustrates the point. He was giving a speech in Albany on the tariff question, a touchy if not dangerous issue. When he finished there was a great burst of applause. One man in the audience supposedly turned to his friend, Mr. Benjamin Knower.

"Mr. Knower!" he said, "that was a very able speech."

"Yes, very able," came the reply.

"Mr. Knower! on which side of the Tariff question was it?"

"That is the very point I was thinking about when you first spoke to me," answered the puzzled Knower.

Van Buren was more a manager of men than a public speaker,

None of the paintings or photographs of Van Buren do him justice. That none convey his charm, graciousness and urbanity, or his political shrewdness and cunning, may itself say something about his character.

operating quietly but with great force and persuasion. He did not have the oratorical flair of a Daniel Webster or the easy speaking style of a Henry Clay, so his influence was felt more behind the scenes. Which explains why some men were very distrustful of him, why when any peculiar circumstances or untoward developments occurred they were sure to see "Mr. Van Buren's sly hand" in them.

As a shrewd observer of the political scene, as an astute judge of men, Van Buren understood the meaning of Andrew Jackson's enormous popularity with the American people long before the election of 1828. He also appreciated what it might mean to his own political ambitions if he could catch hold of Jackson's long coattails. But Van Buren was not a political hack, limited simply to the gratification of his electoral ambition. He recognized that with Jackson he might help direct the country, and the party gathered behind him, along lines compatible with his philosophy of government—a philosophy he claimed was based on the principles and doctrines of Thomas Jefferson. Intellectually, like Jefferson, Van Buren was committed to the doctrine of states' rights, namely that those powers not expressly delegated by the Constitution to the federal government were reserved to the states and the people. He vigorously opposed a strong central government in Washington; he believed in rigid economy when budgeting national expenditures; and he tended to oppose tariffs and public works sponsored by the federal government. Public works, he felt, should be subsidized by the states, just as New York had done in building the Erie Canal. After all, he argued, if New York could finance public improvements, so, too, could all other states.

In addition to reasserting Jefferson's governmental creed, Van Buren hoped to bring about the "substantial reorganization" of Jefferson's old party, to unite the North and the South, to forge an alliance between what he termed the planters of the South and the plain people of the North, to form what would become the Democratic party. Such a "reorganization" would furnish, he wrote, "a complete antidote for sectional prejudices"; moreover, it would quiet the "clamour [against] Southern Influence and African Slavery."

So, in the winter of 1826-1827, in order to reorganize Jefferson's old party and, naturally, to support Jackson's election to the presidency against the incumbent, John Quincy Adams, Van Buren initiated several alliances with politicians from other sections of the country.

There were a number of men involved, many of them Congressmen. The most prominent included Thomas Hart Benton, Senator from Missouri; Thomas Ritchie, editor of the Richmond *Enquirer* and the head of the Richmond Junto, Virginia's equivalent of the Albany Regency; and, perhaps most important of all, John C. Calhoun of South Carolina.

Calhoun was the first man Van Buren spoke to about reorganizing the party. They met late in December 1826 at the home of William H. Fitzhugh in Georgetown, right outside Washington. Van Buren sat leisurely in an oversized chair, one leg dangling over the other, calmly reviewing the need for structuring a reinvigorated party around Jackson so that his election would really mean something. In passing, Van Buren ventured that such a condition would diminish sectional tensions over slavery. For Calhoun, this was a telling point.

As the little man continued speaking Calhoun peered intently at him, his nimble brain catching all the subtle nuances of the New Yorker's arguments. A Jackson victory, Van Buren concluded, "as the result of his military services without reference to party . . . would be one thing. His election as the result of a combined and concerted effort of a political party, holding, in the main, to certain tenets and opposed to certain prevailing principles, might be another and far different thing."

Calhoun was extremely impressed by Van Buren's suggestions, particularly since it was understood that he would be Jackson's vice-presidential running mate. Finally, he rose from his chair and as a gesture of consent stretched out his hand, which Van Buren quickly grasped. From this simple beginning, from this alliance between a planter of the South and one of the "plain people" of the North, the Democratic party eventually emerged. True, the two men could not speak for the majority of voters of the North and the South, but they had tremendous influence among many politicians from their respective sections, and their advice and arguments would be given great weight. In time Calhoun would come to represent the special interests of the South. He became the defender and pleader for what he called the South's "peculiar institution"—slavery. It is interesting therefore that now, in 1826, in arguing the merits of a revitalized alliance between North and South, Van Buren should mention the cessation of Northern criticism of "African slavery" as an important consequence.

Like Van Buren, John C. Calhoun had been born in 1782—March 18th, to be exact. But there the similarity ends. That Calhoun and the Little Magician came from very different sections of the country was extremely meaningful in the long run. He was born in the South Carolina uplands near the Savannah River. Educated at Yale College, he studied law at Tapping Reeve's school at Litchfield, Connecticut, and was admitted to the South Carolina bar. He began his political career with a speech in 1807 at a public meeting in which he denounced Britain's aggressions against American maritime rights. He was elected to the South Carolina legislature and then to the U.S. House of Representatives.

Calhoun's appearance in Congress in 1810, along with Henry Clay of Kentucky, Felix Grundy of Tennessee, and Peter B. Porter of New York, brought together a group of Congressmen who were highly nationalistic and intensely anti-British. For the wrongs committed by England against the United States since the Revolution, such as the impressment of American seamen and the seizure of American ships on the high seas, these young Congressmen urged the country to declare war and thereby redress these terrible indignities to the nation's honor. Because of their belligerency they were called "War Hawks." By their oratorical and organizational skills they eventually succeeded in prodding the Congress into a declaration of war.

Shortly after the War of 1812, James Monroe won election as President of the United States and named Calhoun his Secretary of War. And a right fine Secretary he was, too. Efficient, intelligent, and imaginative, he used his talents and position to strengthen national defense. He was the administration's most nationalistic spokesman, arguing, pleading, cajoling Congress for funds to improve the country's defenses.

But by the 1820s Calhoun's intense nationalistic feeling for the country as a whole began to wane. He became convinced that the Northern section of the nation was taking advantage of the Southern section, particularly with respect to the tariff—the tax on foreign imports. The increased industrialization of the North after the War of 1812 brought steady demands from manufacturers for tariff protection of their products from foreign competition. Northerners wanted foreign goods taxed to jack up their prices, so that lower-priced domestic products could enjoy a wider market at home. Southerners argued that such tariffs were unfair. They sold their staple crop, cotton, on a world market in which the price was determined by the laws of supply and demand but were forced to buy manufactured products at home on a closed market protected by tariff laws. To Southerners, therefore, tariffs, enacted by

Congress, were nothing more than a government subsidy paid to Northern manufacturers out of the pockets of Southern planters and farmers.

Quickly responding to the temper of his constituents, to the needs of his section of the country, Calhoun denounced Congressional efforts to raise tariff rates. Also, cotton prices had been declining steadily for the past few years, and he blamed this slide on the tariff rates enacted by Congress in 1824. And as the price of cotton continued to fall, Calhoun's youthful ideals about a strong central government and federally financed fortifications and public works fell with it. By 1826 he was no longer an ardent nationalist but rather a sectionalist, a man devoted to the needs and problems of his own section, the South. With enormous energy and intellectual power he set about defending the rights of the states.

As he grew older, Calhoun became more and more the theoretician, more and more the advocate of states' rights. His disposition grew sour as he contemplated the future of South Carolina, the South, and its "peculiar institution," slavery. To some observers he was "the cast-iron man," who looked as though he had never been born; and because of the intensity of his feelings he looked as though he could never be extinguished, never consumed. After the 1828 election, when he became Jackson's Vice-President and presided over the Senate, he would stare fixedly at whoever was speaking, concentrating on every word. Sometimes his dark eyes would flash with anger or disagreement if he sensed danger to his ideas or to the South. When he spoke, it was close, rapid, theoretical. Listeners said it was extremely interesting to hear him talk because there was a never failing evidence of high intellect. But after a while listeners turned away, for Calhoun lost the power to communicate with people. More and more he grew to live in "utter intellectual solitude." When he met friends, he didn't converse with them, he harangued them. And he did it everywhere—in the street, in the Senate, by the fireside. He spoke rapidly in whole paragraphs, pausing briefly to allow his listener a word or two in response. But he either dismissed what had been said to him or twisted it into what he wanted to hear. The pause over, Calhoun would begin his lecture anew.

Yet Calhoun had not achieved political distinction because he turned men away. He was in fact a man of powerful intellect, deep convictions, and political astuteness with strong support from South Carolina and other leaders from the South as well as wide respect throughout the nation.

This handsome, highly romantic portrait shows John C. Calhoun before frustration, resentment and anger etched his face. Contemporaries always noticed the black, flashing eyes.

Which explains why Van Buren had gone to him in 1826 and spoken ardently for a revival of a North-South alliance as the basis of a revitalized party which would elect Jackson in 1828. Calhoun was designated Jackson's vice-presidential running mate and expected to succeed Old Hickory in the White House whenever the General stepped down.

But there was one danger Calhoun did not bring up in his conversation with Van Buren. It went back to 1818, when Jackson had invaded and seized Spanish Florida. Calhoun, who was the Secretary of War at the time, took offense at the action. Not that he cared much about the Spanish or wasn't glad to see Florida eventually annexed by the United States. What bothered him was Jackson's failure to consult him and gain his permission before the invasion. The General had bypassed him. He had gone over Calhoun's head to the President. So miffed was the Secretary that he counseled President Monroe to reprimand Jackson. Monroe rejected this advice, but fortunately for Calhoun did not broadcast it. Otherwise, Jackson, who was extremely sensitive about his military exploits and reputation, would have nailed Calhoun as an enemy and the South Carolinian would never have been designated as the General's vice-presidential running-mate ten years later.

There were rumors of Calhoun's true feelings about the Florida invasion, but nothing substantial—nothing to cause Van Buren to back away from him as a collaborator in restructuring the old Jeffersonian party. In any event, as of 1826 Van Buren and Calhoun agreed to bring their supporters into alliance behind Jackson and to encourage as many other national leaders to join them as possible. Van Buren promised to write his allies in Pennsylvania. In addition, the Little Magician offered to tour the South in the spring of 1827 to assure Southern politicos of Northern goodwill.

In concluding this North-South alliance the collaborators did not forget the West. And aside from Jackson himself, the most important Westerner to be drawn into the combination that finally became the Democratic party was Thomas Hart Benton of Missouri.

Benton was a big, powerful-looking man with an ego twice the size of his physique. He had black, curly hair, side whiskers, and a long nose that wandered crookedly down his face. When he spoke he *sounded* powerful, too powerful to be contradicted. He was a great talker, too—loud, forceful, a bit bombastic at times, but very effective.

Benton was born at Harts Mill, near Hillsboro, North Carolina, on

March 14, 1782—the same year as Van Buren and Calhoun—and attended the University of North Carolina, then called Chapel Hill College, where he studied law. He moved to Tennessee in 1806, was elected to the state senate three years later, and became Jackson's aide-de-camp during the Creek War. Unfortunately, Benton and Jackson fell into a terrible quarrel that ruptured their relations for many years. It began as a dispute over a very obscure point of honor between Jesse Benton, Thomas's brother, and Billy Carroll, a brigade inspector in Jackson's army. It ended with Jackson slumped on a barroom floor, his shoulder shattered by a slug and his left arm pierced by a bullet that buried itself near the bone.

After the gunfight Nashville was no longer a healthy place for the Bentons. Jackson's friends took his wounding as an unkind deed for which they felt they must have adequate satisfaction. "I am literally in hell here," Thomas Hart Benton wrote shortly afterward. He had, he said, "the meanest wretches under heaven to contend with—liars, affidavit-makers, and shameless cowards. All the puppies of Jackson are at work on me; but they will be astonished at what will happen; for it is not them, but their master, whom I will hold accountable. . . . I am in the middle of hell, and see no alternative but to kill or be killed; for I will not crouch to Jackson; and the fact that I and my brother defeated him and his tribe, and broke his small sword in the public square, will for ever rankle in his bosom and make him thirst after vengeance. My life is in danger; nothing but a decisive duel can save me, or even give me a chance for my own existence; for it is a settled plan to turn out puppy after puppy to bully me, and when I have got into a scrape, to have me killed somehow in the scuffle, and afterwards the affidavit-makers will prove it was honorably done."

Benton was a sensible man. He didn't have to wait to be killed to know what he must do. He resigned his commission in the army at the close of the War of 1812 and headed west to Missouri. Benton rose quickly in Missouri politics. When the state was admitted into the Union in 1821, Benton became one of its U.S. Senators. In Congress he soon demonstrated his prowess as a skillful parliamentarian. He knew how to weave and maneuver during Senate debates to get his way. Most important of all, he was an extremely influential Western politician. If Jackson had ambitions for the presidency, and if he were ever elected President, Benton could be a valuable friend. So, since both men became U.S. Senators in the 1820s, it wasn't long before Benton and

Jackson met in Washington. Ten years had passed since their quarrel. Would they lunge at one another? Would they draw pistols? No one was quite sure what would happen. But Jackson, an older man who wanted the presidency and understood Benton's potential usefulness, stepped up to his old enemy and asked him about the health of his wife. Amazed and somewhat pleased, Benton responded quickly and returned the inquiry. That's all that happened. The meeting was as brief as it was unexpected. A few days later Jackson called at Benton's lodgings, and not finding him home left his card. Then, the next time the Missouri Senator saw the General, he bowed. Jackson shot out his hand. The two men shook hands and dissolved their old hatred. In the political wars ahead each found the other a bastion of strength and support.

But poor Jesse, Thomas's brother, never forgot and never forgave. In the presidential election of 1828 he was still trying to injure Jackson. He wrote a pamphlet vilifying the General, attempting to prove he was unfit to sit in the White House. It was especially mortifying for him to know that his own brother had deserted to his enemy. He never forgot that.

But Jesse had one satisfaction. The bullet fired so long ago at Jackson still lodged in the old man's arm, giving him at times considerable discomfort. As the years passed, the bullet flattened itself against the bone and threatened to cause paralysis. Another ten years and the pain was so intense that it was decided the bullet had to be removed. So, with Jackson fully conscious and gritting his teeth, the doctor probed and dug into the arm and finally caught hold of the flattened metal and pulled it out. Jackson was almost unconscious when the operation ended. In jest, someone standing nearby offered the souvenir to Thomas Hart Benton, supposedly the owner of the bullet. The Senator refused, observing that Jackson had acquired legal title to it in common law by twenty years' possession. But it had been only nineteen years.

"Oh, well," said Benton, "in consideration of the extra care he had taken of it—keeping it constantly about his person, and so on—I'll waive the odd year."

It was Benton's tremendous influence among Western Congressmen, as well as his debating and parliamentary talents in the Senate, that led Van Buren to solicit his support in 1827 in the creation of the Democratic party. Benton quickly agreed to the alliance since he could not abide Adams. Besides, it would help him reestablish his friendship with Jackson now that Jackson was this party's presidential candidate. So the alliance between the North and the South was extended to include the West. The Democratic party would be a national party.

The leaders of this revitalized party—and there were dozens more besides Van Buren, Calhoun and Benton—were all first-rate politicians. They were expert organizers. And the organization was structured from top to bottom, from local "Hickory Clubs" in the communities to central corresponding committees in the states that sought to unify the efforts of the Jacksonians on the national (Congressional) level. Hundreds of newspapers were founded. Politicians knew that the press was perhaps the greatest unifying political force as well as very influential in shaping the public mind. With a newspaper, said Van Buren, "we can endure a thousand convulsions. Without it, we might as well hang our harps on the willows."

At one meeting of Jacksonian Congressmen it was agreed that they would sponsor "a chain of newspaper posts, from the New England States to Louisiana, and branching off through Lexington to the Western States." So rapid was this journalistic expansion that it was officially announced in 1828 that there were six hundred newspapers—most of them political—published in the country, fifty of them dailies, a hundred fifty semiweeklies and four hundred weeklies. In the presidential election of 1828 the country was literally wrapped in political paper. The American people were battered with millions of words telling them what they must do and how they must vote to save the Republic.

But it takes money to run a campaign and manage a national party, and costs run high when the communications media are extensively used. So the Democrats developed or improved a wide variety of techniques to raise money to pay political costs. At local meetings and conventions the delegates were usually taxed a fixed amount to meet printing costs. One Ohio county central committee requested each ward "to appoint a fund committee . . . for the purpose of receiving . . . contributions . . . and that the same be paid over to the treasurer of the general committee of the county." Elsewhere, public dinners and banquets were held to defray costs. As usual, large contributions were solicited from those who could afford it or whose interest depended on Democratic goodwill. And frequently, newspaper editors were designated official printers to Congress or to state legislatures to print documents, reports, journals and the like, which brought the newspapers a sizeable subsidy.

Most of the money was used to encourage greater public participation in the elective process. Now that there were so many voters, politicians began devising new schemes and methods to capture the mass electorate. One way they learned to win the electorate was to nominate for office men of wide popular appeal. A Hero, for example, like General Andrew Jackson. Someone attractive. Someone who could excite enthusiasms in the people. Someone who possessed charisma. Another way was to provide an attractive election campaign. So these politicians developed a number of new and flashy schemes to amuse and delight the masses. In the process they recast the style and tone of American politics. As they had initiated the modern political system, they also created the modern political campaign style.

For example, they introduced songs and slogans into election campaigns. They inaugurated parades, barbecues, tree plantings, dinners, rallies. They provided buttons and clothes to designate one's party and candidate; and through a chain of newspapers covering the nation they turned out a mountain of party propaganda, including cartoons, songs, and funny stories. These politicians believed that the public responded to stimulation, so the bigger the stimulus the bigger the response. The Age of Jackson marked the beginning of the kind of electioneering which employed gimmicks of all kinds to arouse and sustain popular interest in the activities of the party.

One of the more effective gimmicks invented by the Democrats was the use of the hickory as a symbol of their candidate and party. Since Jackson was known as Old Hickory it was an easy and obvious symbol. But as the Democratic party began to take organizational shape, hickory sticks, hickory canes, hickory brooms shot up across the country, at crossroads, on steeples, on steamboats, in the hands of children—everywhere. Poles made of hickory were erected "in every village, as well as upon the many city streets." Many of them were standing as late as 1845, rotting mementoes of democracy's advance. Local Democratic clubs and militia companies also organized ceremonies to plant hickory trees in their village and town squares as part of their campaign to heighten public interest in the election.

Barbecues were also popular in stimulating public interest. In Baltimore a "Grand Barbecue" was arranged by the Democrats ostensibly to commemorate the successful defense of the city against British attack during the War of 1812. But it actually became a barbecue for Andrew Jackson. Three bullocks were roasted and each man at the affair was expected to wear a hickory leaf in his hat to show his political preference. The festivities began with the firing of a cannon, followed by a "thrilling" parade of over seven hundred men—"gentlemen of the exchange, blacksmiths, tanners, carpenters, masons, butchers and men from all trades . . . in fact the best part of the bone and sinew of the town was there.'' After the parade someone called for a cheer. But for whom? The brave defenders of the city during the late war? Without a moment's pause, the crowd instinctively cheered for Andrew Jackson.

These scenes of contagious and raucous enthusiasm for Old Hickory—the sort of thing that happened later at Jackson's inauguration—were carefully staged by Democrats. They didn't simply happen. They were made to happen. They were believed to be essential in "creating" popular majorities for Democratic candidates—all the candidates, not Jackson alone. "Van Buren has learned you know that the *Hurra Boys* were for Jackson . . .'' wrote one critic, "and to my regret they constitute a powerful host.''

To encourage the *Hurra Boys* and whip up even greater excitement for the General and his party, some politicians toyed with the idea of bringing Jackson himself to their meetings, although that clearly violated tradition and ran the risk of provoking resentment. Presidential candidates were expected to stay home and keep their mouths shut, leaving it to others to solicit votes for their candidacy. So, being a proper and politically cautious man, Jackson refused all invitations to display himself publicly—all, that is, except one. He chose to accept an invitation of the Louisiana Central Committee to attend a ceremony in New Orleans on January 8, 1828, to commemorate his victory over the British in 1815. Ostensibly the celebration was nonpolitical, so Jackson could attend without eliciting a barrage of criticism from those who opposed his election. Even so, the ceremony was arranged and publicized to remind the American people of their "undying gratitude'' to the Hero. Representatives from many state Democratic delegations attended, along with the General. As reported in the newspapers, the celebration was "the most stupendous thing of the kind that had ever occurred in the United States.'' The welcoming ceremony, the speeches, parades, and dinner were unlike anything ever seen before. "The World has never witnessed so glorious, so wonderful a Celebration—'' exclaimed a participant, "never has *Gratitude & Patriotism* so happily united, so beautifully blended—& it will form a bright page in American history.''

The delight with which the people responded to this new brand of electioneering encouraged politicians to program a wider assortment of entertainments, including songs, jokes, cartoons, funny stories, poems and puns. The newspapers carried some of the best jokes and funny sayings, most of which poked fun at the incumbent President, John Quincy Adams, and his Secretary of State, Henry Clay.

"Hurrah for Jackson," said one man.

"Hurrah for the Devil," replied another who opposed Jackson's election.

"Very well," retorted the Democrat. "You stick to your candidate and I'll stick to mine."

One story was told of a man who found the friends of Adams like the Frenchman who boasted that King Louis had spoken to him.

"What did the King say to you?" asked an awed friend.

"He told me to get out of his way," replied the delighted Frenchman.

And there were puns. Most of them were pretty ghastly, like the following:

Question: "Why is Adams on ticklish grounds?"
Answer: "Because he stands on slippery Clay."

Sometimes the politicians simply pandered to the worst instincts and tastes of the electorate, but it was all done to awaken interest and concern in politics, to bring people to the polls to register outrage or faith or enthusiasm. And the great number of new voters who exercised their franchise during the Jacksonian era and who flocked to Washington to cheer their approval of Old Hickory upon his inauguration justified all the efforts of professional politicians and did, in fact, link them closer to the operation of government. Seeing these masses, reading the constant rise of the number of voters exercising the ballot, and looking at the candidates elected to office—every one of them, not simply Jackson alone—provided all the proof needed to argue that popular government had indeed arrived in the United States.

4

The National Republican Party

DEMOCRATIZING THE ELECTORAL process was not the accomplishment of the leaders of the Democratic party alone. Other politicians had a hand in bringing the masses into political action. These men opposed the Democratic party and called themselves National Republicans. They were led by such distinguished statesmen as Henry Clay, Daniel Webster, and, to a more limited extent, the incumbent President, John Quincy Adams.

They called themselves National Republicans because of their emphasis on the role of the federal government in directing the nation's economic growth. They reaffirmed the philosophy of Alexander Hamilton, which defined federal power as broadly as possible, and they pursued a series of goals which had originally been formulated by Henry Clay when he was a Congressman from Kentucky.

Fun-loving, hard-drinking, quick to accept a bet, Henry Clay was a hail-fellow, affable, delightful man whom everyone enjoyed and respected. Tall and thin, with great hollows gouged in both cheeks and a thin, almost invisible line marking the location of his mouth, Clay looked like a west-country farmer. But when he spoke, either in public or private, one realized what a remarkable man he was, how keen his political talents, how wide-ranging the thrust of his mind.

Clay was born in Virginia in 1777, clerked in several law offices until he obtained a license, and then moved to Kentucky. He was elected to the U.S. Congress, where his brain and tongue won him an immediate reputation as a persuasive and influential legislator. Although quite young—he was barely 33—he was chosen Speaker of the House of Representatives, and, as leader of the War Hawks faction just prior to the War of 1812, he placed his friends and allies on important committees to better control the operation of the House affairs and win a declaration of war against Great Britain.

After the war he became a leading critic of the Monroe administration, largely because he was denied the cabinet post he wanted. In an effort to embarrass the administration, he led the fight to win Congressional censure of Jackson for the General's invasion of Spanish Florida. Clay denied personal hostility to Jackson or Monroe. In a speech before a packed House of Representatives he said he was simply doing his duty, acting from principle. Other members, he continued, "may bear down all opposition . . . even vote the general the public thanks; they may carry him triumphantly through this House. But, if they do, in my humble judgment, it will be a triumph of the principle of insubordination—a triumph of the military over the liberties of the people."

Quite predictably, when Jackson read this speech, he erupted into a towering passion. Warned beforehand that Congress might censure him for invading foreign soil without authorization, he raced to Washington to defend his actions, which he believed perfectly legal because they had been sanctioned by President Monroe. "The hypocracy [sic] & baseness of Clay . . ." Jackson wrote to a friend, "make me despise the Villain. . . . I hope you will roast him in the West."

That was the beginning of Jackson's long hatred for Henry Clay. And it intensified over the years. In any event, the censure failed and Jackson always remained highly sensitive to any criticism of his Florida campaign.

In a series of speeches Clay delivered before the Senate in 1824, he outlined several proposals—subsequently called the "American System"—which became the fundamental program of the National Republican party. To begin with, Clay urged building public works at federal expense. Federal construction of roads, bridges, highways, canals would help bind together all the great sections of the nation—East, West, North, and South. For example, the farmer in the West

54

could, with improved transportation, more easily ship his produce to the cities in the East. With the money he received from the sale of his produce he could buy the Eastern manufactured goods he needed. Thus, both the Western farmer and the Eastern manufacturer would prosper, and the ties uniting the nation would be strengthened.

To encourage American industry, Clay proposed a protective tariff so that manufacturers could withstand the fearful competition of foreign goods, particularly British goods, when, after the War of 1812, Britain began dumping her products on the American market. Also, Clay favored a sound banking system supported by the federal government, with stable currency and ready credit which could expand and contract according to the needs of business. He therefore strongly favored continuing the Second National Bank, chartered in 1816, which was operating very efficiently under the able direction of its president, Nicholas Biddle.

Clay claimed his American system—internal improvements, tariff protection, sound currency, and credit—would benefit all geographical sections and economic classes of the country and quickly establish the nation in the front ranks of modern industrial societies. But his program required direct governmental action; it meant strengthening the central government and enlarging its powers to direct and influence the financial affairs of the American people. Those who saw advantage and merit in the American System gravitated to the National Republican party. Those who worried about enlarging the power of the federal government entered the Democratic party.

There was another side—a noneconomic side—to the principles and program of the National Republicans. That side was largely the contribution of John Quincy Adams, running for reelection against Jackson in 1828. He believed the federal government should be responsible for the nation's intellectual and cultural progress. He advocated founding a national university, since knowledge, he said, was the first instrument for the betterment of man. In addition, he proposed building an astronomical observatory to study the phenomena of the heavens. In Europe there were upward of 130 such "light-houses of the skies," he wrote, while in America there was not one. Moreover, he urged systematic and scientific exploration of both the western territories and the entire northeastern coastline to discover and publicize the resources and capabilities of the American continent. Adams also proposed establishing a naval academy similar to West Point (this was achieved much later by a Democratic administration), a Department of the In-

The set mouth, gaunt expression and sharp angles of Henry Clay's face are softened somewhat in this idealized portrait. It does show, however, his commanding presence and self-confidence.

terior, a more effective patent law to protect inventors, and an improved and uniform standard of weights and measures to replace the hodgepodge currently (and still) practiced.

Unquestionably, Adams was an intellectual giant. Unfortunately, he was also a political pigmy. Short and balding, he looked as dour and forbidding as the most stereotyped of colonial Puritans. "I am a man of reserved, cold, austere and forbidding manners," he frankly admitted in his diary. "My political adversaries say, a gloomy misanthrope; and my personal enemies an unsocial savage. With a knowledge of the actual defects in my character, I have not the pliability to reform it."

Son of John Adams, the revolutionary patriot and second President, John Quincy Adams was raised to become President of the United States. He was expected to be a great man, and it placed a terrible burden on him all the days of his life. His mother, the extraordinarily intelligent and strong-willed Abigail Smith Adams, took him to Bunker Hill as a young boy to see the site of the famous engagement between American patriots and British soldiers so that he would understand the obligations and sacrifices the cause of liberty and freedom entailed. She had him read ancient history day after day because she felt it was the best way to inspire him with a sense of public duty as well as teach him the lessons of statesmanship. To further his education he was sent to Russia at the age of fourteen to serve as private secretary to Francis Dana, who had been sent by Congress as minister to the court of Catherine the Great. After fourteen months, young Adams journeyed to Paris, where he served as his father's secretary until 1785. The elder Adams, at the time, was United States minister to France. Between mother and father, John Quincy Adams had been programed for the highest public service, and they expected him to fulfill their ambitions for him. In repeated letters to his mother he assured her he wanted to be a "good boy" and become the man she desired.

Returning to the United States, Adams attended Harvard College, studied law, and in 1791 was appointed minister to the Netherlands by President George Washington. Later he headed the missions to Portugal, Prussia, and Russia and served as one of five commissioners who negotiated the peace treaty with Great Britain that ended the War of 1812. Appointed Secretary of State by President James Monroe in 1817, Adams climaxed a successful diplomatic career by becoming a brilliant Secretary, probably the greatest Secretary of State in American history. With Jackson's military help, Adams won the diplomatic battles to

This late daguerreotype, taken a year before John Quincy Adams's death,
documents everything ever said about him as a brooding, sour-faced misanthrope.

acquire Florida and established a strong American presence in the far northwest, thus transforming the United States into a continental power. He was also the principal architect of the Monroe Doctrine.

In 1824 Adams had run for the presidency. Because there were many other candidates, including Jackson, Clay, and William H. Crawford, no one received a majority of electoral votes. And so, following the requirements of the Twelfth Amendment to the Constitution, the election was thrown for decision to the House of Representatives. On the first ballot the House chose Adams the sixth President of the United States, fulfilling the dream of his aged father and late mother.

Adam's first act as President was to choose Henry Clay to be his Secretary of State. The announcement of this appointment horrified the Jacksonians. "Corrupt bargain!" they raged. Before the House election, they claimed, Clay had obviously offered to throw his support to Adams in return for the secretaryship because that post usually led immediately to the presidency. At least it had for the last twenty years. In the Senate, John Randolph of Roanoke roasted both Adams and Clay in a wild speech full of Latin quotations, literary allusions, European history, and practically everything else the Virginia Senator carried in his intellectual baggage. "Let Judas have his thirty pieces of silver," he roared. This way they could buy "a Potter's field in which to inter this miserable Constitution of ours, crucified between two gentlemen." He ended his speech with a shocker, including a wild analogy to the novel *Tom Jones*. "I was defeated, horse, foot, and dragoons—cut up—and clean broke down—by the coalition of Blifil and Black George—by the combination, unheard of till then, of the Puritan and the black-leg."

Black-leg! Now it was Clay's turn to rage. Immediately he challenged Randolph to a duel. Randolph accepted with an announcement that he had no intention of making Mrs. Clay a widow. On April 6, 1826, the two hotheads met across the Potomac River from Georgetown near a place called Little Falls Bridge. It was late in the afternoon. The weapons: pistols. The distance: ten paces.

As the two men took their places the sun was just beginning to set behind the Virginia hills. On signal by the second, both men fired. Both fortunately missed. Randolph's bullet struck the stump behind Clay, and Clay's bullet kicked up the dirt behind Randolph. Thomas Hart Benton, who had been trying to prevent the duel and had come along as a witness, now tried to stop the fight. But Clay waved him aside. "This is child's play," he sneered.

Benton then asked Randolph to disengage but was again refused. So the seconds reloaded the pistols. Again the signal was given and again two shots rang out. Clay aimed to kill but the eccentric Randolph raised his arm high and fired into the air. As he did so, he said, "I do not fire at you, Mr. Clay."

There was a pause. Then Randolph walked toward his adversary and extended his hand, which Clay clasped with great vigor. In a voice half choked with emotion, Clay exclaimed, "I trust in God, my dear sir, you are untouched: after what has occurred I would not have harmed you for a thousand worlds."

Randolph looked down at his coat. Clay's second shot had torn a hole through it and come dangerously close to Randolph's hip. Laughing, almost like a maniac, the Virginian said, "You owe me a coat, Mr. Clay."

So ended this ridiculous duel. But it silenced neither Randolph nor the Jacksonians. In the presidential campaign two years later in which Adams ran for reelection, the issue raised most often by the Jacksonians was the so-called "corrupt bargain" charge. And the more Clay protested his innocence the more he convinced people of his guilt.

Clay tried desperately to help Adams defeat Jackson in 1828, but it was a losing propositon almost from the very beginning. The election was reduced to two candidates and so the possibility of final selection again falling to the House of Representatives seemed very remote. And with Jackson's great popularity, the managerial skill of the Democrats, and the burning issue of "corrupt bargain," the outcome seemed a foregone conclusion. Still Clay kept up a good running battle for Adams, refusing to believe that the American people would prefer a "military chieftain" over a President and statesman of proven talent in the tradition of Washington, Jefferson, and Madison. Employing every political device he knew to be effective, Clay prepared to purge the government of all officeholders who opposed the Adams administration. "Henceforth," he wrote one friend, "I think the principle ought to be steadily adhered to of appointing only friends to the Administration in public offices. Such I believe is the general conviction in the Cabinet." But President Adams publicly denounced any attempt to use patronage—rewards of public office—to influence politics. He solemnly promised to appoint men whom he believed worthy of office, irrespective of party. But he later admitted he was "importuned to serve my friends and reproached for neglecting them, because I will not dismiss, or drop from Executive offices, able and faithful political opponents to provide for my own partisans.''

Such noble sentiments only made Clay's job more difficult. Patronage is the very lifeblood of political parties, unless there are large financial contributors who are willing to subsidize the tremendous costs of campaigning. And parties financed by wealth function for wealth. So, in a sense, patronage distribution was a splendid means of preventing political control by the rich. Those who worked for a successful candidate could expect a reward once he took office. Realistic politicians like Clay understood this. Not so John Quincy Adams.

Fortunately, Clay was not alone in his efforts to reelect Adams in 1828. He had the considerable assistance of a number of stalwarts, the most important of whom was Daniel Webster of Massachusetts. Between them they constructed a firm base on which to erect their new National Republican party.

Daniel Webster had a strange career. Like Calhoun he started out by going in one political direction and ended up going another. Where Calhoun began as a nationalist and slowly evolved into a states' righter and finally a secessionist, Webster started as an advocate of the states and their rights and then shifted to a strong nationalistic position.

"Black Dan,'' they had called him as a boy. At a tavern one day in Concord, General John Stark, who had fought at the Battle of Bennington during the Revolution, peered at the young Daniel Webster and then with all the candor of age fortified by several stiff drinks said: "Daniel, your face is pretty black, but it isn't so black as your father's was with gunpowder at the Bennington fight.''

True, Daniel Webster was quite dark, so swarthy in fact that some people jokingly told him he looked like an Indian. But when he opened his mouth and started to speak he made sounds such as no Indian—or anyone else for that matter—could imitate. It was a big voice, a bit higher-pitched than one might expect, but rich-sounding and very compelling. By 1825, he was the greatest speaker in New England, and was invited to give an address at the laying of the cornerstone for a monument on Bunker Hill to commemorate the fiftieth anniversary of the famous battle. A great crowd, including General Lafayette, who was then touring in the United States, turned out to hear "Black Dan.''

As Webster rose to speak, the crowd, estimated at ten thousand, hushed to hear every word. He began slowly, reviewing for his audience the many changes that had taken place during the last half century,

The hypnotic stare, bushy eyebrows, bulging forehead, combined with a monumental voice and magnificent delivery, made the "Godlike" Daniel Webster America's greatest orator.

describing how the country had prospered and how the people had advanced under a free government. At one point he turned to the small group of surviving veterans of the Bunker Hill battle and addressed himself directly to them. "Venerable Men," he began. Then he stopped and looked at the few old men seated in the place of honor. "But alas! you are not all here," he continued. "Time and the sword have thinned your ranks."

Having paid due respect to the past, Webster turned to the future, which was the real theme of his speech. The fate of popular government, he said, depends on the success of the political experiment in the United States. "The last hopes of mankind, therefore, rest with us"—with the Union. "Let us cultivate a true spirit of union and harmony. Let us act under a settled conviction, and an habitual feeling, that these twenty-four States are one country." But this nationalistic position was relatively new for Webster, for he had started political life as an intense advocate of states' rights.

Webster had been brought up in New Hampshire, where he was born in 1782—the same year as Van Buren, Calhoun, and Benton. (It was a remarkable year—1782!) Educated at Dartmouth College, he became a lawyer and was elected to Congress from New Hampshire on a platform that condemned the War of 1812—called "Mr. Madison's War" by many New Englanders—and even hinted at secession. The merchants and shipowners of New England had been making money trading with Britain, and the war jeopardized their profits. In a public letter addressed to President Madison, Webster wrote: "We shrink from the separation of the states as an event fraught with incalculable evils." But if it comes, he continued, the fault will rest with the administration and its fire-eating friends from the South and West. Supported by shipping and mercantile interests who were staunchly hostile to the administration and the war, Webster had no difficulty winning election to Congress for several terms.

After the war, when men like Clay and Calhoun were publicly arguing for a strong national government, Webster defended the states and their rights. Like his constituents, he insisted that the national government possessed only limited powers. He emphatically opposed federally sponsored internal improvements, protective tariffs and a national bank.

In 1816 Webster moved from New Hampshire to Boston because he felt Massachusetts held many more opportunities for a rising lawyer and politician. Indeed, almost overnight, his career shot forward. Soon he was arguing cases before the United States Supreme Court. After his successful performance before this court in the Dartmouth College case, he was hired to argue *McCulloch* vs. *Maryland* and *Gibbons* vs. *Ogden.* All these decisions were historic. Many of them, as announced by Chief Justice John Marshall, were culled directly from Webster's arguments.

Webster's success in the courts, usually in defense of business interests in Massachusetts, rapidly advanced his political career. Besides allowing him to buy stock in their corporations and paying him substantial legal fees, Massachusetts businessmen supported his bid for election to Congress starting in 1823, first as Representative and then as Senator. And his unique speaking and legal talents promptly vaulted him to the front ranks of Congressional leadership.

But where initially New England had had heavy investments in shipping and mercantile interests and had objected to the tariff—along with all the other features of Clay's American System—now, in the period following the War of 1812, New England had turned to industry and had begun shifting her capital from shipping to manufactures. Consequently, protecting northeastern manufactures from lower-priced foreign goods by means of a tariff seemed a matter of necessity. In time Henry Clay's entire American System became exceedingly attractive to New England—internal improvements, bank, tariff, everything.

As the interests and needs of his constituents slowly changed, so too did Webster's ideas about the role of government in aiding the economic well-being of the nation. Soon he had changed his position and was arguing for the tariff, at least on those commodities that competed with New England manufactures. Soon he was advocating the merits of the national bank. Indeed, he accepted a retainer's fee from the bank to argue its interests in and out of Congress. Soon he was a full-fledged defender of Clay's entire American System. And, most particularly, he became an ardent nationalist. Gone were his ideas about states' rights. His speeches more and more proclaimed the indissoluble bond between liberty and union. His position stood in stark contrast to the states' rights and secessionist ideas of John C. Calhoun.

Webster had given John Quincy Adams his support in the 1824-25 House presidential election, and he had joined very enthusiastically with Clay to create the National Republican party to try to reelect Adams in 1828. One of the first actions taken by Webster and Clay was to begin a search for that essential ingredient of party building: money. "It seems to me," Clay advised Webster, "that our friends who have the ability should contribute a fund for the purpose of aiding the cause."

Webster was an excellent fund raiser—after all, he had many well-heeled friends—and most of the money either went to Clay himself for dispersal or was distributed as Clay directed. Much of the money went to newspapers to buy support. "The course adopted by the Opposition, in the dissemination of Newspapers and publications against the Administration and supporting presses," declared Clay, "leaves to its friends no other alternative than that of following their example, so far at least as to circulate information among the people." Like the Democrats, Clay and Webster understood the need of influencing the people and persuading them to vote the National Republican ticket.

Clay and Webster also exhorted their friends around the country to organize themselves by forming local committees and holding state conventions. Webster toured New England to ensure its loyalty to Adams and later accepted speaking engagements in Pennsylvania and New York to influence those crucial states. He constantly urged his supporters to "*bestir* themselves" and "rally friends."

And Clay was no less active. "It is a part of the system of the friends of General Jackson," he wrote one partisan, "to make demonstrations—speak boldly—claim every body and every State, and carry the election by storm. The circumstance most to be deprecated is that this system has too much success in dispiriting our friends. You ask my opinion as to the project of a convention in Virginia to nominate, in January next, electors for Mr. Adams. It appears to me to be an excellent project, and one that can not fail to have a good effect."

The National Republicans did indeed hold state conventions, and local rallies and county meetings too. "Political meetings are continually taking place in the different Towns of the State [New Jersey]," explained one National Republican, "where Resolutions are passed and Delegates appointed to attend at Trenton to fix on the Electoral Ticket." At these conventions, central committees and correspondence committees were appointed to keep in communication with similar committees in other states. These interacting committees gave the National Republicans the semblance of a national political organization.

Unfortunately these efforts were woefully uneven throughout the country. The National Republican party was almost nonexistent in the South because of its tariff stance, and in the West the Adams supporters

65

were exceedingly slow in setting up party machinery, resulting occasionally in no machinery at all. Although Clay was admired in most of the West—he was sometimes called "Harry of the West"—it was Jackson who had captured Western affection. Adams as a candidate, on the other hand, was a distinct liability—colorless, drab, unexciting. According to one Western National Republican, the Democrats were "an organized corps, active and well disciplined"; as for his own party, he said, "we have a great many well wishers . . . but no organization."

It was in New England and the middle states of New Jersey, New York, Pennsylvania, Delaware, and Maryland that the National Republicans were strong. The newspapers were particularly effective in chewing over the details of Jackson's "two" marriage ceremonies. Some editors were indignant. "Ought a convicted adultress," wrote one of them of Rachel, "and her paramour husband to be placed in the highest offices of this free and christian land?" Some stories appearing in newspapers came right out of the gutter and were the inventions of desperate editors. "General Jackson's mother was a COMMON PROSTITUTE," read one such item, "brought to this country by the British soldiers! She afterward married a MULATTO MAN, with whom she had several children, of which number General Jackson IS ONE!!!" Old Hickory's reputation as a duelist and gunfighter was also given considerable newspaper coverage. He was maligned as a bully and ruffian, a street brawler, cockfighter, and gambler.

The intensity and scurrility of the propaganda during the 1828 presidential election undoubtedly resulted because both national parties were trying to adjust to the circumstances of a changing society and the vast numbers of new voters they were attempting to control and manage. The Democrats' overwhelming success in winning Jackson's election to the presidency set an example and encouraged both parties to even greater managerial feats in future elections.

But the significance, finally, in the development of party structure and technique was that it got the mass of American voters to participate in the process of selecting the people who run the government. However much Democrats and National Republicans debased the art of debating issues and presenting candidates for office to the electorate, they did bring the people and the government closer together. And that was one of the most lasting and important contributions of the Jacksonian age.

BOOK II

ISSUES AND ANSWERS

(overleaf) The great issues of the day—slavery, union, the Bank, presidential power—were argued and debated in Congress before packed galleries. In this painting, *The Reply to Hayne*, Webster delivers his famous anti-nullification speech, while Calhoun, perched in the presiding officer's chair (in the shadow, left), listens intently.

5

Who Shall Hold Office?

THE ADMINISTRATION OF Andrew Jackson lasted two terms. It stretched from his inauguration on March 4, 1829, until Martin Van Buren, his hand-picked successor, replaced him on March 4, 1837. But to a very large extent the entire fifty-year period between the War of 1812 and the Civil War was the Age of Jackson. And all the experiments in democracy, the alterations of the political process, the extensions of the franchise, the attacks on privilege and deference, the swelling spirit of popular rule—all these were summed up in the phrase "Jacksonian Democracy." It was as though the United States had formed a circle around Jackson to receive the signals and impulses he radiated. Indeed, many of the political vibrations that rocked and jolted the nation during the first half of the nineteenth century resulted directly from his actions and decisions.

Jackson's dynamic force was felt even before he became President— the Florida invasion was only one example—and it would continue to be felt after he left the White House. But the really significant phase of his life, the period in which he had the greatest impact, transpired during the Hero's actual presidency. For his administration grappled with several issues which in their resolution had a profound influence on the course of American life and institutions. These issues included involving more people in the actual running of the government through the rotation system; the problem of holding the Union together; the problem of the Indians; and the struggle for power between the President and the Congress, which resulted in a restructured government.

The first issue was simple and direct: Who shall hold government office? When the masses of people converged on the capital to witness Jackson's inauguration, a large corps of Democratic party newspapermen also streamed into the city to claim their rewards for a contest well fought. They knew they had been valuable to both party and candidate as publicists of the cause, and they were present to receive their just recognition—jobs. From New Hampshire came the brilliant Isaac Hill, a short, lame and cadaverous-looking man who edited the *Patriot* and had helped organize a strong and effective party for Jackson in his state. It was said at the time that he was "determined to revolutionize [New Hampshire] before the end of 1828"—and he practically succeeded. From Kentucky came the wizened, prematurely gray but much talented Amos Kendall, editor of the *Argus of Western America*, who had labored so successfully to unite several party factions in Kentucky behind Jackson to steal that state right out from under Henry Clay's nose.

Other politically important editors who arrived in Washington to share the electoral victory included scholarly Nathaniel Greene, editor of the Boston *Statesman*; quiet Gideon Welles of the New Haven *Journal*; jovial Mordecai M. Noah, editor of the New York City *National Advocate*; energetic Dabney S. Carr of the Baltimore *Republican*; and "from everywhere else," fumed Daniel Webster, "somebody else." It was a large contingent of journalistic and political talent that had come to Washington to "assist Jackson in the establishment of popular rule." Soon these men were meeting daily at the house of Reverend Obadiah B. Brown, a friendly, affable man who doubled as clerk in the Post Office Department during the week and as a minister in the Baptist church on Sundays. Together, they prepared their suggestions and projects for the President to inaugurate "the people's government."

When the group stood outside the east portico of the Capitol on inauguration day and heard Jackson talk about reforming the government by removing the "unfaithful and incompetent," every one of them must have quivered with joy and anticipation. The "rascals" would be thrown out and they, the friends of the masses, would share the rewards, the "spoils" of victory. And true enough, one way or another, either directly or indirectly, they were handsomely repaid. A few of them even exerted a powerful influence on the Jackson administration.

The most powerful was Kendall. Jackson appointed him Fourth Auditor of the Treasury, and from this position he cleared out many of the friends of Adams and Clay and replaced them with certified Democrats. Later he was named Postmaster General, at which time Jackson elevated that post to cabinet level. Henceforth the Postmaster General would control an enormous amount of the federal patronage, and from this position he could pay political debts.

Kendall was also instrumental in winning the President's approval for establishing a new journal in Washington to serve as the official mouthpiece of the Democratic party. As editor, Francis P. Blair was brought in, a mousy-looking man, hardly weighing more than a hundred pounds, who had been Kendall's newspaper associate in Kentucky. On December 7, 1830, the Washington *Globe* began publication, and immediately won national recognition as the voice and mind of the Democratic party, officially approved by Jackson and the leaders of the party in Congress. Blair was a superb editor whose slashing style of writing thoroughly pleased the President.

Isaac Hill, another rough-and-tough-talking editor, was named Second Comptroller of the Treasury. In this office he expected to imitate the style of Kendall in distributing jobs. But he didn't get far, for the Senate refused to confirm his appointment, whereupon he returned to New Hampshire and won election to the United States Senate. As he strolled around the Senate floor he savored every moment of his revenge.

Kendall, Blair, Hill, and several other men became part of a group subsequently known as the "Kitchen Cabinet." This group of unofficial advisers to the President supposedly came to visit Jackson by way of the back stairs through the kitchen. However they got to the President, they successfully claimed his attention and influenced his actions because their ideas almost always mirrored his own. They were all professionals in party politics and they understood how men were managed or manipulated, rewarded or punished to implement the operation of government.

On one particular matter these men were absolutely agreed: the need to "reform" the government by a change of personnel. For these journalists it was a matter of practical politics, the reward for services

Washington seen from across the Potomac seems quiet and rural, yet during this era it was the setting for spectacular Congressional brawls that changed the fate of the nation.

rendered. But for Jackson it was a matter of principle, a matter of democratizing the operation of government. What he wanted understood was that the pervasive notion, traditionally followed up to this time, that government service was the right of the elite—the well educated or the upper class—would no longer be valid under his administration. Jackson believed that government jobs should be open to all. The masses—educated or not, wealthy or not, wellborn or born in obscurity—might not only vote, but hold office as well. Moreover, he contended that it was important in a republic that there be a regular turnover of personnel in government; otherwise office holders become inefficient and corrupt. In time, said Jackson, a bureaucracy emerges which is totally divorced from the people.

His administration would be based on what he called "the principal of rotation." And he proudly proclaimed it to the entire nation in his first annual message to Congress, delivered in December 1829, less than a year after taking office. He flatly stated that the "duties of all public officers are . . . so plain and simple that men of intelligence may readily qualify themselves for their performance. . . . In a country where offices are created solely for the benefit of the people no one man has any more intrinsic right to official station than another." Offices were not established, he continued, to give support to "particular men" at the public expense. No wrong is therefore done by removing them from office, "since neither appointment to nor continuance in office is a matter of right."

To Jackson the principle of rotation directly addressed the problem of how and by whom the government should be run. Jackson believed that through rotation the federal government in Washington could be made to respond directly to the changing demands of the American people as expressed by their ballots. Thus, each new administration, elected by the people, should bring in its own corps of supporters to make certain the policies of that administration were honestly and fairly implemented. Most important, rotation meant that a great many more people would get an opportunity to serve the government. The more people actively involved in the affairs of the nation, the more democratic the system, and the more the problems of the nation get to be widely known and understood. It was an old Jeffersonian principle: Greater participation by the electorate in government safeguards the nation from arbitrary and dictatorial rule. Rotation comes closest to the ideal of making government and its problems available to the largest number of people. But though it was an old principle, Jackson's way of hammering at its importance was new and seemed revolutionary at the time.

Rotation also strengthens the party—the best bulwark of democracy—by placing in the hands of politicians the distribution of jobs (patronage) as rewards, and this nurtures the party organization. But there are dangers: Rotation can be an easy excuse and justification for political head chopping, for regarding government jobs as "spoils" won in a war in which enemies are punished and friends rewarded. When this is the attitude, the best, most efficient, and most dedicated public servants will frequently be removed to make room for party workers whose only interest in office is the money or power involved. When rotation is administered by incompetents or thieves, then everyone suffers and the democratic system is dangerously compromised.

For some politicians, of course, "spoils" is all rotation really means. But to the politician devoted to public service it doesn't mean that at all. Van Buren provides a good example of a politician who used patronage intelligently and with a view to its salutary impact on the operation of government. In New York State he had built his political organization, the Albany Regency, on the skillful use of patronage. In the process he encouraged the careers of such distinguished men as William L. Marcy, Silas Wright, Jr., Benjamin F. Butler, and John A. Dix. But Van Buren ignored the claims of stupid or dishonest politicians and recognized only those men whose intelligence, integrity, ability, and loyalty were outstanding. His machine, as a consequence, was rarely operated by political hacks.

Not that it was simple or easy to dispense patronage with intelligence and skill. Men like Van Buren were hounded for jobs, and it was frequently impossible to shake loose a determined office seeker. Shortly after Jackson's election, Van Buren was designated Secretary of State. In no time the Little Magician was deluged by office seekers. He happened to be in New York City staying at the City Hotel. One young man went looking for him and found the bar in the City Hotel crowded with politicians who had come to "pay their respects" to the Secretary-designate. After a while the doors of the dining room were thrown open and a clerk came in, mounted a chair, and called out:

"Gentlemen who desire to see Mr. Van Buren will please walk into the dining-room."

"We thundered in—" reported the young man, "fifty or sixty of us;

politicians in and out of place; those wanting to get in, those to stay in. We were all hail fellows well met, and there was a roar of jovial talk and banter. Politicians, you know, are friendly to every body; for no man knows who can or who can not forward his views, nor how soon a man now powerless may be in a position to help.''

After a while a waiter entered the room and said, ''Gentlemen, Mr. Van Buren requests your cards.''

Everybody broke out laughing. There was a general fumbling in pockets.

''Cards?'' said the young man. ''What does he want cards for? I have no card with me. I shall write a note.''

While the other office seekers kidded him about his naïveté, the young man scribbled a note which said: ''Sir, I am the bearer of two letters of introduction to you: one from my uncle, Mr. — —, and the other from my friend, the Hon. — —.''

The young man folded his note and placed it on the tray with the cards. The waiter took the tray and withdrew. After a time he returned and solemnly announced:

''Gentlemen, Mr. Van Buren sends his compliments and says he is fatigued with his journey, and requests the honor of your company this evening at eight o'clock, one and all.''

As everyone started to leave, the waiter called to the young man and asked him to wait. Suddenly he became the lion of the room.

''You are a made man,'' said one. ''You'll get the best office in the gift of the government. Not a doubt of it.''

The crowd slowly dispersed. The young man sat some minutes wondering how long he would have to wait and what he would say when he met the great man. ''Without having heard any one enter, I looked up at length, and lo! there, on the opposite side of the fire-place sat the Magician!''

The Little Magician, the Red Fox of Kinderhook, the master builder of the Democratic party! The young man approached his quarry; there was a shaking of hands; the letters were presented and Van Buren read them carefully as though studying each word. After a moment or two Van Buren refolded the letters and said in a voice that was reassuring and almost seductive: ''I highly esteem your uncle, and also your friend. No men in the State stand higher in my regard than they. If I can do anything to oblige them or forward your views, it will give me great pleasure.''

What suavity! what style! thought the young man. A hack politician would have blurted out something like "What can I do for you?" or "As soon as I have something I'll get in touch with you," or "Tell your uncle I'll keep you in mind" or some such. Not Van Buren. Although he knew what the young man was about, he spoke with a subtlety that respected the sensibilities both of himself and the office seeker.

Not unexpectedly, the young man became a clerk in the State Department. He enjoyed a long tenure though he saw many men come and go. Each time there was a new Secretary of State, he did not know for days, sometimes weeks, whether he would be retained. Yet he lasted eight years. Then one morning shortly after a new administration had begun, "a gentleman entered my office, and, presenting his commission, informed me, with the utmost politeness, that I was no longer in the service of the government, and that I saw before me that dread being—terror of all office-holders—A SUCCESSOR!

"I have seen many heads taken off in my time,"he said, "but never one quite so neatly as my own."

When Van Buren arrived in Washington early in 1829 to take up his post as Secretary of State, there was another horde of office seekers waiting for him at his hotel. Even though it was after dark they spotted his coach, surrounded it, and pursued him to his room, where he flopped on a sofa to recover from the tedious journey. Soon the room was filled with people jammed together from wall to wall, and for the next hour they pressed their demands upon him, finally leaving when Van Buren informed them he must go to pay his respects to the President.

Jackson was not better off. In fact his situation was worse. Applicants came right to the White House door and demanded to see "their" President. They were taken directly to him to plead their need. Since this was the "People's government," the people felt no constraint about going directly to the top man and informing him of their wishes. Jackson was so inundated with demands for jobs that he wrote there were five hundred applicants for every office available. Nevertheless he said he was "determined to hear with caution, examine well, and grant offices to none but such as was honest and capable."

Thus, in the early years of the Jackson administration, there appeared to be a mad scramble for office, with politicians of all stripes and talents competing for every favor imaginable. Jackson's enemies circulated stories that during the first year of the "People's government" some two thousand government workers were removed. To men in office from the preceding administration, it seemed like a Democratic "Reign of Terror." There was no other way to describe it. Said one: "Terror . . .

reigned in Washington. . . . The great body of officials awaited their fate in silent horror, glad when the office hours expired at having escaped another day." There were reports that one man "cut his throat from ear to ear, from the mere terror of being dismissed" while another "has gone raving distracted."

The suspicion and fear of a thoroughgoing purge were aggravated by some Democrats themselves. One of Van Buren's lieutenants in the United States Senate, William L. Marcy, a man of integrity and ability, told his colleagues in the Senate flat out that the removals were justified. "To the victor belong the spoils of the enemy," he baldly asserted, leaving himself open to much misinterpretation. The statement seemed to prove everything Jackson's enemies contended about the removals.

In New York City a man of considerably less integrity, one Samuel Swartwout, described the principle of spoils in very direct and simple terms precisely as he understood it. Unfortunately his letter, later published to the dismay of Jacksonians everywhere, reinforced the position of those who argued that the President's system was simple spoilsmanship. "I hold to your doctrine fully," Swartwout wrote, "that no d——d rascal who made use of his office or its profits for the purpose of keeping Mr. Adams in, and General Jackson out of power, is entitled to the least lenity or mercy, save that of hanging. . . . Whether or not I shall get any thing in the general scramble for plunder, remains to be proven; but I rather guess I shall. . . . Your man, if you want a place, is — —. . . . Make your suit to him, then, and you will get what you want."

Cadaverous, vacant-eyed, slack-jawed, Swartwout did in fact get his share of the plunder. He was an old friend of Jackson's and one of the President's earliest supporters in New York City. Swartwout wanted to be Collector of the Customs House in New York because that was where much "loot" could be found. The President obligingly gave him the job, but not before Van Buren protested vigorously. Swartwout was a crook, he told the President, who would surely bring disgrace to the administration if given such a sensitive and lucrative post. But one of Jackson's most outstanding characteristics was his fierce loyalty to friends (as well as ferocious animosity toward enemies) and so he refused to believe Van Buren or remove Swartwout. A few years later it was discovered that Swartwout had stolen over a million dollars from the Customs House. He fled to Europe to escape capture and imprisonment. Jackson was deeply offended by his friend's betrayal. "Can he live after this?" he raged, "or will he cut his own throat?"

The Swartwout incident confirmed in the minds of critics that the Jackson administration had inaugurated a spoils system by which the government was being plundered by political hacks as a reward for services rendered the party. "The government," stormed one man, "formerly served by the *elite* of the nation, is now served, to a very considerable extent, by its refuse."

Despite the criticism and the few scandals that surfaced during his administration, Jackson kept insisting that rotation was basically democratic and consistent with the nation's republican form of government. The old system of appointments and removals meant a policy of "elitist" control of the government, said Jackson, and he was more than ever convinced of the need for rotation.

But the furor over the spoils system convinced most Americans that the President had indeed instituted democratic government for the nation. Whether true or not, that's what they believed. To the ordinary citizen, the common man, it seemed that "the people" themselves had finally assumed control of their government. No wonder, then, that this period of American history came to be designated "The Rise of the Common Man." It dovetailed perfectly with remembered scenes of Jackson's inauguration when thousands of "plain folk" converged on Washington to witness the commencement of the "People's government."

Democratic politicians and newspapermen, quite naturally, propagated this notion. Their newspapers rang with claims that Jackson and his party represented the great masses of the electorate and that their victory terminated rule by the "elite." And who were the elite? They were the few, the wellborn, the "aristocracy." They were the rich who had controlled the government long enough. Their day was now over, and their places assumed by the common people. Democracy had arrived in America!

Whether democracy had *really* come to America can be debated. In fact many present-day historians have gone to great pains to prove the phrase "Jacksonian Democracy" a contradiction in terms. But they miss the important point. The people at the time *believed* democracy had come to America and they believed it in part because it was repeated to them over and over, especially during the furor over removals. Thus, one of the important accomplishments of the politicians of the Jacksonian age was the democratic style and tone they generated, even though true democracy for all Americans—including women, blacks, and Indians—was a long way off.

Actually, the rotation system as practiced at this time did not remotely resemble what was described by either the friends or the enemies of Jackson's administration. Its true history was something else. First of all, Jackson did not introduce the system. There was nothing new to removing men from office who were the appointees of one's political opponents. That had been going on for years. Every intelligent man knew this. Even John Quincy Adams's Postmaster General admitted it. "For an administration to bestow its patronage without distinction of party is to court its own destruction." Nevertheless, Jackson's critics honestly contended that his removals were so massive that he had, indeed, invented a spoils system. But here again they were wrong. There never was a purge, never a bloodletting, never a reign of terror. In fact, by no definition was Jackson a spoilsman. Only 919 out of 10,093 government employees were removed during the first eighteen months of his administration. For the entire eight years of his presidency a little more than ten percent of all officeholders were replaced. When these figures are considered in light of normal replacements due to death and resignation or those whose contracts had expired, plus people dismissed for incompetence and dishonesty, they constitute a very creditable record. Certainly this does not represent the actions of a spoilsman who wants to remove everyone in sight and replace him with his friends.

In fact there were many instances when Jackson refused to permit the removal of particular individuals for political reasons. One that received considerable publicity involved Solomon Van Rensselaer. Van Buren had him removed as postmaster of Albany, New York, because he had a long record of political hostility to Van Buren's Regency. Van Rensselaer came to Washington to complain to Jackson, and caught up with the President at a dinner in the White House.

"Sir," said Van Rensselaer to the President, "I have been removed as postmaster of Albany but there is something I wish to show you." With that Van Rensselaer began unbuttoning his jacket.

"What are you doing, Sir?" said the startled Jackson.

"I want you to see my wounds, Sir, received while defending my country against the British during the late war. And my thanks is removal from my office, the only position I have to sustain me in my old age."

Jackson's response was immediate. "Button your jacket," he commanded. "You are still the postmaster."

OFFICE HUNTERS FOR THE YEAR 1834.

A highly effective political cartoon lambasts Jackson, the demon, for corrupting the nation by dangling political plums in front of office seekers who twist, turn and jump to grab at electoral spoils.

When Van Buren heard he had been overruled, he went to Jackson to protest. He explained to the President that Van Rensselaer had been a serious and persistent political enemy in the state capital and would use the office to their disadvantage. But Jackson was adamant. "That man has taken British lead in his body. I will not remove him."

It made a pretty story when it got out, and it proved to the American people once more that a patriot, a noble and just man, was President of the United States.

If removals were relatively few, then was the notion that the common people had taken over the operation of government nothing but political propaganda? Not exactly—although the propaganda didn't hurt. As a matter of fact the government was indeed democratized—or opened to a larger number of Americans—but not through a system of removals or rotation.* The infusion of new employees to government service resulted from a vastly increased government payroll. Over a ten-year period, from approximately the middle of the 1820s through most of Jackson's two terms, government expenditures doubled from eleven and a half million dollars per annum to nearly twenty-three million. And much of the distribution of new jobs thus created was in fact carefully controlled and managed by skillful Democrats. For example, the Constitution requires that a census be taken every ten years, and the 1830 census became an excellent opportunity to strengthen the party through the appointment of census takers. Amos Kendall was largely responsible for the superb manner in which the Democrats realized the possibility of gaining popular favor. As early as 1829 he was instructing state leaders about the necessity of building a strong party apparatus at the local level. The initial step in any organizational plan, he advised, should be a "private meeting" of members of the legislature with "all the good and true men" in the state, plus the appointment of a central committee and the designation of "trusty agents in every county." And, in selecting these trusty agents, he went on, "you may hold out to them the hope, that if they are active in organizing and training the party, they will probably receive the appointment to take in the census, and efficient means must be taken to reserve it to them, thus proving that fidelity to the cause shall not go without its reward."

As thousands of new faces joined the government service, small

---

*One modern study (see Further Reading) argues that in terms of education and social standing, Jackson's appointments were little different from John Adams's and Thomas Jefferson's.

wonder then that Jackson's enemies presumed there had been a massive execution of incumbent officeholders.

Although the spoils controversy during Jackson's administration may appear insignificant to us today, actually it was extremely important. Its importance gets to the very heart of government. First of all, in raising the issue Jackson hoped to establish the principle of rotation as a means of strengthening democratic government. Its discussion, pro and con, added to the general climate of democracy that characterized the age. It seemed to document the notion that popular government had been established. As Jackson said—and it has not been said better—office is created for the benefit of the people, not the support of officeholders. Next, in practical terms, the great expansion of the personnel of the government during the 1830s meant many more people were actually engaged in the operation of government. This was a healthy development. So, in fact, Jackson's objective—to draw fresh blood into the government—was at least partly achieved. Finally, and perhaps most important of all, the spoils question directly confronted the problem of how and by whom the government should be run. Jackson offered one way. He called it "rotation." But his way can, and in time did, lead to abuses when it was made to serve only the party and not the people, and when incompetents and criminals took charge of the government's business.

To reformers of the late nineteenth century, the abuses resulting from Jackson's way were solved by civil-service legislation. But that way also created problems. Where will the two major parties—upon whom the country is absolutely dependent for its governmental functions—obtain the means to operate if the patronage is denied them? The answer is obvious. They will turn to the rich, both individual and corporate. And, as the 1970s' scandals of the Nixon administration—the Watergate, milk-fund, selling of ambassadorships, and ITT affairs—surely demonstrated, that alternative is a dangerous and frightening one.

The problem remains. Its importance is clear. Any government can be subverted by its servants. Perhaps the solution lies in getting a great many more people to contribute their time and modest sums to keep the two parties operating honestly and efficiently. If, in time, this does happen, then the Jacksonian objective of drawing the people and their government closer together will have been achieved.

6

The Problem of Union

THE ONLY ISSUE that ever seriously endangered the safety of the Union was slavery. In 1861 the Civil War finally fissured the nation and, in the prophetic words of Daniel Webster, "drenched [the land] in fraternal blood." The scar of that rupture remained red and angry for decades. Indeed, the full consequence of that unhappy era in terms of racial strife remains to this day.

The first serious explosion in the country over slavery occurred during Jackson's administration. But because of Jackson's strong presidential leadership, a willingness on both sides to compromise, and a desire to "save the Union," bloody conflict and secession were prevented, at least temporarily. But as historian William W. Freehling has pointed out, the controversy that erupted in 1832 during Jackson's administration was a "prelude" to the convulsion that shattered the nation thirty years later. When war finally came many Americans wistfully looked back to the Age of Jackson and remembered how their President had guided the country away from secession and its bloody consequence. They wished somehow to summon him from the grave. So, in the presidential election of 1860, many of them went to the polls and voted for Jackson, even though it was foolish and a bit crazy. Maybe they thought that act of desperation would express their need for his kind of leadership and would somehow rescue them from their predicament.

The controversy that boiled out of the Jackson era occurred a little over forty years after the creation of the American nation, and seriously raised questions about the continuance of the Union. But the problem was not a simple one. It got all tangled up with related issues such as the personal ambitions of rival politicians, sectional antagonisms, the antislavery crusade in the North and the anger and hostility that that crusade engendered in the slaveholding South, states' rights and nullification ideas, and the problem of the tariff. To understand what happened in this first crisis over preserving the Union, it is necessary to examine a few of these tangled strands in more detail.

Take political rivalries—the jealousies and opposing ambitions of men who were competing to become Jackson's successor as President.

John C. Calhoun, the spokesman for Southern interests, had been elected Vice-President as Jackson's running mate in 1828, and it seemed to him and to a great many other people, especially his friends, that he would succeed Jackson in the White House in four or eight years, depending on whether the President wanted one or two terms in office. But almost immediately he ran afoul of the presidential ambitions of Martin Van Buren. This, plus his own foolish mistakes, eventually alienated him from Jackson and the Democratic party and drove him to words and deeds that endangered the Union.

When Jackson appointed Van Buren Secretary of State, Calhoun suddenly saw his rival rise up before him. To cut the Secretary back to size, Calhoun embarked on a desperate scheme to force the dismissal of Jackson's cabinet and arrange the appointment of a new cabinet which would exclude Van Buren and his friends. He went about it by attempting to goad the Secretary of War, John Eaton, into resigning; once Eaton was got rid of, it would be easy to push out the rest. Calhoun's scheme went like this: Eaton's wife, Margaret (Peggy) O'Neale Timberlake, had an unsavory past, and Calhoun and his wife set out to embarrass Eaton by deliberately snubbing Peggy. As the soul of Southern propriety and rectitude, Calhoun, and his wife, refused to socialize with her, and they prevailed upon their friends, those both inside and outside the cabinet, to follow their example. This kind of pressure was expected to drive the Eatons from Washington.

But Calhoun's plot backfired. While Van Buren went out of his way to associate with the Eatons, Jackson defended Peggy, seeing in her something of his beloved Rachel, whose life had been shortened, he said, because of similar treatment. "What divine right," Jackson stormed, "let females . . . establish a secrete [*sic*] inquisition and decree who shall, & who shall not, come into society—and who shall be sacraficed [*sic*] by their secrete slanders." Eventually Eaton did resign because of the embarrassment, and the entire cabinet was, in fact, replaced, all of which acutely distressed Jackson because it made him and his administration look foolish.

For this he had Calhoun to thank, and he did not take it kindly. He soon discovered additional reasons to resent his Vice-President. Jackson learned that years before, Calhoun, as Secretary of War in the Monroe administration, had sought his censure because of the Florida invasion. It is not particularly clear how Jackson first learned the truth. There had been rumors for years. But all along the General thought Calhoun had been his defender who had tried to block the censure efforts inside Monroe's cabinet. Now in 1830 he learned differently. He was given documentary evidence that showed what Calhoun had really done. Jackson confronted Calhoun with the evidence and asked for an explanation. Responding in a fifty-two-page letter, Calhoun sputtered a defense which left no doubt that he had been guilty of a gross hypocrisy. The President replied with a curt, "No further communication with you on the subject is necessary." Calhoun then made the further mistake of going public with the controversy, printing copies of letters by the various participants, and ending up by accusing Van Buren of reviving the incident in order to stab him in the back and replace him as Jackson's successor in the White House. The public disclosure of these letters infuriated the President because it was calculated to injure his reputation with the people. But friends assured him the Vice-President did himself more harm than anyone else.

As his political fortunes plunged, as his presidential prospects dimmed, Calhoun became reckless—reckless particularly about slavery, for he had nothing to lose. Always in the background, smoldering behind many political debates of the day, lurked the dread issue of slavery. And now Calhoun chose to concentrate on that issue and force a public discussion of it. In the past, in defending the South and what he called its "peculiar institution"—slavery—he had disguised his identity. Now, his immediate presidential hopes dashed, he was openly arguing Southern "rights," particularly the extreme idea of the right of a state to void or nullify any federal law that jeopardized its interests, whatever those interests might be.

Congress passed a particularly high tariff bill in 1828, which was immediately dubbed the Tariff of Abominations and generated cries of secession from the Union by some Southern hotheads. Calhoun returned to his plantation in South Carolina burdened with the need to do something about what he called the "illegality" of forcing such federal legislation as the new tariff down the throat of a reluctant state. He felt he must articulate a theory by which a state could protect itself against the tyranny of the central government. In short, he must devise a method whereby the minority could defend itself against an overbearing majority.

What finally resulted was a paper entitled "Exposition and Protest," which was passed in 1828 by the South Carolina legislature without mentioning the author's name. In it Calhoun not only condemned protective tariffs, but, more importantly, developed the doctrine of nullification. This theory argued that if the federal government passed legislation detrimental to the interests of a state—a tariff, for example—then the state could pass its own law declaring the federal law inoperative within its boundaries. Thus federal legislation would be "nullified" within that state. If three-fourths of all the states nullified, then the law would be void everywhere, just as if the Constitution had been amended. Through the process of nullification, Calhoun argued, the rights of the minority would be protected. In a republic, he said, majority rule must always be tempered by minority rights.

But suppose the federal government refused to allow its laws to be nullified by a single state? Then, said Calhoun—and he said it reluctantly—the state had the right to secede from the Union. But, he insisted, he had advanced the doctrine of nullification to *prevent* secession, to prevent the dismemberment of the Union.

Some of these ideas got a thorough public and national review when a stormy debate broke out in the U.S. Senate in January 1830. Daniel Webster of Massachusetts and Calhoun's spokesman, Robert Y. Hayne of South Carolina, verbally tangled over the composition and nature of the Union.

This historic Webster-Hayne debate was provoked by a resolution restricting the further sale of public lands. But almost immediately the debate moved from the question of public lands and sectional rivalries to the all-embracing questions of the continuance of the Union and the troubling problem of slavery.

In a closely argued and meticulously constructed speech, Hayne defended slavery, states' rights, and Calhoun's doctrine of nullification.

If the Union is to be maintained, Hayne argued, the rights of the South, particularly the right to continue owning slaves, must be respected, and any effort to jeopardize those rights would necessitate some extreme form of state action, nullification first, secession if nullification failed. The idea of nullification was based on viewing the Union as simply a confederation of independent states. Thus, Hayne argued, each state was sovereign within its own boundaries and not absolutely subject to federal law. His speech was so powerful, so logical in its arguments— given its premise about the composition of the Union—that Webster, in composing his "reply," was offered assistance by one justice of the Supreme Court. But Webster was confident and waved the assistance aside. "I shall grind him into a powder," Webster said of Hayne, "and blow him away."

The Senate was packed with spectators to hear the "Godlike Daniel." They filled the gallery and spilled over onto the Senate floor itself. It was quite unusual, if not startling, to see women seated on the same floor with the august body of Senators, adding a touch of color to the surroundings with their bright bonnets and stylish dresses.

Once the upper house had been called to order, Webster rose to seek recognition. The presiding officer, Vice-President Calhoun, recognized him, and the drama was under way.

Webster always began a speech slowly, his right hand resting on his desk, his left hanging limply at his side. The magnificent head would then start to turn from side to side to catch the attention of all the spectators in the gallery, his bushy eyebrows and deep-set eyes producing a hypnotic gaze that held his audience in a paralytic grip. Once he had launched into his speech, his voice would swell with emotion for dramatic effect at one moment and then diminish to a whisper to underscore his meaning at the next. As he became more animated his left hand would work itself behind his back and reach under his coattail, while his right hand swung through the air in great looping gestures as though he were trying to pull his audience closer to him. At one point in this speech Webster directly attacked Hayne's states' rights and nullification positions, saying: "I go for the Constitution as it is, and for the Union as it is. It is, Sir, the people's Constitution, the people's government, made for the people, made by the people, and answerable to the people."

Government for and by the people! Never mind the states and their rights. It is the people who count. The people, indivisible, under the *federal* government.

The speech went on for two days. It reached a peak of high drama that electrified the gallery when Webster shook his finger at Vice-President Calhoun and roared that the Union was composed of people, not states. Then came the overwhelming climax, a statement so noble and true that even today it has the power to move a reader and say something important about the life of the nation. "While the Union lasts," he said, "we have high, exciting, gratifying prospects spread out before us, for us and our children. Beyond that I seek not to penetrate the veil. God grant that in my day, at least, that curtain may not rise! God grant that on my vision never may be opened what lies behind! When my eyes shall be turned to behold for the last time the sun in heaven, may I not see him shining on the broken and dishonored fragments of a once glorious Union; on States dissevered, discordant, belligerent; on a land rent with civil feuds, or drenched, it may be, in fraternal blood! Let their last feeble and lingering glance rather behold the gorgeous ensign of the republic, now known and honored throughout the earth, still full high advanced, its arms and trophies streaming in their original lustre, not a stripe erased or polluted nor a single star obscured, bearing for its motto no such miserable interrogatory as 'What is all this worth?' nor those other words of delusion and folly, 'Liberty first and Union afterwards'; but everywhere, spread all over in characters of living light, blazing on all its ample folds, as they float over the sea and over the land, and on every wind under the whole heavens, that other sentiment, dear to every true American heart—Liberty *and* Union, now and forever, one and inseparable!"

Liberty *and* Union! You can't have one without the other, said Webster. Without Union there is no liberty for anyone. If a state can nullify a federal law, it can crack the Union. And once the Union is cracked, it will split again and again until the United States becomes nothing more than a collection of petty sovereignties. In this weakened condition the nation would be subjected to European domination.

It was a stupendous speech, everyone agreed to that; but leaders of both parties were quite disturbed over this sudden public quarrel concerning the nature of the Union and the place of slavery within American society. If allowed to continue, it would certainly worsen the already tense situation in the mounting sectional wrangling and cause serious

89

rifts within the country. In consultation with Van Buren, Jackson quickly recognized his duty to put a stop to it. He abhorred the idea of nullification. As an intense nationalist he rejected it out of hand. As President he felt he must make his position clear to both Congress and the American people.

Jackson got his opportunity on April 13, 1830, when the Democrats held a commemorative celebration to honor the birthday of Thomas Jefferson. After receiving his invitation to the dinner he conferred with Van Buren, who urged him to let the members of his party know—and that included the nullifiers—that the Union must not be threatened or endangered. It was rumored that the friends of Calhoun—and perhaps Calhoun himself—planned to use the occasion to enlist the support of other states in their extreme interpretation of states' rights. Jackson agreed with Van Buren that the time had arrived to stop them. He went to the dinner exhilarated with a sense of impending battle.

The dinner was held at the Indian Queen Hotel. A full portrait of George Washington and two busts of Thomas Jefferson decorated the hall. Numerous evergreens were placed around the room. The diners sat at two parallel tables, with a cross table at the head "which promoted festivity and sociality." When the dinner ended the President was asked to give a toast. Jackson rose and lifted his glass. Then slowly his gaze moved from person to person as though he were looking for someone in particular. Indeed, he was. When the eyes of everyone in the room were riveted on him, Jackson turned and stared directly at John C. Calhoun. Raising his glass a bit higher, he fired his volley squarely into the face of the nullifier.

"Our *Federal* Union," he cried: "*It must be preserved.*"

Utter silence gripped his listeners. His intent and meaning were thunderously clear.

The Vice-President followed with his toast. "The Union," Calhoun declared: "Next to our liberty, the most dear; may we all remember that it can only be preserved by respecting the rights of the States and distributing equally the benefit and burden of the Union." Then came the political master, Martin Van Buren. "Mutual forbearance and reciprocal concession," he said: "Through their agency the Union was established. The patriotic spirit from which they emanated will forever sustain it."

As far as Jackson was concerned, Calhoun's public avowal of nullification had separated him from the community of men dedicated to the defense and preservation of the federal Union. Calhoun's words and

In later life, Calhoun's obsession with the need to protect slavery and the rights of the South gave him this staring, somber look.

actions, he felt, were motivated by his selfish needs and political ambition. The Vice-President was willing to sacrifice party and country for self-serving ends. His present course, wrote Jackson, proved "Calhoun a *villain*."

Just how far Calhoun was prepared to go to demonstrate his independence—and in party terms, disloyalty—became evident shortly after Jackson re-formed his cabinet. The President appointed Van Buren minister to Great Britain, but when the Senate voted on confirmation the result was a tie, 23 to 23, with Southern nullifiers joining Clay, Webster, and other National Republicans in voting against confirmation. The tie-breaking vote lay with the Vice-President, John C. Calhoun.

The angry man could not resist the temptation to strike at his rival. Hating Van Buren and tormented by a need for revenge, Calhoun voted to reject the nomination, even though it meant calling down on his head the wrath of Jackson and the other Democratic leaders. After casting his vote, Calhoun turned to a friend and said, "It will kill him, sir, kill him dead. He will never kick sir, never kick." True, Calhoun had killed a minister, but at the same time he effectively removed himself as Jackson's successor to the presidency—a removal, as it turned out, that proved permanent.

Jackson immediately notified party leaders that he wanted Van Buren as his vice-presidential running mate when he sought reelection to the presidency in 1832. "I have no hesitation in saying that Calhoun is one of the most base hypocritical and unprincipled villains in the United States," said Jackson. He wrote Van Buren that his rejection was a personal attack on the executive, which "the people will properly resent . . . by placing you in the chair of the very man whose casting vote rejected you."

Calhoun was now beyond the pale. Even as Vice-President he no longer counted in Jackson-dominated Democratic circles. He was without a party. His national leadership was gone. As such he became an extremely dangerous man, a man intent on one thing—the interests of his section, the South. And that meant slavery. Every skill he had, every intellectual tool he possessed, was now concentrated on the protection and defense of the South's "peculiar institution." John C. Calhoun would hasten the rush toward confrontation between the North and South.

But apart from the rivalries of ambitious politicians as a factor in opening up the slavery controversy and thereby endangering the Union, two other extremely important developments took place during the 1820s and 1830s that set the North and South on a collision course. Simultaneously, there arose a great demand in the North to end slavery, while in the South there was a rising determination to preserve slavery at all costs.

The antislavery mood in the North had been building for decades. Even in the colonial period there had been opposition to the institution, particularly among Quakers. By the 1770s and 1780s, most of New England had declared slavery illegal, with New York, Pennsylvania, and New Jersey following in the 1780s and 1790s. In the Northwest Territory (the area which later became the states of Michigan, Ohio, Indiana, Illinois, and Wisconsin) the Northwest Ordinance of 1787 forbade slavery; and in 1820, as part of the Missouri Compromise, it was prohibited north of 36° 30′ in the Louisiana Purchase. Furthermore, the Constitution permitted Congress to terminate the importation of slaves— though only after 1808.

This small beginning of the antislavery crusade received a jolting thrust forward during the Jacksonian era. The fact that most western European nations had abandoned slavery had a profound impact on Americans. England abolished the institution in the 1830s, and all the Latin American countries, with the exception of Cuba and Brazil, emancipated their slaves. That a supposedly advanced, civilized, modern and democratic society like the United States could still tolerate the "peculiar institution" in the middle of the nineteenth century seemed monstrous to most Northern liberals.

In the 1820s vocal denunciation of slavery erupted across the tier of Northern states. Several newspapers were founded with the specific purpose of advancing the cause of emancipation by stirring up public opinion over the horror and savagery of the slave institution. In the same way that politicians were founding newspapers to create and control voting majorities, abolitionists were imitating the technique to start a movement that would purge the nation of the brutal institution. The first important paper was the *Genius of Universal Emancipation*. It was a Baltimore journal whose editor, Benjamin Lundy, complemented his writing against slavery by organizing antislavery societies. Lundy was especially active in his organizing work, and indeed the abolitionist crusade might never have succeeded as well as it ultimately did without the intensive effort devoted to organizing people into formal groups, collecting money, and providing abolitionist propaganda that was circulated around the country. Like party politicians, abolitionists organized themselves into militant cadres to slay the slavery beast.

Lundy's newspaper was founded in 1821, and in it he urged the use of reason in persuading Southerners to abandon the slave system. He did not advocate involving the federal government to solve the problem. Soon, however, a more strident editorial voice was heard. William Lloyd Garrison, who learned his trade by writing for Lundy, believed in a more aggressive approach to abolition. His was a raucous, fiery voice demanding the *immediate* end of slavery. His radicalism—he went to prison on one occasion—brought about an estrangement from Lundy. Garrison moved to Boston, where in 1831 he founded his *Liberator* newspaper, the mood and tone of which were sounded with the first issue. "I am aware," Garrison editorialized, "that many object to the severity of my language; but is there not cause for severity? I *will be* as harsh as truth, and as uncompromising as justice. On this subject, I do not wish to think, or speak, or write, with moderation. No! No! Tell a man whose house is on fire, to give a moderate alarm; tell him to moderately rescue his wife from the hands of the ravisher; tell the mother to gradually extricate her babe from the fire into which it has fallen—but urge me not to use moderation in a cause like the present. I am in earnest—I will not equivocate—I will not excuse—I will not retreat a single inch—AND I WILL BE HEARD.''

The fact that the Constitution of the United States recognized slavery—it allowed three-fifths of the slaves to be counted in determining each state's representation in the House of Representatives, did not allow Congress to restrict the importation of slaves until 1808, and provided for returning fugitive slaves to their masters—only proved to Garrison how basically evil the American political system really was. Indeed, he called the Constitution "an agreement with hell and a covenant with death." This denunciation of the supreme law of the land, during a period of intense nationalism in which the signers of the Declaration and the framers of the Constitution were virtually deified, did not help the antislavery cause in the North. There were some Americans—even ardent abolitionists—who regarded Garrison as an extremist, a radical, a lunatic, whose sole purpose was the destruction of the American system of government.

What they especially disliked was the physical violence that began to attend the crusade. The mood was turning ugly. Frequently, at antislavery meetings, abolitionists lost their tempers and insulted the country or jeered at prominent men of the past, like Washington and

Jefferson, who had owned slaves. Sometimes fistfights broke out when anti-abolitionists attended the meetings to foment trouble. Bricks, stones, and other missiles were hurled at people. Garrison himself was roughed up and dragged through the streets by a Boston mob who resented his attack on the Constitution. And Elijah P. Lovejoy, an abolitionist newspaperman, was murdered by a mob in Alton, Illinois, in 1837.

To advance immediate abolition throughout the United States, Garrison had founded the New England Anti-Slavery Society in 1832, and a year later the American Anti-Slavery Society, a national organization to coordinate and direct efforts to end slavery. Among the most notable men and women who were drawn to the abolitionist crusade were Theodore Dwight Weld, Wendell Phillips, Lewis and Arthur Tappan, Gerrit Smith, and Sarah and Angelina Grimké, two sisters from an aristocratic, slave-owning South Carolina family who had moved to the North because of their intense hatred of slavery. Weld became the Anti-Slavery Society's most pungent publicist and lecturer. Angelina Grimké, his wife, was of enormous help, particularly in gathering materials from newspapers to document the horrors of slavery, and in her fervent speeches on the lecture circuit advocating abolition.

Thanks to the organization, agitation, lecturing, and publishing of these converted, conscientious, devoted, and dedicated abolitionists, the antislavery movement spread rapidly throughout the North, heating up the political climate and generating an atmosphere of controversy. But not everyone was a Garrisonian. Not all were extremists. In fact, most Americans who had any antislavery feelings at all did not advocate immediate emancipation. They preferred a systematic, orderly, slow freeing of slaves, extended over a period of years in which the slave owners would be financially compensated for their loss. They feared that the sudden termination of the slave system would cause many social and economic problems for the entire nation. Others would go no further than opposing the extension of slavery into the territories of the United States. Probably they had no regard for black people and were motivated by a selfish economic desire to restrict the territories to free (white) labor. And there were other Northerners who were downright opposed to abolition. Many of these were poor whites living in Northern cities who hated the freed black men because they competed with them for available (usually unskilled) jobs. Therefore they wished to keep the blacks in bondage.

The danger, apparent to every responsible political leader in both

One of the horrors of slavery was the auction block. A mother and infant are being sold to the highest bidder. Behind, the flag of the Republic, symbolizing the "land of the free," makes a mockery of American democracy.

parties, was that the issue of slavery might suddenly blow up the country, as Garrison and other extremists seemed to be advocating. This catastrophe had to be avoided at all costs. The essential task, as most politicians saw it, was to hold the Union together. This they understood. This they saw very clearly. They were not trying to protect slavery, though many of them were socially conservative, unconcerned about the plight of the slaves. That they recognized their duty as politicians to preserve the Union did not mean they advocated slavery; it did not mean that national politics was ruled by proslavery sentiment. The key phrase had been sounded by Jackson: "Our Federal Union: It must be preserved." Nevertheless, extremist abolitionists in the North were watching their opportunity to detonate their bomb.

There were extremists in the South, too.

The rise of the abolitionist movement naturally roused white Southerners to a defense of their way of life. At the time of the drafting of the Constitution it had not been uncommon to find many Southerners apologetic about slavery, declaring the institution moribund and certain to die in the immediate future through a natural evolutionary process. But the evolutionary process took a different direction. At the beginning of the nineteenth century the South experienced an economic trans- formation that locked it permanently to the slave system. The invention of the cotton gin in 1793 by Eli Whitney, a Connecticut Yankee, provided the transformation by revolutionizing cotton processing. Now both short-haired and long-haired cotton could be grown profitably all over the South, not simply along the Atlantic coastal area. Cotton thus became the staple of the entire South, its cash crop. And growing cotton necessitated a large work force in the fields, which Southerners argued could be satisfied only by the slave system. It is interesting to note that cotton production from 1790 to 1810—a twenty-year span—rose from 3,000 bales a year to 178,000 bales and that the number of slaves in the South during the same period jumped from 700,000 to 1,200,000. The percentage of cotton exported tripled during this same period. By the 1830s approximately half the nation's total exports consisted of one commodity: cotton.

This economic dependence upon slavery, plus the mounting attacks by abolitionists, converted white Southerners from apologists for, to defenders of, the "peculiar institution." By the Jacksonian era they had completely abandoned their previous and more ambiguous position. Gone was the apology, gone the ambiguity. John C. Calhoun now argued that slavery was "a positive good." Southern clergymen now cited the Bible to prove divine approval of the system. Throughout history, argued one defender, all great civilizations were based on slavery. It was practically the *sine qua non* for material and cultural progress. "At the slaveholding South all is peace, quiet, plenty and contentment," wrote another. "We have no mobs, no trades unions, no strikes for higher wages, no armed resistance to the law, but little jealousy of the rich by the poor." Not only that, "there is no rivalry, no competition to get employment among slaves, as among free laborers. Nor is there a war between master and slave. . . . The institution of slavery gives full development and full play to the affections."

Thus, at the very moment that abolitionism was spreading in the North and throughout the world, a determination to perpetuate slavery gripped the South. And as abolitionist propaganda increased in volume and effectiveness, slave owners grew more and more apprehensive, defensive, angry—and frightened. Many Southern whites lived in communities where they were outnumbered by blacks, sometimes by twenty to one. They lived in fear and dread that black men one day would rise up in fury and massacre all whites, just as had occurred a few years before on the island of Santo Domingo in the Caribbean. Southerners became so fearful of this possibility that they were suspicious of everything said, done, or even remotely suggested about their slaves.

There were just enough slave insurrections to make Southern fears something more than illusion. One was the Denmark Vesey Conspiracy that had occurred in Charleston, South Carolina, in 1822. Vesey was a free mulatto who, with Gullah Jack, an old African witch doctor, supposedly convinced thousands of blacks to murder all white men in Charleston and rape their women. Actually not more than a hundred slaves were involved and it is doubtful the conspiracy was ever a serious one. Nevertheless, word of a "servile insurrection" spread among slave owners and immediately five companies of South Carolina soldiers were called out. There were many arrests and during the next two months thirty-five slaves were hanged and another thirty-seven banished from the state. The "conspiracy" crushed, Charleston slave owners breathed a sigh of relief. They were certain they had barely escaped the horrors of rape, murder and theft. "Let this never be forgotten," wrote one man, "that our NEGROES . . . are the *anarchists* and the *domestic enemy*; the *common enemy of civilized society*, and the barbarians who would, IF THEY COULD, become the DESTROYERS *of our race*."

In the next few years there were several other slave disturbances, none serious but all frightening Southerners half out of their wits. Then, in 1831, came the Nat Turner Rebellion. This was a major uprising, the most important slave insurrection in American history. And this knocked the Southerners into a perpetual state of shock and terror.

Nat Turner, with nearly a hundred slaves, murdered about sixty whites—more than half of them women and children—in Virginia. Turner was a remarkable man. In the minds of some, a religious fanatic. He had a dream, a messianic dream that he was destined to save his people, to free his fellow slaves. But such dreams often lead to violence, deliberate or not. In Turner's case it was deliberate.

The revolt he led happened at a place appropriately called Jerusalem in southeast Virginia along the North Carolina border. It started on Sunday, August 22, 1831. Within a day almost all the white men, women, and children of this quiet rural area were slaughtered. As the slaves moved from farm to farm they gathered guns, swords, and other weapons. Only one white family is known to have survived. They were spared, said Turner in his *Confession*, because they "thought no better of themselves than they did of the negroes."

As soon as the alarm was sounded, heavy reinforcements of the local constabulary rushed to the area and suppressed the rebellion. There was a savage massacre. Slaves were killed on the spot, without arrest and without trial. Members of a vigilante group swore they would kill "every black person they saw in Southampton County." A contingent of black prisoners was summarily beheaded by one military unit and the heads placed on poles for the edification and instruction of other slaves. It is not known how many blacks were butchered in the massacre— possibly several hundred.

The horror of this killing—of whites by blacks, not the other way around, of course—swept the South. "Fear was seen in every face," went one North Carolina report, "women pale and terror-stricken, children crying out for protection, men fearful and full of foreboding." This hysteria completed the radicalization of many Southerners. Now more than ever they defended slavery and their particular way of life. They would not countenance criticism of any sort. They insisted abolitionists be silenced lest they trigger additional insurrections.

In such a tense and emotionally charged situation there was always the danger that a simple incident or a seemingly trivial event might touch off an explosion that would permanently damage the nation.

It was not long in coming. On the surface it did not appear that slavery was involved. But it was there. It was always there, lurking, subtly poisoning everything that was taking place.

The event that started the rush toward confrontation began in 1832 as a dispute over the tariff. But it quickly developed into a controversy that raised again the doctrine of nullification and threatened to lead to Southern secession. It brought the nation close to war.

Since the early 1820s, the tariff had been a source of irritation and discord between the North and South. Passage of a tariff on imported manufactures was almost guaranteed to ignite tempers and drive Southerners into "calculating the value of the Union." Their reaction to the Tariff of Abominations in 1828 had proved how dangerous and unpredictably treacherous the issue could be. Party leaders were leery about adjusting the duties in the foreseeable future. Inequitable though some of the rates might be, the country was living with them, and therefore it was monumentally injudicious at this time to fool around with them.

But fool with them they did. Hoping to correct past mistakes, Congress passed the Tariff of 1832. Although it removed some of the abominations of the 1828 law, Congress did not lower the rates to any significant degree. The tariff wall remained relatively high. But many Democrats voted for it on the assumption that an improved bill might quiet passions in the South. Jackson signed it for the same reason. But the nullifiers—men like Calhoun and his friends in South Carolina— were not quieted. On the contrary, they demanded total surrender on the issue, an end to all protective tariffs. All their fears and frustrations, all their concern for slavery, states' rights, and the Southern way of life were now embodied in this single issue. Counting on Southern discontent over tariff rates as support for their contemplated defiance of the government, the nullifiers proceeded to organize themselves in South Carolina to test the ties of union.

In Washington, John C. Calhoun wrote the Governor of South Carolina, James Hamilton, Jr., urging him to apply his doctrine of nullification and declare the new tariff inoperable in South Carolina. "The Union," he wrote, "of which the Constitution is the bond, is a union of States, and not of individuals." A state may declare an act of Congress null and void within its borders, said Calhoun, and this action is binding on all the citizens of the state. Simultaneously, he argued that the federal government had no authority to coerce a state.

The restraint Calhoun had once exercised—based on his expectation that he would follow Jackson into the White House, provided of course that he did not alienate Northern sensibilities—was now gone. Van Buren had replaced him as Jackson's successor. Now Calhoun urged radical measures to solve the South's problems. He urged nullification—and, if necessary, secession.

Governor Hamilton called a special session of the state legislature to respond to the "outrage" of the federal government in legislating a new tariff. Acting decisively and under the control of the well-organized nullifiers, the legislature in turn called for an elected convention to meet on November 19, 1832, to act in the name of the state.

The convention, as expected, adopted the ideas of Calhoun and passed an Ordinance of Nullification on November 24, 1832, by a vote of 136 to 26. The Ordinance declared the tariff laws of 1828 and 1832 null and void and forbade the collection of tariff duties within the borders of South Carolina. It went on to warn the federal government that if force were used against the state to require it to obey the law, then South Carolina would quit the Union. Once that happened it was expected the rest of the South would also secede.

President Jackson was shocked and angered by the action of his native state. He believed the "nullies," as they were called, were deliberately baiting him in their desire to cause trouble. But did they not realize, he wrote, that as President he had sworn to uphold the Constitution and faithfully execute the laws of the United States, that his duty was clear, that he had no choice? The tariff was law, and, "by the eternal," he would uphold the law even against the state of his birth. In a Proclamation dated December 10, 1832, he spoke directly to the people of South Carolina. He praised them but he also warned them. He would not tolerate defiance of the national government, he said. "Those who told you that you might peacefully prevent [the] execution [of federal law] deceived you. . . . Their object is disunion. But be not deceived by names. Disunion by armed force is *treason*. Are you really ready to incur its guilt?"

While Jackson tried to warn the people of South Carolina against an illegal act which would force his hand to execute his constitutional duty, he took other more direct actions to prevent possible secession and civil war. First he wrote to known unionists within the state to gain their help and cooperation. In particular he corresponded with Joel R. Poinsett, the former minister to Mexico, who had formed a Union party within the state to oppose the action of the "nullies," especially their secessionist intent. In one letter to Poinsett, Jackson said: "I repeat to the union men [in South Carolina] again, fear not, *the union will be preserved* and treason and rebellion put down, when and where it may shew [*sic*] its monster head."

Jackson also checked out the federal government's military strength just in case it was needed, even for purposes of demonstration. He alerted naval authorities in Norfolk, Virginia, to prepare a squadron to send against South Carolina if the use of force proved necessary. He notified the federal commanders of the several forts in the Charleston harbor to prepare for a possible emergency. And he hurried several thousand troops to the southern border of North Carolina, to move into South Carolina at his command if the state tried to carry forward its defiance of federal law.

Meanwhile, Calhoun resigned as Vice-President on December 28, 1832, a little over two months before his term legally expired. In a complicated maneuver, he got himself elected U.S. Senator by the South Carolina legislature; thus the state's most effective speaker and parliamentarian was stationed inside Congress to protect the state's interests. He replaced Robert Y. Hayne, who was brought home and elected to the Governor's chair. This switching of personnel was expected to demonstrate South Carolina's determination to fight on at every front. Having Calhoun in the Senate meant that the chief nullifier had a national forum whereby he could lambast the federal government, the North, Jackson, the Democratic party, and anyone else who dared to force South Carolina to obey any law she deemed contrary to her interests.

But it was not the tariff that really bothered the South, although clearly such legislation provided a focus for resentment. The real issue was slavery, upon which everything else depended. For that reason the controversy was recognized as a serious and dangerous development which could tear the Union apart.

Fortunately, the politics of brinkmanship attempted by South Carolina and John C. Calhoun were answered by the masterful politics of President Andrew Jackson. His response to the threat of secession was nothing short of brilliant. As he repeatedly said, he was determined to preserve the Union. While he prepared for the possibility of bloodshed he did everything within his power to work out a compromise by which both sides could back off gracefully. Besides aiding and encouraging the unionists within South Carolina to provide a balance to the "nullies" within the state, he went to Congress and urged a policy of conciliation. Henry Clay was one of the first to respond. The Senator from Kentucky, after consulting with a number of Congressmen to find a compromise that would encourage South Carolina to abandon nullification without penalizing Northern interests, introduced a new tariff bill in 1833.

This so-called Compromise Tariff of 1833 provided a ten-year truce—its most important provision—during which time the tariff rates would be slowly reduced. At the same time another bill was passed providing the necessary military assistance to insure obedience to the law. This was called the Force Bill—or, by Southerners, the Bloody Bill.

South Carolina immediately accepted the compromise. Its nullifying convention reassembled on March 11, 1833, and repealed the Ordinance of Nullification against the tariff laws. But then, to save face, it nullified the Force Bill. Since it was a meaningless gesture Jackson allowed South Carolina this conceit. For the sake of the Union he could afford to be generous.

South Carolina retreated from its defiance because the state had tried the doctrine of nullification and found it wanting. Not another Southern state had supported her and she could not risk going it alone. The reason for her isolation most probably was the lack of enthusiasm in the other slaveholding states for nullification. It was a doctrine of dubious validity. But had South Carolina actually seceded—a right held to be fully constitutional by other Southern states—and had the issue been other than economic, it might have been a different story altogether. South Carolina never nullified again. The next time she chose to act, she seceded. And war resulted.

None of the basic problems facing the nation, such as slavery, sectional antagonisms between the North and South, or the constitutional rights of the states vis-à-vis the federal government, were solved by the nullification controversy. What was accomplished through strong executive leadership and a spirit of compromise, which is the very essence of politics, was avoidance of armed conflict and the breakup of the Union. It was a notable achievement. Unfortunately, these ingredients were not present thirty years later when these problems were finally submitted to the test of arms.

7

The Indian Problem

IF PARTY LEADERS during the Jacksonian era failed to solve the problem of slavery, the same can not be said of their handling of the Indian problem. This issue they solved with a vengeance, much to the satisfaction of Americans at the time. But the effects of that solution have had a terrible impact on the nation right down to the present. What is particularly sad is that the solution to the Indian problem was an ugly contradiction to the general democratic mood of the Jacksonian age.

For some modern Americans there is only one word to describe the nation's historic policy toward the Indians: genocide—the calculated, ruthless, seemingly insane determination to exterminate a whole race of people. One modern historian, Bernard W. Sheehan, summed it up when he wrote: "The white man is guilty. He has been charged with the destruction of the American Indian, the evidence has been presented, and the verdict returned for all to see." Another recent historian has observed that it is rather fortunate that our present concern and sympathy for the Indians came when it was too late to do anything about it, too late to reverse the history of a hundred years. If Americans had it to do all over again, he said, most probably they would not hesitate to repeat the policies of the past. After all, the Indians stood in the way of the progress of the majority, could not or would not adapt to the changing society, occupied desired land—in short, failed to become cultural white men. So they had to be eliminated, one way or another.

The concern of many Americans today for the plight of the Indians is properly humane and sympathetic, perhaps a bit romantic, and not a little tinged with an overly simplistic view of history, namely the wicked-white-man interpretation. Somehow, it is assumed, things could have been different had there been decency and respect shown the Indians for their property and cultures. Had the white men been less greedy, less racist in their thinking, had the Indians been better protected, especially by the federal government, the treaties kept, the dishonest agents weeded out and punished, somehow the Indians as Indians could have endured; two cultures or maybe even an intermingling of cultures might have resulted. But it just didn't work out that way—and the reasons say a great deal about the nature of the democracy of the Jacksonian era.

It is interesting to note that not until political democracy was achieved in America—the creation of a mass electorate, the rise of the common man, the respect for the popular will, the notion that political leaders must serve as representatives of the people, and the rest—not until then did the country decide to get rid of its Indians. And it fell to Andrew Jackson, the symbol of the great democracy, to run the Indians off their ancestral lands and dump them unceremoniously in remote and desolate corners of the United States where they barely survived. In order to understand how this calamity occurred it is necessary to understand white-red relations from the very start of the nation's history.

White America's policy from the beginning was a curious mixture of the benign and the malevolent. This contradictory attitude commenced with the arrival of the British in North America. Colonists fluctuated from outright warfare—seizing land and driving the Indians from white society—to missionary endeavor to Christianize the Indians, educate them, share with them the benefits of Western civilization, and welcome them into the white community. Sometimes Indian land was stolen, sometimes legitimately obtained through purchase and treaty.

During the American Revolution, the ambiguous policy of Americans changed. Because most Indians allied themselves with the British, Americans felt justified in punishing the Indians for their mistake of judgment by forced cessions of land. But the Indians resisted this policy—resisted it so successfully that the government was obliged

106

to return to a policy of land purchase to get the cessions it wanted.

Even so, many Americans practiced only one policy toward the Indians: theft and, when necessary, homicide. To them, Indians were inferior. All Americans wanted was their land. They felt the Indians had no rights white men need respect.

When the Constitution was adopted, establishing a government committed to freedom and liberty, the situation of the Indians living within the territorial limits of the United States contradicted the ennobling ideas of both the Declaration of Independence and the Constitution. But the Founding Fathers who won independence from Great Britain and wrote the Constitution lived in what they believed was an Age of Enlightenment. They were convinced that men of reason, intelligence, and goodwill could come together, and in a spirit of compromise and accommodation resolve whatever issues divided or troubled them. They were committed to rational solutions of men's problems. Therefore, they reasoned that Indians were not inferior to white men. In their view, these "noble savages" simply existed on a lower stage of development and one day would catch up to modern society—provided the white man's civilization was brought to them. In exchange for land the Indians would receive the blessings of Western civilization. What could be fairer than that?

Under President George Washington and his Secretary of War, Henry Knox—for it was the War Secretary whose office handled the Indian problem—the national policy of the United States was formulated to "civilize" Indians and absorb them into the Union. Washington said he sought "to advance the happiness of the Indians and to attach them firmly to the United States." He, like others of his time, hoped that with the application of this policy the Indian would "cease his wandering ways," adopt the practice of private property as the white man understood it, farm like white Americans, raise oxen, sheep, and other domestic animals, build comfortable houses, educate his children, and embrace Christianity.

President Thomas Jefferson continued this policy. As he said to a delegation of Indians who visited him in the capital, "Let me entreat you on the lands now given you to begin every man a farm, let him enclose it, cultivate it, build a warm house on it, and when he dies let it belong to his wife and children after him." Like Washington, Jefferson simply ignored the agricultural aspects of Indian society. Both Presidents assumed the Indians knew little, compared to whites, about farming and working the land. Thus, if the Indians would adopt white men's ways, Jefferson said to them, then "you will unite yourselves with us, and we shall all be Americans. You will mix with us by marriage. Your blood will run in our veins and will spread with us over this great island." But if the Indians refused to accept civilization, what then? Why then they were doomed. "We shall be obliged to drive them," said Jefferson, "with the beasts of the forest into the Stony [Rocky] Mountains."

This policy of assimilation or integration of the two races reflected the stubborn hope and belief of the early Presidents. It was quite appropriate to the men of the Age of Enlightenment. But it just didn't work out. For while the United States was making dramatic, even revolutionary advances—a population doubling in ten years, with many new Western states added to the Union, canals and other public works being built so rapidly as to constitute a transportation revolution—with all these accomplishments advancing the prosperity and happiness of the nation, the Indians had remained indifferent to the benefits and opportunities of Western civilization except to adopt its worst vices. They continued their "wandering ways." They refused the invitation to become cultural white men. They were obviously going nowhere, while the white man was pressing further along the road of progress and improvement. Civilization, Americans finally concluded, was simply not meant for the red man. He couldn't handle it.

Though the nation pulsed with democratic spirit during the 1820s and 1830s, the idea of equality was never extended to include Indians. Furthermore, the concept of assimilation between the two races was now reckoned a failure and repeatedly attacked by a number of politicians who seemed to reflect the popular attitude. Henry Clay, for example, as Secretary of State under President Adams, had stated that "it was impossible to civilize Indians. It was not in their nature. They were essentially inferior to the Anglo-Saxon race . . . and their disappearance from the human family will be no great loss to the world." And Henry Clay was not alone. Many Americans agreed with this racist attitude, arguing that the Indians were incapable of self-improvement and only blocked the natural expansion and progress of the civilized white man. There was only one thing to do under the circumstances, and that was to remove this obstacle so that the civilized race could have all the territory it needed to fulfill its destiny.

Removal! Send the tribes out of the country. Send them west. Send them where they would cease to take up valuable land and thus interfere with the nation's growth and development. And the sooner it was done the better.

By the time Andrew Jackson was elected President many Americans demanded an end to Indian presence in white society. As the popularly elected President, the representative of the democracy, Jackson was expected to solve the problem. And from the very start of his administration he indicated a readiness to oblige. In his first annual message to Congress in 1829, Jackson noted that some Southern tribes had attempted to create independent governments within the limits of Georgia and Alabama. But these states extended their laws over the Indians, arguing that the Indians were occupying land within their sovereign jurisdictions. The Indians rejected this argument and appealed to the United States government for protection. They appealed for help to their old enemy, that Indian fighter par excellence, Andrew Jackson.

These Southeastern tribes were not savages. They were not weak aborigines defenseless before aggressive states. The truth of the matter, though few white men cared to acknowledge it, was that some Indian tribes had made real "progress in the arts of civilized life," to quote from Jackson's own message. The President knew this and admitted it. He knew the Southern tribes had made notable advances, especially the Cherokees. Many Cherokees lived in fine houses, cultivated large plantations and even owned slaves—just to prove how "civilized" they really were. They had schools and a newspaper and their own written language. They tended to act like members of an independent, sovereign power, capable of conducting its own affairs. But the trouble was that they occupied land within the boundaries of several states. Indeed, some fifty-three thousand Cherokees, Creeks, Chickasaws and Choctaws extended over thirty-three million acres of land in the southern and southwestern section of the United States east of the Mississippi River.

White men in general, and the states of Georgia and Alabama in particular, were contemptuous of Indian pretensions to civilization and independence. All they knew was that red men blocked their territorial progress by occupying land they wanted. So they insisted on removal— beyond the Mississippi River if possible, below ground if not.

The success of some tribes in adapting to the white man's civilization did not alter the fundamental belief of Americans at this time that Indians generally were inferior and that their disappearance from the

109

human family, as Clay said, would be no great loss. Even men of goodwill, men friendly to Indian rights, men not greedy for Indian land, slowly came to the conclusion that removal or annihilation were the only alternatives facing the Indians. Either they moved west of the Mississippi River and got out of harm's way or they would be buried—literally destroyed—they themselves and their cultures. "Say to the [Indians]," Jackson wrote at this time, "where they now are, they and my white children are too near to each other to live in harmony and peace. Then game is destroyed & many of their people will not work, & till the earth. Beyond the river Mississippi where a part of their nation have gone, their father has provided a country, large enough for them all, and he advises them to remove to it. There, their white brethren will not trouble them . . . and they can live upon it, they and all their children as long as grass grows or water runs in peace and plenty. It will be theirs forever."

Jackson had little choice in deciding on a policy of removal. According to a distinguished historian of American Indian policy, Francis Prucha, the President had only four courses of action open to him. The first choice was to kill the Indians outright. Simply send in the army and by brute force exterminate the race. While many frontiersmen strongly and eagerly approved such a policy, it was never even remotely contemplated by Jackson or any responsible official within his administration.

His second choice was to attempt the assimilation or integration of the white and red races, as the earlier Presidents had anticipated. But by the 1820s it was abundantly clear that this policy was unacceptable. Most white men in America had a long history of racism. They regarded other races as inferior and were not about to accept assimilation, no matter what the Founding Fathers hoped. Consequently, any attempt to mingle the races was foredoomed to failure. Southerners were especially adamant on this point. If assimilation were possible with the red men, would assimilation with the black men be far behind?

Jackson's third choice was to protect the Indians where they lived. They would be islands within white society, safeguarded by treaties, and, necessarily, by military force to keep white men from encroaching on the red men's territory. Those who opposed removal favored this alternative. Even today critics of the removal policy feel some variation of this choice should have been attempted by the American government. But the standing army needed for such an operation against avaricious

110

whites would have been enormous, more than was possible in the 1830s. The country would have become an armed camp.

The fourth choice was removal, and to Jackson this policy was the only answer to the unyielding antagonism that existed between the white and red races. And to a large extent the policy was adopted to protect the Indians and their cultures against inevitable extinction if they stayed where they were. Jackson told Congress that the white man had the means to destroy the Indians unless they moved—and on that score there could be no doubt. "That this fate surely awaits the Indians if they remain within the limits of the States," he said, "does not admit of a doubt. Humanity and national honor demand that every effort should be made to avert so great a calamity."

It is difficult to believe—indeed mind-boggling—that Andrew Jackson, the Indian fighter, the stern commander of the Creek Indian War, actually acted out of concern for the well-being of the Indians and for their civilization. Of course, it is unquestionable that he also responded to what he knew the American people demanded. But he could have sat on his hands, done nothing and let "nature" take its course, which undoubtedly would have meant annihilation for the Indian. Instead, as his private letters and official papers and messages repeated many times, he was most anxious to preserve Indian life and culture, and the only way he felt it could be done was to separate the races—separate them forever.

It has been said that Jackson hated Indians. That it was blind hatred, nothing else, which prompted his action. Those who make this charge forget that he raised an Indian boy from infancy. The infant had been discovered in the arms of his dead mother in 1813 in the Creek village of Tallushatchee after a particularly bloody battle during the Creek War. Jackson had asked other Indian women to care for the boy, but they refused. "All his relations are dead," they said; "kill him too." But the General spurned this advice, named the child Lincoyer, and took him back to the Hermitage, where he raised him and gave him a good education. Unfortunately the boy died of tuberculosis at the age of seventeen. But, if Jackson hated Indians how then did he take one into his home and treat him as a member of the family?

Still, that he did not hate Indians does not mean Jackson was their devoted friend and protector. As President he regarded them as a responsibility, which meant preventing their destruction. So, in 1829, he asked Congress to pass legislation creating an Indian Territory west

111

of the Mississippi River outside the limits of any existing state or territory. This new Territory would be guaranteed to the Indians as long as they occupied it, each tribe having a distinct control over a portion of it. There they could have their own government; they would be subject to no other control from the United States except what was necessary to preserve peace on the frontier and between the several tribes. The emigration would be voluntary, said Jackson, for it would be "as cruel as unjust" to force them "to abandon the graves of their fathers and seek a home in a distant land." But if they did refuse to leave, Jackson warned, then they must be subject to the laws of the states within which they resided. And, in view of the declared intentions of many states, that was a very unpleasant prospect.

The immediate problem was Georgia. That state had already planned to do something about the Indians living within her borders. And the Cherokee Nation was the special target. In December 1829 the state legislature passed a law extending the authority of the state over the lands held by the Indians within her borders. But the Cherokees resisted. Not by brandishing tomahawks. Not by going on the warpath and killing and burning. But by the most "civilized" manner possible: The Cherokees sued Georgia in the United States Supreme Court. And they hired one of the best constitutional lawyers in the country to argue their case for them.

The case arose when an Indian named Corn Tassel was apprehended and tried in a Georgia court for killing another Indian. Corn Tassel was found guilty and sentenced to be hanged. The Cherokees—in the case *Cherokee Nation* vs. *Georgia*—appealed to the Supreme Court on the grounds that Georgia lacked jurisdiction over the tribe. John Marshall, the Chief Justice of the United States, declared that the Cherokees were not an independent nation as understood under the Constitution but rather a "dependent domestic nation." In other words, that Indian tribes were dependent upon the federal government, not the states.

But Georgia paid no heed to Marshall. Just a few days before the decision was handed down, Corn Tassel was executed. Still the Cherokees resisted. In another case the Indians again appealed to the Supreme Court. Again it involved a Georgia law. This particular law forbade white men from residing among Indians without obtaining a license from state authorities. Two missionaries named Worcester and Butler disobeyed the law and were arrested and imprisoned. In the case *Worcester* vs. *Georgia*, John Marshall declared the Georgia law unconstitutional, stating that Georgia had no constitutional right to extend her authority over the Cherokee Nation. Andrew Jackson supposedly said when he heard the decision, "Well, John Marshall has made his decision. Now let him enforce it." This may sound like Jackson, but there is no real evidence he ever said it.

But whatever Jackson said, he was determined to initiate the policy of removal, even as the Congress prepared to act. His Secretary of War wrote to several army generals stationed in the Southwest in 1829 and ordered them to arrange Indian agreement to the government's policy of removal. "A crisis in our Indian affairs has arrived," he wrote, because of the action by Georgia. This action was certain to be imitated by other Southern states that wanted to get rid of Indians. The President, he continued, was convinced that the only way they could escape destruction "is *for them to emigrate.*" But Jackson wished to avoid trouble, the Secretary said. Therefore the generals must convince "the chiefs and influential men" of the Southern tribes with reason and logic of the necessity of removal. If the chiefs could be brought around, "the rest would implicitly follow." Avoid a general council, he continued, because then those who oppose the idea could raise objections and influence others. Instead, if the chiefs could be spoken to individually and privately they might be persuaded by forceful argument. The generals should say something to the effect that the "President views the Indians as the children of the Government. He sees what is best for them; and that a perseverance in their refusal to fly the dangers that surround them, must result in their misery, and final destruction."

Two themes were hammered at by the Jackson administration: The policy of removal adopted by the President was necessary to preserve Indian life and culture; and refusal by the Indians to remove themselves would result in the destruction of the race. That a government of free men could threaten the destruction of a race of people to accomplish its will is a sad commentary on democracy in the Age of Jackson.

Whether the Indians agreed to their own removal no longer mattered. The white men had determined they must go, and go they would, *now.* Responding to Jackson's request, Congress passed the Indian Removal Act in 1830. According to this act, Indian lands within the existing twenty-four states were to be exchanged for new lands west of the Mississippi River. Nothing was said about forcing the Indians to go if they resisted relocation. On the surface the legislation appeared decent and humane. Then, a few years later, in 1834, Congress enacted the

Indian Intercourse Act, setting up the Indian Territory which later became the state of Oklahoma. The Indians were expected to live in this Territory, where they were promised perpetual protection from the white man.

Thus, the solution of the Indian problem seemed easily resolved in the cooperative act of Congress and the administration, both responding to the nation's desire to expand westward without the presence of the Indian impediment. There were some objections. Petitions came from college students and some religious groups such as Quakers, Methodists, and Congregationalists, begging the government to protect the Indians in their claims to their own land as well as to allow them the exercise of their own laws and customs. To do otherwise, said these petitioners, would be unjust and oppressive. But this token concern for the Indians nowhere matched the concern for the slaves which was mounting at precisely the same moment in time. The verdict of Americans in the Jacksonian age was that Indians belonged out west on the plains, where they could be ignored and forgotten.

So under Jackson, under the great democratic leader of the American people, the tragic and horrible removal of the Indians began. Whatever the intentions of those responsible for the policy, the actual removal was a frightful injustice which brought sickness, starvation, and death to thousands of human beings.

Some Indians readily complied with the dictates of the government. They ceded their lands in the East, packed their belongings, and headed west into the treeless, waterless, arid plains. Andrew Jackson himself signed over ninety treaties with various tribes—Northern as well as Southern—accepting their eastern lands in exchange for western lands in the Indian Territory.

Not all tribes were so obliging. The Alabama Creek Indians had to be forcibly removed, many of them in chains. The Chocktaws were booted out of Mississippi in the dead of a bitter winter with little provision for their needs. Sometimes Indians were tricked into signing away their lands and possessions, tricked through drink or empty promises. Several times suspicion and distrust and the impatience of the white man triggered Indian wars. For example, when the hungry Sac and Fox Indians in Illinois returned to their ancestral lands to plant grain and escape starvation, the white settlers in the region suspected an attack and proceeded to slaughter them. This was the famous Black Hawk War which Abraham Lincoln participated in. An even more serious conflict occurred in 1835 when the Seminole Indians in Florida, led by a young and able chieftain named Osceola, refused to comply with the treaty they had signed and emigrate. Troops were dispatched to Florida by the President. But the Seminoles, adept at guerrilla warfare, stubbornly resisted, and so a long, ugly war dragged on for years in the Everglades. Even after Osceola was captured under a flag of truce, the Indians continued to fight. But it was hopeless. Although it cost the government over fifteen million dollars, the Seminoles were eventually subdued, their lands taken from them, and most, but not all, of the tribe driven westward.

But a special horror awaited the Cherokees in Georgia. They refused to budge and President Jackson had to threaten them. "You cannot . . . flourish in the midst of a civilized community," he told them. "You have but one remedy. . . . Remove to the west." Using every legal weapon available to them they delayed the removal for several years, but finally in 1838 they were forcibly expelled from their lands. Georgia militiamen were sent into their country. These militiamen were not disposed to treat the Indians kindly, and quickly demonstrated that they meant business. Prison stockades were erected "for gathering in and holding the Indians preparatory to removal." From these forts soldiers with rifles and bayonets went out in search of Indians, flushing them out of house and cabin and bringing them to the stockades as prisoners. Indian families at dinner, wrote one observer, "were startled by the sudden gleam of bayonets in the doorway and rose up to be driven with blows and oaths along the weary miles of trail which led to the stockade. Men were seized in their fields, women were taken from their wheels and children from their play."

Frequently, the captured Indians would turn for one last look at their homes as they reached the top of a hill or ridge only to see them in flames, set afire by the lawless rabble who followed the soldiers and scavenged for loot. These outlaws stole the cattle and other livestock; they robbed graves in their desire for silver pendants and other valuables. One Georgia volunteer who later served in the Confederate army said: "I fought through the Civil War and have seen men shot to pieces and slaughtered by thousands, but the Cherokee removal was the cruelest I ever saw."

Within a single week the efficient Georgia militiamen had rounded up over seventeen thousand Cherokees. These bewildered Indians, homeless, destitute, and hungry, could hardly understand what had

Savagery, greed and utter contempt for human life are nowhere better illustrated than in the story of the Indians' removal from their

ancestral lands. The *Trail of Tears* shows the proud and mighty Cherokees on their long trek into the alien territory of the West.

happened to them. They were herded into a concentration camp. Many sickened and died. In June the first contingent of about a thousand Indians was taken to steamboats and sent down the Tennessee River on the initial leg of the westward trip, a journey the Cherokees came to call "The Trail of Tears." Then they were boxed like animals into cars drawn by two railroad locomotives. Again there were many deaths because of the oppressive heat and the cramped conditions in the railroad cars. The Cherokees walked the last leg of "The Trail of Tears" until they reached their final destination beyond the western border of Arkansas. In all it was an eight-hundred-mile journey.

A handful of Indians hidden away in the uppermost reaches of the mountains was impossible to get at, and because of this tactical problem an incident occurred which produced in Cherokee annals one of its great heroes. According to the best eyewitness accounts, a Cherokee woman was attacked by two soldiers and in self-defense she killed both with a hatchet. An Indian named Tsali took the weapon from the woman and hid it under his shirt so that she would not be charged with the "crime." The American general in charge of the troops served notice on the mountain Cherokees, of whom Tsali was a member, that they must produce someone who could be punished for the homicides. The Cherokees were all for rejecting the demand and taking their chances of escaping capture in their cloud-hidden heights. But Tsali said he was prepared to offer his life for his people, and a white trader and friend of the tribe named William Thomas advised the Indians to accept Tsali's offer—but with conditions. The general was then informed that Tsali would be surrendered to the Americans for punishment in return for permission for the rest of the Cherokees to remain in the mountains unmolested. Since the general was anxious to avoid a difficult campaign in the mountains, he agreed to recommend the proposal to his superiors in Washington. Meanwhile Tsali was brought in by a contingent of Cherokees and handed over to the Americans. In one of the most ghastly displays of American justice, the contingent of Cherokees who had accompanied Tsali were required to execute him. Tsali, his brother, and his eldest son were lined up before a firing squad and shot.

For years the white trader, William Thomas, attended the prolonged negotiations to win over both the state and the United States to the proposal of allowing this tiny band of Cherokees to remain undisturbed in their mountain hideaway. Since so few Indians were involved, since the land they occupied was unattractive and inaccessible, the state and federal governments finally gave their consent and Tsali's sacrifice was rewarded. The descendants of those Cherokee stalwarts still live in those mountains today.

The remainder of the Cherokee Nation was not so fortunate. It has been estimated that some four thousand of them died on "The Trail of Tears." Along the way the Cherokees were cheated and robbed by agents, speculators, contractors, lawyers, and anyone wielding local police power. Food provided by the governments disappeared or arrived in short supply. "Oh! the misery and wretchedness that presents itself to our view in going among these people," wrote one man. "Sir, I have witnessed entire families prostrated with sickness—not one able to give help to the other; and these poor people were made the instruments of enriching a few unprincipled and wicked contractors." By the middle of June 1838, the general in charge of the Georgia militiamen reported that no Cherokees remained on Georgia soil except as prisoners in the stockade. It was a very efficient operation, the practical annihilation of a once great people.

All told some sixty thousand Indians were removed beyond the Mississippi, and of that number perhaps fifteen thousand Indian men, women, and children died in transit. It is one of the most disgraceful episodes in American history. Protests from reformers and hundreds of church groups fluttered into Congress denouncing removal. But once the red men were transported across the Mississippi, it was presumed by many men of goodwill that the Indians and their cultures were at last safe. In his last message to Congress Andrew Jackson stated that he thought he had finally settled the Indian problem to the satisfaction of all, that he had saved the race from extinction. "This unhappy race," Jackson said, "are now placed in a situation where we may well hope that they will share in the blessings of civilization and be saved from that degradation and destruction to which they were rapidly hastening while they remained in the States. . . . Our own citizens . . . will rejoice that the remnant of that ill-fated race has been at length placed beyond the reach of injury or oppression, and that the paternal care of the General Government will hereafter watch over them and protect them."

A democratic government freely elected by the people had solved the Indian problem to its own satisfaction. The paternal care of the federal government that Jackson spoke about never occurred. When the American people were ready to move again, across and beyond the Mississippi, the Indians were forced once more to get out of the way.

119

There was resistance and bloodshed until the prostrate red men could fight no more. Herded into reservations in some of the most desolate sections of the United States, the Indians were practically forgotten, since they no longer had the will nor the strength to protest their fate. Miraculously, many of the tribes survived (just barely), and their cultures too.

And so, in a terrible contradiction, a young republic just starting to emerge as a powerful democratic nation resolved one of its problems by the near extinction of an entire race of people, who, they thought, stood in their way. Yet at the time, many politicians in Congress and in the White House believed they had placed the Indians in a position of safety by settling them across the Mississippi, beyond what Jackson called "the reach of injury or oppression." They thought what they did was their only possible course of action. And maybe, despite everything that happened, maybe it was.

BOOK III

THE GROWTH
OF PRESIDENTIAL POWER

(overleaf) When Jackson tangled with members of Congress during the early 1830s, he restructured the government's balance of power. Here Jackson takes his cane to the many-headed "Hydra of Corruption," the Bank of the United States. In the center, Van Buren explains his distaste for dissention. The individual heads of the Hydra represent state branches of the Bank; the largest head—wearing a top hat—pictures its president, Nick Biddle.

8

The President Vetoes

PERHAPS THE SINGLE most important political event of Jackson's entire administration was the Bank War. Jackson's "War"—and that is the best word to describe his actions—against the Bank of the United States had a staggering impact on the course of American history.

The War reshaped the nation's political future. In fact, in terms of party history, it overshadowed all other events during the middle period of the nineteenth century—roughly the years from 1816 to 1850. It brought about the creation of a new political party, the Whig party. It fashioned the character of the Democratic party with respect to leadership, organizational discipline, and popular following for over a generation. It exalted such things as party loyalty to the point where most issues in the immediate future would be determined in Congress strictly by party vote. And it demonstrated that the President could be a politician of the great mass of American voters as well as head of the party.

Most important, the War altered the fundamental structure of government. The conflict between the supporters and opponents of the Bank, fought both in Washington and across the country, resulted in a vast expansion of presidential power. The fight that ensued between

123

the President and the Congress profoundly changed the relationship between the executive and legislative branches. The operation of government as originally conceived by the Founding Fathers, with its delicate system of checks and balances and its dependence on the supremacy of Congress in originating laws, was altered to such an extent that Henry Clay called it a "revolution . . . tending towards a total change of the . . . character of the Government."

And the War had an economic impact, too. It indirectly produced an enormous expansion of credit and paper money which propelled the nation into an era of significant industrial growth and development. The creation of this capital advanced the full implementation of the industrial revolution.

The Second Bank of the United States, frequently referred to as the BUS, had been created by Congress immediately after the War of 1812. Its capital stock—which was different from its deposits—was assigned at thirty-five million dollars, one-fifth of which was purchased by the United States government and four-fifths by the public, making it a quasi-public institution—partly owned by the government and partly by private individuals. According to its twenty-year charter, the BUS was permitted to expand from its main headquarters on Chestnut Street in Philadelphia and establish branch banks in the leading cities of the country. When full-grown it was like a vast octopus, with its head in Philadelphia and its tentacles reaching to Boston, New York City, Charleston, Cincinnati, Pittsburgh, New Orleans, Savannah, Washington, St. Louis, Natchez, Portland, Buffalo, Nashville, and Baltimore—in all a total of twenty-six branches. Calling it an octopus is not to imply anything sinister; this is just an easy way to describe its far-flung influence and power by the time Jackson became President.

The BUS was run by a board of directors, five appointed by the President of the United States and twenty elected by the stockholders. In actual practice, however, the affairs of the Bank were managed by its president, who was elected by the stockholders.

The Bank not only accepted savings from private depositors, but it also served as the depository for all government monies. In other words, the United States government handed over its funds to the BUS for its care and use. That made the BUS an economic powerhouse. Because it had so much money and so much power, it was the financial center of the United States.

124

Furthermore, the authority of the Bank to issue bank notes (paper money or IOUs) which could be redeemed in specie (gold and silver) automatically increased the supply of currency in the country. When more money was needed all the Bank had to do was issue more notes. Thus the BUS could expand and contract credit at will. This control of currency and credit supply helped American business because when business needed to expand, money or credit were available as loans from the Bank. Of course, if the Bank wanted to be nasty and refuse loans it could cripple business and cause a recession. In this way—through the instruments of credit and money supply—the BUS centralized and controlled the financial operations of the entire country. It had enormous power for good or evil.

The funds of the federal government which the Bank held on deposit did not simply sit in the Bank's vaults; they were invested. Millions of dollars put to work to make millions more. And these millions were shared by those people at home and abroad who were wealthy enough to own the Bank's stock. Of course the government was a stockholder, too. But four-fifths of the stock was held by private individuals who were well-off for the most part. So to some people it seemed unfair that money taken by the government from *all* the people in the form of taxes was invested by the BUS to make additional money for the wealthy few.

But the government did enjoy certain real and immediate advantages from its arrangement with the BUS. The Bank helped in the collection of taxes. It transferred government funds from one section of the country to another without charge. It also served as a depository for government funds. Despite these advantages, its ability to control the entire fiscal structure of the country seriously disturbed some Americans.

Andrew Jackson was one. He did not like the staggering power available to the Bank through its control of credit and currency. He did not like its ability to act with or without government approval, with or without public support. Like any corporation, the Bank's principal concern was the welfare of its stockholders, not of the public at large. Worse, said Jackson, this financial clout could be employed "to control the Government and change its character." It could be used to influence the political process—by "buying" elections for example—to get what it wanted.

The president of the BUS at this time was Nicholas Biddle. Here was a man who had everything: brains, looks, money, family, taste, and tremendous financial savvy. He came from a well-to-do Philadelphia family, graduated Princeton at the age of fifteen as valedictorian (he could have graduated a year earlier but the trustees of Princeton thought that too young), toured Europe, and served as temporary secretary to James Monroe, who was then the American minister to Great Britain. Upon returning to the United States, Biddle learned law, won election to the Pennsylvania legislature, married an heiress, and was finally appointed to the board of directors of the BUS by President James Monroe. The brightest, most articulate, best-informed member of the board, Biddle was elevated to the presidency of the Bank in 1823.

But Biddle had his faults. He was arrogant. There were also questions about his integrity. Not that he slipped his hand into the till on occasion to augment his income. Rather, some things he initiated violated the terms of the charter. For example, he was not above lending the Bank's money to the Bank's "friends" and refusing loans to those he considered hostile. He showed favoritism to privileged Congressmen, several of whom, including Daniel Webster, received retainers from the Bank.

In his first annual message to Congress, in 1829, Jackson took notice of the BUS. He did it in two short paragraphs. But those paragraphs eventually touched off a War that shook the nation and profoundly affected the processes of government. In the message Jackson said the Bank had "failed in the great end of establishing a uniform and sound currency." He also said he doubted its constitutionality and expedience. But Congressmen hearing these comments could hardly believe Jackson was serious. The Bank a failure at establishing a sound currency? That was absurd. Whatever its sins or faults, the BUS had indeed stabilized and strengthened the currency. Jackson was simply exaggerating.

Yet it was soon clear that the President wanted changes in the Bank's operations. Since the charter was due for renewal in 1836 he invited Congress to begin thinking of reform. He was not out to kill the Bank. Not now, at least.

But Jackson's dislike of the Bank went deeper than he told Congress. As a young man he had gotten involved in a land speculation scheme and accepted some IOUs which turned out to be worthless. Only through luck and hard work did he finally extricate himself from financial disaster. But forevermore Jackson hated IOUs, speculation, paper money, and banks themselves. "I do not dislike your Bank any more than all banks," he later told Biddle quite bluntly. And the reason banks were so high on his hate list was that they speculated in land and

126

paper money, and frequently issued paper in excess of their gold and silver reserves. And where bank speculation ran unchecked, bank failures were extremely common, taking with them the savings of innocent people and wiping them out.

Another thing: Jackson did not believe in credit. Every man should pay his debts just as he himself had done in his youth, when he had nearly collapsed into bankruptcy. Consequently he objected to the paper-issuing, credit-producing aspects of banking. If people paid what they owed in hard money, said Jackson, the country would be better off. Of course it was impossible to get rid of all banks. They were a necessary evil. But Jackson did feel something should be done about the largest of them—the BUS—particularly since it had been created by the federal government. As President, he now had his chance.

Curiously, Biddle wasn't disturbed by Jackson's message to Congress. He told a friend he was convinced the President was essentially friendly to the BUS! After all, he had had a recent conversation with Jackson in which he told the President that he thought he could have enough of the government's money put aside to pay off the national debt by 1833, something Jackson devoutly wished. And not only pay it by 1833 but pay it on January 8, the anniversary of the Battle of New Orleans. It would be a kind of gift to the President to help celebrate the great event.

The conversation had taken place in the White House. Jackson, looking grave, had gestured his guest to sit near the fireplace. Biddle tried to be pleasant and gracious. Elegantly dressed in the latest fashion, he exuded a sense of social and financial power that came very naturally to a member of the privileged class.

"I feel very sensibly the services rendered by the Bank at the last payment of the national debt," said Jackson to Biddle at one point, "and shall take an opportunity of declaring it publicly in my message to Congress."

"We shall all be proud of any kind mention in the message," Biddle replied, "for we should feel like soldiers after an action commended by their General."

"Sir," said the sly Jackson, "it would be only an act of justice to mention it."

Actually the President had no intention of commending the Bank in his annual message to Congress. Quite the contrary. Still, when the message was published, Biddle chose to interpret it as basically

127

friendly. Had the President really meant to make trouble, he thought, he certainly would have devoted more than two short paragraphs to the question.

If Biddle failed to understand Jackson's intention, many people around the country got it—and liked what they got. One New York Congressman wrote: "I have twice read Andrew's message & think it a very good one, for the best of all reasons, because in all important points his Dox agrees with my Dox, which you know is the only way of determining what is orthodox & what heterodox—I shall vote against rechartering the great bank. It is capable of raising too high a pressure for the safety of those who may come within the sphere of its action."

The Bank was too powerful, he was saying. Too dangerous. And any number of people around the country agreed with this Congressman. But they had other objections as well. They felt the Bank was a monopoly with special privileges granted to it by Congress, by which the rich who owned its stock got richer and everybody else paid the bill. Such privileges ran contrary to the spirit of this democratic age, violating the generally accepted notion of the times that everyone should have an equal opportunity to get ahead.

One man summarized other complaints which he heard around the White House. He listed the Bank's "corrupting influence" because of its enormous wealth, particularly since it had Congressmen on its payroll; "its patronage greater than that of the Government"—and the Jacksonians were very sensitive about patronage because they understood its importance to the functioning of a democracy; and, he concluded, "its power to embarrass the operations of the Government—& to influence elections."

Influence elections! Here now was one of the things that really rankled. Here perhaps was the true reason for the Bank War. During the presidential election of 1828 there had been reports that the Bank had used its money against Jackson to assist the reelection of John Quincy Adams and other National Republicans. For example, it was asserted that money had been spent in Kentucky to buy votes among roughnecks and river bums for Adams, and that the branch bank of the BUS in Louisville had contributed $250 to the National Republican party. T.P. Moore, the Democratic party's chief organizer in Ohio, informed Jackson that "Mr. Clay presses the United States branch Bank." That last remark may have been ambiguous, but it was enough to quicken Jackson's already aroused suspicions.

These were trifling incidents, although irritating to Democrats. But when Isaac Hill, the Jacksonian newspaperman and party organizer in New Hampshire, publicly alleged partisan political actions by the Portsmouth branch of the BUS, he fired the shot that touched off the Bank War—or so Webster, Clay, John Quincy Adams, and many other contemporaries later contended.

Here's what happened. According to the Democrats in New Hampshire, Jeremiah Mason, president of the Portsmouth branch of the BUS and a close friend of Daniel Webster, had been discriminatory in awarding loans, refusing the applications of the friends of General Jackson. In addition the branch interfered in the election of Democrats through its financial contributions to the campaigns of National Republicans. In sum, as Hill curtly informed Biddle himself, the "friends of General Jackson have had but too much reason to complain of the branch bank at Portsmouth." They demand "that this institution . . . may not continue to be an engine of political oppression." Mason lent money to his own brother-in-law in Boston, said Hill, but "our" merchants who needed only "two or three thousand dollars" were refused.

As repeated to Jackson and reported in the Democratic press, the lending practices of the Portsmouth branch (which probably reflected the general policy of the BUS, they said) constituted an attack "on the plain people of the North" while the "vested interests" of the upper classes were pampered and subsidized. It was a conspiracy, snapped the Jacksonian newspapers, of wealth against the common good, a "contest between the Bank and the People."

Rather cleverly, the Democrats transformed a complaint about the Bank's political discrimination against their party members into a struggle between the interests of the rich and powerful on the one hand and the interests of the vast numbers of ordinary folk on the other. Partisan politics had spawned a democratic crusade.

Most unwisely, Biddle just ignored Hill's letter of complaint. But when the accusations were repeated by Levi Woodbury, the Democratic Senator from New Hampshire, and Samuel D. Ingham, Jackson's new Secretary of the Treasury, Biddle could not ignore them. Nevertheless, his written replies to Woodbury and Ingham were unbelievably inept and can only be described as demonstrations of bad temper. He categorically denied any interference by the Bank in the recent election and attributed the "personal rancor" against Mason to his vigor in enforcing the payment of debts.

To satisfy himself that his conclusions were correct, Biddle took a trip to Portsmouth to investigate the charges. Not surprisingly, his preconceived opinions were amply supported by the people he interrogated. The entire affair, he concluded, was a "paltry intrigue got up by a combination of small bankrupts & smaller Demagogues." All of which he subsequently reported to Ingham, adding gratuitously that it was none of the Secretary's business what the political opinions and actions of the Bank's officers were!

Ingham showed the letter to Jackson. The President read it slowly, studying the tone of the letter. When he finished reading it he returned it to Ingham and after a long pause instructed his Treasury Secretary to inform Biddle that the President of the United States "reserves his constitutional powers . . . to redress all grievances complained of by the people of the interference by the Branches with the local elections of the states, and all their interference with party politicks, in every section of the country."

According to most contemporaries, the Portsmouth incident began the Bank War. Even if one challenges this oversimple explanation of a major historical event, the Portsmouth affair certainly initiated the rhetoric and tone—thanks to Hill, Woodbury, and many other politicians, as well as an efficient Democratic press—which converted partisan political complaints against the Bank into a democratic crusade for social, economic, and political justice. Out of their pique over the Bank's failure to support their election, Democrats found an issue by which they could champion the cause of the people against the rich, or, as they put it, "the Democracy against the Aristocracy." Of course they identified their opponents, the National Republicans, as the party of the "aristocracy."

But what resulted from the crusade was never contemplated by the promoters of the Bank War. What resulted was a number of significant—indeed "revolutionary"—changes in the structure and process of government.

The influence of party politics on the life of the BUS became absolutely clear when Biddle decided to ask Congress for a renewal of the Bank's charter in 1832, four years before its current charter expired. He was opting for a trial of strength between the President and the Bank, even though he was warned that in such a trial "the Bank will go down—For Gen J's popularity is of *a sort* not to slaken at present."

Then why did Biddle permit such an action, when it might cause his

Bank's destruction? Quite simply, many National Republicans wanted him to request an early renewal of the charter because they could then make an election issue of it; this, they felt, could aid their reelection in 1832. Or, since Jackson was also seeking reelection, he might see it to his advantage not to allow the matter to become an issue and thus permit the Bank to have its recharter. Obviously Biddle could ill afford to disregard the wishes of the National Republicans, for, "The friends of the Bank in Congress," he was told, "expect the application to be made."

So Biddle asked for recharter. And immediately his action was interpreted by the Democrats as a challenge to the reelection of Andrew Jackson. "Now as I understand the application at the present time," wrote Roger B. Taney, Jackson's Attorney General, "it means in plain English this—the Bank says to the President, your next election is at hand—if you charter us, well—if not—beware of your power." Biddle was deliberately baiting the President, said Taney. He dared Jackson to "do his d——dest."

The application for recharter instantly roused Jackson's fighting instincts. When an assistant spoke to him about being forced under the circumstances to grant recharter, Jackson started raging. "I will prove to them that I never flinch," he stormed, "that they were mistaken when they expect to act upon me by such circumstances." As far as the President was concerned, Biddle's latest action only confirmed his belief that the Bank interfered with the political process and was therefore dangerous to the government and the people. An institution so monstrous had to be destroyed. Not changed, not reformed. Executed!

In his letters the President began to refer to the Bank as a monster, a "hydra-headed" monster, equipped with horns, hooves, and tail, and so dangerous that it impaired "the morals of our people," corrupted "our statesmen," threatened "our liberty," subverted "the electoral process," and sought "to destroy our republican institutions." The Democratic press repeated Jackson's litany and explained to the people how Biddle's request for recharter actually disguised an attack upon the President and the great American electorate. "The Jackson cause," they trumpeted, "is the cause of democracy and the people, against a corrupt and abandoned aristocracy." And why is the President opposed, they asked rhetorically. Because "he supports the interests of the WHOLE PEOPLE—because he will not uphold corrupt monopolies— because he will not become suppliant to the Aristocracy of the land! *This*

Thomas Hart Benton was Jackson's most important floor manager in Congress. As one friendly politician observed of their Bank war, "They were the chief destroyers of the *monster*."

is why he is opposed. And who are his opposers? Do they class with the farmers and mechanics? No. Do they class with the useful—the laboring men of the country? No. They are the rich—the powerful—the men who grind the faces of the poor, and rob them of their hard earnings. Men who live on their *twenty per cent extortions* from the poorer classes. *These* are the opposers of Andrew Jackson."

"Let the cry be heard across the land," stormed the Washington *Globe*, the principal Democratic newspaper. "Down with bribery—down with corruption—down with the Bank." That also meant "down with the National Republicans," the friends of the Bank.

So the issue was joined. Biddle demanded recharter now. Jackson insisted the Bank must go. In January 1832, a bill for recharter was introduced into Congress and the two parties—the National Republicans and Democrats—lined up for battle. In the Senate, Henry Clay, the presidential candidate of the National Republican party, and his colleague Daniel Webster took the lead in guiding the bill's safe passage through Congress, while Jackson's friend and supporter Thomas Hart Benton, Senator from Missouri, commanded the opposition. Biddle, of course, was on the scene using "his" money and influence to aid the Bank's cause. He ordered petitions sent to Congress from every state in the Union. He bought advertising space in newspapers to argue the Bank's position. He reminded influential politicians of past favors.

And Biddle's efforts paid off. On June 11, 1832, after a long debate, the bill for recharter passed the Senate by a vote of 28 to 20; a month later, on July 3, by a vote of 107 to 85 it rode through the House of Representatives. Biddle was overjoyed. "I congratulate our friends most cordially upon this most satisfactory result," he wrote. "Now for the President."

Jackson was waiting. Debilitated by the hot, sticky July weather, the President looked like a ghost when the Bank bill came to his desk for signing. Some feared he was close to death. He was sixty-five years old and recently had had another "bleeding of the lungs," probably caused by an abscess from his old wounds. He had barely enough strength to get out of bed. Van Buren came to see him one day and was startled by the President's appearance. The old man lay on a couch, gasping for breath. As Van Buren walked into the room Jackson glanced up, his face brightened, and he grasped his friend's hand. "The bank, Mr. Van Buren, is trying to kill me," he said in a whisper. Then, pressing Van Buren's hand very tightly, he added, "*but I will kill it.*"

His message vetoing the Bank bill was ready. It had been prepared by several members of his Kitchen Cabinet, most notably Amos Kendall, Roger B. Taney, Andrew Jackson Donelson, who was the President's nephew and personal secretary, Levi Woodbury, and, of course, Jackson himself. And what they produced was a remarkable state paper of transcendent historic significance. Indeed, it was the most important veto message ever written. It changed and amplified the fundamental power of the President.

The Bank veto was sent to Congress on July 10, 1832. It hit like a thunderclap. Jackson cited not only constitutional, but social, political, and economic reasons against the recharter. He said the Bank of the United States enjoyed exclusive privileges that gave it a monopoly of foreign and domestic exchange. Government must never grant exclusive privileges to any institution or individual, he continued, for that necessarily creates inequities and in the United States there must be equality for all. Only a relatively few people own stock in the BUS, yet they divide profits from investment of government funds which are collected from all the people. Worse, some eight million dollars' worth of shares of this stock are held by foreigners, said Jackson. "By this act [passed by Congress] the American Republic proposes virtually to make them a present of some millions of dollars." Over and over in the veto message, like the intense nationalist he was, Jackson reiterated his concern over this foreign influence within the Bank—and through the BUS, the entire country.

In writing the veto the way he did, Jackson accomplished something that was quite unprecedented. Previous Presidents had used the veto a total of nine times! In forty years under the Constitution only nine bills had been killed by a President. And only three of these nine dealt with important legislation. In every instance the President vetoing a particular bill had claimed it violated the Constitution. It was generally believed that a question of a bill's constitutionality was the *only* reason to apply the veto. Jackson disagreed. In his veto he now declared that a President could kill a bill for any reason—political, social, economic, or constitutional—when he felt it harmed the nation. If he thought a measure detrimental to the people's welfare, Jackson insisted the President had a right and a duty to veto that measure.

The implications of Jackson's interpretation of the veto power were enormous. The President was now taking on powers that had always belonged to Congress. This was immediately recognized by men like

Clay and Webster. For in effect what Jackson said to the Congress in the Bank-bill veto was this: Before passing any law, you had better be sure I am not opposed to it, because if I am, I have the power to kill it.

Thus, according to Jackson's view, Congress must carefully consider the President's wishes on all legislation *before* enacting it, or risk a veto. This interpretation of presidential prerogatives essentially changed the relationship between the legislative and executive branches of government. For, from the beginning of the nation under the Constitution, the legislative branch of the government—the Congress—had been considered preeminent. In the minds of most, it was Congress that embodied and secured representative government—not the President. Now Jackson seemed to be disputing that. Of course Congress can override a presidential veto, but that requires a two-thirds vote from both houses. Overriding is almost impossible to obtain because of party loyalty; it usually happens only when there are lopsided majorities of the party opposed to the President in both houses. As a result, few presidential vetoes have been overturned since Jackson's time. In effect, then, Jackson was claiming that the power of the President was the equivalent of two-thirds of both houses of Congress! His interpretation of the veto would alter the basic equality between the branches of government as written into the Constitution by the Founding Fathers. Instead of a 50-50 relationship between the chief executive and Congress, it would become a 67-33 relationship in the President's favor.

Continuing his veto message, Jackson next declared that the Bank in his opinion was unconstitutional. That was a shocker. For Supreme Court Justice John Marshall had declared the Bank constitutional in 1819 in the case *McCulloch* vs. *Maryland*. He had decreed that the implied-powers clause of the Constitution authorized Congressional action in creating the BUS.

"To this conclusion," said Jackson in his veto, "I cannot assent." Both houses of Congress as well as the executive must decide for themselves what is or is not constitutional before taking any action, whether that action consists of voting for a bill by Congress or signing it by the President. "It is as much the duty of the House of Representatives, of the Senate, and of the President," Jackson continued, "to decide upon the constitutionality of any bill or resolution which may be presented to them for passage or approval as it is of the supreme judges when it may be brought before them for judicial decision."

135

National Republicans wondered what Jackson was up to now. Was he attempting to make himself and the Congress coequal with the courts in determining the constitutionality of Congressional legislation? If that was true, he was undertaking still another fundamental alteration in the structure of government.

Although Jackson was challenging the Court's exclusive right to determine constitutionality, he was speaking before, not after, the fact. After the fact the Court decides; before the fact, he was saying, both the President and the Congress have a duty to determine in their own minds the constitutionality of specific legislation and to act accordingly. Jackson was contending that just because the Court declares a bill constitutional does not mean Congress *must* vote for such a bill when one is introduced or that the President *must* sign it if, in their good judgment, they honestly believe the bill unconstitutional. And, on the Bank question, Jackson did not agree with the Court's earlier position. Since the matter was subject to legislative and executive action, he simply claimed the right to think and act as an equal and independent member of the government.

If this doctrine was not electrifying enough to jolt some members of Congress right out of their seats, the final paragraph in the message certainly was. And it did! "It is to be regretted," said Jackson, "that the rich and powerful too often bend the acts of government to their selfish purposes. Distinctions in society will always exist under every just government. Equality of talents, of education, or of wealth can not be produced by human institutions. In the full enjoyment of the gifts of Heaven and the fruits of superior industry, economy, and virtue, every man is equally entitled to protection by law; but when the laws undertake to add to these natural and just advantages artificial distinctions, to grant titles, gratuities, and exclusive privileges, to make the rich richer and the potent more powerful, the humble members of society— the farmers, mechanics, and laborers—who have neither the time nor the means of securing like favors to themselves, have a right to complain of the injustice of their Government.''

This was a call to war. It was political propaganda of the highest order, guaranteed to stir men to action. Jackson had converted partisan complaint against the Bank into a struggle between the rich and poor. As champion of the common man—what he called the farmer, mechanic, and laborer—the President was prepared to do battle with the institution that most represented the privileged classes in America. There is almost a touch of demagoguery to the message, in that it can be interpreted in its final paragraph as an invitation to class conflict. But what magnificent propaganda it was! What red-hot controversy!

The message was effective. It caught the spirit of the times and expressed it in forceful language. It recognized that there were differences in society and always would be, but it declared that the government must never interpose to help one class over another and thereby aggravate these differences. When it does interfere, by such actions as creating the Bank, it creates "artificial" distinctions. This generates inequality, which produces injustice. Despite all the differences that existed in society, Americans of the Jacksonian period believed in human equality in the abstract, which they felt could be realized in the concrete as equal opportunity. Perhaps that, after all, is the essence of American democracy, even today.

Jackson ended his veto message by declaring his belief that there were no necessary evils in government. "Its evils exist only in its abuses," he said. "If it would confine itself to equal protection, and, as Heaven does its rains, shower its favors alike on the high and the low, it would be an unqualified blessing. In the act before me there seems to be a wide and unnecessary departure from these just principles."

Friends of the Bank were aghast at the tone and language of Jackson's message, let alone its principles. Nicholas Biddle likened it to "the fury of a chained panther biting the bars of his cage." It was, he said, "a manifesto of anarchy, such as Marat or Robespierre might have issued to the mobs" during the French Revolution.

The battle now moved back to Congress. Clay, whose American System dictated the need for sound currency and credit through the efforts of a strong bank, and Webster, who as the principal spokesman for American capitalism advocated a central bank, undertook the difficult next step of trying to convince Congress to override Jackson's veto.

Both Houses of Congress were jammed with spectators when the debates began. In the hall of Representatives visitors had to listen very carefully because the acoustics were so poor. Sounds skidded around the walls before ascending into the great dome ceiling that rose sixty feet above the floor. Otherwise the chamber was a model of governmental splendor, with a Brussels carpet covering the floor, crimson curtains over the windows and also beneath the low gallery, and a vast quantity of brass spittoons located around the room within firing distance of every Representative. Huge brass candlesticks adorned the Speaker's desk, over which hung an immense canopy of crimson silk with a superimposed gilt eagle. Columns of Potomac marble topped by white Corinthian capitals supported the semicircular hall and provided a majestic setting for the dramatic debates which were about to begin.

The Senate appointments were even more luxurious. Because there were fewer members than in the House, the atmosphere had an intimacy that encouraged powerful exchanges among the strong-willed, opinionated, and colorful personalities who made up the Senate. When Webster rose to denounce Jackson's veto message it was a foregone conclusion that he would deliver a mighty blast. The gallery hushed when he began to speak.

"According to the doctrines put forth by the President," intoned the glowering Webster, "although Congress may have passed a law, and although the Supreme Court may have pronounced it constitutional, yet it is, nevertheless, no law at all, if he, in his good pleasure, sees fit to deny it effect; in other words, to repeal and annul it." More than that, Webster continued, Jackson "claims for the President, not the power of approval, but the primary power, the power of originating laws."

Not exactly. Rather Jackson claimed the right to be a partner in the power of originating laws, a power he argued was lawfully his under the Constitution by virtue of his veto authority. But even this was a departure from the past. Up to this time, the power of originating laws had always been presumed to be lodged exclusively with the Congress. So Webster rejected Jackson's claim. "We have arrived at a new epoch," he warned. "We are entering on experiments with the government and the Constitution, hitherto untried, and of fearful and appalling aspect."

Henry Clay agreed with Webster. And when he asked to speak there was even greater excitement among visitors in the galleries. For Clay was a gut fighter, a verbal brawler whose slashing attacks on his victims delighted his audience because they were always so deliciously nasty and personal. He called Jackson's action a "perversion of the veto power." This power, he said, was "not expected . . . to be used in ordinary cases. It was designed for instances of precipitate legislation, in unguarded moments." It was to be used rarely, if at all, something all previous Presidents had understood. Jackson's interpretation, on the other hand, was "hardly reconcilable with the genius of representative government."

The Democrats hooted at Clay's criticism. Thomas Hart Benton, Jackson's staunch ally in the Senate and a man so opposed to paper money that he was called "Old Bullion," defended the President's message and chided the opposition for its lack of respect for Jackson. He rebuked them particularly for their abusive language. But Clay, in reply, laughed at Benton's present solicitude for the General. He remembered back to 1813, he said, when Benton, Benton's brother Jesse, and Jackson had a disagreement that ended in a gunfight in Nashville. At least, taunted Clay in a sneering tone that brought laughter from the galleries, "I never had any personal rencontre with the President. I never complained of the President beating a brother of mine after he was prostrated and lying apparently lifeless." Nor, he continued, had he ever said that if Jackson were elected President, Congressmen would have to protect themselves by carrying knives and pistols.

"That's an atrocious calumny," cried Benton, springing to his feet.

"What," retorted Clay, "can you look me in the face, sir, and say that you never used that language?"

"I look," said Benton, "and repeat that it is an atrocious calumny, and I will pin it on him who repeats it here."

Clay flushed with rage. "Then I declare before the Senate that you said to me the very words."

"False! False! False!" screamed Benton.

Other Senators jumped to their feet, fearful the two men would attack one another. Ladies in the galleries let out cries of apprehension while the men roared their excitement at the possibility of a fistfight on the floor.

The chair gaveled for order. After a few anxious moments the dignity of the Senate was restored.

"I apologize to the Senate," said Benton, "for the manner in which I have spoken—but not to the Senator from Kentucky."

Clay responded quickly. "To the Senate I also offer an apology—to the Senator from Missouri, none!"

Despite the great burst of oratorical power of such Bank men as Webster and Clay, Congress was unable to override Jackson's veto. On July 16, 1832, both houses adjourned. Since there would be a presidential election in the fall, the members were terribly concerned about what the Bank War might mean in political terms. And because of the veto, Jackson had placed the issue squarely before the American people and asked them for a decision. Since Clay had already been nominated for the presidency by the National Republican party and Jackson was the declared favorite of the Democrats, the electorate had a clear alternative. It was either Clay and the Bank—or Jackson and no Bank.

The decision was up to the American people.

9

The Issue Goes to the People

THE PRESIDENTIAL ELECTION of 1832 was one of the most innovative elections in American history. To start with, this was the first (and one of the very few) elections in which the American people were actually invited to decide an important issue. The electorate was frankly told that the life of the Bank of the United States hung on their choice between the two presidential candidates, Jackson and Clay. The election would decide the fate of the BUS. In most presidential elections it is the individual candidate and his party who normally attract the most attention and concern. There may be a platform with promises of legislation to be enacted or reforms to be initiated, but they are not binding and it is rare that an administration fulfills its entire pledged platform. It is even rarer that a significant national question is taken to the people directly with an understanding that however they vote, their decision will be absolute. Probably most voters don't wish to face such an awesome responsibility. They believe such decisions should be left to politicians; after all, that's what they get paid to do. Then if they make a wrong decision, or one that offends a majority of the people, they will be turned out of office.

Politicians understand all this and normally do their utmost to spare the public the burden of decision. The 1832 election was something of an exception.

This election was also significant in that it inaugurated the practice by the major parties of holding national nominating conventions to choose their presidential and vice-presidential candidates. Local conventions and state conventions had become regular practice in many sections of the country in the past few years. But there had never been a national convention. Prior to 1832, presidential candidates had been nominated by caucuses—meetings of Congressional members belonging to the same party, who named their candidate by majority vote—or by state legislatures that usually put forward favorite sons. These techniques were ultimately discarded because they did not seem democratic enough (caucuses) or because they appeared too parochial and local (state nominations). A national convention, comprising delegates from every state in the Union, was expected to provide a more representative device in keeping with a changing, modern society; it would necessarily involve a great many more people from all sections of the country— every state in fact—in the process of choosing presidential candidates. It was another step in the continued democratization of American institutions.

Still another unique feature of the 1832 election was the appearance of the first third party in American history. The Anti-Masonic party began in New York because of a murder in 1826. Suddenly, people became conscious of the existence of a secret society in their midst, the Masonic Order, which, it was alleged, had arranged the abduction and probable murder of a poor stonecutter who had published a book revealing Masonic secrets. Masons were believed to be rich. So the murder was seen as a plot by the "aristocracy" to protect their clandestine organization. The more these agitated New Yorkers inquired about Masonry, the more their suspicions were aroused. They convinced themselves that Masons held all the important positions in politics, law, and business, and that no one could "get ahead" without becoming a member of this secret, undemocratic society.

Soon a political witch-hunt commenced. Anti-Masonic newspapers were founded to fan the fury of the masses. Organizations were formed with the avowed purpose of removing all Masons from political office. During the next few years this furor spread from New York into Pennsylvania, Vermont, and parts of Indiana and Ohio. Some commentators saw the agitation as an ugly aspect of a changing society in

141

which those "on the make" raged against the alleged advantages of privileged classes. Whatever the reason, the movement expanded rapidly, stimulated by the organization and political skills of such men as Thaddeus Stevens, Thurlow Weed, William Seward, John C. Spencer, Samuel A. Foot and Henry Dana Ward. Anti-Masonic parties were organized in several states to screen political candidates and make certain they were free of Masonic taint. When it was discovered that both Jackson and Clay were Masons, the Anti-Masons rejected the candidates of the two major parties and decided to run their own candidate for President.

On September 26, 1831, the Anti-Masons met in Baltimore and held America's first national presidential nominating convention. Thirteen states were represented by 116 delegates at the convention, and they nominated William Wirt of Maryland for President and Amos Ellmaker of Pennsylvania for Vice-President.

But the national convention was not invented by the Anti-Masons. It was something a great many politicians had been talking about for several years. Indeed, back in 1826 Van Buren had suggested a national convention to nominate Jackson in order to strengthen the organization of the emerging Democratic party. Nothing came of the idea at the time because there were fears that a fight over naming the Vice-President might develop, which would seriously injure the fledgling party.

Now in 1832 such fears no longer existed. And because of the continued demand for a more representative, more democratic, method of selecting presidential candidates, the convention system seemed ideal. So it was seized upon by the two major parties.

The National Republicans acted first. They held their convention in Baltimore on December 21, 1831. In all, 155 delegates attended, representing eighteen states, and Henry Clay of Kentucky and John Sergeant of Pennsylvania were chosen to head the ticket. At this convention the delegates voted by roll call—each man rising from his seat when his name was called and declaring the name of his candidate.

A few months later another National Republican convention met in Washington, D.C. to name its candidate. This was a local convention, not a national one. But what made this meeting unique and important was the dramatic appearance of the candidate himself to accept the nomination. Henry Clay was their choice. And suddenly, there he was, standing in their midst, smiling and expressing his pleasure over their action. In a short speech he conveyed "the deep and grateful sense which I entertain for the distinguished proofs which you have . . . given to me of your esteem and confidence." If elected, he promised to maintain the people's interest at home and abroad, eradicate corruption, and uphold the Constitution and the laws. And so from this modest beginning would later come the long tradition of acceptance speeches by presidential candidates who would urge the party to fight hard and promise to carry out a program to advance the nation's interests "at home and abroad."

Another unusual aspect of this convention in Washington was the decision to write a party platform. Basically, the members adopted Clay's American System at the same time that they condemned what they called "Jackson's spoils system." They also demanded better trade relations with the West Indies.

The Democrats held their convention on May 21, 1832. Some 334 delegates—more than twice the number at the other two conventions—representing every state but Missouri (whose delegates could not reach the convention in time) met in Baltimore. There was no question about the presidential nomination. The incumbent president was their only choice. So instead of nominating him, the delegates simply said they "concurred" in the many nominations Jackson had already received from several states.

The real question for the Democrats was the vice-presidential nomination. Jackson wanted Van Buren. But not every Democrat was exactly crazy about the Little Magician, particularly the old friends of John C. Calhoun. Yet what could they do other than desert the party? Jackson had named his choice. So be it. On the second day the delegates duly rubber-stamped it. Jackson and Van Buren became the Democratic ticket.

The convention system, as adopted by the Anti-Masons, National Republicans, and Democrats, succeeded in a number of important objectives. The selection of candidates was conducted in a more open and democratic manner than ever before. More people were involved in the process, and, in time—once the system took hold—they represented every section, state, class, and economic interest and most political views in the nation. The convention eliminated the proliferation of candidates which had frequently happened when selection had been left to individual states. It therefore protected the parties against factionalism and the almost certain defeat at the polls which is its natural consequence. The convention also provided the best technique of forcing politicians to close ranks behind the designated ticket even when not everyone is enthusiastic about a particular candidate—as was the case with Van Buren. Party harmony, unity, and loyalty are essential for electoral success, and the convention system, more than anything else, provided this. In an age when the franchise increased rapidly, some process was needed to direct, channel, and guide this vote, lest it be dispersed and weakened over a wide variety of factions and candidates. If the weight of the majority vote is to be felt effectively it must be held together as a majority, not fragmented into a number of minority groups, such as occurred in Europe. The purposes of democracy were therefore well served by the invention of the convention system, just as Van Buren had predicted. It still thrives today, although not everyone is totally happy with it.

In the presidential campaign of 1832 which followed the nominating conventions, the Democrats cleverly argued that the Bank's money was the principal issue, that its financial strength was such that it could always sweep aside popular opinion to get what it wanted. It could bowl over the government too—even influence the election decisively in Clay's favor. This was a genuine fear among Democratic politicians, not a fake issue concocted for popular consumption. "The U.S. Bank is in the field," reported Senator William L. Marcy of the Albany Regency, "and I cannot but fear the effect of 50 or 100 thousand dollars expended in conducting the election in such a city as New York." The fear was repeated in other parts of the country. "The Bank is scattering its thousands here to affect us," reported a New Hampshire man. A Western Democrat declared: "I fear the Bank *influence* more than anything else. I have no doubt that the Bank managers will expend a large sum of money." Said another: "If the Bank, a mere monied corporation, can influence and change the results of our election at pleasure, nothing remains of our boasted freedom except *the skin of the immolated victim.*"

So the contest, as far as the Democrats saw it, was a struggle between unbridled financial power, privilege, and elitist rule in support of Henry Clay on the one hand, and equality, liberty, and popular rule in support of Andrew Jackson on the other. "The Jackson cause," they trumpeted, "is the cause of democracy and the people, against a corrupt and abandoned aristocracy."

One can be very suspicious of such campaign arguments. One can question the motivation behind these exaggerated statements about what

144

the opposition represented. But that's not the historical significance of this election. What was important was the tone and spirit the Democrats generated during this campaign. Their exaggerated boasts and wild claims saturated the atmosphere with cries against privilege, deference, and elitism and in support of popular rule. The people were wise and virtuous in all things, said the Democrats, and their will the only criteria for a free nation. This upsurge of admiration and respect for the people, this vocal affirmation of the merits of a mass electorate, replaced traditional notions of rule by the "few and the wellborn." Like the controversy over "spoils," this election provided the opportunity for politicians to create an ambience of political rhetoric that encouraged the growth of the democratic spirit.

The Democratic party was not alone in this endeavor. The National Republicans made their contribution too, only their bugaboo was not the "monster Bank" but what they called the "corrupt and arbitrary rule" of Andrew Jackson. And his recent veto flouting Congress' decision to recharter the Bank was the latest example, they said. To the National Republicans the election of 1832 was a struggle for representative government against the machinations of a dictator. "THE KING UPON THE THRONE: *The People in the Dust!!!*" read one newspaper headline. Andrew Jackson "has set at utter defiance the will of the people as strongly expressed by their Senators and Representatives . . . he has exercised a power that no Monarch in Europe dared attempt . . . he has, by his frequent exercise of power which should never be ventured upon but in the most extreme cases, proved himself to be the most absolute despote [*sic*] now at the head of any representative government on earth." This nation was created, said the National Republicans, to escape monarchical rule. The Founding Fathers, in their wisdom, provided representative government through the establishment of a Congress elected by the people. And now what's happened? Now what have we got? Now, to subvert republican rule, a President has emerged, elected by the electoral college, who uses the veto to assume power expressly delegated to the Congress. Unless he is hurled from office by the judgment of the people, warned the National Republicans, the nation under executive rule will rapidly collapse into a dictatorship.

The spoils system Jackson had "inaugurated" was another case in point, another example of presidential "despotism." The National Republicans claimed that Jackson had driven men of ability and dedication from office and replaced them with political hacks intent on finan-

GRAND FANTASTICAL PARADE, NEW-YORK, DEC 2ᵈ 1833

"Come yet thee o'eved the made of a lath."

These Butions the tinner and Dick the Butcher and Smith the weaver is rigged as Princs He rip"

"with such coercions I'll not march with them this file."

Shakespeare.

Humor, absurdity, and downright zaniness—such were political campaigns, as shown in this cartoon, "Grand Fantastical Parade." The flag at the left says: "OUR GENERAL!! May he *soon* meet his *reward* in Heaven for his *everlasting* services on EARTH."

cial gain. In so doing, they said, he was sinking the government into corruption, its integrity irreparably damaged. Only the voters could restore the system to its republican purity and simplicity by directing the removal of Democrats and their replacement with National Republicans, who were devoted to public service and representative Congressional government.

There was still time. "One more opportunity—*perhaps the last*—is yet afforded us," commented a National Republican newspaper in Ohio, "of strangling the monster of despotism before it shall have attained its full growth, and checking the full tide of corruption before it shall have become too strong to be resisted. The power still remains in our hands. Let us so use it as men who are to render an account to our God, to our country, to the world—and all will be well."

Both parties accepted the principle that the great masses of plain people throughout the United States should rule. Whereas, thirty years earlier, Alexander Hamilton had called the people a "beast" and John Adams and other Founding Fathers expressed fears that anarchy was the natural consequence of democracy, in the Age of Jackson these fears evaporated in a celebration of the mass electorate.

One of the important aspects of the 1832 election was the degree to which both parties now attempted to encourage popular participation in the electoral process. They were extraordinarily inventive in persuading people to vote, building on the initial efforts of politicians in the 1828 election. They conducted barbecues, rallies, parades, and the like, recognizing that these techniques tended to bring the people out and get them to vote—and, after all, that was one of the things democracy was supposed to be about. The traditional notion that voting should be confined to the educated or wellborn was forever gone.

Parades became fixtures of American elections and were conducted by all parties, even by men who thought them crude, vulgar, and tasteless displays of the human condition in its worst setting. One of the best such demonstrations in the 1832 election took place in New York City and was described by Michel Chevalier, a Frenchman traveling through the United States at the time. It was a parade stretching a mile long, he wrote. "The Democrats marched in good order, to the glare of torches; the banners were more numerous than I had ever seen them in any religious festival; all were in transparency, on account of the darkness. On some were inscribed the names of the democratic societies or sections: *Democratic young men of the ninth or eleventh ward*; others

147

bore imprecations against the Bank of the United States; *Nick Biddle* and *Old Nick* were figured largely. Then came portraits of General Jackson afoot and on horseback; there was one in the uniform of a general and another in the person of the Tennessee farmer, with the famous hickory cane in his hand. Those of Washington and Jefferson, surrounded with Democratic mottoes, were mingled with emblems in all designs and colors. Among these figures an eagle, not a painting, but a real live eagle, tied by the legs, surrounded by a wreath of leaves, and hoisted upon a pole, after the manner of the Roman standards. The imperial bird was carried by a stout sailor, more pleased than was ever any city magistrate permitted to hold one of the strings of the canopy in a Catholic ceremony. From further than the eye could reach, came marching on the Democrats. I was struck with the resemblance of their air to the train that escorts the viaticum in Mexico or Puebla. The American standard-bearers were as grave as the Mexican Indians who bore the sacred candles. The Democratic procession, also like the Catholic procession, had its halting places; it stopped before the homes of the Jackson men to fill the air with cheers, and halted at the doors of the leaders of the Opposition, to give three, six or nine groans.''

The National Republicans matched the Democrats in organizing parades and rallies. The bigger the better, they said. At one demonstration ten thousand people supposedly attended. ''We looked around,'' wrote one reporter, ''and we saw the mariner and the merchant, the storekeeper and the mechanic, the manufacturer and the day laborer—all glowing and gratified at the eloquence of the orators.'' The rally turned out to be a particularly ''glorious one for our cause. It reanimated our friends, added warmth to their patriotism—and has given fresh ardour to their exertions.'' And at a ''great meeting of naturalized Irish citizens'' held in Philadelphia and described as a ''bumper'' crowd, Jackson was repudiated by the overwhelming sentiment of the audience. ''Thousands upon thousands were there,'' reported one man, and ''we consider this meeting as a death blow to the administration in this quarter. . . . It is evident that the mass of the people—the bone and sinew of the city and county—the patriotism and purity of the community, are opposed to the re-election of Andrew Jackson.''

There was now an exuberance, an ''ardour'' to the electoral process that generated huge crowds at all party functions. Barbecues were especially attractive. Even when they lost local elections, as the Democrats did in Kentucky, the politicians seemed to think a barbecue was in order. ''There seems to be no way of convincing these fellows,'' snapped the Louisville *Journal*, a National Republican paper, "that they are fairly beaten. They have one sort of answering for every thing. If we show them that we have elected our Lieutenant Governor by a majority of nearly 30,000, *they reply by swallowing a pig*. If we show them that we have gained great strength in the Senate, and added to our superiority, *they reply by devouring a turkey*. If we show them that we have obtained a majority of two-thirds in the House of Representatives, *they reply by pouring off a pint of whiskey or apple-toddy*. There is no withstanding such arguments. We give it up."

If Democrats were quick to swallow a pig to reply to political argument, the National Republicans showed a remarkable flare for political cartooning as a device to ridicule the opposition. Political cartoons developed into an art during this Jacksonian age. One of the most striking, entitled "Uncle Sam in Danger," showed the good Uncle sitting in a chair, his arm lanced, with blood and gold and silver coins flowing from the wound into a basin held by Amos Kendall. "Dr." Jackson stands over the victim, a scalpel in his hand. "Hold the Bason [*sic*] Amos," says Jackson, "this is merely an Experiment but I take the Responsibility." To one side of the picture Van Buren comments that he cannot give an opinion on the operation, while on the other side stands a citizen who laments: "Twixt the Giniril (since He's taken to Doctring) and the little Dutch Potercary, Uncle Sam stands no more chance than a stump tailed Bull in fly time."

One popular cartoon showed Jackson receiving a crown from Van Buren and a scepter from the devil; another portrayed Jackson, Van Buren, and others attired as burglars, aiming a large battering ram at the Bank's front door; and a third, depicting the spoils system, had a fearsome red devil flying over the country with strings attached to his fingers, feet, and tail, and tied at the other end to spoilsmen who bounced and jumped as the devil jiggled the strings. Presumably Jackson was the devil and the Democrats his puppets.

All of the cartoons and other gimmicks measured the distance politicians had traveled away from serious discussions of important public issues. The tactics marked the level of "debate." A striking pamphlet can influence voters, remarked one commentator, "and so does a well-conducted newspaper; but a hickory pole, a taking cry, a transparency, a burst of sky rockets and Roman candles (alas! that it should be so!) have a potency over a large third of our voters that printed eloquence can not exert."

Perhaps politicians showed keen insight into the public mind by amusing them with hickory poles and Roman candles rather than frightening them with serious talk about the one issue that had been taken directly to them for resolution. It was one thing to talk about democracy, equal opportunity, aristocracy, and privilege, and something else to prove that the Bank had failed to establish a uniform and sound currency or that paper money was a threat to the Republic and that the people by their vote must rid the country of both. Better to cheer Old Hickory—or razz Harry of the West. That way the seriousness of the matter could be concealed and forgotten.

When the hoopla and ballyhoo ended at the polls, Jackson won a thumping victory. He received a total of 688,242 popular votes, or 55% of the total, while Clay took 473,462 votes (37%) and Wirt 101,051 (8%). In the electoral college it was a sweep. Jackson won 219 votes, Clay 49, and Wirt 7. Wirt carried Vermont and Clay took Massachusetts, Rhode Island, Connecticut, Delaware, and Kentucky, and a majority of the Maryland electoral vote. All the rest went to Jackson except South Carolina which, because of the nullification furor, gave her 11 votes to John Floyd of Virginia.

Even though they had been told they were deciding the fate of the Bank, the American people, in casting their ballots, most likely did not vote against the Bank or against Henry Clay as much as they voted *for* Andrew Jackson. The simple truth of the matter is that the masses loved Jackson and had confidence in him and trusted him. He had succeeded in making them feel he was their representative, their leader. And if he directed the dissolution of the Bank then they would follow along, however worried they might be about the financial consequences. "Who but General Jackson would have had the courage to veto the bill rechartering the Bank of the United States," asked one man, "and who but General Jackson could have withstood the overwhelming influence of that corrupt Aristocracy?" Soon there was talk of a third term. "My opinion is," said the defeated William Wirt, "that he may be President for life if he chooses."

Jackson himself saw his election as a mandate from the people to proceed further than his simple refusal to permit recharter of the Bank and to kill it outright, or at the very least cripple it. So the presidential election of 1832 signaled the beginning of the end of the great Bank of the United States. But it also signaled the continued democratization of the electoral process. The masses of American voters were courted and flattered, urged to exercise their ballot in the interest of improved republican government. Many of the politicians who sponsored the electoral nonsense that typified the 1832 campaign may have been quite cynical about the ''democracy,'' the ''wisdom'' of the people, and other such slogans they bandied around the country. But whether they were cynical or not, whether they believed their democratic mouthings or not, is irrelevant. What is important is that they created—for whatever reason—a climate of respect and regard for the popular will. The sound and tone of ''democracy'' engulfed the country. The air was saturated with it. And it endured. It became a permanent part of American politics.

This, then, was one of the great contributions of the Jacksonian era.

10

The President Becomes
the Head of the Government

THE ELECTION OF 1832 was filled with the shouts and sounds of a free people raucously engaged in conveying their will to their elected government. But the election actually proved several things. It proved that Andrew Jackson was not only the head of his party, who could dictate the issues the party must support, but also that he was a masterful politician who knew how to lead the great numbers of American people. The election proved the President of the United States could be—and indeed should be—a leader of the masses. The entire electorate was his constituency. He was its representative. Gone forever was the older notion of an aloof chief executive whose responsibility to the people was only vaguely understood.

And much of this had come about because of the Bank War. It provided the occasion by which Jackson during the election campaign could go to the people and ask for their support against the "monster" in order to safeguard their liberties and protect their government. The War started the process whereby the relations between the people and the central government, and among the several branches of government, underwent structural changes. Those changes continued after the election. Indeed, once the election ended and Jackson was assured of four more years in office, he decided to remove the government's deposits from the BUS, and that decision set in motion a chain of events that produced still another vast increase in the power of the chief executive.

Supposedly, Jackson first expressed his decision to remove the deposits to Francis P. Blair, editor of the Washington *Globe*. It was shortly after the election. The two men were sitting in the White House. Blair was complaining to Jackson that despite the electoral victory and the people's "mandate" to do something about the wicked practices of the Bank, Czar Nick Biddle was spending public funds "to frustrate the people's will." The tiny editor sputtered as he spoke. "He is using the money of the government for the purpose of breaking down the government," Blair charged. "If he had not the public money, he could not do it."

Whether Biddle was actually using public money to "break down the government"—whatever that meant—hardly mattered. The President was quite prepared to believe the worst. Thus, as Blair spoke, piling one accusation of impropriety on top of another, Jackson became visibly agitated. The muscles of his jaw tensed. His eyes flashed. Finally he exploded. "He shan't have the public money!" Jackson stormed. "I'll remove the deposits! Blair, talk with our friends about this, and let me know what they think about it."

When Blair returned with the information requested of him a few days later he was surprised to find Jackson calm and quite composed, almost to the point of nonchalance. "Oh," said Jackson, "my mind is made up on *that* matter. Biddle shan't have the public money to break down the public administration with. It's settled. My mind's made up."

That was typical of Jackson. First came the explosion, the tantrums, the wild threats. But once he made up his mind a mood of calm settled over him, sometimes giving people the wrong impression of his attitude. The decision reached, he was now prepared to act. Jackson summoned his cabinet and informed the members of his intentions. Since by law the Secretary of the Treasury, not the President, was authorized to remove the deposits, and since the incumbent Secretary opposed removal, Jackson decided to appoint a new Secretary and "kick" the present one "upstairs" by making him Secretary of State. William Duane, an intense, fidgety, sharp-featured man, was chosen as the new Treasury Secretary because he was known to oppose the Bank and could be expected to do what the President instructed. In a weak moment Duane also agreed to resign his office if he found Jackson's directions impossible to obey.

But once sworn into office, Duane slowly changed his mind about the removal of the deposits. His pride was the chief reason. He did not like the way it was simply presumed that he would do as he was instructed, as though his opinions didn't matter in the least. Finally, since the law clearly placed the responsibility for the public funds in his hands, he decided he was not going to have the responsibility taken from him and was not going to be told—even by the President—what to do. So he went to Jackson.

The President was in his office, sitting at his desk and reading several reports. He greeted his Secretary warmly and the two men sat down together near the window to catch the slight breeze that stirred the hot, humid air. When Duane finished his statement, the President just stared at him, flabbergasted.

"But you said you would retire if we could not finally agree," said the President after recovering from the shock.

"I indiscreetly said so," Duane replied, "but I am now compelled to take this course."

The words angered the old man, as though they had been deliberately chosen to offend him. Still, he did not wish to quarrel with his Secretary and so he tried to reason with him. But Duane would not yield.

"A secretary, sir," said Jackson at one point, "is merely an executive agent, a subordinate, and you may say so in self-defense."

"In this particular case," responded Duane, "congress confers a discretionary power, and requires reasons if I exercise it. Surely this contemplates responsibility on my part."

Duane had a point. The law clearly stated that Duane must report to Congress any decision regarding the deposits. Congress was in recess, and so he felt he should do nothing until Congress reconvened the following December, when he could make his report as the law required.

Jackson seethed. "How often have I told you," he continued, "that congress cannot act until the deposits are removed."

Duane asked for a delay—at least ten weeks.

"Not a day," barked the President, "not an hour."

Now there was only one recourse, and the President quickly took it. Duane was promptly notified in writing that "your further services as Secretary of the Treasury are no longer required." In his place Jackson appointed Roger B. Taney, who had been serving as Attorney General.

This incident may seem trifling. Actually it was extremely important. It was another action which served to strengthen the presidency. It was one more Jacksonian stroke that altered the relations between the executive and the legislature and contributed to the growth of presidential power. To begin with, the purse strings of public funds are held by Congress. This is clearly written in the Constitution. In fact the purse strings are placed in the hands of the House of Representatives, whose members are directly elected by the people. Under the charter of the Bank of the United States, Congress permitted the Secretary of the Treasury to act in its place and remove the government's money if he felt it was necessary. Congress had authorized the Secretary of the Treasury, *not* the President. What is more, the law specifically stated that the Secretary must notify the Congress of his actions. Jackson, in ordering the removal, assumed control of public funds. This action was constitutionally questionable but obviously one which would add to his prerogatives and enhance his powers if he got away with it.

Another reason why this Duane incident is important is Jackson's presumption that he could dismiss at will any member of the cabinet. Since all cabinet posts are created by act of Congress and appointments to them require confirmation by the Senate, there was some question as to whether the President could remove a cabinet officer without receiving prior consent from the Congress. This was particularly true of the Secretary of the Treasury because of his handling of public funds, which fall under the exclusive control of the Congress. Jackson, by his action, settled the question for himself and for all future Presidents. He assumed absolute power to remove cabinet officers without even notifying Congress, much less obtaining its consent. Jackson was asserting exclusive control over the entire executive branch at the same time he was insisting on the right to share some of the powers of the legislative branch.

Here, again, Jackson was breaking with the past, striking off in a new direction. Previous Presidents had resolved difficulties with their cabinet officers by getting them to resign. It was less messy that way, and it also skirted the constitutional question of the President's removal power. But Jackson hit the question head on. His dramatic dismissal of Duane set a precedent. In effect he was defining his authority in such a way as to strengthen presidential prerogatives. And anyone who disagreed with his definition could expect to be summarily bounced out of office.

Duane's dismissal caused quite a storm. There was a barrage of complaints from National Republicans over the President's action. Again, they charged, he was destroying representative government in the United States. "Executive despotism," they called it. They were even more outraged when Jackson appointed Roger B. Taney the new Secretary, and Taney, though not yet confirmed by the Senate, ordered the removal of the government's deposits from the BUS. His order went out in September 1833 and the Congress was not scheduled to reconvene until December 1833. To National Republicans the action appeared to be an outright and illegal assumption of power. Technically, they said, Taney was not the Secretary since he had not been confirmed, but here he was moving public funds in obedience to the President's order.

By the time Congress reconvened, the removal operation was well under way. Actually, Taney did not pull all of the government's money out of the BUS in one fell swoop. His policy was more subtle. He directed that all future money collected by the government in taxes, land sales, tariff revenues, and the like be placed in selected state banks, called "pet banks" by the opposition. For operating expenses the government drew out its remaining funds from the BUS until they were exhausted. Thus, removal was a gradual process and calculated to prevent undue shock to the banking system.

Once back in session, the Senate, under the leadership of Clay and Webster, was spoiling for a fight. An unconfirmed Secretary was directing the dispersal of public funds. What's more, the House of Representatives, which held the purse strings, had the year before voted a resolution declaring the government's deposits safe within the vaults of the BUS and requesting that they be left there. But Jackson had blithely disregarded this resolution and had ordered his Secretary to begin removal. Oh, the clamor and tumult of the Congressional debates once the session got under way. The frustration! the anger! The Senate finally took its fury out on poor Taney. It refused to confirm him as Secretary of the Treasury.

Some Congressmen then argued that since Taney had never been confirmed, he had never been Treasury Secretary and therefore his order for removal lacked legal force. But that argument had no effect on the President and he went right ahead with removal, appointing Levi Woodbury of New Hampshire as the new Secretary of the Treasury and instructing him to continue Taney's policy.

Then came an unexpected shock. Not from Jackson but from Czar Nick. As frustrated and angry as any Senator or Representative, Biddle

156

ached to wreak revenge on his tormentor. "This worthy President," he wrote, "thinks that because he has scalped Indians and imprisoned Judges* he is to have his way with the Bank. He is mistaken." To demonstrate what he meant, Biddle called for a general curtailment of loans throughout his entire banking system. Those seeking loans would be denied; those in debt to the Bank would be called upon to pay what they owed.

Biddle's order was so sudden and its financial effect so devastating that it pitched the country into an economic panic. Which was precisely what Biddle wanted. If he brought enough pressure and agony to the money market there would be such a public outcry that Jackson would be forced to restore the deposits. And maybe the charter, too. Nothing can be accomplished, Biddle wrote, unless there is "distress in the community. Nothing but the evidence of suffering abroad will produce any effect in Congress. . . . Our only safety is in pursuing a steady course of firm restriction—and I have no doubt that such a course will ultimately lead to restoration of the currency and the recharter of the Bank."

Within a few months Biddle reduced loans by more than eighteen million dollars. State banks were directed to pay what they owed the "monster," and pay in hard cash. This squeeze staggered the commercial and manufacturing centers of the country, which needed capital for expansion. "The distress among the merchants is truly appalling," commented one businessman. Dealers and merchants in New York City were reported to be "in very great distress nay even to the verge of General Bankruptcy." "Things are getting worse and worse here," one New Yorker informed Biddle. By the end of January 1834 the pressure was described as "as great as any community can bear." "Bankruptcy to the North is almost general," exclaimed Senator John Tyler from Virginia in February 1834, "and where the present state of things will end it is impossible to say."

Biddle's arbitrary and disruptive action seemed to prove every accusation Jackson and the Democrats had ever leveled against the BUS. Here was raw, naked power, exercised by one man, who could virtually bring down the financial community throughout the nation without answering to anyone except his money-hungry board of directors. Of course friends of the Bank responded by accusing Jackson

---

*During the Battle of New Orleans Jackson arrested the federal district judge for issuing a writ of habeas corpus releasing a man the General believed dangerous and had had imprisoned.

of abuse of power, to which the Democrats replied that Jackson had at least been elected to his office by the people of the United States, that he exercised legitimate authority granted under the Constitution, and that his actions proceeded from his concern for the welfare of the people, not the mercenary interests of the wealthy few. Again and again, Democrats interpreted the Bank War in terms of Jackson as champion of the people versus Biddle the spokesman of the money power.

During the winter and spring of 1833-34, Jackson received repeated pleas from businessmen to give in to Biddle so that he would end the curtailment. They assured the President that he had demonstrated his great popularity with the masses and had won a stupendous electoral victory. "But give Biddle his charter," they begged, "or he will ruin us." One delegation told the President that they were close to bankruptcy, that they were insolvent.

"Insolvent do you say?" snorted Jackson. "What do you come to me for, then? Go to Nicholas Biddle. We have no money here, gentlemen. Biddle has all the money. He has millions of specie in his vaults, at this moment, lying idle, and yet you come to *me* to save you from breaking. I tell you, gentlemen, it's all politics."

Indeed! And no one knew that better than Andrew Jackson. Yet it was the kind of politics that ultimately served the democracy, for the Bank War revealed the inherent dangers and impropriety of government participation in financial operations that enrich or benefit one class of citizens over all others. Jackson saw, too, how the Bank had been used to serve political ends, such as the 1832 campaign of Henry Clay, and he repeatedly warned how threatening the consequences of such involvement could be to the liberty of the nation.

As a matter of fact the Bank War led immediately into a realignment of political parties. Under the combined pressure of Jackson's removal policy and Biddle's financial squeeze, a new political combination slowly emerged in the winter of 1833-34. All those who hated and feared Jackson and the aggressiveness of his presidency—National Republicans, Bank men, Southern nullifiers, states' righters, friends of Calhoun, Democrats who could not accept removal of the deposits— joined together to form a new political party. They called it the "Whig" party, which is the classic name used to designate opposition to concentrated political power in the hands of the chief executive. The name was first employed in the newspapers and received national attention when Henry Clay used it in a speech attacking Jackson which he delivered in the Senate on April 14, 1834.

The old National Republicans, who had originally coalesced in support of a vigorous federal government to advance the economic and intellectual well-being of the nation, now found their ranks swelled by men who disagreed with their political philosophy but who joined them for a variety of reasons: Jackson's use of presidential power, or his Bank policy, or the way he handled the nullification controversy, or the spoils system—all the things he had done to curtail Congressional authority and thereby, it seemed, representative government. Many were former Democrats—especially Southern Democrats—who believed he had indeed misused his office. Others were Northern businessmen who thought Jackson's reckless assault on the Bank would financially damage the nation. Soon the Whig newspapers were attacking Jackson as "King Andrew the First" and describing him as a despot plotting to extinguish the liberties of the nation. Cartoons showed Jackson garbed as an emperor, with a crown on his head and a scepter in his hand. Under his feet was the tattered Constitution. The Whigs contended they were locked in a deadly struggle with a tyrant who confused his own will with the people's. Their duty was to alert the people to their danger and pull the tyrant down.

Despite the formation of the Whig party, despite their attacks, despite the anguished cries of bankrupt merchants because of the panic, Jackson would not change the thrust and direction of his presidency nor budge from his resolve to kill the Bank. "I have it *chained*," he raged, "*the monster must perish*." To give in to Biddle now, he argued, would be to surrender the freedom of the nation to a money changer who did not represent them or care for their interests.

Led by Henry Clay, the Whigs in Congress began a systematic attack on Jackson, accusing him of subverting the republican system of government. They charged him with seeking to transform the country into a dictatorship. "The premonitory symptoms of despotism are upon us," said Clay in one speech before the Senate; "and if Congress do not apply an instantaneous and effective remedy, the fatal collapse will soon come on, and we shall die—ignobly die—base, mean, and abject slaves; the scorn and contempt of mankind; unpitied, unwept, unmourned."

Clay's speech infuriated Jackson. "Oh, if I live to get these robes of office off me," he seethed, "I will bring the rascal to a dear account."

There is a story, undoubtedly apocryphal, that years later Jackson on his deathbed was asked if there was anything he had left undone. "Yes," gasped the dying man, "I didn't shoot Henry Clay and I didn't hang John C. Calhoun."

159

Jackson was the first President lampooned by his enemies as a monarch, fully ensconced in a throne room and adorned with the robes and symbols of royalty.

KING ANDREW THE FIRST.

KING
ANDREW
THE FIRST,
" Born to Command."

A **KING** who, possessing as much power as his Gracious Brother *William IV.*, makes a worse use of it.

A **KING** who has placed himself above the laws, as he has shown by his contempt of our judges.

A **KING** who would destroy our currency, and substitute *Old Rags* payable by no one knows who, and no one knows where, instead of good *Silver Dollars*.

A **KING** born to command, as he has shown himself by appointing men to office contrary to the will of the People.

A **KING** who, while he was feeding his favourites out of the public money, denied a pittance to the *Old Soldiers* who fought and *bled* for our independence.

A **KING** whose *Prime Minister* and *Heir Apparent*, was thought unfit for the office of ambassador by the people:

Shall he reign over us,
Or shall the PEOPLE RULE?

The Congressional debates over the removal of the government's deposits from the BUS and Jackson's misuse of presidential power ran on for over three months, the longest single debate in either House or Senate since the government had begun. The seriousness of the matter, the eloquence of the speakers, and the excitement generated by the contest between the President and the Congress drew great crowds of people to Washington.

Washington was still the city of "magnificent distances," which was one of the earliest descriptions of the capital. Government buildings and private homes dotted a sprawling terrain whose streets stretched like spokes of an enormous wheel from the main thoroughfare that connected the White House with the Capitol. Cows pastured undisturbed in the open areas between residences. There was space available for expansion. It was a city planned for the future.

The Senate was the great attraction, for all but one of the great political leaders of the age were clustered there. (Jackson, staying with at least one tradition, remained away from the Senate chamber.) Perched high in his presiding chair was the new Vice-President, Martin Van Buren, looking very composed and debonair. Sprawled in his chair on the floor below him sat Henry Clay, frequently impatient with what he heard in the debate and jumping from his seat to prowl among his colleagues or wander to the Senate table to sample the contents of the snuffbox. Daniel Webster looked grave and worried, his deep-set, luminous eyes peering out under a massive brow. Thomas Hart Benton, the leader of the Senate Democrats, sat among a pile of papers and books ready to demand the floor whenever the attack upon the President descended to low-swinging invective. And then there was John C. Calhoun, his face lined with frustration and disappointment—Jackson's enemy and the outcast of the Democratic party. Because the Senate chamber was small and its acoustics excellent, every snarling, vicious word snapped around the room like the crack of a whip and kept the galleries quiet and unusually attentive.

Both sides claimed to speak for the cause of democratic government, the Whigs in denouncing executive usurpation, the Democrats in assaulting the power of the rich as represented within and without the halls of Congress. Not only Jackson but leaders of both parties suffered savage tongue-lashings. It was something the galleries thoroughly enjoyed. On one occasion during this long debate, Thomas Hart Benton, in a four-day speech, cut up Henry Clay rather badly, and in the process

161

reminded the nation that Jackson had just won an overwhelming popular vote of confidence while Clay had been rejected, put down, defeated. "The senator from Kentucky," he thundered, "calls upon the people to rise, and drive the Goths from the Capitol. Who are those Goths? They are General Jackson and the democratic party—he just elected President over the senator himself, and the party just been made the majority in the House of Representatives—all by the vote of the people. It is their act that has put these Goths in possession of the capitol to the discomfiture of the senator and his friends; and he ought to be quite sure that he felt no resentment at an event so disastrous to his hopes, when he has indulged himself with so much license in vituperating those whom the country has put over him."

But Clay was more than a match for Benton. He returned sarcasm for ridicule, stinging rejoinder for biting accusation. But he never forgot that Jackson was his true target. "Everything [is] falling," he declared in one powerful thrust at the President, "everything [is] going down, down, down." It was a struggle "between the will of one man and that of twelve millions of people. It is a question between power—ruthless, inexorable power—on the one hand, and the strong deep-felt sufferings of a vast community, on the other."

At one point in the debate Clay demanded the attention of Martin Van Buren, the presiding officer. In his most sarcastic voice he "implored" the Magician to go to Jackson and on bended knee "exert his well-known influence" over the President and insist upon the restoration of the deposits. When the speech ended, Clay returned to his seat and smiled at his Whig friends, rather pleased at the digs he had scored at the expense of the Democratic leadership. Everyone turned to Van Buren to catch a reaction but the little man let no meaning slip over his face. Instead he quietly gestured another Senator to take his seat as presiding officer as he hopped down to the floor. Then he walked straight across the chamber toward Clay. There was no mistaking where he was headed and suddenly it occurred to everyone in the room that a fearful brawl was about to take place on the Senate floor between the Vice-President of the United States and the nation's most distinguished Senator.

Seeing Van Buren approach, suspecting the worst, Clay slowly rose from his seat and stared at the approaching figure. Could it be that the Vice-President, that soul of courtesy and amiability, was about to strike him or demand in ugly phrases satisfaction on the dueling grounds? Clay could not imagine what to expect, nor could the spectators who watched in hypnotic fascination. Still Van Buren came on, still headed straight for the Kentucky Senator. Finally he reached Clay's side. The silence in the room now reached thunderous proportions. There was the little man from New York staring up at the tall, gaunt orator from Kentucky. But Van Buren did not rebuke Clay with violent word or action. He bowed. Then, in a mocking voice, he said, "Mr. Senator, allow me to be indebted to you for another pinch of your aromatic Maccoboy." The words snapped the tension and the Senate breathed a sigh of relief as Clay, dumbfounded, waved his hand toward the gold snuffbox he always had on his desk. He was too amazed to utter a word. Van Buren took a pinch of snuff, applied it to each nostril, and then leisurely returned to the Vice-President's chair, winking at Senators as he went. It was a sly, characteristic rejoinder to the Westerner's sarcasm.

The dispute in all its many ramifications had now become a titanic political free-for-all. Democratic leaders organized mass meetings throughout the nation to denounce the "aristocratic" Senate and its master, the "monster" Bank. For their part, Whigs arranged the submission of hundreds of petitions to Congress demanding the renewal of the Bank's charter so that the economic panic could be terminated. One outraged Whig from Cincinnati wrote directly to Jackson. "Damn your old soul, remove them deposites back again, and recharter the bank, or you will certainly be shot in less than two weeks and that by myself!!!"

The "aristocratic" Senate—so named by the Democrats because the Whigs held a slight majority in the upper house—climaxed the furious antics of the past several months by bringing forward a resolution of censure against the President of the United States. So strong was the new Whig coalition and so distressing the economic havoc caused by Biddle's squeeze that on March 28, 1834, under the masterful leadership of Henry Clay, the Senate agreed by a vote of 26 to 20 to officially censure Andrew Jackson for removing the government's deposits from the Bank of the United States without the express authorization of the United States Congress. This, according to Clay, constituted a gross misuse of presidential power.

"It's all politics," Jackson had once said. Now he knew how true his words were. Now he knew how deep a political wound could penetrate, for the censure was a savage blow to his pride. He was crushed by the Senate's action. Always a proud man, a man who guarded his reputation with fierce concern, he was genuinely grieved by the censure.

But not for long. Within a few days the old fighting spirit stirred within him. His blood was up. Although sixty-seven years old and physically quite infirm, he could still summon the will to shout his defiance. With the help of a number of his advisors he began writing a "Protest" message to defend himself before the Senate, but more particularly to defend himself and his actions before the American people.

In the nineteenth century Presidents did not appear in person before Congress. So Jackson's "Protest" had to be read to the Senate, the words droned out by the clerk. And even though the reading lacked dramatic force, the words themselves were so potent—indeed revolutionary—that many Whig Senators, astounded at the appalling doctrines Jackson pronounced in his message, sat staring in utter disbelief.

The President's "Protest" began by accusing the Bank of having grown rotten with financial power, power to control the destiny of individuals and government. "So glaring were the abuses and corruptions of the Bank . . ." he said, "so palpable its design by its money and power to control the Government and change its character, that I deemed it the imperative duty of the Executive authority . . . to check and lessen its ability to do mischief. . . . The [censure] resolution of the Senate . . . presupposes a right in that body to interfere with this exercise of Executive power."

Jackson was a superb politician; he composed his message not simply for the edification of Congress but for the enlightenment and education of the American people. The message was a political document as well as one of the most important and influential state papers ever prepared by a chief executive. Because it was an instrument of propaganda, Jackson felt it important to reiterate his claim that the power of appointing, controlling, and removing those who executed the laws belonged exclusively to the Chief Executive—even though those appointed were confirmed by the Senate and their duties included reporting to the Congress. The Secretary of the Treasury, continued Jackson's "Protest," in a specific reference to William Duane, was subject to the "supervision and control" of the President, and the law establishing the Bank of the United States could not change the relation between the President and his Secretary. Thus, he had had full authority to remove Duane without first obtaining Congressional approval.

Then Jackson dropped the bomb, the thing that had Senators aghast. It separated his administration from everything that had gone before. It changed the whole direction of government. Although it may not sound very important or exciting on first reading because future generations accepted its meaning without question, it actually marked a new beginning in American political history. "The President," declared Jackson, "is the direct representative of the American people." More than that, he is "elected by the people and responsible to them."

Direct representative of the American people! Elected by the people and responsible to them! Those statements convulsed the Whigs. Those doctrines certainly did not accord with the practice or beliefs of previous Presidents. Where was it written in the Constitution and the law, asked the Whigs, that the President was the representative of the people? Where was it written that he was responsible to them? Jackson was obviously repudiating his responsibility to the Congress, where the law and tradition placed it. He was embarked on yet another adventure to strengthen his power by claiming a special relationship to the people—a relationship which he shared with no one else. *Republican government meant leadership by the legislature,* argued the Whigs. *Leadership by the executive meant despotism.*

The entire tone of the "Protest" constituted a dangerous challenge to the traditional theory of legislative government which had, until this moment, been the basis of the American system. As such it could not go unanswered. The biggest Whig guns were trundled out to demolish Jackson's seemingly "monarchical" position and the bombardment began almost immediately. For, without question, they caught all the nuances of the "Protest" in terms of their meaning in relation to the traditional structure of American government.

Daniel Webster was now regarded as the "Great Expounder and Defender of the Constitution"—a title conferred on him by those who considered him "Godlike." It therefore fell to him to open the attack in the Senate and answer Jackson's outrageous contentions.

"Again and again we hear it said," Webster began, "that the President is responsible to the American people! that he is responsible to the bar of public opinion! For whatever he does, he assumes accountability to the American people! . . . And this is thought enough for a limited, restrained, republican government! An undefined, undefinable, ideal responsibility to the public judgment!" Webster paused, his features darkening by the intensity of his feelings. "I ask again, Sir. Is this legal responsibility? Is this the true nature of a government with written laws and limited powers?"

165

Then Webster confronted Jackson's revolutionary idea that the President was the direct representative of the people, that the executive was in effect the "tribune of the people." Again, Webster denied the principle. "Connected, Sir, with the idea of this airy and unreal responsibility to the public is another sentiment, which of late we hear frequently expressed; and that is, *that the President is the direct representative of the American people.*" At this point Webster was almost shouting. "This is declared in the Protest," he argued. "Now, Sir, this is not the language of the Constitution. The Constitution no where calls him the representative of the American people; still less their direct representative. It could not do so with the least propriety." The obvious proof was the manner of presidential elections.* "He is not chosen directly by the people, but by a body of electors, some of whom are chosen by the people, and some of whom are appointed by State legislatures. Where, then, is the authority for saying that the President is the *direct representative of the People*? . . . I hold this, Sir, to be a mere assumption, and dangerous assumption."

Webster concluded with a vigorous rejection of Jackson's entire theory. "And if he may be allowed to consider himself as the SOLE REPRESENTATIVE OF ALL THE AMERICAN PEOPLE, then I say, Sir, that the government . . . has already a master. I deny the sentiment, therefore, and I protest against the language; neither the sentiment nor the language is to be found in the Constitution of this Country."

The Whigs broke out in wild applause. The hurl and sweep of his language drove them to a near frenzy. With his consummate eloquence, Webster had put it to the President in clear and precise phrases, so that when his speech was printed in the newspapers for the instruction of the American people they would understand: Jackson was deliberately restructuring the government to the advantage of the executive branch, and such restructuring endangered their freedom and liberty, for it was a well-established fact that republican government demanded a strong legislature. Jackson's contentions were the beginning of executive despotism.

Next it was John C. Calhoun's turn to blast away at the President's pretensions. As he rose to speak the Senate and gallery were unusually crowded. Once Jackson's Vice-President, he was now a man without a

---

*See footnote concerning electoral college, page 15.

party. Everyone knew he hated Jackson, but they also knew he was a distinguished political theoretician and whatever he said about the Constitution would have enormous intellectual power.

Calhoun did not fail them. In a lengthy, involved, and strongly argued speech, he assailed the President's claims. Jackson "tells us again and again with the greatest emphasis," Calhoun began, "that he is the immediate representative of the American people. He the immediate representative of the American people! . . . What effrontery! What boldness of assertion! Why, he never received a vote from the American people. He was elected by electors . . . and of course is at least as far removed from the people as the members of this body, who are elected by Legislatures chosen by the people."

"Why all this solicitude on the part of the President to place himself near the people?" Calhoun asked. "The object cannot be mistaken. It is preparatory to further hostilities—to an appeal to the people . . . to enlist them as his allies in the war which he contemplates against this branch of the Government." Calhoun wasn't telling the Senate anything it didn't know. What he did emphasize was the fact that Jackson's appeal to the people masked his attack on the original structure of the government as provided by the Founding Fathers. For, while previous Presidents had understood and appreciated that the seat of government was the Congress, and while they had consequently functioned like prime ministers, as the heads of a coordinate branch of the government—one of the three equal branches—Jackson, on the other hand, now claimed he was the head of the entire government and the spokesman of the American people.

Surely this was pernicious doctrine, concluded Calhoun. It was the destruction of tripartite government. The end of republicanism. The triumph of despotism.

Henry Clay spoke next. Like the others before him Clay denied the President's assertions about his responsibility. "I deny it absolutely," said the Senator. "All are responsible to the law." What Jackson was attempting, he argued, was a "revolutionary" change in government. Everyone who knew anything about the Constitution and the intentions of the men who wrote it could see that. But Clay's speech was not only bitter, it was insulting. The administration, he said, was expiring in agony. If a phrenologist were to examine Jackson's head he would find "the organ of destructiveness prominently developed. Except an enormous fabric of Executive power, that President has built up nothing. . . . He goes for destruction, universal destruction.''

Despite the arguments and eloquence of this triumvirate—Webster, Clay, and Calhoun—Jackson's novel concept found ready acceptance with the electorate, for the people did in fact think of the President as "their representative"—the man who runs the government. It was an idea whose time had arrived. Perhaps Jackson instinctively knew it, considering his political skills, and knew the people would accept it. Eventually even the Whigs capitulated to it. Said one Senator: "Until the President developed the faculties of the Executive power, all men thought it inferior to the legislature—he manifestly thinks it superior; and in his hands the monarchical part of the Government (for the Executive is monarchical . . .) has proved far stronger than the representatives of the States."

In introducing and ultimately finding acceptance of his theory, Jackson altered the essential character of the presidency. As the representative of the American people, the President from this time on became the true head of the government. That meant he would formulate national policy and direct public affairs. Enacting new laws was no longer the sole province of Congress. Instead, the President would present to Congress the needs of the people as he understood them, and ask for the necessary legislation. It was now up to the President to have some vision of the nation's future growth and development (that is if he had any stature as a statesman), formulate the vision into a specific program, and then present the program to Congress for funding and approval.

For all intents and purposes Andrew Jackson was the first modern President. He strengthened the presidency, redefined its role, and profoundly altered its relationship to the people. He used the executive office for purposes of national leadership. Under Jackson the people and their government were brought closer together.

Yet some of the most imaginative politicians of the age did not understand or appreciate what Jackson had done. Some of his closest friends, like Martin Van Buren, had grave doubts about the "Protest." Van Buren feared it might be misunderstood as a denial of the right of Congress to provide for the custody, safekeeping and disposition of the property and public money of the United States. He worried that some might think Jackson had in effect seized this right for the Chief Executive. Van Buren urged him to write a second message and dis-

This 1845 daguerreotype was taken a few months before Jackson's death. Ailments caused by early duels and military wounds bothered him most of his long and active life.

claim any such intention. He felt their political friends might desert them on account of Jackson's policies and actions.

But Jackson was very calm and sure of himself. "Mr. Van Buren," he replied, "*your* friends may be leaving you—but my friends *never* leave *me.*"

By the spring of 1834 the Bank War itself began to move in Jackson's favor. It started when the President, in one more piece of nastiness toward Biddle, ordered the BUS to hand over the funds, books, and accounts (which belonged to the government) relating to pensions for Revolutionary War veterans. In the past the government's money was paid to the veterans by the Bank. Jackson now directed that the payments be handled by the Secretary of War.

Biddle refused. He told the government the money and the accounts were his to handle as he saw fit. But this was very high-handed even if he had been goaded by Jackson. He was saying in effect that he considered himself above government direction, at least above any direction demanded by the President of the United States.

The Democrats lashed poor Biddle over this latest defiance. *He* was the tyrant, they said, not Jackson. Biddle had produced the panic and now he boldly refused a government order to relinquish the pension money. Who exactly did Biddle think he was? Could no government official, no law, command his obedience?

Now even Webster saw the danger. No further argument was needed, he said, to convince the public that the Bank of the United States was a dangerous monopoly and must be dissolved. Still Biddle persisted in his refusal to part with the money. It could not be removed by presidential fiat, he said. It was his to handle as he had always done. And not only did he refuse to give it up, he refused to pay the veterans. Again he thought he could apply financial pressure to get what he wanted. But it was a grave political blunder. All he succeeded in doing was to deepen public resentment toward him and his institution. Without realizing it, and certainly without wishing it, Biddle was helping the President kill his Bank.

Finally, the House of Representatives, where the Democrats held a majority, brought the long War against the BUS to an end. A series of four resolutions was brought in from the Ways and Means Committee, chaired by James Knox Polk of Tennessee, one of Jackson's protégés. The first resolution said the Bank should not be rechartered. The

Democrats lined up solidly behind it and the House overwhelmingly passed it, 134 to 82. The second resolution said the deposits should not be restored to the Bank. Here some Democrats were troubled by the entire removal policy and so the vote was closer, although the measure passed, 118 to 103. The third resolution counseled that the government's money should remain in the state or "pet" banks. It passed by an almost identical vote, 117 to 105. The final resolution called for the selection of a committee to investigate the Bank's affairs and find out the reasons for the panic. By the most lopsided vote of all, the House passed it, 175 to 42.

Jackson glowed. "I have obtained a glorious triumph," he enthused. The vote in the House "has put to death that mammoth of corruption and power, the Bank of the United States."

Criticized by friends and supporters and stung by sharp public reaction to his latest actions, Biddle slowly loosed his financial squeeze. Within a few weeks the panic began to ease. More loans were allowed, more currency made available. It was remarkable, noticed many, how the will of one man could so absolutely control the economy of the nation. Finally, in July 1834, the board of directors of the BUS unanimously instructed Biddle to end the curtailment, and shortly thereafter the panic evaporated. The directors reacted to the temper of public opinion. They knew Biddle was thoroughly despised by the American people. They were now concerned for the life of the Bank.

Without the charter and without the government's funds the Bank slowly died. It was a demeaning death. When Jackson declared that the Bank's notes would no longer be acceptable for payment of taxes owed the government, it was one more nail in the coffin and Biddle began "winding up the Bank's affairs, quietly and certainly." The branch banks became independent state institutions. Finally, after 1836 when the original charter expired, the central bank in Philadelphia ceased to be a national bank and became just another state institution.

The destruction of the Bank of the United States terminated any central control over the nation's banking system, and state banks now enjoyed a vast measure of freedom. So they began issuing millions of dollars of paper money. As a consequence they fueled a mighty spurt of industrial growth and expansion. Since a nation must have capital to become industrialized, one result of the Bank War was extremely important in producing the capital that advanced the creation of America's industrial society.

As for the BUS, its power gone, its commanding position as a financial center was assumed by wealthy Wall Street banks in New York City. And it finally went down in bankruptcy in 1841. Philadelphia ceased being the financial capital of the country. That title now belonged to New York, as Chestnut Street, the site of the BUS, gave way to Wall Street.

In a real sense the Bank War ended a few years later when the Senate, now controlled by Democrats, agreed to "expunge" its 1834 censure of Jackson. For several years the Democrats had tried to expunge but could not overcome Whig opposition. Finally, on January 16, 1837, their ranks swelled by victories in recent elections, they succeeded in passing a resolution to erase the censure from the Senate journal. By a vote of 24 to 19 they directed that black lines be drawn across the words of censure adopted in 1834.

The Whigs were outraged. "It is not in the power of your black lines to touch us," shouted one Whig Senator at his Democratic colleagues. "Remove us. Turn us out. Expel us from the Senate. Would to God you could. Call in the praetorian guard. Take us. Apprehend us. March us off." Webster assured everyone that the action of defacing the Senate journal was unconstitutional, but it remained for Henry Clay to send the fury of Whig resentment and anger ricocheting around the Senate chamber. With almost uncontrolled passion he denounced President Jackson as a tyrant. "He has swept over the Government, during the last eight years, like a tropical tornado," thundered Clay. "Every department exhibits traces of the ravages of the storm. . . . What object of his ambition is unsatisfied? . . . What more does he want? Must we blot, deface, and mutilate, the records of the country, to punish the presumptuousness of expressing an opinion contrary to his own? . . . Black lines! Black lines!" They were black lines surrounding the announcement that liberty was dead in America—constitutional government gone.

When the Whigs had drained themselves of passion and bitterness, Senator Benton was again on his feet to move that the resolution be carried out. As the clerk of the Senate turned to carry out the order most of the Whigs walked out of the chamber to demonstrate their disapproval. Then the galleries set up a commotion. They began hissing the action of the clerk.

Outraged by the hissing, Benton sprang to his feet, his right fist shaking toward the demonstrators. "Bank ruffians! Bank ruffians!" he called out to them. "Seize them, sergeant-at-arms!"

Order was quickly restored and the clerk proceeded to his task. He took the appropriate journal from the shelf, turned to the page of March 28, 1834, when the censure resolution was passed, and carefully drew broad black lines around it. Across its face he wrote: "Expunged by order of the Senate, this 16th day of January, in the year of our Lord, 1837."

It was one of the last legislative actions taken during the administration of Andrew Jackson, a triumph for the Democrats, an action of humiliation for the Whigs.

11

Power and Politics

MARCH 4, 1837, marked Andrew Jackson's last day in office as President of the United States. His eight-year tenure encompassed some of the most important changes in American political history. There would be additional changes in the next several years but to many the brightest, happiest times were those when Old Hickory sat in the White House. They were years of hope and promise. They were the "go ahead" years.

As Jackson prepared to leave the White House and return to his home in Tennessee, he rather enjoyed his reputation as a President who had accomplished a great deal in converting the United States government from an elitest republic into a representative democracy. Not that he had broadened the franchise in any way. But because of his presence, what he symbolized to the nation, and the manner in which the Democratic party capitalized on his popularity, more ordinary citizens were concerned and actually involved in the functioning of their government than ever before. Never a modest man, Jackson appreciated his own achievements as President and he appreciated the depth and intensity of popular feeling toward him. Even Whigs recognized the extraordinary bond between the masses and this fierce, cantankerous old man. The "less informed—the unsophisticated classes of people," wrote one partisan Whig, "believed him honest and patriotic; that he was the friend of the *people*, battling for them against corruption and extravagance and opposed by dishonest politicians. They loved him as their friend."

Throughout his administration, Andrew Jackson had exercised a leadership new to presidential history. He dared to claim that he was the head of the government. He presumed to set national policy. Furthermore, he insisted that the needs of the American people were best served by strong presidential leadership, meaning the President must be the leader of his party as well as the head of the government.

In augmenting presidential power, Jackson opened a Pandora's box. For presidential power can be used for good or ill, depending on who exercises it. In the course of American history it has been used by some to advance the needs of the people, but it also has been used to subvert constitutional government.

The statesmen of the American Revolution had been very suspicious of a strong Chief Executive. To them, executive power was tantamount to monarchical power, and they had had their fill of monarchical rule. King George III, of late and unlamented memory, was the obvious example of the kind of executive they did not want. When they wrote their Declaration of Independence they listed, point by point, all his abuses of power that had compelled them to rebellion. Consequently, when they came to frame the instrument for their governance—the Articles of Confederation—they abolished the executive office. They believed in legislative government, in their minds the equivalent of representative government. To safeguard the liberty of the people, Congress and only Congress must rule!

The failure of the Articles of Confederation after a six-year trial emphasized the need for a stronger central government. The men who attended the Constitutional Convention in Philadelphia in 1787 understood that one of the weaknesses of the original document was the lack of an executive, so in their new instrument they provided a separate and distinct executive branch. They were still committed to representative government with a strong legislature elected by the people and holding tight the purse strings, but they now created a system of three equal branches—executive, legislative, and judicial—and provided each with the means of checking the others in order to prevent misrule or tyranny.

George Washington was an excellent first President under the Constitution. Not only did he fully implement all the powers provided him by the Constitution, but he infused the office with a style and tone that gave it dignity and importance, something desperately needed to overcome the resentment and suspicion generated by the misdeeds of English sovereigns. Washington jealously guarded his own authority but he was also careful to respect that of the Congress. This worked both ways, for Congress also appreciated the separation of powers and the vigilance necessary for republican government.

Washington's administration constituted the first step in the long development of presidential power. Thomas Jefferson aided the process. A superb politician, he worked his will through his friends on the various committees in both houses of Congress. More important, he decided to buy Louisiana even though there was some question of the constitutionality of such a purchase, a question expressed by himself and members of Congress. Without prior approval by anybody, Jefferson proceeded to make the purchase. And he did it, despite momentary hesitation, because he believed the future greatness and immediate preservation of the Union depended on the acquisition of this territory.

But the first *major* alteration of executive power came with the administration of Andrew Jackson. He redefined the presidency both in its relationship to Congress and to the people. He claimed primacy in government. Of the three equal parts—and they did remain equal despite his innovations—he insisted he was the first among equals, that he was the popular voice, responsible for national policy. No longer a prime minister deferential in all respects to the Congress, he acted as the head of state, the national leader, the formulator of national issues.

This altered interpretation of presidential authority was later strengthened by such notable statesmen as Lincoln, the two Roosevelts, and Woodrow Wilson. Not until World War II did the presidential office undergo yet another and even more fundamental change. It was global war, and the threat of global war that could extinguish life on this planet, that brought a vast expansion of presidential power. By the time the process seemed halted in 1974 by the resignation of Richard Nixon, Presidents had waged undeclared wars, bombed neutral nations, impounded funds appropriated by Congress, and insisted on sweeping claims of executive privilege. What had arrived was what Arthur M. Schlesinger, Jr., has termed an "imperial" presidency.

This concept of limitless executive power, rejected by the nation through the demanded resignation of Richard Nixon, gravely endangered the entire constitutional system of government. Fortunately, the Watergate scandal which ultimately drove Nixon from office terminated (let us hope) this unlawful and loathsome interpretation of presidential power.

But the presidency initiated by Jackson was something else. He represented the concept of a strong president who takes charge of the government, defines the issues, and leads Congress and the nation in achieving the successful resolution of those issues.* It is this kind of presidency that is so essential to the nation's progress and social betterment. Since the adoption of the Constitution it has been the strong President, with a vision of the country's future development, sensitivity to its immediate needs, and the will to eliminate economic and social inequality and injustice, who has secured the legislation that has enhanced the happiness and prosperity of the American people. For it is the President who must decide national priorities and present to Congress the issues requiring legislative attention. To do this he must be a skillful politician as well as a strong-willed executive, for he cannot obtain needed legislation without attracting sufficient votes to win Congressional passage of his program. And his effectiveness in securing votes will depend in large measure on the extent of his party support. In other words the President must be the leader of his party as well as leader of the government if he is to serve the American people successfully.

This type of presidential leadership evolved during the Jacksonian era. To a large extent it happened at this time because Jackson was the kind of man who could exert such leadership and because he was so popular and enjoyed the trust and confidence of the electorate. Also, this leadership developed because Jackson dramatically changed the presidential veto power† and made it a legislative tool. As a consequence, the character of the presidency was also changed.

Furthermore, the kind of leadership Jackson inaugurated was assisted

---

*After Jackson, the notion that the President is in charge of the government became a fact accepted by the American people. A single example will document this.

In 1837 a major depression struck the country. The President, Martin Van Buren, was blamed—after all, he was in charge of the government—and in the next presidential election he was badly defeated. Yet the previous depression, in 1819, had no such effect on the President. James Monroe was not blamed for the catastrophe. Not only was he reelected to office, but it was an overwhelming triumph. He received all electoral votes but one. Obviously something had happened between the presidencies of James Monroe and Martin Van Buren.

†Jackson vetoed twelve times. That's minuscule by today's standards but those twelve constituted more than all the vetoes of his six predecessors combined. In addition, Jackson was the first President to use the pocket veto. This is a special veto by which the President may kill legislation by withholding his signature from a bill after Congress has adjourned. If Congress is still in session a bill automatically becomes law ten days after it is passed, with or without the President's signature.

by the revival of a vigorous two-party system and by the intense political activity going on during this period. The recently enfranchised masses were organized into political cadres and marched to the polls to register their preference among the party candidates. In the progress of democracy in America and in the elimination of privilege, the two-party system was a principal contributing agent. It was through this system that voters found the most convenient and effective way of expressing their will.

Also important was the arrival of a new breed of politician who preached the doctrine of popular rule. The politicians of both parties during the Age of Jackson loudly affirmed the merits, virtue, and wisdom of the mass electorate. Traditional notions of deference, privilege, and place, as well as notions about rule by the few, well-educated, or wellborn, dissipated before the democratic blasts about equality of opportunity, the right of every white adult male to vote and hold office, and the indestructibility of a popularly supported government.

President Jackson aided this growth. Not through any direct action of his so much as by the style and tone of his administration. The style bespoke popular rule. It celebrated the masses, even though the nation had a long way to go in providing equal rights for everyone, especially Indians, women, and blacks. Thus, what has been termed ''Jacksonian Democracy'' is nothing more than the commitment, at long last, to the principal of popular rule. The old fears of the Founding Fathers that democracy could lead to anarchy were finally laid to rest in the shouts and cheers for ''the majesty of the people.''

One partisan summed it all up when he said that Andrew Jackson gave ''an impulse . . . to the democracy of America [which] will always continue to be felt, and impel the government in a more or less popular direction.''

The Jacksonian era, therefore, established the fundamental political practices and patterns for the future. It was a new departure in the structure and operation of government. It represented the political beginnings of modern America.

It was also a period in American history when equality of opportunity for all was demanded. The American people wanted to ''go ahead,'' and they savagely resented anything or anyone who had an advantage which could slow them down. So they were on their way. Nothing seemed impossible for them, nothing beyond their grasp. That this age of promise and hope should end in the slaughter that was the Civil War seems a tragic conclusion.

For Andrew Jackson it ended, in a sense, when his chosen successor, Martin Van Buren, followed him as the eighth President of the United States. The day of the inauguration was bright and cloudless. Thousands of people lined Pennsylvania Avenue to witness the beginning of a new administration. But really they had come to salute the departure of the old, for to them there was a deeper and more sentimental attachment to the old than the new.

In the White House, Jackson left his top-floor room for the first time in several weeks, since the onset of his most recent illness. He was just eleven days away from his seventieth birthday and he was a tired and worn-out old man, very infirm and rarely without pain. His face registered his suffering. Though his cheeks were shrunken and he moved stiffly he carried himself with a certain brittle strength. His bearing was always dignified and "presidential," and those glittering eyes notified everyone around that an indomitable, strong-willed, and fiery-tempered curmudgeon still lay coiled behind them.

Jackson slowly made his way out of the White House and seated himself in a carriage beside Van Buren for the drive to the Capitol. For him it was heartening to know that the country trusted him enough to accept Van Buren as his successor. Some politicians said that Van Buren's electoral victory the previous fall was Andrew Jackson's third election as President of the United States. In voting for Van Buren the people once again expressed their faith in Jackson.

As the carriage carrying the two Presidents headed along Pennsylvania Avenue the spectators just stared at the two men. There were no shouts, no applause, no cheers. Just silence. Then, in a profound gesture of respect, they removed their hats. They did it on impulse. They did it without thinking. Thomas Hart Benton was so impressed that he afterward wrote: "For once the rising was eclipsed by the setting sun."

When the two men reached the Capitol a passage was made for them through the immense crowd. Jackson alighted from the carriage and walked steadily through the mass, his tall white head very erect and uncovered. When he reached the top of the portico and could be seen by the vast throng, a "murmur of feeling" generated from the crowd and kept growing in volume until it became a roar. "It was a cry," recorded Benton, "such as power never commanded, nor man in power received. It was affection, gratitude and admiration. . . . I felt an emotion which has never passed through me before." Touched by the demonstration, Jackson turned and bowed to the people below him. It was a simple gesture but it seemed to carry great meaning. The masses responded with a great burst of applause and shouts. Then he took his seat to watch the proceedings.

Van Buren stepped forward to take the oath of office from the new Chief Justice of the United States, Roger B. Taney. This, too, gave Jackson immense satisfaction. He "never forgot his friends," and at the first opportunity he had rewarded Taney for his loyalty, dedication, and ability. On the death of Chief Justice John Marshall he had nominated Taney to fill the vacancy. The number of Whigs in the Senate had long since been diminished, so Taney was duly confirmed by the Democratic majority. It more than made up for Taney's rejection as Secretary of the Treasury a few years before.

After the oath, Van Buren read his inaugural address. At one point he spoke specifically about Jackson. "In receiving from the people," Van Buren said, "the sacred trust twice confided to my illustrious predecessor, and which he has discharged so faithfully and so well, I know that I can not expect to perform the arduous task with equal ability and success. . . . For him, I but express with my own, the wishes of all—that he may yet live long to enjoy the brilliant evening of his well-spent life."

Now it was over for Jackson. Now it was time to retire to the Hermitage. Three days after Van Buren's inauguration the ex-President headed for home, back to Tennessee. He rested along the way and visited many old friends. Because of his many stops it was several weeks before he finally reached Nashville. Wherever he appeared crowds congregated. They seemed to appear from nowhere. As soon as the word passed that General Andrew Jackson was in the vicinity, large numbers of people materialized in an instant. Their genuine affection really stirred the old man. When he spoke to them—and he usually did, because he liked to talk to people—he said he was particularly proud that as President he had "killed the money power" in the country that was oppressing the people. He was also proud that he had put down nullification and saved the Union. But more than all that, he felt he had championed the cause of the ordinary citizen, that he had been a true representative of all the people.

When he finally reached the Hermitage, just outside Nashville, many of his friends were waiting for him. The old men were lined up in front, the boys in the rear. Jackson got out of his carriage, but not without considerable effort. He listened courteously to a welcoming address by a friend. He replied with deeply felt sentiments of his appreciation, after which he shook hands with his old associates. Then one man stepped forward and made a short speech, something to the effect that "the children of his old soldiers and friends welcomed him home, and were ready to serve under his banner." Whenever he called, they would be there.

The words were barely spoken when Jackson began to tremble. His frame shook. Tears streamed down his aged cheeks. The reference to the children was more than he could bear.

"I could have stood all this," he stammered; "but this, it is too much, too much."

The crowd gathered around him and for several minutes there was a general outburst of tears, sentiment, and happy words.

This tough old man was weeping for joy, the joy of satisfaction, of knowing his efforts as soldier and politician had found favor with the people.

Jackson lived on for eight more years. He watched the country suffer through an intense economic depression during most of Van Buren's administration but he was pleased that it held out against establishing another national bank. Economic freedom for the individual, he said, depended on maintaining a divorce between the government and the country's banking operation. In its broadest terms this policy of divorce is called "laissez-faire," a policy the country generally pursued for the remainder of the century.

The depression lasted four or five years and slowed the economic progress of the nation—but did not stop it. By the early 1840s the nation was on the move again.

The depression knocked Van Buren out of the presidency. He was defeated for reelection in 1840 by William Henry Harrison, the Whig candidate who had a reputation as a military hero and an Indian fighter, just like Jackson. But within a month of his inauguration Harrison died of pneumonia and was succeeded by his Vice-President, John Tyler of Virginia, a former Democrat whose economic views strongly resembled Jackson's. In Congress, Henry Clay tried to translate his American System into law, including the establishment of another national bank, but Tyler wielded the mighty veto power and struck down all of Clay's efforts. Some Whigs wanted to impeach the President—they called Tyler "His Accidency"—and they might have tried, if they had had the votes to win conviction.

The decade of the 1840s witnessed a rapid territorial expansion of the United States, which Jackson heartily endorsed. His old friend and protégé, Sam Houston, had gone to Texas and had been instrumental in winning independence for Texas from Mexico. Both Houston and Jackson wanted to bring Texas into the Union but sectional rivalry and the problem of slavery delayed the negotiations. Said Jackson: "Texas [is] the key to our future safety. . . . We cannot bear that Great Britain have a Canedy [*sic*] on our west as she has on the north." Several years passed before the political problems standing in the way of annexation could be resolved. But the Congress finally passed a joint resolution inviting Texas into the Union. As one of his last acts as President, Tyler arranged the formal entry of the new state early in March 1845. Jackson was overjoyed when he heard the news. "All is safe at last," he wrote.

Jackson was also happy to live to see the election of another protégé, James Knox Polk of Tennessee, as America's eleventh President. What added to his pleasure was the fact that Polk had defeated Henry Clay, a candidate for the presidency for the third and last time. Polk was elected on a platform of geographical expansion, for an expansionist surge gripped the country. It was called "Manifest Destiny." The term was coined by John L. O'Sullivan, editor of the *United States Magazine and Democratic Review*, when he wrote that it was the "manifest design of Providence" that Americans would possess "this continent." In other words, God Himself intended this continent for Americans. All others must leave.

Manifest Destiny was an expression of a swelling nationalistic fervor in the country. But there was a danger to it. It could stumble the nation into war. Some Americans demanded the annexation of Oregon. "Fifty-four forty or fight," they cried. But to press for expanding the nation's boundaries to the 54° 40' line could mean war with England because of her claim to the Oregon territory. Jackson spoke for many fierce nationalists when he said that Polk would maintain the rights of the country, hopefully without resorting to war. "If not," the old man said, "let war come. There will be patriots enough in the land to repel foreign aggression, come whence it may, and to maintain sacredly our just rights and to perpetuate our glorious constitution and liberty, and to preserve our happy Union."

Polk avoided war with England by agreeing to compromise. The Oregon country was sliced in two at the forty-ninth parallel, the northern half becoming part of Canada.

The sharing of the Oregon Territory and the annexation of Texas did not lessen the expansionist fever. California beckoned. But that meant wresting it from Mexico. So be it. In May 1846 the United States declared war against Mexico.

So the Age of Andrew Jackson opened and closed with a bang! The age began with the raucous shouts of an enthusiastic electorate proclaiming the inauguration of Jackson to the presidency—and in the process nearly wrecking the White House. And the age closed with the crackle of gunfire that started the Mexican War and initiated the long, tragic drift into secession and civil war. For the victory against Mexico not only brought in California, but New Mexico, Arizona, Utah— virtually the entire Southwest as it presently exists. And with that, a struggle ensued between the North and the South over whether this enormous territory would be closed or open to slavery. Off and on for a dozen years the struggle raged, only to be resolved in the disaster of the Civil War. The Age of Jackson was over.

Andrew Jackson did not live to witness the hostilities against Mexico. By the spring of 1845 he could no longer keep up the fight. His body throbbed. His head never stopped aching. He coughed incessantly. In addition he began to swell with the dropsy. On June 2, the swelling got so bad that an operation was performed by Dr. Esselman from Nashville. This gave him some relief but it left him prostrate and debilitated.

On Sunday morning, June 8, the doctor visited Jackson at the Hermitage and found him sitting in his armchair. One look and the doctor knew "the hand of death was upon him." Family and friends were summoned. An hour or so later he fainted. Quickly he was moved to his bed, but his family and servants thought he was dead and began wailing their grief.

But the old man hung on. He raised his eyelids. He heard the wails. "My dear children," he whispered, "do not grieve for me; it is true I am going to leave you; I am well aware of my situation; I have suffered much bodily pain." He then took leave of his family, kissing each one and giving each his blessing.

Although the effort was an agony, he spoke again. "My dear children, and friends and servants, I hope and trust to meet you all in heaven, both white and black." There was a pause and he repeated this last phrase, "both white and black," looking at his servants "with the tenderest solicitude." Then he turned and as though in a stupor he just stared at his granddaughter, Rachel.

About noon a neighbor and old comrade in his military and political

183

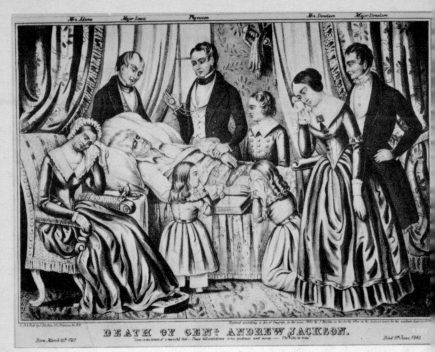

The final scene of Jackson's life in a sentimental rendering. After Old Hickory's death, one of his slaves was asked if he thought the General had gone to heaven. The man thought a moment and replied, "If he wants to go to Heaven who's to stop him?"

wars, Major William B. Lewis, rushed to his side. "Major," said the dying man, "I am glad to see you. You had like to have been too late." Seeing Lewis reminded him to send farewell messages to Thomas Hart Benton, Sam Houston, and other absent friends. Then Jackson lapsed into long silence, his eyes drifting upward into his head. After a few moments, his adopted son took his hand and whispered in his ear, "Father, how do you feel? Do you know me?"

The eyes opened once more. "Know you?" Jackson replied. "Yes, I know you. I would know you all if I could see. Bring me my spectacles."

After the eyeglasses were adjusted to his head, he spoke of his imminent death. Whereupon everyone in the room burst into tears. The servants standing on the porch and looking in through the windows sobbed and wrung their hands.

Jackson spoke again. "What is the matter with my dear children? Have I alarmed you? Oh, do not cry. Be good children, and we will all meet in heaven."

These were his last words. He closed his eyes and lay still. At six o'clock his head fell forward and was caught by Major Lewis. The Major listened for his breathing but heard none. Jackson died quietly.

Major Lewis removed the pillows on which Jackson had been propped. He noticed that the expression of pain so long etched on the General's face had disappeared. The warrior was at rest.

A day later Sam Houston arrived at the Hermitage with his young son. He rushed to the room containing the open coffin. When he saw the corpse he fell on his knees, sobbing. He buried his face on Jackson's breast.

After a moment Houston composed himself and drew the boy to his side. "My son," he said, "try to remember that you have looked upon the face of Andrew Jackson."

Further Reading

ALL HIS LIFE Andrew Jackson was a controversial figure. He still is. Historians have been arguing for more than a hundred years about the man and the period of American history which bears his name. Consequently, many of the things said in this book would cause a few modern historians to howl their disagreement. Some of them even think Jackson and the Jacksonian era an unmitigated disaster for the nation. Edward Pessen, for example, in his *Jacksonian America: Society, Personality, and Politics* (Homewood, Ill., 1969), called the Jacksonian age an age of materialism, of vulgarity, of only *seeming* deference to the common man by a number of *un*common men who really ran things.

At almost every point of the Jackson story different historians take opposite positions, and so this bibliography is constructed to give the reader an opportunity to examine the various contending views.

If Pessen is darkly negative about this era, Arthur M. Schlesinger, Jr., is brightly positive. His *The Age of Jackson* (Boston, 1946), which won a Pulitzer prize in 1946, is still the best overall statement of the era and has not been matched in interpretation or sheer narrative power. To see things from the side of the National Republicans and Whigs (rather than the Democratic side), one should read Glyndon G. Van Deusen, *The Jacksonian Era 1828-1848* (New York, 1959).

Treating Jackson himself there are two admiring biographies: Marquis James, *The Life of Andrew Jackson* (Indianapolis and New York, 1938), which is extremely well written; and my own *Andrew Jackson* (New York, 1966). James Parton, *The Life of Andrew Jackson* (New York, 1860), is long (three volumes), very old, but very good, and ends with an unfavorable interpretation of Jackson.

John C. Calhoun gets the same treatment. A three-volume biography, *John C. Calhoun* (Indianapolis and New York, 1951) by Charles Wiltse, is laudatory; a short biography, *John C. Calhoun: Opportunist* (Gainesville, Fla., 1962) by Gerald Capers, is highly critical. No modern biographies exist of Van Buren or Webster and most of the older ones are limited in value. *The Life of Henry Clay* (Boston, 1937) by Glyndon G. Van Deusen can be read with profit. An excellent biography of Thomas Hart Benton is William N. Chambers' *Old Bullion Benton: Senator From the New West* (Boston, 1956).

The revival of political parties during the Age of Jackson is narrated in Richard McCormick, *The Second American Party System: Party Formation in the Jacksonian Era* (Chapel Hill, N.C., 1966), and Richard Hofstadter, *The Idea of a Party System: The Rise of Legitimate Opposition in the United States, 1780-1840* (Berkeley, Cal., 1969). The Hofstadter book is especially useful and most original.

On the matter of rotation or spoils, James Parton is so critical that he says if all Jackson's other public acts had been perfectly wise and right, "this single feature of his administration would suffice to render it deplorable rather than admirable." Sidney H. Aronson, in *Status and Kinship in the Higher Civil Service: Standards of Selection in the Administrations of John Adams, Thomas Jefferson, and Andrew Jackson* (Cambridge, Mass. 1964), argues that there was little difference between the men chosen for federal office by these three Presidents.

The politicians' handling of the slavery question is probably the most difficult of all to resolve. Ten years ago Richard H. Brown wrote an article, "The Missouri Crisis, Slavery, and the Politics of Jacksonianism," *South Atlantic Quarterly*, LXV (Winter, 1966), pp. 55-72, in which he argued that the question of slavery had a great deal to do with the political alliances concluded during this era. The notion of slavery's significance (rather than the tariff's) in the nullification controversy was developed in William W. Freehling, *Prelude to Civil War: The Nullification Controversy in South Carolina, 1816-1836* (New York, 1965). The argument that national politics of the 1830s were determined by proslavery considerations is forthrightly advanced in Douglas T. Miller, *Then Was the Future: The North in the Age of Jackson, 1815-1850* (New York, 1973).

Abolitionism is traced in a very comprehensive survey by Louis Filler, *The Crusade Against Slavery, 1830-1860* (New York, 1960). A valuable collection of essays on the subject has been edited by Martin Duberman and entitled *The Antislavery Vanguard: New Essays on the Abolitionists* (Princeton, 1965).

Since the turn of the century there has been a growing sympathy among white Americans for the plight of the Indians. This sympathy probably reached its peak in the 1970s. An excellent collection of statements about the Indians has been edited by Francis Paul Prucha: *The Indian in American History* (New York, 1971); this contains a reprint of an important article by Bernard W. Sheehan, "Indian-White Relations in Early America." The best brief survey of Indian history is William T. Hagan, *American Indians* (Chicago, 1961). A sympathetic account of removal is Grant Foreman, *Indian Removal: The Emigration of the Five Civilized Tribes of Indians* (Norman, Okla., 1953), as well as his *The Last Trek of the Indians* (Chicago, 1946). Because of their illustrative material two books are especially valuable: *The American Heritage Book of Indians* (New York, 1961) by William Brandon, and Oliver LaFarge, *A Pictorial History of the American Indian* (New York, 1956). On the Cherokees specifically, see Louis Filler and Allen Guttmann, eds., *The Removal of the Cherokee Nation: Manifest Destiny or National Dishonor* (Boston, 1962). The contribution of the Indians is excellently described by Alvin M. Josephy, Jr., in *The Indian Heritage of America* (New York, 1968).

The Bank War used to be the most hotly disputed issue among Jacksonian historians, but so much was said about it in so concentrated a time span that everyone got pretty sick of it, even though the question of its meaning and importance was never resolved. A brief study is my own *Andrew Jackson and the Bank War* (New York, 1967). Strongly anti-Jackson and pro-Bank is Thomas Govan's biography *Nicholas Biddle* (Chicago, 1959). Also unsympathetic to Jackson and his banking policies is Bray Hammond, *Banks and Politics in America from the Revolution to the Civil War* (Princeton, 1957).

189

Whether democracy really advanced during the Jacksonian era and whether Jackson and his party had anything to do with it are probably the most intensely debated questions now before Jacksonian scholars. This book argues "yes" on both counts. Edward Pessen is probably the one historian who disagrees vehemently, arguing that democracy not only did not advance during this period but actually took a step backward; *Riches, Class, and Power Before the Civil War* (Lexington, Mass., 1973) is his most recent statement on the subject. Although Douglas T. Miller does not deny the rise of democracy in terms of politics during the Jacksonian era, he does insist that aristocracy also grew stronger. His description of the emergence of a new moneyed elite in New York is found in *Jacksonian Aristocracy: Class and Democracy in New York, 1830-1860* (New York, 1967). Lee Benson, *The Concept of Jacksonian Democracy: New York as a Test Case* (Princeton, 1961), argues that both parties—not simply the Democrats as is sometimes claimed—were responsible for the egalitarianism of the period.

The strengthening of presidential power during Jackson's administration is really the subject of my *Andrew Jackson and the Bank War* (New York, 1967); the book's subtitle is *A Study in the Growth of Presidential Power.* Very suggestive is Leonard D. White, *The Jacksonians: A Study in Administrative History 1829-1861* (New York, 1954). Arthur M. Schlesinger, Jr., *The Imperial Presidency* (Boston, 1973), is particularly concerned about the recent rise of presidential power, but he does go back in time and look at the contributions of earlier presidents.

Finally, there are several good general histories of this period, a number of which take an opposite point of view from the one expressed in this book. Furthermore, they discuss social, cultural, and constitutional developments. They include: John R. Howe, *From the Revolution Through the Age of Jackson: Innocence and Empire in the Young Republic* (Englewood Cliffs, N.J., 1973); Douglas T. Miller, *The Birth of Modern America, 1820-1850* (New York, 1970); and Raymond H. Robinson, *The Growing of America: 1789-1848* (Boston, 1973).

Index

Abolition, 85, 93-98; organization, 93-95; leadership, 93, 94, 95
Adams, Abigail, 57
Adams, John, 34, 36, 57, 82 note, 147
Adams, John Quincy: presidential candidate, 55, 59, 65-66; program, 55, 57; appearance, 57; education and early career, 57; appointed Secretary of State, 57; acquires Florida, 59; and Monroe Doctrine, 59; elected President, 59; appoints Clay Secretary of State, 59; criticized, 59; and patronage, 60-61; incidental mentions of, 25, 32, 34, 41, 48, 52, 53, 71, 80, 108, 128, 129
Age of Jackson, 3, 7, 9, 14, 37, 50, 69, 84, 113, 147, 178, 183
Age of the Common Man, 18, 79, 106
Alabama, 4, 24, 109, 114
Albany, N.Y., 39, 80
Albany Argus (New York), 38
Albany Regency, 38, 42, 75, 80, 144
Alton, Ill., 95
American Anti-Slavery Society, 95. *See also* Abolition

American Revolution, 4, 16, 18, 19, 24, 35, 37, 61, 106, 170, 175
American System, 54-55, 64, 137, 143, 181
Anti-Masonic party, 141-42, 143
Argus of Western America (Kentucky), 70
Aristocracy, 14, 16, 79, 129, 130, 131-32, 136-37, 141, 150, 158, 161, 163. *See also* Privilege
Articles of Confederation, 175

Baltimore, 70, 93, 124, 142, 143
Baltimore and Ohio Railroad, 11
Bank of the United States, Second, 55, 64; Jackson's War against, 123ff; early history, 124; organization and operation, 124-25; recharter requested, 130-31; recharter approved, 133; recharter vetoed, 133-35; veto sustained, 139; and election of 1832, 140ff; deposits removed, 153-64; House support, 156; resolutions against, 170-71; end of, 171-72

191

193

France, 57
Franklin, Benjamin, 24
Freehling, William W., 84
French Revolution, 137

Garrison, William Lloyd, 94-95
Gatsby's Hotel, 34
*Genius of Universal
    Emancipation* (Baltimore), 93
George III, 175
Georgetown, 42, 59
Georgia, 32, 109; and removal of Indians,
    112-13, 115-19
Gibbons vs. *Ogden*, 64
Globe (Washington, D.C.), 71, 133, 153
Goodyear, Charles, 13
Governmental change during the
    Jacksonian era, 3, 18, 66, 70, 74,
    82, 83, 123-24, 130, 134-36,
    152-53, 155, 164-68, 174-76, 177
Great Britain, 9, 15, 24, 43, 54, 57, 63,
    92, 93, 106, 107, 126, 182. *See
    also* British armed forces
Great Lakes, 10
Great Plains, 11
Greene, Nathaniel, 70
Grimké, Angelina, 95
Grimké, Sarah, 95
Grundy, Felix, 43
Gulf of Mexico, 24

Hamilton, Alexander: as Secretary of the
    Treasury, 36; ideology, 36-37, 53,
    147; interpretation of Constitution,
    36, 38
Hamilton, James, Jr., 101-2
Harrison, William Henry, 39, 181
Hayne, Robert Y., 87-88, 103
Hermitage, 27, 29, 111, 180, 185
Hill, Isaac, 71; appearance, 70; attacks
    BUS, 129-30; quoted, 129
Hillsboro, N.C., 46
Houston, Sam, 182, 185

Howe, Elias, 13

Illinois, 4, 10, 11, 93, 114
Illinois and Michigan Canal, 10
Immigrants, 10
Indian Intercourse Act, 113-14
Indian Queen Hotel, 90
Indian Removal Act, 113. *See
    also* Indians
Indian Territory, 111-12, 114
Indiana, 4, 10, 15, 93, 141
Indians, 19, 79; as issue, 17-18, 70, 105;
    Jackson's campaigns against, 23,
    24; frontier attacks by, 24, 25;
    United States policy toward, 105-7;
    early relations with whites, 106-7;
    Enlightenment view of, 107; policy
    of assimilation, 108, 110; removal
    policy developed, 108-9; removed to
    West, 111-12, 114-19; wars,
    114-15; number removed, 119. *See
    also* individual tribes
Industrial changes during the Jacksonian
    era, 9, 10, 11, 14, 43
Industrial Revolution, 9, 124
Inequality during the Jacksonian era, 16,
    17, 106, 108, 178
Ingham, Samuel D., 129, 130
Insane asylums, reforms of, during the
    Jacksonian era, 17
Internal improvements. *See* Public works
International trade, 9
Inventions during the Jacksonian era,
    13-14
Irish, 148

Jack, Gullah, 99
Jackson, Andrew: quoted, 22, 28, 29, 32,
    54, 70, 74, 77, 78, 81, 82, 86, 90,
    92, 102-3, 110, 111, 112, 113, 115,
    119, 120, 125, 126, 127, 131, 133,
    134, 135, 136, 137, 153, 154, 158,
    159, 164, 165, 170, 171, 181, 182;

195

197

Photo credits

Grateful acknowledgment is made for the use of illustrations:

Collection of the Boatmen's National Bank of St. Louis: title page
Faneuil Hall, Boston: 67
Harper's Weekly: 96-97
Library of Congress: 26, 62, 146, 169, 184
The Metropolitan Museum of Art; gift of I.N. Phelps Stokes,
Edward S. Hawes, Alice Mary Hawes, Marion Augusta Hawes, 1937:   58
The New-York Historical Society: 30, 121, 160
The New York Public Library, Picture Collection and Prints Division: 1, 12,
40, 72-73, 81, 91, 132
United States State Department: 56
Woolaroc Museum, Bartlesville, Oklahoma: 116-117
Yale University Art Gallery, gift of John Hill Morgan: 45

About the Author

As Professor of History at the University of Illinois, Robert V. Remini has twice been named Outstanding Teacher of the Year. His scholarship on the Jacksonian period appears in several of his books, including *Martin Van Buren and the Making of the Democratic Party*, *The Election of Andrew Jackson*, *Andrew Jackson* (a biography), *Andrew Jackson and the Bank War*, and *The Age of Jackson* (documents). He is consultant to "The Papers of Andrew Jackson," the official project which will publish all of Jackson's important papers and correspondence.

Born in New York City, Mr. Remini earned his M.A. and Ph.D. degrees at Columbia University. He served on the editorial board of the *Journal of American History*, published by the Organization of American Historians. He now lives in Wilmette, Illinois, with his wife and three children.

Workbook for

The Human Body in Health and Disease

Workbook for
The Human Body in Health and Disease

Sixth Edition

Ruth Lundeen Memmler, M.D.

*Professor Emeritus, Life Sciences;
formerly Coordinator, Health, Life Sciences, and Nursing,
East Los Angeles College, Los Angeles, California*

Dena Lin Wood, R.N., B.S., P.H.N.

*Staff Nurse, Memorial Hospital of Glendale,
Glendale, California*

Illustrated by Anthony Ravielli

J.B. Lippincott Company   Philadelphia

London   Mexico City   New York   St. Louis   São Paulo   Sydney

Sponsoring Editor: Patricia Cleary
Developmental Editor: Joyce Mkitarian
Design Director: Tracy Baldwin
Cover Photo Illustration: Eric Pervuknin and Kathy Ziegler
Cover Designer: Anthony Frizano
Production Supervisor: J. Corey Gray
Production Editor: Rosanne Hallowell
Compositor: Circle Graphics
Text Printer/Binder: Kingsport Press
Cover Printer: The Lehigh Press, Inc.

ISBN 0-397-54605-X

6 5 4 3

Preface

Workbook for The Human Body in Health and Disease, Sixth Edition, is designed to assist the beginning student in learning the basic information required of those in the health occupations. While it will be most effective when used in conjunction with the sixth edition of *The Human Body in Health and Disease,* it is also applicable to other textbooks in basic anatomy and physiology.

The continued emphasis on physiology is reflected in the exercises and problems presented in this revision. There is maximum coordination with the parent textbook, and the chapter sequence follows that of the textbook. The Practical Applications portions of the workbook, as in the previous edition, use clinical situations to test the student's understanding of a subject. Comparing the normal with the abnormal helps to fix the basic facts that underlie the care and cure process, and may also help the student to gain some understanding of disease prevention and health maintenance.

The exercises were prepared with the aim of helping the student to learn, and not merely to test knowledge. A certain amount of repetition has been purposely incorporated as a means of reinforcement.

Contents

Workbook for
The Human Body in Health and Disease

1

Introduction to the Human Body

I. Overview

Living things are organized from simple to complex levels. The simplest living form is the **cell**, the basic unit of life. Specialized cells are grouped into **tissues** that in turn are combined to form **organs**; these organs form **systems**.

The systems include the skeletal system, the framework of the body; the muscular system, which moves the bones; the circulatory system, consisting of the heart and blood vessels that transport vital substances; the digestive system, which converts raw food materials into products usable by cells; the respiratory system, which adds oxygen to the blood and removes carbon dioxide; the integumentary system, the body's covering; the urinary system, which removes wastes and excess water; the nervous system, the central control system which includes the organs of special sense; the endocrine system, which produces the regulatory hormones; and the reproductive system, by which new individuals of the species are produced.

All of the cellular reactions that sustain life together make up **metabolism**, which can be divided into **catabolism** and **anabolism**. In catabolism, food is broken down into smaller molecules with the release of energy. This energy is stored in the compound **ATP** (adenosine triphosphate) for use by the cells. In anabolism, simple compounds are built into substances needed by the cells.

All the systems work together to maintain a state of balance or **homeostasis**. The main mechanism for maintaining homeostasis is negative feedback, by which the state of the body acts to keep conditions within set limits.

It is essential that a special set of terms be learned in order to locate parts and to relate the various parts to each other. Imaginary lines called **planes of division** separate parts of the body into regions in much the same way that the Equator, the Tropics of Cancer and Capricorn, and the Arctic and Antarctic Circles divide the earth into zones. Further divisions of the earth by lines of latitude and longitude make it possible to pinpoint locations accurately. Similarly, separation into areas and regions within the body, together with the use of the special terminology for directions and locations, makes it possible to describe an area within the human body with great accuracy.

The large internal spaces of the body are the **cavities**, in which various organs are located. The **dorsal cavities** are further divided into the cranial cavity and the spinal canal. The **ventral cavities** are the thoracic and abdominal cavities. The lower portion of the abdominal cavity is the pelvic cavity.

The metric system is used for all scientific measurements. If you learn to "think metric" you will find it easier to use than the older systems used in the United States because it is based on multiples of 10.

II. Topics for Review

A. Body systems
B. Body processes
C. Body directions
D. Body cavities
    a. Dorsal and ventral cavities
    b. Regions in abdominal cavity
E. The metric system

III. Matching Exercises

Matching only within each group, print the answers in the spaces provided.

Group A

extracellular	anabolism	physiology
organs	homeostasis	cells
systems	tissues	pathology

1. The building phase of metabolism is ___anabolism___

2. The study of disease is ___pathology___

3. A combination of specialized groups of cells forms ___tissues___

4. The study of how the body functions is ___physiology___

5. A combination of various tissues forms parts having a special function that are called ___organs___

6. Several different parts and organs grouped together for specific functions form ___systems___

7. The basic units of life are called ___cells___

8. A state of balance in the body is ___homeostasis___

9. Fluids located outside the cells are described as ___extracellular___

Group B

epigastric region	ventral	distal
umbilicus	lateral	medial
proximal	thoracic region	transverse

1. To indicate nearness to the midsagittal plane, use the word _medial_

2. A part that is away from the midline (or toward the side) is _lateral_

3. To indicate that a part is near or toward the point of origin, use _proximal_

4. A part that is away from the point of origin is _distal_

5. A horizontal or cross section is also said to be _transverse_

6. The central region of the abdomen just below the breast bone is the _epigastric_

7. Another name for the navel is the _umbilicus_

8. The upper or chest portion of the ventral body cavities is the _thoracic region_

9. The word that means *toward the belly surface* is _ventral_

Group C

| caudal | cranial | posterior |
| sagittal plane | proximal | transverse plane |

1. To say *toward the origin of a part,* use the word _proximal_

2. To indicate that a part is toward the rear use _posterior_

3. The word that means nearer the tail region is _caudal_

4. To indicate that a part is nearer the head use the word _cranial_

5. A plane that divides the body into superior and inferior parts is a(n) _transverse_

6. A plane that divides the body into left and right parts is a(n) _sagittal_

Group D

| urinary system | integumentary system | skeletal system |
| endocrine system | reproductive system | respiratory system |

1. The system that includes the hair, nails, and skin is the _integumentary_

2. The bones, joints, and related parts form the system called the _skeletal_

3. Another name for the excretory system is the _urinary_

4. The system of scattered organs that produce hormones is called the _endocrine_

5. The system that includes the sex organs is the _reproductive_

6. The lungs and bronchial tubes form the system called the _respiratory_

Group E

spinal canal   cranial cavity   diaphragm
negative feedback   nervous system   pelvic cavity

1. The cavity in the lower part of the abdominal cavity is the _____pelvic_____

2. The muscular partition between the two ventral body cavities
   is the _____diaphragm_____

3. A system that controls and coordinates the body is the _____nervous system_____

4. The upper part of the dorsal body cavity is the _____cranial cavity_____

5. The lower part of the dorsal body cavity is the _____spinal canal_____

6. A mechanism for maintaining homeostasis is _____negative feeback_____

IV. Labeling

For each of the following illustrations, print the name or names of each labeled part on
the numbered lines.

1. _cranial-superior_
2. _transverse_
3. _midsagittal_
4. _inferior_
5. _dorsal, posterior_
6. _ventral, anterior_
7. _frontal plane_

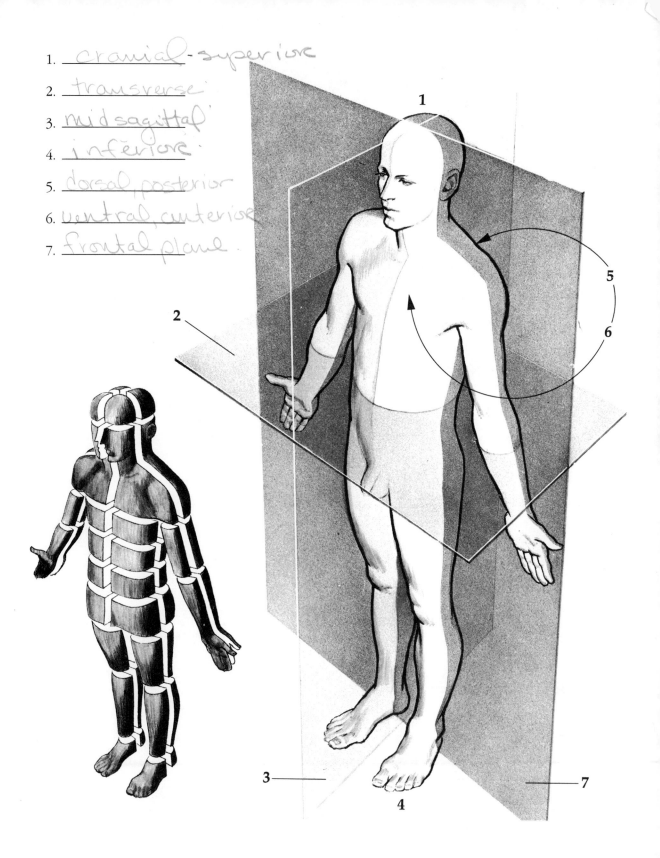

Body planes and directions

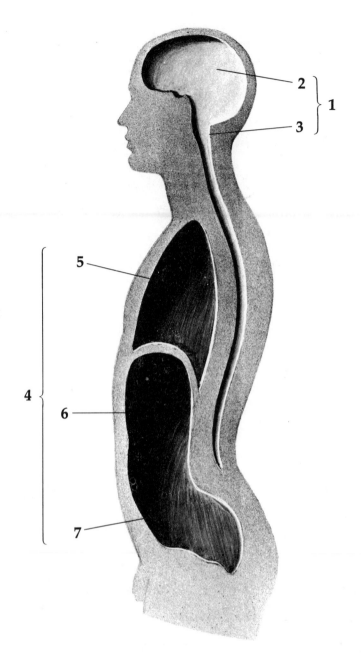

Side view of body cavities

1. _____Dorsal_____
2. _____cranial cavity_____
3. _____spinal canal cavity_____
4. _____Ventral_____

5. _____thoracic_____
6. _____abdominal_____
7. _____pelvic_____

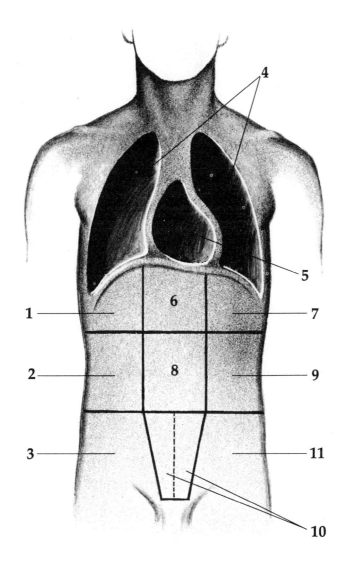

Front view of body cavities and the regions of the abdomen

1. right hypochondriac
2. " lumbar
3. " iliac
4. pleural sacs for lungs
5. pericardial " for heart
6. epigastric

7. left hypochondriac
8. umbilical
9. left lumbar
10. hypogastric
11. left iliac

V. Completion Exercise

Group A

Print the word or phrase that correctly completes each sentence.

1. The energy compound of the cell is ___ATP (no)___

2. Groups of specialized cells are organized into ___tissues___

3. Regions and directions in the body are described according to the position in which the body is upright, with the palms facing forward. This is called the ___anatomic___

4. The midline plane that divides the body into right and left halves is the ___midsagittal___

5. Planes that divide the body into upper and lower parts are called ___transverse___

6. The plane that divides the body into front and rear parts is the ___frontal___

7. The space that encloses the brain and spinal cord forms one continuous cavity, the ___dorsal body cavity___

8. The space that houses the brain is the ___cranial cavity___

9. The elongated canal that contains the spinal cord is known as the ___spinal cavity___

10. The ventral body cavities include an upper space containing the lungs, the heart, and the large blood vessels, which is called the ___thoracic cavity___

11. The lower ventral body cavity is quite large and is called the ___abdominal___

12. The large ventral body cavities are separated from each other by a muscular partition, the ___diaphragm___

13. The large lower ventral body cavity may be subdivided into nine regions, including three along the midline. The uppermost of these midline areas is the ___epigastric___

14. All of the chemical reactions that maintain the cell make up ___metabolism___

Group B

Print the word that correctly completes each sentence about the metric system.

1. The standard unit for measurement of volume, slightly greater than a quart, is a(n) ___liter___

2. The number of grams in a kilogram is ___1000___

3. The number of centimeters in an inch is ___2.5___

4. The number of milliliters in 0.5 liters is ___500___

5. The standard unit for measurement of length is the ___meter___

VI. Practical Applications

Study each discussion. Then print the appropriate word or phrase in the space provided.

Group A

1. The gallbladder is located just below the liver. The directional terms that best describe this relationship include ___inferior to liver, right hypochondriac___

2. The kidneys are located behind the other abdominal organs. This relationship may be described as ___posterior, lumbar___

3. The tips of the fingers and toes are farthest from the region of origin of these digits, so they are said to be the most ___distal___

4. The entrance to the stomach is nearest the point of origin or beginning of the stomach, so this part is said to be ___proximal___

5. The ears are located away from the midsagittal plane or toward the side, so they are described as being ___lateral___

6. The head of the pancreas is nearer the midsagittal plane than its tail portion, so the head part is more ___medial___

7. The diaphragm is above the abdominal organs; it may be described as ___sup. to hyp. + ep. reg.___

Group B

On the ward in which postoperative patients are being cared for you are asked to study certain cases and answer the following questions.

1. Mr. A had an appendectomy. The area of the abdomen in which the appendix is located is in the lower right side and is known as the ___right iliac region___

2. Mrs. B had a history of gallstones. The operation to remove these stones involved the upper right part of the abdominal cavity, or the ___right hypochondriac___

3. Miss C was injured in an automobile accident. In addition to a number of fractures, she suffered a ruptured urinary bladder. The area involved, in the lower midline part of the abdomen, was the ___hypogastric region___

4. Mr. B required an extensive exploratory operation that necessitated incision through the navel. This portion of the abdomen is the ___umbilical region___

none of the above

2

Chemistry, Matter, and Life

I. Overview

Chemistry is the physical science that deals with the composition of matter. To appreciate the importance of chemistry in the field of health, it is necessary to know about atoms, molecules, elements, compounds, and mixtures. Though exceedingly small particles, atoms possess a definite structure: the **nucleus** contains **protons** and **neutrons**, and surrounding the nucleus are the **electrons**. An **element** is a substance consisting of just one type of atom. Union of two or more atoms produces a **molecule**; the atoms may be alike (such as the oxygen molecule) or different (sodium chloride, for example), and in the latter case the substance is called a **compound**. To go a step further, a combination of compounds, each of which retains its separate properties, is a **mixture** (salt water is one example). Chemical compounds are constantly being formed, altered, broken down, and recombined into other substances. Water is a vital substance composed of hydrogen and oxygen. It makes up more than half of the body and is needed as a solvent and a transport medium. Hydrogen, oxygen, carbon, and nitrogen are the elements that constitute about 99% of living matter, while calcium, sodium, potassium, phosphorus, sulfur, chlorine, and magnesium account for most of the remaining 1%. Proteins, carbohydrates, and lipids are among the compounds formed from these elements. Some atoms play a vital role in the diagnosis and treatment of disease. The isotopes of atoms that give off rays are said to be radioactive, and in this form have the ability to penetrate and destroy tissues; thus they are useful in the treatment of many types of cancer.

II. Topics for Review

A. Atoms and elements
B. Molecules and compounds
C. Water, solutions, and suspensions
D. Chemical bonds
E. Acids and bases
F. Radioactivity
G. Organic compounds

III. Matching Exercises

Matching only within each group, print the answers in the spaces provided.

Group A

chemicals	organic	nucleus
chemistry	atoms	pharmacology

1. The smallest complete units of matter are called _____

2. The science that deals with the composition of all matter is _____

3. The study of all aspects of drugs is called _____

4. Aspirin, penicillin, and all other drugs are classified as _____

5. The part of the atom containing most of its mass including protons and neutrons is the _____

6. The chemical compounds that characterize living things are described as _____

Group B

radioactivity	isotopes	elements
molecule	compounds	mixture
neutrons	electrons	protons

1. The positively charged particles inside the atomic nucleus are _____

2. The noncharged particles within the atomic nucleus are _____

3. The negatively charged electric particles outside the atomic nucleus are the _____

4. Substances composed of one type of atom are called _____

5. Elements existing in forms that are alike in their chemical reactions but that differ in weight are called _____

6. The word that refers to emission (giving off) of rays from disintegrating isotopes is _____

7. The unit formed by the union of two or more atoms is the _____

8. Substances that result from the union of two or more different atoms are known as _____

9. The combination of various compounds that remain intact and retain their properties is designated a(n) _____

Group C

carbohydrates	cations	acid
electrolytes	anions	water
proteins	buffer	pH

1. Positively charged ions are called _____

2. Negatively charged ions are _____

3. Compounds that form ions when in solution are called _____

4. Compounds of nitrogen, carbon, oxygen, and hydrogen are called _____

5. Simple sugars are classified as _____

6. A substance which helps to maintain a stable hydrogen ion concentration in a solution is a(n) _____

7. The universal solvent is _____

8. The symbol for hydrogen ion concentration is _____

9. A substance that donates a hydrogen ion to another substance is a(n) _____

Group D

element	covalent	phospholipids
suspension	colloidal	amino acid
atomic number	solution	

1. Nitrogen is an example of a(n) _____

2. An element can be identified by its _____

3. A building block of proteins is a(n) _____

4. The group of lipids that contains phosphorus in addition to carbon, hydrogen, and oxygen is the _____

5. A chemical bond formed by the sharing of electrons is called _____

6. A mixture in which substances will settle out unless the mixture is shaken is a(n) _____

7. Cytoplasm and blood plasma are examples of a type of suspension described as _____

8. Salt water is an example of a(n) _____

Group E

ionic	neutrons	decomposed	neutral
radioactivity	carbon	lipid	enzyme

1. A pH of 7.0 is termed _____

2. A type of protein that acts as a catalyst in metabolic reactions is a(n) _____

3. Another name for a fat is a(n) _____

4. Cancer therapy includes the use of needles, seeds, or tubes containing isotopes that possess _____

5. An electrolyte is formed by a bond described as _____

6. The greater weight of a given isotope is due to the presence of a larger number of _____

7. Elements cannot be changed into something else by physical or chemical methods; that is, they cannot be _____

8. Organic chemistry is based on the element _____

IV. Labeling

For each of the following illustrations, print the name or names of each labeled part on the numbered lines.

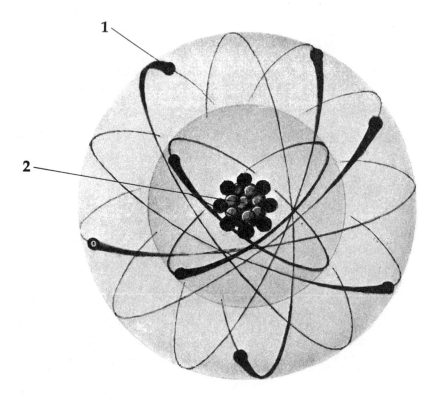

Oxygen atom

1. _____   2. _____

14

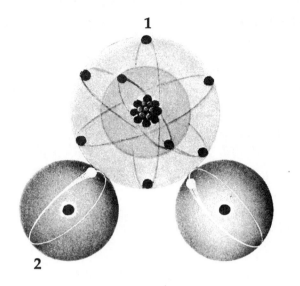

Molecule of water

1. _____ 2. _____

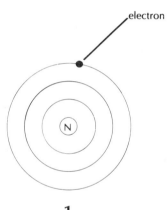

electron

1

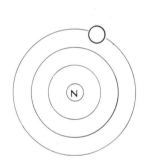

3

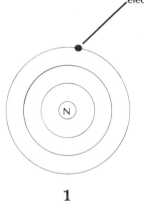

2

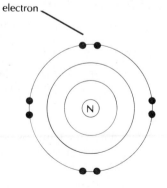

electron

4

Cations and anions

1. _____ 3. _____

2. _____ 4. _____

V. Completion Exercise

Print the word or phrase that correctly completes each sentence.

1. The four elements that make up about 99% of living cells are carbon, hydrogen, and oxygen plus _____

2. Most people keep a shaker of salt on the table. Salt is an example of a combination of two different elements. Such a combination is called a(n) _____

3. Compounds first found in living organisms, as for example starch in potatoes, are classified as _____

4. An element that is part of the air we breathe also is part of the water we drink. This element is _____

5. The smallest particle of salt obtainable that would still have the properties of salt is the _____

6. The salt in salt water will regain its properties if the water is boiled. Since water and salt do not combine chemically, this solution is an example of a(n) _____

7. If we could remove a single electron from a sodium atom, or could add a single electron to a sodium atom, the result would be an atom with either a positive or a negative charge, known as a(n) _____

8. Numerous essential body activities are possible owing to the property of certain compounds to form ions when in solution. Such compounds are called _____

9. The name given to a chemical system that prevents changes in hydrogen ion concentration is _____

VI. Practical Applications

Review assigned clinic charts to learn about the kinds of tests performed. You will find that most of these studies are based on principles of chemistry and physics.

1. Mr. B complained of shortness of breath. Several studies were done including a visible tracing of the electric currents produced by his heart muscle. Such a record is called a(n) _____

2. Joan, age 4, was brought to the clinic by her mother because she experienced attacks of fainting and unconsciousness. As an aid in diagnosis, a graphic record of her brain's electric current was obtained. This brain wave record is called a(n) _____

3. A routine test done on Ms. J showed glucose in her urine—an abnormal finding. Glucose is one of a group of compounds found in certain foods and classified as _____

4. Mr. K's urinalysis showed the presence of albumin. Albumin is an example of compounds found in the body that contain nitrogen, carbon, hydrogen, and oxygen. These compounds are classified as

_____

3

Cells and
Their Functions

I. Overview

The cell is the basic unit of life; all life activities result from the activities of cells. The
study of cells began with the invention of the light microscope and has continued with
the development of electron microscopes. Cell functions are carried out by specialized
structures within the cell called **organelles**. These include the nucleus, ribosomes, mitochondria, Golgi apparatus, and endoplasmic reticulum (ER).

An important cell function is the manufacture of **proteins**, including enzymes (organic
catalysts). Protein manufacture is carried out by the ribosomes in the cytoplasm according to information coded in the deoxyribonucleic acid (DNA) of the nucleus. DNA is
also involved in the process of cell division or **mitosis**. Before cell division can occur,
the DNA must double itself so that each daughter cell produced by mitosis will have
exactly the same kind of DNA as the parent cell.

The cell membrane is important in regulating what enters and leaves the cell. Some
substances can pass through the membrane by **diffusion**, which is simply the movement
of molecules from an area where they are in higher concentration to an area where they
are in lower concentration. Water can diffuse rapidly through the membrane by the
process termed **osmosis**. For this reason, cells must be kept in solutions that have the
same concentrations as the cell fluid. If the cell is placed in a solution of higher concentration (a hypertonic solution) it will shrink; in a solution of lower concentration (a
hypotonic solution) it will swell and may burst. The cell membrane can also selectively
move substances into or out of the cell by **active transport**, a process that requires
energy (ATP) and carriers. Large particles and droplets of fluid are taken in by the
processes of **phagocytosis** and **pinocytosis**.

When cells change genetically (mutate) so that they multiply out of control, the result
is a tumor. A tumor which spreads to other parts of the body is termed **cancer**. The
causes of cancer include chemicals, ionizing radiation, and irritants. Heredity is also a
factor in the development of cancer.

II. Topics for Review

A. Cell structure
B. Protein synthesis
C. Cell division (mitosis)
D. Movement of materials across the cell membrane
E. Cells and cancer

III. Matching Exercises

Matching only within each group, print the answers in the spaces provided.

Group A

semipermeable	isotonic	diffusion
enzymes	mitosis	active transport
osmosis	filtration	

1. The protein substances that assist in the cell's chemical reactions are the _____

2. The process of body cell division is known as _____mitosis_____

3. The membrane of the cell is said to be _____

4. The spread of molecules throughout an area is known as _____Diffusion_____

5. Water molecules diffuse through the cell membrane by the process of _____Osmosis_____

6. The passage of solutions through a membrane as a result of mechanical force is called _____

7. A solution that has the same concentration of molecules as the fluids within the cell is described as _____

8. The cell uses energy to move substances across the membrane in a process called _____

Group B

mitochondria	ribosomes	cilia
lysosomes	nucleolus	cell membrane
flagellum	ER	

1. A system of membranes throughout the cell is the _____

2. A small globule within the nucleus is the _____

3. Small bodies in the cytoplasm that act in the manufacture of proteins are _____

4. The outer covering of the cell is the _____

5. The organelles that convert energy to ATP are _____

6. A long whiplike projection used in cell locomotion is a(n) _____

7. Small bodies in the cell that contain digestive enzymes are _____

8. Small hairlike projections from the cell used to create movement around the cell are called _____

Group C

| ATP | nucleotide | centriole |
| DNA | genes | RNA |

1. The chemical in the nucleus that makes up the chromosomes is _____

2. The organelle that is active in cell division is the _____

3. The energy compound of the cell is _____

4. A building block of nucleic acids is a(n) _____

5. The hereditary factors in the cell are _____

6. The nucleic acid that carries information from the nucleus to the ribosomes is _____

Group D

edema	pinocytosis	carcinogen
hypertonic	hypotonic	active transport
mutation	osmotic pressure	

1. A cell may take in so much water it will burst if it is placed in a solution that is _____

2. A cell takes in droplets by the process of _____

3. The force that draws water into a solution is called _____

4. A solution with a salt concentration greater than 0.9% is described as _____

5. An accumulation of fluid in the tissues is called _____

6. A change in the genetic material of a cell is a(n) _____

7. The cell membrane is described as selectively permeable because it can carry out _____

8. A cancer-causing chemical is a(n) _____

IV. Labeling

For each of the following illustrations, print the name or names of each labeled part on the numbered lines.

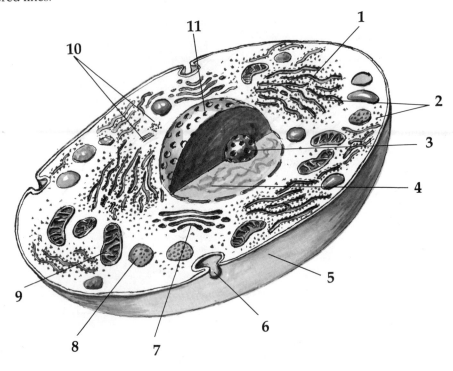

A typical cell

1. _____

2. _____

3. _____

4. _____

5. _____

6. _____

7. _____

8. _____

9. _____

10. _____

11. _____

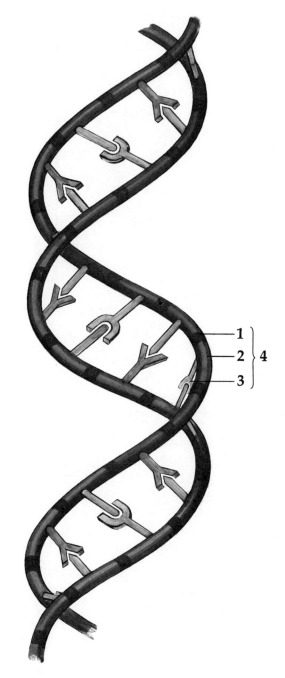

The basic structure of a DNA molecule

1. _____

2. _____

3. _____

4. _____

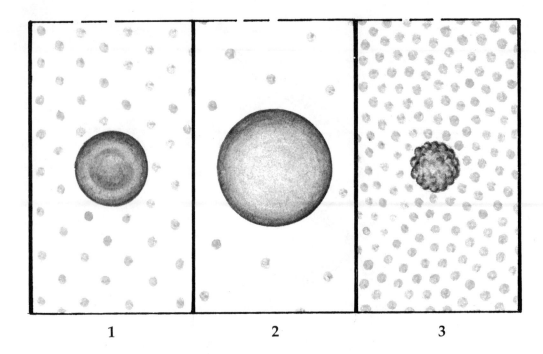

1   2   3

Osmosis

Describe the solutions shown in each picture.

1. _____

2. _____

3. _____

V. Completion Exercise

Print the word or phrase that correctly completes each sentence.

1. The general term that describes all the chemical reactions by which food is made usable by the cells is _____

2. Groups of similar cells that function together for the same general purpose make up _____

3. The metric unit that is used to measure cells is the _____

4. Small structures within a cell that perform special functions are called _____

5. The control center of the cell which contains the chromosomes is the _____

6. Chromosomes are composed mainly of _____

7. The energy compound of the cell is _____

8. Before a cell can divide the chromosomes must _____

9. The number of daughter cells formed when a cell undergoes mitosis is _____

VI. Practical Applications

Study each discussion; then print the appropriate word or phrase in the space provided.

Observations you might make while touring a hospital laboratory include the following:

1. The janitor in the laboratory was using a cleaning solution that contained ammonia. You will recall that this would cause ammonia molecules to spread throughout the room. This movement of molecules from an area of high concentration to other areas where concentration is low is called _____

2. One of the laboratory technicians was trying to separate solid particles from a liquid mixture. He poured the mixture into a paper-lined funnel. The liquid flowed through the funnel while the solids remained behind on the paper. This process is called _____

3. A laboratory worker was carefully measuring certain salts in order to prepare a normal saline solution. Normal saline is used to replace lost body fluids because the concentration is nearly the same as that inside the cells. Such a solution is said to be _____

4. While doing a complete blood count a technician noted that some of the red blood cells had ruptured. The solutions used were tested to determine whether they were too dilute. Osmosis of water into a cell could be the cause of cell breakage. When a red blood cell bursts it is said to _____

5. A student was learning how to do blood smears. Upon examination of the blood with the microscope he found that many red blood cells appeared shrunken. The explanation was that he was proceeding so slowly that the liquid part of the blood was evaporating, leaving a highly concentrated solution. Such a solution is described as being _____

4

Tissues, Glands, and Membranes

I. Overview

The cell is the basic unit of life. Individual cells are grouped according to function into **tissues**. The four main groups of tissues include **epithelial tissue**, which forms glands, covers surfaces, and lines cavities; **connective tissue**, which gives structure and holds all parts of the body in place; **nerve tissue**, which conducts nerve impulses; and **muscle tissue**, which produces movement.

The simplest combination of tissues is a **membrane**. Membranes serve several purposes, a few of which are mentioned here: they may serve as dividing partitions; may line hollow organs and cavities; and may anchor various organs. Membranes that have epithelial cells on the surface are referred to as epithelial membranes. Two types of epithelial membranes are mucous membranes, which line passageways leading to the outside, and serous membranes, which line body cavities and fold over the internal organs.

Many diseases directly affect membranes. The common cold, for example, is an inflammation of the mucosa of the nasal passages. Membranes also serve as pathways for the spread of disease, as may occur in some disorders of the reproductive system.

It may happen that the normal pattern of cell growth is disrupted by the formation of abnormal cells; this abnormal growth is a **tumor**. If the tumor is confined locally and does not spread, it is called a benign tumor; if it spreads from its original site to other parts of the body, it is called a malignant tumor. Most benign tumors can be removed surgically; malignant tumors are usually treated by surgery, radiation, or chemotherapy, or by a combination of these methods.

II. Topics for Review

A. Classification of tissue
B. Functions of the four main groups of tissues
C. Types of glands
D. Epithelial membranes
E. Origin of tumors
F. Characteristics of tumors

III. Matching Exercises

Matching only within each group, print the answers in the spaces provided.

Group A

cartilage	tissues	bone
adipose	cilia	squamous
exocrine	layered	secretions

1. Groups of cells similar in structure and function are called ___tissues___

2. An important function of epithelium is the production of ___secretions___

3. Dust and other foreign particles are moved along the airways by tiny hairlike projections from epithelium called ___cilia___

4. The type of connective tissue that stores fat and serves as a heat insulator is called ___adipose___

5. One of the hard connective tissues that has the important function of acting as a shock absorber and as a bearing surface to reduce friction between moving parts is ___cart.___

6. Osseous tissue is similar to cartilage in its cellular structure. In development, cartilage gradually becomes impregnated with calcium salts to form ___bone___

7. Flat, irregular epithelial cells are described as ___squames___

8. The term *stratified* means ___layered___

9. Glands that secrete through ducts are called ___exocrine___

Group B

ligaments	marrow	neuron
mucus	collagen	transitional
cartilage	secretions	fascia

1. Mucus, digestive juices, and sweat are examples of ___secret.___

2. Dust and other inhaled foreign particles are trapped in a secretion called ___mucus___

3. Layers of fibrous connective tissue around muscles are called ___fascia___

4. A crepelike type of epithelium that is capable of great expansion is called ___trans.___

5. The strong connective bands that support joints are called ___lig.___

6. The main fibers in connective tissue are made of a flexible white protein called ___collagen___

7. The tough, elastic substance found at the ends of long bones is _____ cartilage _____

8. Blood cells are produced in the red _____ marrow _____

9. Another name for a nerve cell is a(n) _____ neuron _____

Group C

myocardium	neurilemma	myelin
voluntary muscle	spasm	visceral muscle
fibers	connective tissue	

1. Areolar, adipose, and osseous tissue all act as the body's supporting fabric and are therefore classified as _____ conn _____

2. The basic structural unit of nerve tissue, the neuron, consists of a nerve cell body plus small branches, which are called _____ fibers _____

3. The ability of certain nerves to repair themselves is due to the presence of a thin coating membrane called the _____ neuril. _____

4. Some nerve fibers, like telephone wires, are encased in a protective covering, or sheath. This fatty insulating material is called _____ myelin _____

5. The thickest layer of the heart wall is formed by cardiac muscle or _____ myocard. _____

6. A general muscle disorder is characterized by involuntary muscle contractions. A single, sudden contraction is called a(n) _____ spasm _____

7. Muscle tissue is classified into three types. That which forms the walls of the organs within the ventral body cavities is called _____ visceral _____

8. Skeletal muscle is usually under the control of the will. It is therefore described as _____ voluntary _____

Group D

suture	malignant	tumor
epithelium	connective tissue	periosteum
benign	tendon	

1. The tissue that forms a protective covering for the body and that lines the intestinal tract and the respiratory and urinary passages is called _____ epith. _____

2. Repair of damaged nerve and muscle tissue is accomplished by the growth of _____ conn. _____

3. A layer of fibrous connective tissue around a bone is the _____ periosteum _____

4. Repeated injury to a single area may trigger the development of abnormal tissue growth at this point. Such a growth is given the general name of _____ tumor _____

5. The size of a scar following the healing of a clean wound may best be reduced by bringing the edges together with a(n) _____ *suture*

6. A band of connective tissue that connects a muscle to a bone is a(n) _____ *tendon*

7. New growths that spread and grow rapidly, often causing death, are said to be _____ *malig,*

8. A growth that does not spread and is usually confined to a local area is said to be innocent or _____ *benign*

Group E

pleura	membrane	mucous membranes
pericardium	lubricants	fascia
peritoneum	serous membranes	

1. Any thin sheet of material that separates two or more groups of substances is classified as a(n) _____ *membran*

2. The membranes that line the closed cavities within the body are _____ *serious membrane*

3. The tough membranes composed entirely of connective tissue which serve to anchor and support organs are the _____ *fascia*

4. The linings of tubes and spaces that are connected with the outside are largely epithelial. They are _____ *mucus*

5. The membrane that covers each lung is known as the _____ *pleur*

6. The special sac that encloses the heart is known as the _____ *perici*

7. The serous membrane of the abdominal cavity is the largest of its kind and is called the _____ *peritoneum*

8. An important function of most epithelial membranes is to produce fluids that serve as _____ *lubricants*

Group F

superficial fascia	periosteum	synovial membranes
parietal layer	perichondrium	mucous membranes
mesothelium	capsules	cutaneous membrane

1. Membranous connective tissues that enclose organs are called _____

2. The tough connective tissue membrane that serves as bone covering is the _____

3. Covering cartilage is a membrane similar to that covering bone. It is called _____

4. Secretions produced by the lining of joint cavities act as lubricants to reduce friction between the ends of bones. These linings are _____

5. The linings of the various parts of the respiratory tract are all _____

6. The tissue that underlies the skin is known as the _____

7. The part of a serous membrane that is attached to the wall of a cavity or sac is the _____

8. The type of epithelium that covers serous membranes is called _____

9. The skin is described as the _____

Group G

sarcoma	lipoma	osteoma
carcinoma	myoma	glioma
nevus	angioma	

1. A benign connective tissue tumor that originates in adipose tissue is called a(n) _____

2. The general term for a tumor composed of blood or lymph vessels is _____

3. A tumor that originates from the connective tissue of the central nervous system is a(n) _____

4. A benign connective tissue tumor that originates in a bone is called a(n) _____

5. A better term for a mole or other small circumscribed tumor of the skin is _____

6. The most common type of cancer is one that originates in epithelium. It is called a(n) _____

7. Cancers that originate in connective tissue usually spread by way of the bloodstream. This type of cancer is called a(n) _____

8. The fibroid originates in the uterus. This innocent tumor is correctly classified as a(n) _____

IV. Labeling

Print the name or names of each labeled part on the numbered lines.

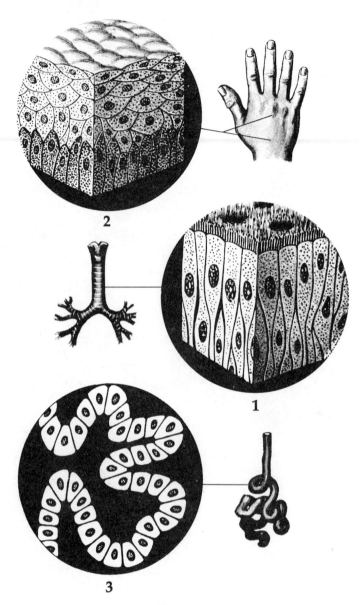

Three types of epithelium

1. _____

2. _____

3. _____

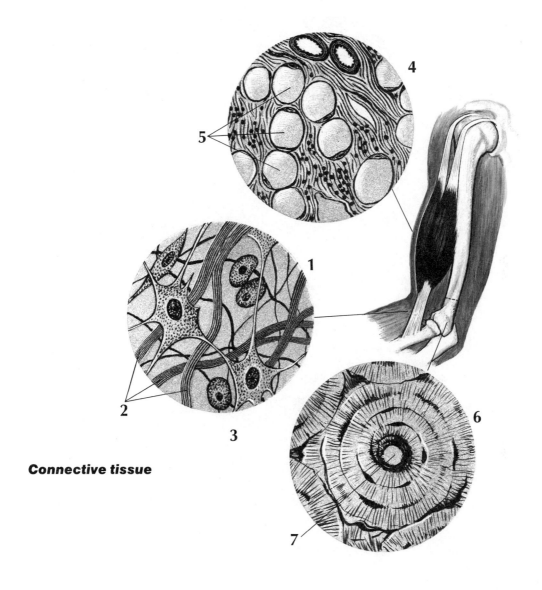

Connective tissue

1. _____   5. _____

2. _____   6. _____

3. _____   7. _____

4. _____

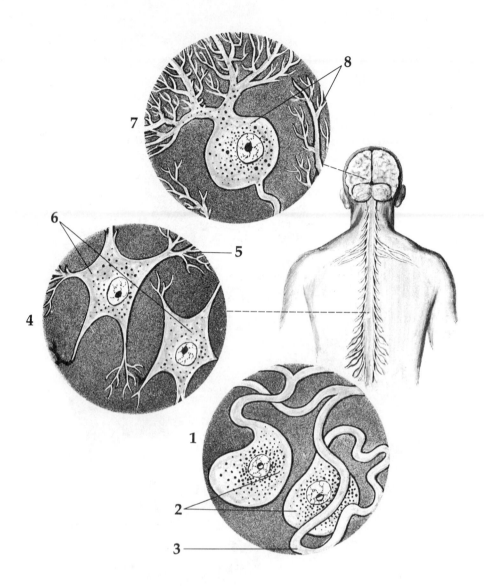

Nerve tissue

1. _____   5. _____

2. _____   6. _____

3. _____   7. _____

4. _____   8. _____

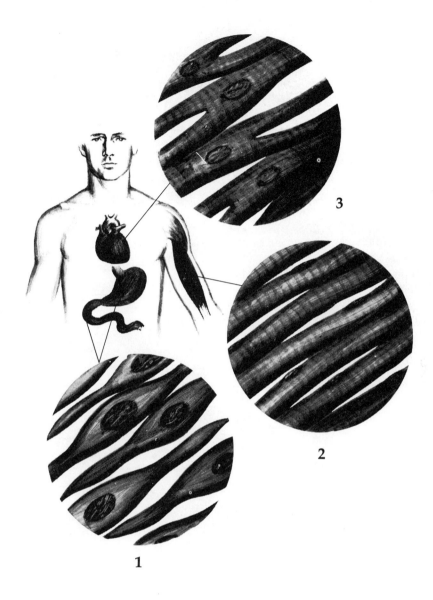

Muscle tissue

1. _____

2. _____

3. _____

V. Completion Exercise

Print the word or phrase that correctly completes each sentence.

1. Another term for the smooth involuntary muscle of most hollow organs is _____

2. The supporting tissue of the body organs is called _____

3. The basic unit of nerve tissue is the nerve cell, the scientific name for which is _____

4. Movement is produced by the tissue known as _____

5. The noun that indicates a layer of serous membrane is _____

6. The lubricant produced by membranes that line cavities connected with the outside is known as _____

7. The microscopic hairlike projections found in the cells lining most of the respiratory tract are called _____

8. The layer of a serous membrane that lines the wall of a cavity or sac is called the _____

9. Layers of fibrous connective tissue that enclose certain internal organs are called _____

10. The tough connective tissue membrane that covers most parts of all bones is given the name _____

11. A lubricant that reduces friction between the ends of bones is produced by the _____

12. The general term referring to cancers that originate in epithelium and are spread through the lymphatic system is _____

13. The malignant tumors that originate in connective tissue and that spread by way of the bloodstream are called _____

14. Among the forms of treatment of certain cancers is the use of drugs. This treatment is known as _____

VI. Practical Applications

Study each discussion. Then print the appropriate word or phrase in the space provided.

Group A

The following patients were seen in the hospital emergency room.

1. Little J, age 7, fell while riding his bicycle. He sustained several gashes on his face. At the emergency center the cuts were

cleansed and sutured. Suturing is desirable because it reduces
the size of the connective tissue replacement, called the

_____

2. Student K, age 16, had sustained a deep cut on his index finger
while he was whittling a piece of wood. Although the cut was
sutured and healed well, he noted loss of sensation on the tip of
the cut finger. However, after a few weeks the sensation began to
return. This was possible because of the thin nerve fiber covering
that aids in the nerve repair process. This membrane is called

_____

3. Baby M, age 3 months, had a history of crying intermittently for
several hours every day. Apparently, he was suffering from
spasms of the visceral muscles of the intestine, a condition
known as

_____

Group B

While observing in an outpatient clinic a student noted the following cases.

1. Baby J experienced difficulty in breathing and had a copious
discharge from his nose. A diagnosis of URI (upper respiratory
infection) was made. The location of the membrane and the
type of discharge indicated that the involved membrane was
one of the

_____

2. Mrs. K complained of a swelling in the left groin. She had
suffered previously from an infection of bone in the middle
back; now it appeared that the infection had traveled along the
fibrous covering of some of the back muscles. Such muscle
coverings are called

_____

3. Mr. B was concerned about swelling and tenderness over his
neck and upper back. His work involved the demolition of old
buildings; he had become careless about personal cleanliness.
Infection now involved the skin and connective tissue under it.
The "sheet" that underlies the skin is called

_____

4. Mrs. J had suffered a painful bump on her ankle. The swelling
involved the superficial tissues and the fibrous covering of the
bone, or the

_____

5. Mrs. C had undergone extensive surgery because of deformities
due to rheumatoid arthritis, an inflammatory disorder of the
membranes lining the joint spaces. These lining membranes are
known as

_____

6. Ms. G experienced abdominal pains following longstanding
infection of the pelvic organs. Connective tissue bands (adhe-
sions) were found to extend throughout the peritoneal surface.
The layer of peritoneum that is attached to the organs is
called the

_____

7. Student N suffered a mild concussion while playing football and it was feared that there might be damage to the brain coverings. These brain and spinal cord coverings are known as _____

8. Mrs. J was quite ill. Her symptoms were those associated with the disease called lupus erythematosus. She complained that it hurt to breathe because the membranes covering the lungs were involved. These membranes are called the _____

Group C

A day in the tumor clinic involves observation of several patients. Among the situations you might encounter are the following.

1. Mr. B was concerned about a small growth on the left side of his face which had not cleared after many months. He thought it might be growing. The physician informed Mr. B that a biopsy was necessary in order to make a positive diagnosis. If the growth proved to be malignant, it would be a(n) _____

2. Mrs. C complained of an irritation in the area of a large dark mole on her right ankle. The doctor advised her to have the mole removed and examined under the microscope, because such a mole may be malignant. This type of cancer is called a(n) _____

3. Mr. K's problem involved multiple rounded growths located just under the skin of his right forearm. These were diagnosed as benign fatty tumors, or _____

4. Ms. G had noticed a small lump in her left breast. A biopsy was done in order to determine whether this was a malignant tumor of the ducts, which could be classified as _____

5. Baby K was under treatment for a large birthmark on his right cheek. This type of tumor, which is composed of blood or lymph vessels, is classified as a(n) _____

5

Disease and Disease-Producing Organisms

I. Overview

Disease may be defined as an impairment or other change from the normal state which prevents some of the tissues and organs from carrying on their required function. The causes are many and varied. Among them are **congenital disorders** or birth defects (which may be hereditary or acquired within the uterus), disorders resulting from **environmental factors** (such as a chemical agent or lack of sunshine), and those due to **neoplasia** (abnormal cell growth). Predisposing causes are another important group of factors that play a part in the development of disease. An understanding of disease incorporates a study of the body including its anatomy (structure) and its physiology (functions) under normal and pathologic (abnormal) conditions. This understanding is aided by use of disease terminology. **Infection,** or invasion of the body by disease-producing microorganisms, including bacteria, fungi, viruses, and protozoa, is the most important cause of disease in human beings. A second major cause of human disease is **infestation,** a type of infection due to parasitic worms. Control of infection depends on understanding how organisms are transmitted and how they enter and leave the body. Public health has been vastly improved through laboratory identification of pathogens and the application of **chemotherapeutic** and **aseptic** methods to prevent or control their spread.

II. Topics for Review

A. Causes of disease
B. Predisposing causes of disease
C. Disease terminology
D. Basis of infection
E. Characteristics of microorganisms
F. Diseases caused by worms
G. Methods of destroying pathogens or of inhibiting their growth

III. Matching Exercises

Matching only within each group, print the answers in the spaces provided.

Group A

hereditary	congenital	therapy
symptoms	acute	chronic
pathogens	malnutrition	signs

1. A lack of essential substances such as vitamins in one's diet is known as _malnutrition_

2. Living organisms that cause many types of illness throughout the world are called _pathogens_

3. Any defect or abnormality present at birth is said to be _congenital_

4. A disorder that is passed on to the infant by way of a parent's reproductive cells is referred to as _hereditary_

5. A relatively severe disorder of short duration is said to be _acute_

6. Diseases that persist over a long period of time are said to be _chronic_

7. Changes in body function that are experienced by the patient are called _symptoms_

8. A course of treatment that is prescribed by the physician is called _therapy_

9. Evidences of disease that can be observed by others are _signs_

Group B

viruses	helminths	curved rod
fungi	rickettsias	cocci
protozoa	bacilli	chlamydias

1. Rod-shaped bacteria are called _bacille curved ro_

2. Spherical bacteria are known as _cocci_

3. The bacterium that causes cholera is classified as a(n) _bacilli_

4. The parasites that cause typhus fever and Rocky Mountain spotted fever are classified as _rickettsias_

5. Mycotic infections are caused by _fungi_

6. Organisms classified as bacteria, though smaller, are the cause of trachoma and parrot fever. They are known as _chlamydias_ _rickettsias_

7. The smallest known infectious agents are the _viruses_

8. The group of microorganisms described as animal-like are the _protozoa_

9. Another name for worms is _helminths_

Group C

etiology   incidence   idiopathic
endemic   epidemic   diagnosis
asepsis   sterilization   syndrome

1. The process that kills every living organism on an object is _sterilization_

2. A condition in which no disease-causing organisms are present is called _asepis_

3. The process of determining the nature of an illness is called making a(n) _diagnosis_

4. A group of signs or symptoms that occur together forms a(n) _syndrome_

5. A disease present at the same time in many people living in the same area is said to be _epidemic_

6. If a disease is characteristically present continuously in a given area it is said to be _endimic_

7. A disorder without known cause, or self-originating, is said to be _idiopathic_

8. The study of the cause of a disorder is said to be its _etiology_

9. The range of occurrence of a disease and its tendency to affect particular groups of persons is said to be its _incidence_

Group D

prognosis   anatomy   pathology
microbiology   communicable   physiology
parasitology   protozoology   bacteriology

protozoology

1. The study of one-celled animals is _bacteriology_

2. The study of organisms that live on or within other organisms at the expense of those organisms is _parasitology_

3. The study that deals with the activities or functions of a living organism and its parts is

4. The study of rickettsias and chlamydias is included in _bacteriology_

5. The study of all microscopic organisms is _microbiology_

6. The science that deals with the structure and relationships of parts of the body is _physiology_
anatomy

7. The study that deals with the nature of disease and includes the changes caused by disease is *physiology*

8. A disease that can be transmitted from one person to another is *communicable*

9. A prediction on the probable outcome of a disease is a(n) *prognosis*

Group E

infection	spore	pasteurization
botulism	dust	gram-positive
acid-fast	chemotherapy	antibiotic

1. The process of heating milk to 145° F for 30 minutes and then allowing it to cool rapidly before it is bottled is *pasteurization*

2. A deadly type of food poisoning due to a rod-shaped bacillus is *botulism*

3. A most effective carrier of microbes present in the atmosphere is *dust*

4. Invasion of the body by pathogenic microorganisms is called a(n) *infection*

5. The organisms that cause tuberculosis and leprosy retain color (stain) after application of an acid. Such organisms are said to be *acid fast*

6. Microorganisms that retain the bluish dye after they have been stained and treated with iodine and a solvent are said to be *gram positive*

7. Treatment of a disease by the administration of a chemical agent is called *chemo*

8. A chemical agent derived from living cells that is used to kill or arrest the growth of pathogens is called a(n) *antibiotic*

9. A resistant form of bacterium is a(n) *spore*

IV. Labeling

For each of the following illustrations, print the name or names of each labeled part on the numbered lines.

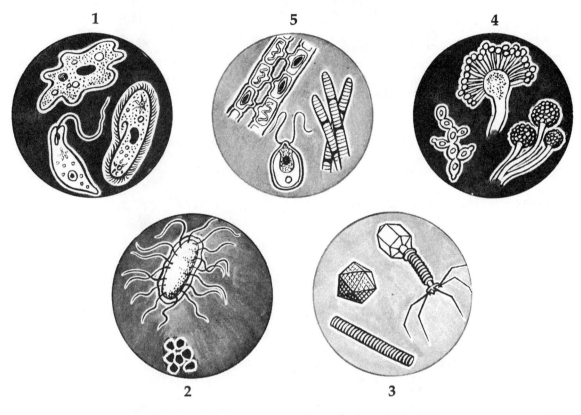

Examples of microorganisms

1. ____Protozoa____   4. ____fungi____
2. ____Bacteria____   5. ____algae____
3. ____viruses____

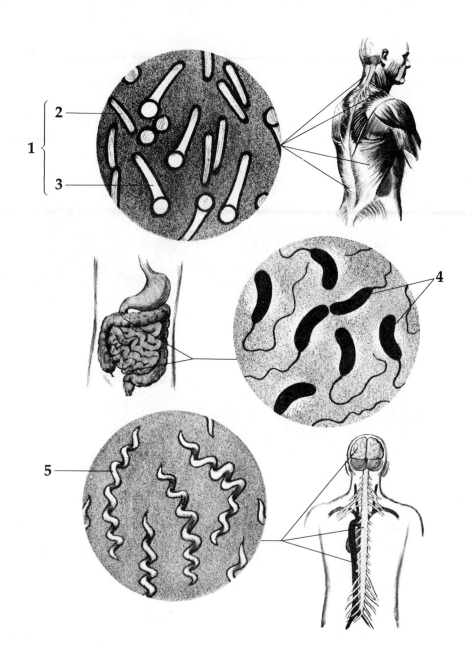

Rod-shaped and curved bacteria

1. _tetanus_
2. _veg. growing form_
3. _spore form_
4. _Asiatic Cholera_
5. _spirochete_

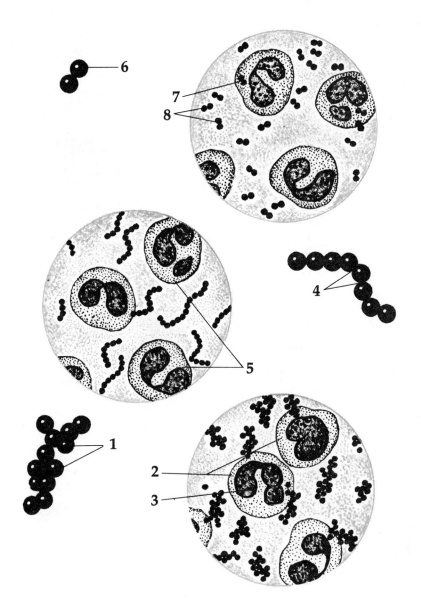

Spherical bacteria

1. _Staphlyococci_
2. _pus cells_
3. _nucleus of leukocyte_
4. _stretococci_
5. _leukocytes_
6. _ciplicocci_
7. _intracellura cocci_
8. _extracellular cocci_

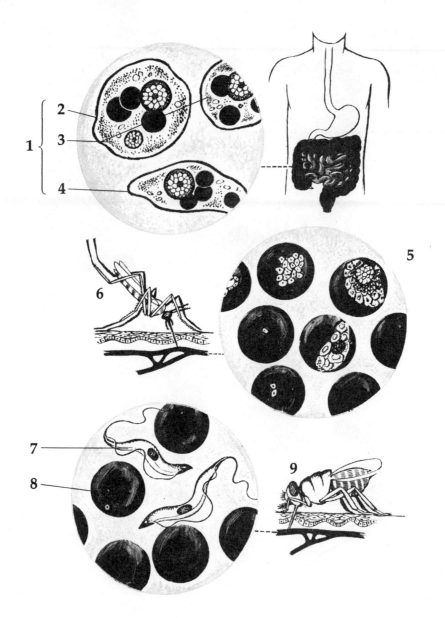

Pathogenic protozoa

1. amebic dysentery
2. protec. wall
3. inactive forms
4. active or motile forms
5. malaria
6. anaphles mosquito
7. trypansoma gambiense
8. erthrocyte
9. tetse fly

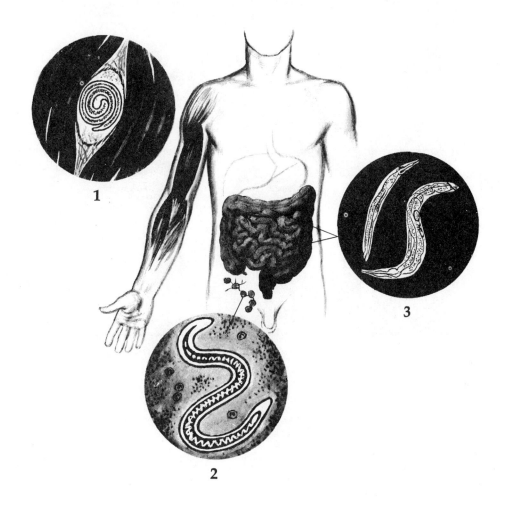

Common parasitic worms

1. _trichina_

2. _filaria_

3. _ascaris_

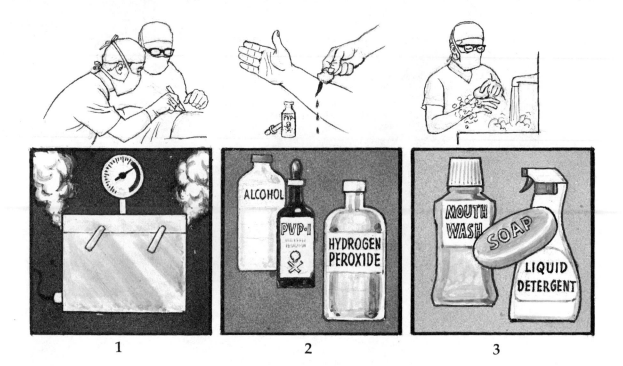

Aseptic methods

1. *Sterilization*
2. *Disinfection*
3. *Antisepsis*

V. Completion Exercise

Print the word or phrase that correctly completes each sentence.

1. A highly prevalent contagious disease, due to infection with diplococci, is called

   gonorrhea

2. Boils, carbuncles, and impetigo are among the infections caused by widespead organisms called

   _____

3. Blood poisoning (septicemia), scarlet fever, rheumatic fever, and other disorders are caused by a group of microorganisms called

   _____

4. Legionnaire's disease, tuberculosis, and tetanus (lockjaw) are caused by rod-shaped microorganisms known as

   _____

5. Chickenpox, hepatitis, the common cold, and many other contagious diseases are caused by submicroscopic organisms known as

   _____

6. Tetanus is caused by an organism that exists in two forms. One of these is the growing vegetative form. The other form is a resting and resistant form, the _____

7. Asiatic cholera is a dread disease found in India, China, and other Asiatic countries. It is caused by a comma-shaped microorganism called the _____

8. Syphilis is a venereal disease that may eventually involve the brain and circulatory organs. It is caused by a cork-screw-shaped microorganism, the _____

9. Bacteria that are pathogenic may cause injury and even death by the action of poisons referred to as _____

10. Included in the class of protozoa called Sporozoa is a plasmodium that causes a worldwide debilitating disease called _____

11. One of the most common parasitic worms is the intestinal roundworm called _____

12. A small roundworm that may become enclosed in a cyst or sac inside the muscles of the pig and be transmitted to man by way of improperly cooked pork is known as the _____

13. The flatworm composed of many segments (proglottids) may grow to a length of 50 feet—hence the name _____

VI. Practical Applications

Study each discussion. Then print the appropriate word or phrase in the space provided.

1. Mrs. K brought her young baby in for follow-up examination of his condition of harelip. Harelip is an example of a birth defect that is acquired by the fetus during development in the mother's uterus. Such defects, along with those that are inherited, are all said to be _____

2. Mr. N, age 81, showed evidence of tissue deterioration. This wear and tear is often described as _____

3. Ms. C required further study of an obscure disorder for which no cause had been found. Such a disease is often referred to as _____

4. Mr. S needed prophylactic (preventive) treatment because he had received several puncture wounds while repairing an old building. He was given an injection to prevent the development of lockjaw. The scientific name for lockjaw is _____

5. Ms. D attended the clinic for treatment of a very sore throat. Laboratory tests showed the presence of spherical bacteria in chains. The scientific name for such organisms is _____

6. Mrs. A brought her young daughter to the clinic for examination of boils (furuncles) that had been appearing on the child's neck with disturbing frequency. Boils are often due to dot-shaped microorganisms that resemble bunches of grapes when examined under the microscope. These organisms are called _____

7. Mr. E came to the clinic because he had suffered from bouts of diarrhea ever since returning from a camping trip that took him into several countries. One common cause of intestinal disorders is a dysentery caused by a one-celled protozoan called _____

8. Mr. J had been camping in a brush-covered area. He now had a high fever and a red rash over large parts of his body. His disease was diagnosed as Rocky Mountain spotted fever, which is most often transmitted by the bite of a _____

9. Mrs. K had a fever, cough, and other symptoms of pneumonia. The suspected portal of entry for the organisms causing her illness is the _____

10. Mr. L came to the clinic for administration of drugs used to treat his condition of Hodgkin's disease, a type of cancer. Drugs used in treatment of cancer are known as _____

6

The Skin in Health and Disease

I. Overview

Because of its various properties, the skin can be classified as an **enveloping membrane**, an **organ**, and a **system**. A cross section of skin reveals its layers of **epidermis** (the outermost layer), **dermis** (the true skin where the skin glands are mainly located), and the **subcutaneous tissue** (the underlayer).

The skin serves the essential functions of **protecting** deeper tissues against drying and against invasion by harmful organisms, **regulating** body temperature, and **obtaining information** from the environment. It also **excretes** water, salts, and some waste in the form of sweat. The pigment **melanin** gives the skin its color; races that have been exposed to the tropical sun for thousands of years have highly pigmented skin. The protein **keratin** in the epidermis thickens and protects the skin, and **sebum**, secreted by the sebaceous glands, lubricates the skin and prevents dehydration. Hair and nails, composed mainly of keratin, are structures associated with the skin.

The appearance of the skin is influenced by such factors as the quantity of blood circulating in the surface blood vessels and its hemoglobin concentration. Much can be learned about the condition of the skin by observing for the presence of **discoloration**, **injury**, or **eruption**. Aging, exposure to sunlight, and occupational activity also have a bearing on the condition and appearance of the skin. The skin is subject to numerous diseases, of which the most common are various types of **dermatitis**, such as eczema and acne.

Being the most visible aspect of the body, the skin is the object of much quackery, and vast sums of money are spent in efforts to beautify it; good general health is, however, the most important part of skin health and beauty.

II. Topics for Review

A. Skin layers
   1. Epidermis
   2. Dermis
   3. Subcutaneous layer
B. Skin glands
   1. Sudoriferous glands
   2. Sebaceous glands
C. Hair and nails
D. Functions of the skin
E. General appearance of the skin
F. Skin diseases

III. Matching Exercises

Matching only within each group, print the answers in the spaces provided.

Group A

epidermis	sebaceous glands	melanin
keratin	sudoriferous glands	dermis
integument	subcutaneous layer	connective tissue

1. In its role as a system, the skin is called the _integument_

2. The protein in the epidermis that thickens and protects the skin is _keratin_

3. Certain glands produce sweat; these are the _sudoriferous_

4. The tissue layer under the skin is the _subcutan_

5. The oily secretion on skin and hair is produced by _sebaceous_

6. Several layers of epithelial cells form the outermost part of the skin, the _epidermis_

7. Since the epidermis is lacking in blood vesels, nutritive sub-stances reach the epidermal cells from the underlying _dermis_

8. The framework of the dermis is composed of _connective_

9. Skin color is due largely to the presence of the pigment called _melanin_

Group B

lesion	receptors	dermis (or corium)
dilate	absorption	ciliary glands
pathogens	infection	fat

1. In its function of regulating body temperature the skin dissipates heat as the blood vessels enlarge or _dialate_

2. Modified sweat glands are found in the eyelid edges. These are known as

ciliary

3. In its role of protecting deeper tissues the skin prevents drying and invasion by

pathogues

4. The skin's function of obtaining information from the environment is due to the presence of a variety of sensory nerve endings. One general term for these is

receptors

5. The subcutaneous tissue is composed of connective tissue and

fat

6. A local wound or injury to the skin is called a(n)

lesion

7. The nerve endings of the skin are located mainly in the

dermis

8. Medications are given by mouth or by injection more often than they are applied to the skin. This is because the skin has limited powers of

absorbtion

9. Following a wound or injury of the skin, pathogens may enter and cause a(n)

infection

Group C

intact ✓	follicle ✓	sebum —
melanin ✓	nerve endings	temperature ✓
corneum ✓	ceruminous	germinativum

1. Dilation of blood vessels brings more blood to the surface so that heat is dissipated into the air. This is one way in which the skin acts to regulate

temperature

2. The skin is an able defender against invasion by pathogens as long as it remains unbroken or

intact

3. Exposure to sunlight causes an increase in the quantity of the pigment

melanin

4. The uppermost layer of the epidermis is the stratum

corneum

5. The modified sweat glands that secrete wax are called

ceruminous

6. The oily secretion of the sebaceous glands is

sebum

7. Obtaining information about the environment is a function of the skin's

nerve endings

8. The deepest layer of the epidermis, which contains living, dividing cells, is the stratum

germinaltivum

9. Each hair develops within a sheath called a(n)

follicle

Group D

crust ✓
jaundice ✓
macule ✓

herpes simplex ✓
vesicle ✓
papule ✓

urticaria ✓
pustule ✓
excoriation

1. Any flat, discolored spot on the skin is called a(n) *macule*

2. A yellowish skin discoloration may be due to the presence of bile pigments in the blood. This condition is called *Jaundice*

3. The name given to a skin lesion produced by scratching is *excoriation*

4. A pimple that does not contain pus is called a(n) *papule*

5. A better term for scab is *crust*

6. A small sac that contains fluid is a blister or *veside*

7. Following the vesicular stage of chickenpox, pus appears in each lesion. This is a(n) *pustule*

8. A viral skin disease that is characterized by many watery blisters is called *herpes simplex*

9. An allergic disorder in which there are itchy patches (hives) is called *urticaria*

IV. Labeling

For each of the following illustrations, print the name or names of each labeled part on the numbered lines.

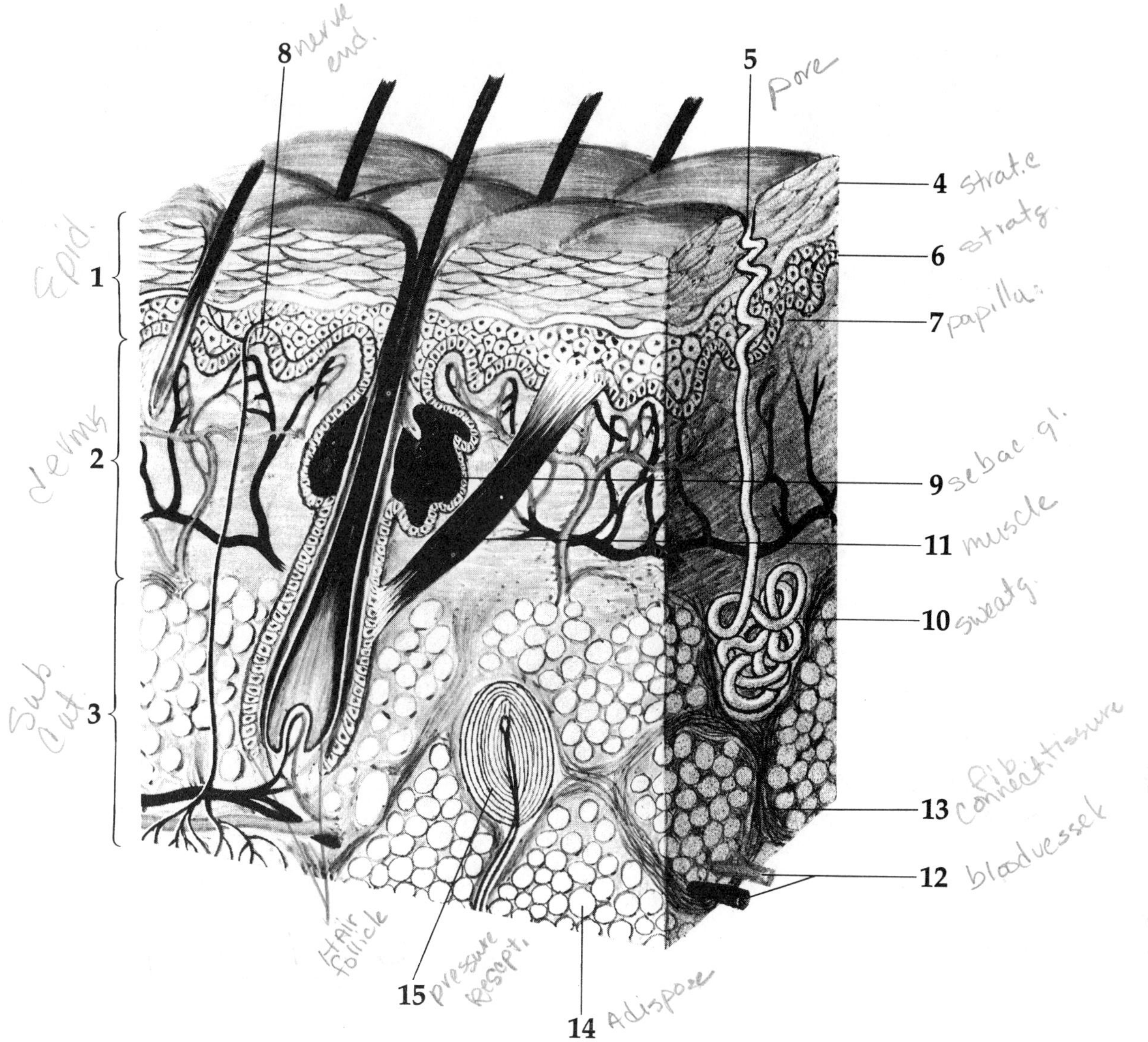
1 epid.
2 dermis
3 Sub cut
4 strat.c
5 pore
6 stratg.
7 papilla
8 nerve end.
9 sebac gl.
10 sweatg.
11 muscle
12 bloodvessels
13 fib. connect. tissue
14 Adispose
15 pressure recept.
Hair follicle

Cross section of the skin

1. epidermus
2. dermus
3. subcutaneous
4. stratum corneum
5. pore
6. stratum germinativum
7. papilla
8. nerve
9. sabecous
10. sweat gland
11. muscle
12. blood vessels
13. fibrous conn. tissue
14. adipose/fat cells
15. pressure receptor

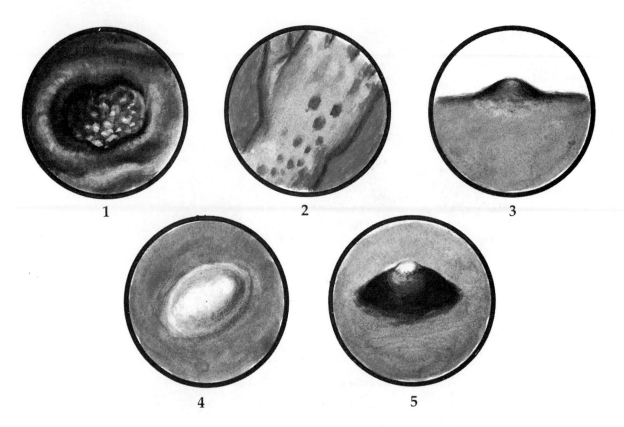

Some skin eruptions

1. ____ulcer____   4. ____vesicle____

2. ____macule____   5. ____pustule____

3. ____papule____

V. Completion Exercise

Print the word or phrase that correctly completes each sentence.

1. The outer cells of the epidermis, which are constantly being shed, are designated the horny layer, or

   ____Stratum corneum____

2. Many kinds of irritants and pathogens may cause skin inflammation. The general term for this disorder is

   ____dermatitis____

3. A comedo is a plug of dirt and oily secretion in the pore of an oil gland. The common name is

   ____blackhead____

4. The pigment of the skin is

   ____melanin____

5. Besides causing sunburn, prolonged excessive exposure to sun-light is thought to be one cause of

Skin cancer

6. One means by which the body protects itself against pathogens is production of skin secretions which are slightly

acid

7. Epidermophytosis, or athlete's foot, is due to infection by

fungi

8. Numerous factors including infection may cause baldness. Absence of hair from any areas where it is normally present is called

alopecia

9. An acute contagious skin disease caused by staphylococci or streptococci may be extremely serious in infants and young children. This disease is

impetigo

10. Overactivity of the sebaceous glands during adolescence may play a part in the common skin disease

acne vulgaris

11. Areas of redness represent a type of skin injury known as

erytherma

12. The nails originate from the outer part of the

epidermis

13. The ceruminous glands and the ciliary glands are modified

sudoriferous

14. Hair and nails are composed mainly of the protein that thickens and protects the skin, called

keratin

15. The blood vessels which nourish the epidermis are located in the skin layer just below the epidermis, called the

dermis

VI. Practical Applications

Study each discussion. Then print the appropriate word or phrase in the space provided.

Group A

These patients were seen in the outpatient clinic.

1. Mrs. A brought her three children to the clinic. The 9-month-old baby had redness of both cheeks, a symptom that the physician described as

erythema

2. The physician also found several tiny blisters on the baby's cheeks, and made the notation on the chart that these eruptions were

vesicles

3. On both the baby's cheeks there were small pimple-like protrusions. The physician referred to them as

papules

4. The physician diagnosed a noncontagious disorder of sensitive skin known as

eczema

5. Mrs. A's 6-year-old son had a number of blisters on his hands that contained pus. Microscopic examination revealed the presence of staphylococci. This contagious skin disease is called _impetigo_

6. The doctor ordered that the boy be kept home from school and that special care be followed to prevent infection in the two younger children. The middle child, age 4, seemed well. The physician was mainly concerned about the baby, since this disorder is highly contagious and may become so serious in a young baby as to be _fatal_

7. Mrs. A wondered why her own skin looked yellower than normal. Questioning indicated that she had become a food faddist and was eating carrots and other deeply colored vegetables to the exclusion of other foods. Mrs. A's condition is called _carotinemia_

8. L, age 15, came to the clinic with his father. The son's skin was marked by pimples and blackheads, and had a roughened appearance. This common disorder of the oil glands is found mainly in adolescents and is called _acne vulgaris_

Group B

1. Mr. K, age 38, was losing his hair. He mentioned that many of his male relatives had a similar problem. The medical term for baldness is _alopecia_

2. Numerous vesicles and ulcers were found on Mrs. D's feet. This disorder is popularly called athlete's foot. A better term is _epidermophytosis_

3. Mrs. J was concerned about a redness and silvery scaling on her elbows that seemed to "come and go"; the name for this disorder is _psoriasis_

4. Mr. M, a laborer, had neglected to give his skin proper care. Now numerous painful nodules were seen in the axillae. These nodules, due to bacteria entering the hair follicles, are called boils, or _furuncles_

5. There was also a deep-seated infection of the subcutaneous tissue on Mr. M's lower back. These infected areas are known as _carbuncles_

6. Fair-skinned Mr. G had spent most of his 40 years in Arizona and southeastern California. He now noticed a firm nodule on the edge of the left ear pinna and said it was increasing in size. A biopsy revealed a malignancy called _carcinoma_

7. Mr. G's teen-age son had large areas of red, peeling skin due to sunburn. The nurse advised him to protect his skin with zinc ointment or another effective _sunscreen_

8. Young Alice J was concerned about her pallor and asked the nurse about cosmetics she might use to improve the color. The nurse suggested that the most helpful thing would be to improve her

   general health

9. The clinic personnel were given careful instructions on the proper method of handwashing. This is desirable because hand-washing is the most effective method of preventing the spread of infectious

   pathogens

7

The Skeleton—
Bones and Joints

I. Overview

The skeletal system protects and supports the body parts and serves as an attachment for the muscles, which furnish the power for movement. The skeletal system includes some 206 bones; the number varies slightly according to age and the individual.

Bones are composed of living tissue and have their own systems of blood and lymphatic vessels and nerves. Bone tissue may be either **spongy** or **compact**. Compact bone is found in the shaft (diaphysis) of a long bone and in the outer layer of other bones. Spongy bone makes up the ends (epiphyses) of a long bone and the center of other bones. **Red marrow** occurs in certain parts of all bones and manufactures the blood cells; **yellow marrow**, which is largely fat, is found mainly in the central cavities of the long bones.

Bone is produced by cells called **osteoblasts** which gradually convert cartilage to bone during development. The mature cells that maintain bone are called **osteocytes**, and the cells that break down bone for remodeling and repair are the **osteoclasts**.

The entire bony framework of the body is called the skeleton. It is divided into two main groups of bones, the **axial skeleton** and the **appendicular skeleton**. The axial skeleton includes the skull, spinal column, ribs, and sternum. The appendicular skeleton consists of the bones of the arms and legs, the shoulder girdle, and the pelvic girdle.

A **joint** is the region of union of two or more bones; joints are classified on the basis of the degree of movement permitted. Connective tissue bands, the **ligaments**, hold the bones together in all the freely movable (synovial) joints and many of the less movable joints.

II. Topics for Review

A. Structure of bone
B. Bone cells
C. Bone formation

D. Functions of bones
E. Bones of the axial skeleton
F. Bones of the appendicular skeleton
G. Landmarks on bones
H. Disorders of bones
I. Types of joints
J. Disorders of joints

III. Matching Exercises

Matching only within each group, print the answers in the spaces provided.

Group A

cartilage   red marrow   yellow marrow
periosteum   calcium salts   appendicular skeleton
axial skeleton   endosteum   osteoblast

1. The bony framework of the head and trunk forms the   _axial_

2. Production of blood cells is carried on mainly in the   _red marrow_

3. The combination of bones that form the framework for the extremities is called the   _append._

4. The fatty material found inside the central cavities of long bones is   _yellow marrow_

5. The tough connective tissue membrane that covers bones is   _periosteum_

6. The somewhat thinner membrane that lines the central cavity of long bones is   _endosteum_

7. The pliability of the young child's bones is due to their relatively large proportion of   _cartilage_

8. A cell that produces bone is called a(n)   _osteoblast_

9. The brittleness of the old person's bones is due to their relatively large proportion of   _calcium salt_

Group B

cranium   occipital bone   parietal bones
ethmoid bone   sutures   sphenoid bone
temporal bones

1. The delicate spongy bone located between the eyes is called the   _ethmoid_

2. The bone which forms the back of the skull, and part of the base of the skull, is the   _occipital_

3. That part of the skull which encloses the brain is the   _cranium_

4. The bat-shaped bone that extends behind the eyes and also forms part of the base of the skull is the _sphenoid_

5. The paired bones that form the larger part of the upper and side walls of the cranium are the _temporal_

6. The two bones that form the lower sides and part of the base of the central areas of the skull are _parietal_

7. The cranial bones join at places called _sutures_

Group C

mandible   maxillae   zygomatic bone
hyoid   nasal bones   lacrimal bone

1. At the inside corner of each eye is a very small bone, the _lacrimal_

2. The only movable bone of the skull is the _mandible_

3. Lying just below the skull proper is a U-shaped bone called the _hyoid_

4. The higher part of each cheek is formed by a bone called the _zygomatic_

5. The two bones of the upper jaw are the _maxillae_

6. The two slender bones that form much of the bridge of the nose are the _nasal bones_

Group D

true ribs   cervical region   floating ribs
lumbar region   diaphysis   thoracic region
rib cage   coccyx   scoliosis

1. The shaft of a long bone is the _diaphysis_

2. The spinal column is divided into five regions; the first seven vertebrae comprise the main framework of the neck, the _cervical_

3. The third section of the vertebral column consists of five bones that are somewhat larger than the first 19 vertebrae; these form the _lumbar_

4. The second part of the vertebral column has 12 bones which make up the _thoracic_

5. Lateral curvature of the vertebral column is a common abnormality. It is called _scoliosis_

6. In the child the tail part of the vertebral column is made of four or five small bones that later fuse; this is the _coccyx_

7. Protecting the heart and other organs as well as supporting the chest are functions of the surrounding framework called the

rib cage

8. The first seven pairs of ribs are called the

true ribs

9. Among the false ribs are two pairs, the last two, which are very short and do not extend to the front of the body. These are the

floating

Group E

patella	epiphysis	radius
ulna	tibia	sesamoid
fibula	olecranon process	

1. The upper part of the ulna forming the point of the elbow is the

olecranon

2. The medial forearm bone is the

ulna

3. The kneecap is also called the

patella

4. Of the two bones of the leg the larger is the

tibia

5. The forearm bone on the thumbside is the

radius

6. The patella is the largest of a type of bone that is encased in connective tissue. It is described as

sesamoid

7. The lateral bone of the leg is the

fibula

8. The end of a long bone is the

epiphysis

Group F

kyphosis	foramina	lordosis
foramen magnum	anterior fontanel	sacrum
spongy		

1. The skull of the infant, being in its formative stage, has a number of soft spots. The largest of these is the

anterior fontanel

2. An excessive anterior convexity of the lumbar curve is called

lordosis

3. The type of bone tissue found at the ends of a long bone is described as

spongy

4. The region of the spinal column below the lumbar region is made of four to five fused bones. It is called the

sacrum

5. An abnormally increased concave curvature of the thoracic spine is called

kyphosis

6. The largest opening in the skull, containing the spinal cord, is the

foramen magnum

7. Openings or holes that extend into or through bones are called

foramina

Group G

impacted fracture　　　osteitis deformans　　　comminuted fracture
greenstick fracture　　　spiral fracture　　　compound fracture
osteomyelitis　　　　　　bursitis

1. An infection of bone caused by pus-producing bacteria is

   osteomyelitis

2. An incomplete break in a bone is most likely to occur in children. It is referred to as a(n)

   impacted

3. The broken ends of the bones are jammed into each other in a(n)

   greenstick

4. When tissues are torn and the bone protrudes through the skin, the person is said to have a(n)

   compound

5. A break in which there is more than one fracture line and in which several fragments are present is called a(n)

   comminuted

6. If the bone has been twisted apart there is a(n)

   spiral

7. An abnormality of body chemistry involving calcium is characteristic of Paget's disease, or

   osteitis deformans

8. Inflammation of a small sac near a joint is called

   bursitis

Group H

costal　　　　　　　shoulder girdle　　　　phalanges
greater trochanter　　calcaneus　　　　　　carpal bones
metacarpal bones　　symphysis pubis　　　ilium
pelvic girdle　　　　processes　　　　　　ligaments

1. The five bones in the palm of each hand are the

   meta carpal

2. The largest of the tarsal bones is the heel bone or

   calcaneus

3. The 14 small bones that form the framework of the fingers on each hand are the

   phalanges

4. In the pelvic girdle, the os coxae is divided into three areas. The upper wing-shaped part is the

   illium

5. The bones of the wrist are the

   carpal bone

6. The clavicle and the scapula are contained in the

   shoulder girdle

7. The os coxae articulating with the sacrum comprise the

   pelvic girdle

8. An adjective that refers to the ribs is

   costal

9. The pubic parts of the two ossa coxae unite to form the joint called the

   symphysis pubis

10. The connective tissue bands that hold bones together at joints are called

ligaments

11. The large, rounded projection at the upper and lateral portion of the femur is the

greater trochanter

12. The prominences on bones that serve as muscle attachments have the general name of

processes

Group I

| articular cartilage | ball-and-socket | abduction | rotation |
| synovial membrane | flexion | hinge | extension |

1. The contacting surfaces of each joint are covered by a layer called the

articular cartilage

2. A bending motion that decreases the angle between two parts is

flexion

3. The lubricating fluid inside a joint cavity is produced by the lining of the cavity termed the

synovial

4. Movement away from the midline of the body is known as

abduction

5. Motion around a central axis is called

rotation

6. The reverse of flexion is

extension

7. The type of joint that allows for circumduction is a(n)

ball + socket

8. The type of joint found at the elbow is a(n)

hinge

Group J

| articulation | diaphysis | osteoporosis | diarthroses |
| rickets | acetabulum | rheumatoid arthritis | |

1. The deep socket in the hip bone that holds the head of the femur is the

acetabulum

2. A deficiency of calcium and phosphorus is the main cause of

rickets

3. The shaft of a long bone is the

diaphysis

4. A most crippling inflammatory disease of joints is

rheum. arthritis

5. The region of union of two or more bones is called a joint or

articulation

6. The more freely movable joints are

diarthroses

7. A common disorder in older women which involves abnormal bone formation is

osteoporosis

IV. Labeling

For each of the following illustrations, print the name or names of each labeled part on the numbered lines.

1. cranium
2. facial bones
3. mandiable
4. clavical
5. scapula
6. sternum
7. humerous
8. costal cartilage
9. vertabral colum
10. illium
11. pelvis
12. knee joint
13. ankle
14. sacrum
15. radius
16. ulna
17. carpals
18. meta carpals
19. phalanges
20. femur
21. patella
22. tibia
23. fibula
24. calcaneus
25. tarsal
26. metatarsals
27. phalanges

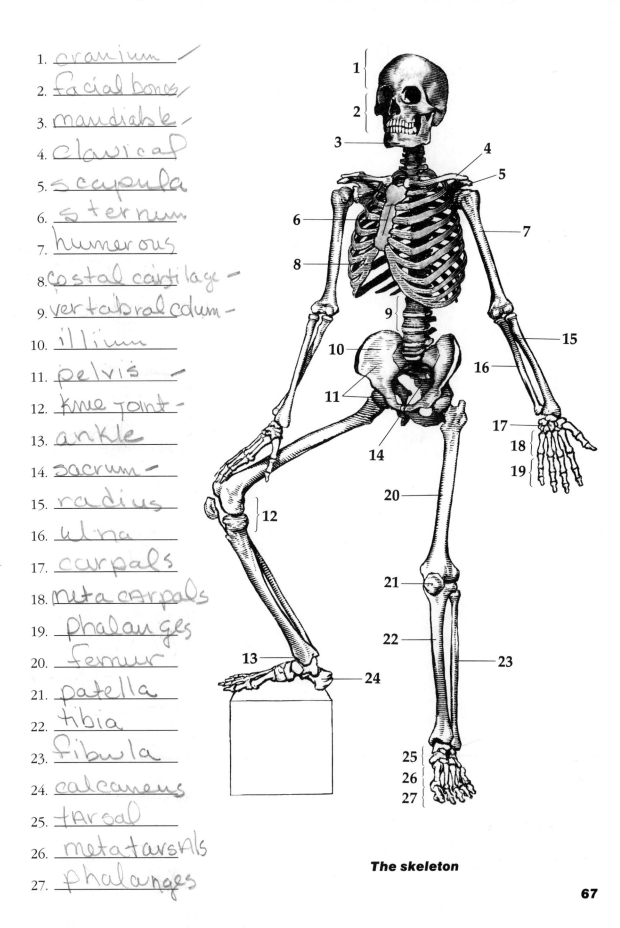

The skeleton

67

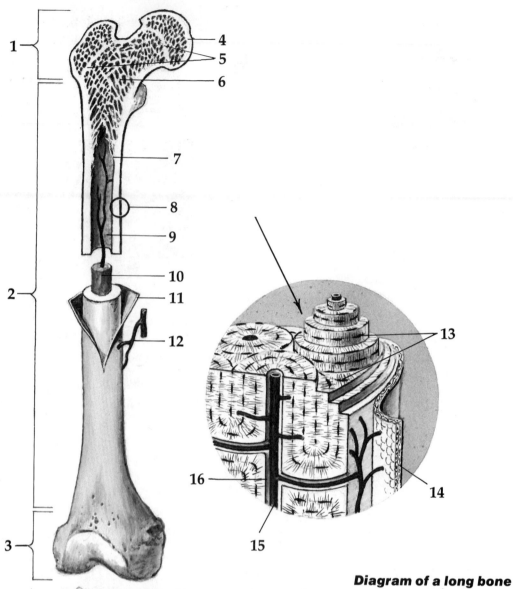

Diagram of a long bone

1. proxi mal epiphysis
2. diaphysis
3. distal epiphysis
4. cartilage
5. growth lines
6. spongy bone (red marrow)
7. endosteum
8. diaphysis (compact) bone)
9. medulary cavity (marrow
10. yellow marrow (Fat)
11. periosteum
12. vein
13. osteocytes
14. periosteum
15. blood vessels
16. canal

1. _frontal_
2. _parietal_
3. _sphenoid_
4. _temporal_
5. _nasal_
6. _maxilla_

7. _zygomatic_
8. _mandiable_
9. _coronal suture_
10. _lambdoidal suture_
11. _occipital_
12. _mastoid process_
13. _styloid process_
14. _ligament_
15. _hyoid_

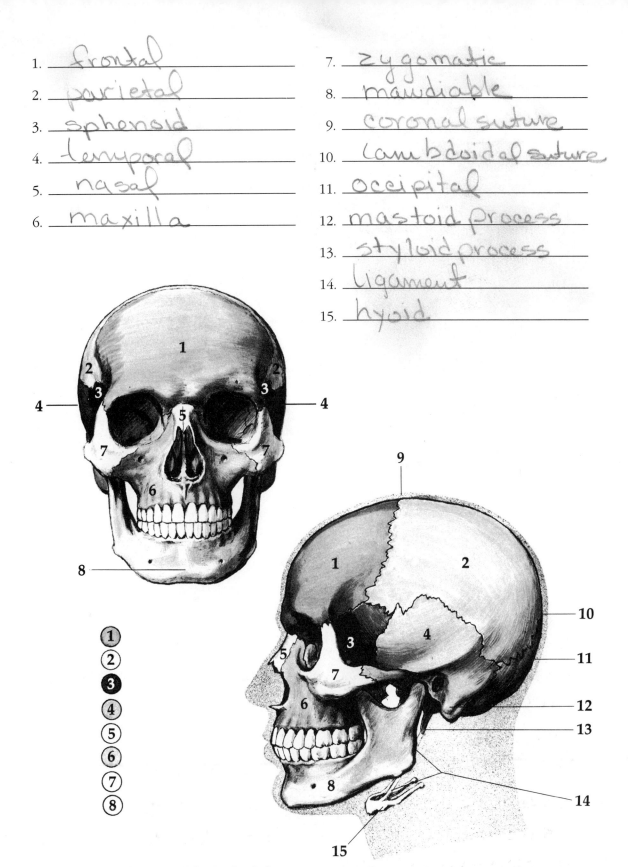

Skull from the front and from the left

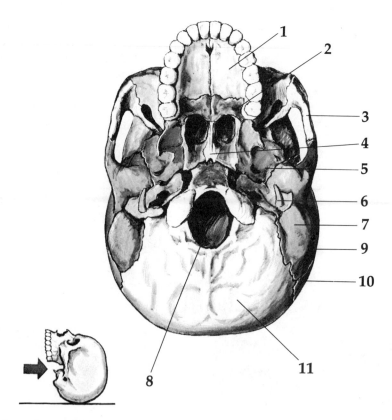

Skull from below, lower jaw removed

1. maxilla
2. palatine
3. zygomatic
4. vomer
5. sphenoid
6. styloid process
7. mastoid process
8. foramen magnum
9. temporal
10. parietal
11. occupital

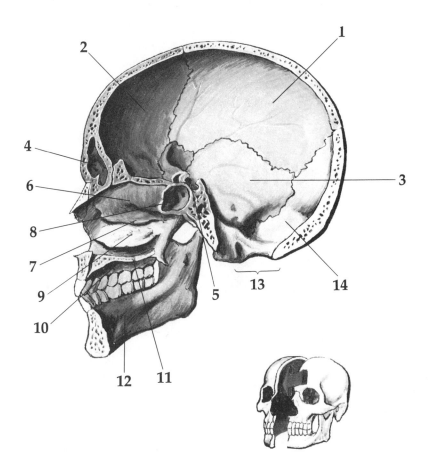

Skull, internal view

1. _parietal_
2. _frontal_
3. _temporal_
4. _frontal sinus_
5. _sella turcia_
6. _superior concha_
7. _middle concha_
8. _sphenoid sinus_
9. _inferior concha_
10. _maxilla_
11. _palatine_
12. _mandiable_
13. _foramen magnum_
14. _occipital_

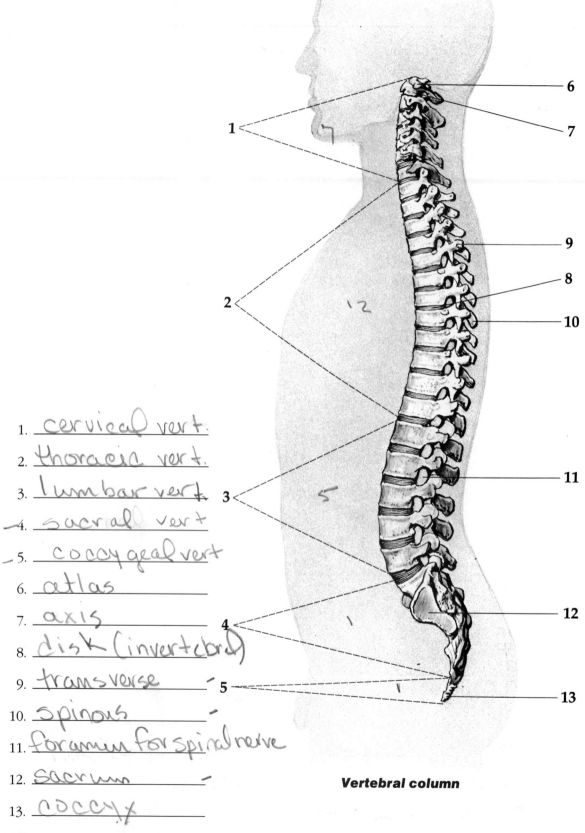

1. cervical vert.
2. thoracic vert.
3. lumbar vert.
4. sacral vert.
5. coccygeal vert
6. atlas
7. axis
8. disk (invertebral)
9. transverse
10. spinous
11. foramen for spinal nerve
12. sacrum
13. coccyx

Vertebral column

72

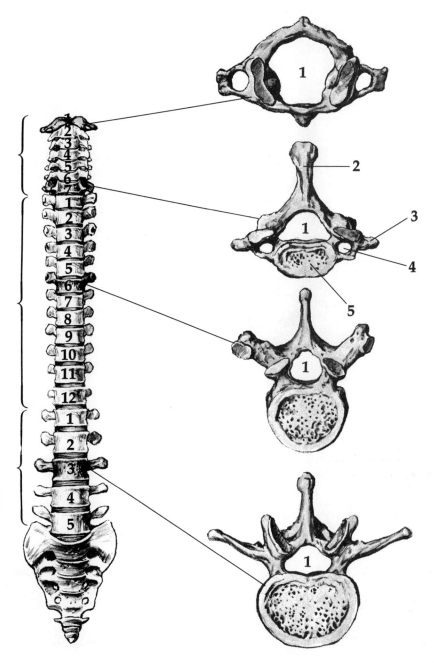

Vertebrae

1. ___vert. foramen___   4. ___transverse foramen___

2. ___spinous process___   5. ___centrum___

3. ___transverse process___

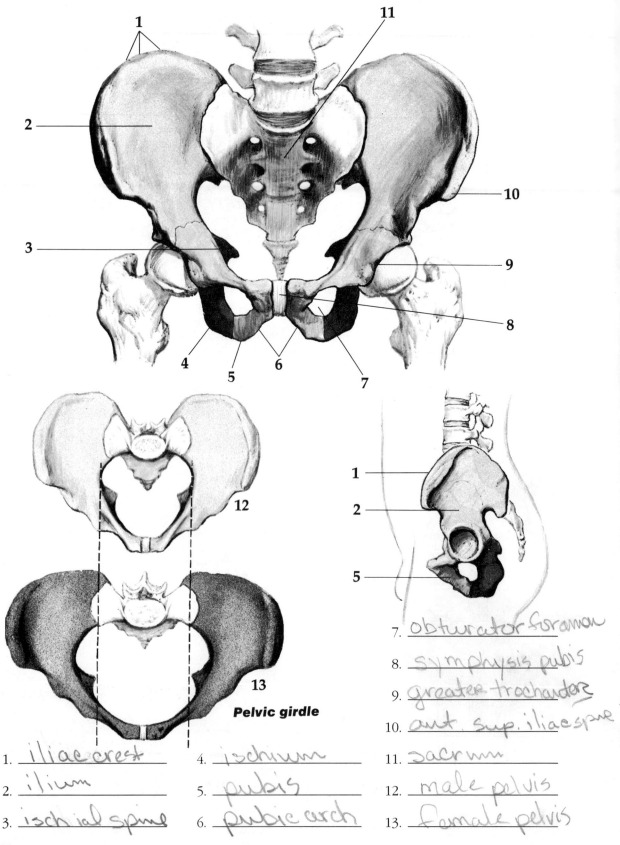

Pelvic girdle

1. iliac crest
2. ilium
3. ischial spine
4. ischium
5. pubis
6. pubic arch
7. obturator foramen
8. symphysis pubis
9. greater trochanter
10. ant. sup. iliac spine
11. sacrum
12. male pelvis
13. female pelvis

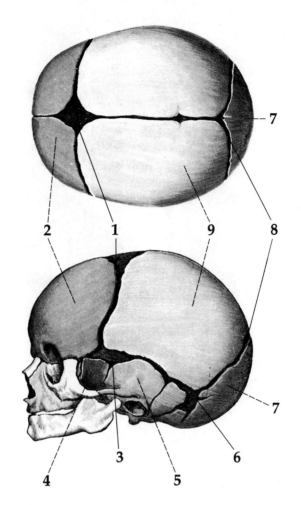

Infant skull, showing fontanels

1. frontal
2. anterior fontanel
3. sphenoid fontanel
4. sphenoid bone
5. temporal
6. mastoid fontanel
7. occipital
8. post. fontanel
9. parietal

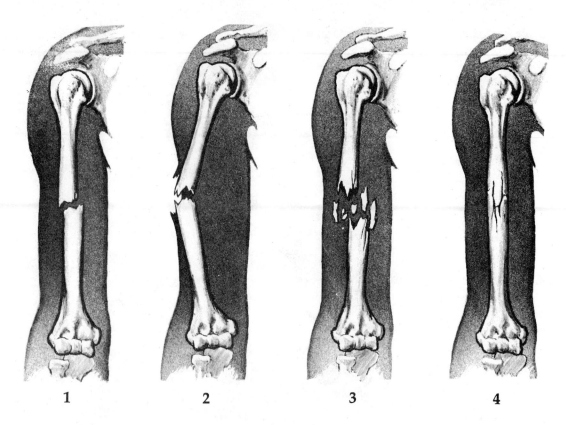

1 **2** **3** **4**

Types of fractures

1. ___Simple___   3. ___comminuted___

2. ___Compound___   4. ___Green stick___

V. Completion Exercise

Print the word or phrase that correctly completes each sentence.

1. During development, secondary bone-forming centers appear across the ends of the long bones. Each end of a long bone is called a(n) _____

2. When bone-forming cells mature and become enclosed in hardened bone material, they are referred to as _____

3. In the embryonic stage of bone development, most of the developing bones are made of _____

4. When bone is resorbed, cells that break down bone become active; these cells are called _____

5. The type of bone tissue that makes up the shaft of a long bone is called _____

6. The hardening of a long bone begins at the center of the

      _____

7. The skull, vertebrae, ribs, and sternum make up the part of the skeleton called the

      _____

8. The cervical and lumbar curves, which appear after birth, are referred to as

      _____

9. A suture is an example of an immovable joint also called a(n)

      _____

10. Pivot, hinge, and gliding joints are examples of freely movable joints also called

      _____

VI. Practical Applications

Study each discussion, then print the appropriate word or phrase in the space provided.

Group A

A group of high school seniors was involved in a serious traffic accident on the way home from the prom.

1. There was a pronounced swelling of the upper right side of Mary's head. X-ray films showed a fracture of the largest skull bone, the

      _____

2. Mary also suffered an injury to one of the two large bones of the pelvic girdle. This bone articulates with the sacrum and is named the

      _____

3. John suffered multiple injuries to his left lower extremity. Protruding through the skin was a splintered portion of the longest bone in the body, the

      _____

4. Susan thought her injuries were the least serious, so she walked several blocks to find help. Then she noticed that her right knee was not functioning normally. Examination revealed a fractured kneecap. Another name for the kneecap is

      _____

5. Harry, the driver of the car, was forcibly thrown against the steering wheel. He suffered fractures of the sixth and seventh ribs, which are included among the

      _____

Group B

Mr. B, age 58, was admitted to the general hospital because of acute pain and swelling of his right great toe. He also complained of a chronic backache. Mr. B underwent a complete physical examination.

1. Mr. B suffered from a disorder of metabolism in which uric acid accumulated in the blood and uric acid crystals were deposited in the joints of his right great toe. This disorder is called

      _____

2. X-ray films showed involvement of the toe joints. The framework of the toes is made up of bones called the

     _____

3. Spurs of bony material were found to be present at the edges of the vertebrae just above the sacrum, which is the part of the spinal column called the

     _____

Group C

Mrs. C, age 36, visited her doctor's office because of swelling and pain in the joints of her hands and fingers. Examination revealed the following:

1. Evidence of inflammation and overgrowth of the lining membrane of the joint cavities, a membrane that is called the

     _____

2. Difficulty in moving the joints of the fingers due to damage to the normally smooth gristle on the joint surface. This layer is called the

     _____

3. That Mrs. C was probably suffering from the common disorder called

     _____

8

The Muscular System

I. Overview

The muscular system is composed of some 600 individual muscles, each of which is a distinct organ. Muscles usually work in groups to execute a body movement. The muscle that produces a given movement is called the **prime mover**; the muscle that produces the opposite action is the **antagonist**. There are three basic types of muscle tissue: **skeletal, smooth,** and **cardiac**. The focus of this chapter is skeletal muscle, which is attached to bones. Skeletal muscle is also called voluntary muscle, because normally it is under the conscious control of the will.

Skeletal muscles are activated by electrical impulses from the nervous system. A nerve fiber makes contact with a muscle cell at the **neuromuscular junction**. From this point, the impulse spreads along the muscle cell membrane, producing an electrical change called the **action potential**. As a result of this electrical change in the cells, the muscle can contract (shorten) to produce movement.

Muscle contraction occurs by the sliding together of protein filaments called **actin** and **myosin** within the cell. These filaments make contact only in the presence of calcium, which is released from the endoplasmic reticulum of the muscle cell when the action potential spreads along the cell membrane. **ATP** is the direct source of energy for the contraction. In order to manufacture ATP the cell must have adequate supplies of glucose and oxygen delivered by the blood. A reserve supply of glucose is stored in muscle cells in the form of a compound called **glycogen**, and additional oxygen is stored by a pigment in the cells called **myoglobin**.

When muscles do not receive enough oxygen, as during strenuous activity, they can produce a small amount of ATP and continue to function for a short period. As a result, however, the cells produce lactic acid which eventually causes muscle fatigue. The individual must then rest and continue to breathe in oxygen, which is used to convert the lactic acid into other substances. The amount of oxygen needed for this purpose is referred to as the **oxygen debt**.

Muscles act with the bones of the skeleton as **lever systems**, in which the joint is the pivot point or **fulcrum**. Exercise and proper body mechanics help in maintaining muscle health and effectiveness. Continued activity delays the undesirable effects of aging.

II. Topics for Review

A. General characteristics of skeletal muscles
B. The mechanism of muscle contraction
C. Muscle attachments
D. Muscle movement
E. Muscles of the head and the neck
F. Muscles of the upper extremities
G. Muscles of the trunk
H. Muscles of the lower extremities
I. Muscle metabolism during exercise
J. Body mechanics
K. Disorders of muscles

III. Matching Exercises

Matching only within each group, print the answers in the spaces provided.

Group A

action potential   contractility   excitability
neuromuscular junction   isotonic   tonus
isometric

1. The capacity of a muscle to respond to a stimulus is known as _excitability_

2. The point where a motor nerve fiber contacts a muscle cell is called the _motorendplate_ _neuro musclar junction_

3. Following stimulation of a muscle cell, the electrical change transmitted along the cell membrane is called a(n) _action potential_

4. The capacity of a muscle fiber to undergo shortening is called _contractility_

5. The normal partially contracted state of muscles is called _tonus_

6. Muscle contractions in which the tone remains constant while the muscle shortens are _isotonic_

7. Those contractions in which there is a great increase in muscle tension without change in muscle length are called _isometric_

Group B

glycogen   actin   lactic acid
calcium   myoglobin   oxygen
ATP

1. The substance that accumulates in muscles working without enough oxygen is _lactic acid_

2. The ion that must be released into the muscle cell before contraction is

calcium

3. The immediate source of energy for muscle contraction is a substance called

atp

4. The compound that stores glucose in muscle cells is

glycogen

5. A protein filament needed to produce contraction in muscle cells is

actin

6. During vigorous exercise muscles build up a need for

oxygen

7. The compound that stores oxygen in muscle cells is

myoglobin

Group C

vasodilation   myosin ✓   prime mover ✓
antagonist   origin ✓   insertion ✓

1. The muscle that produces a given movement is the

Prime mover

2. The end of a muscle that puts a body part into action is the

insertion

3. A need for oxygen in muscle tissue produces a change in the blood vessels that brings more blood to the tissues. This change is called

vasodilation

4. The end of a muscle attached to a more fixed part of the body is the

origin

5. A protein needed for contraction in muscle cells is

myosin

6. The muscle that must relax during a given movement is the

antagonist

Group D

biceps brachii ✓   pectoralis major ✓   deltoid ✓
latissimus dorsi ✓   triceps brachii ✓   trapezius ✓
sternocleidomastoids ✓   axilla

1. Working together, the two muscles on either side of the neck flex the head on the chest. They are the

sternocleidomastoids

2. Movement of the shoulder is a function of the

trapezius

3. A powerful extensor of the arm (at the shoulder) used in swimming is the

latissimus dorsi

4. The muscle capping the shoulder and upper arm, often used as an injection site, is the

deltoid

5. A muscle on the front of the arm acts as a flexor of the elbow and a supinator of the hand. It is the

biceps

6. The large muscle on the back of the arm extends the elbow, as when delivering a blow (in boxing). Since it has three origins, it is called the

triceps

7. The large muscle of the upper chest flexes the arm across the body; it is called the

pectoralis major

8. The pectoralis major and the latissimus dorsi both form part of the walls of the

axilla

Group E

gastrocnemius   levator ani   epimysium
aponeurosis   tendons   diaphragm
torticollis

1. Muscles may be attached to bone by cordlike structures called

tendon

2. Some muscles are attached to bone by a sheet of

aponeuroiss

3. The connective sheath enclosing an entire muscle is the

epimysium

4. The chief muscle of respiration is the

diaphragm

5. The chief muscle of the calf of the leg is the

gastrocnemius

6. The muscle of the pelvic floor that aids in defecation is the

levator ani

7. Injury or spasm of a sternomastoid muscle may cause a condition called

torticollis

Group F

sacrospinalis   intercostals   gluteus maximus
buccinator   sartorius   quadriceps femoris
iliopsoas

1. Located between the ribs are muscles that aid in respiration, called the

intercostals

2. The muscle that forms the fleshy part of the cheek is the

buccinator

3. The longest muscle of the spine is the

sacrospinalis

4. Much of the fleshy part of the buttock is formed by the

gluteus max.

5. The powerful flexor of the thigh is the

iliopsoas

6. The muscle that extends the knee, as in kicking a ball, is the

quadriceps femoris

7. The thin muscle that travels down and across the medial surface of the thigh is the

sartorius

Group G

muscular dystrophy   ptosis   atrophy
myositis   bursitis   myalgia

1. A term that means muscular pain is   *myalgia*

2. A progressive muscle disorder that is more frequent in male children and often leads to complete helplessness is called   *musc. dyst.*

3. A common early symptom of myasthenia is drooping of the eyelids, or   *ptosis*

4. Inflammation of a synovial fluid sac is   *bursitis*

5. A wasting or decrease in the size of a muscle, usually from lack of activity is   *atrophy*

6. Acute inflammation of muscle tissue is   *myositis*

IV. Labeling

For each labeled muscle in the following drawings print the name on the appropriate numbered lines.

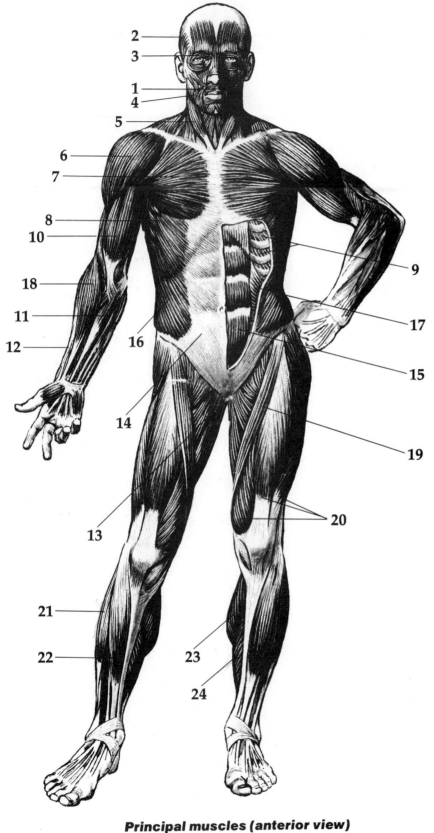

Principal muscles (anterior view)

1. orbicularis oris
2. temporalis
3. orbicularis oculi
4. ~~triangularis~~ *masseter*
5. sternocleidomastoid
6. deltoid
7. pectoralis major
8. biceps brachii
9. intercostals
10. biceps
11. flexor carpi
12. extensor 4
13. adductor longus
14. abdominal apon.
15. rectus abdominis
16. external oblique
17. internal oblique
18. brachio radialis ~~extensor carpi~~
19. sartorius
20. quadriceps
21. peroneus longus
22. tibialis
23. gastronemius
24. soleus

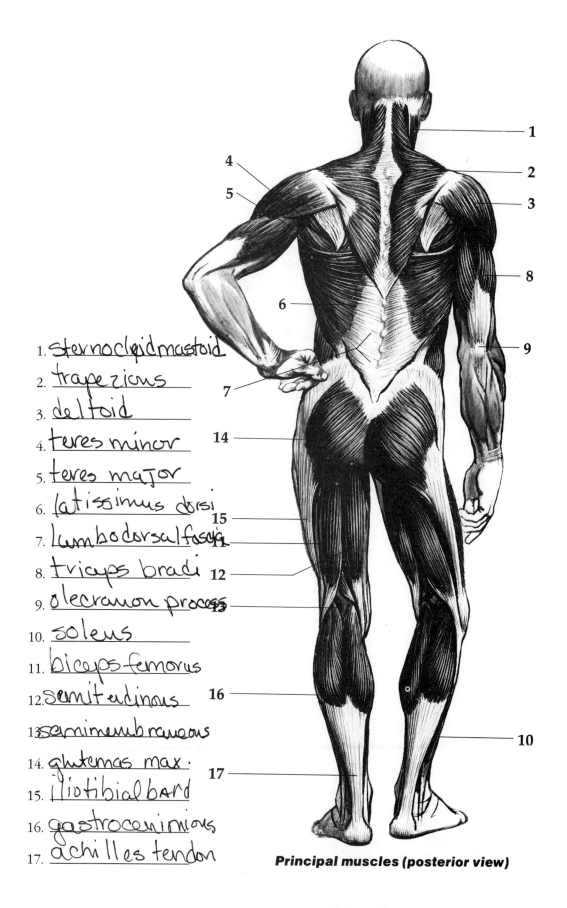

1. sternocleidmastoid
2. trapezious
3. deltoid
4. teres minor
5. teres major
6. latissimus dorsi
7. lumbodorsalfascia
8. triceps bradi
9. olecranon process
10. soleus
11. biceps femorus
12. semitedinous
13. semimembraneous
14. glutemas max.
15. iliotibial bard
16. gastrocenimious
17. achilles tendon

Principal muscles (posterior view)

85

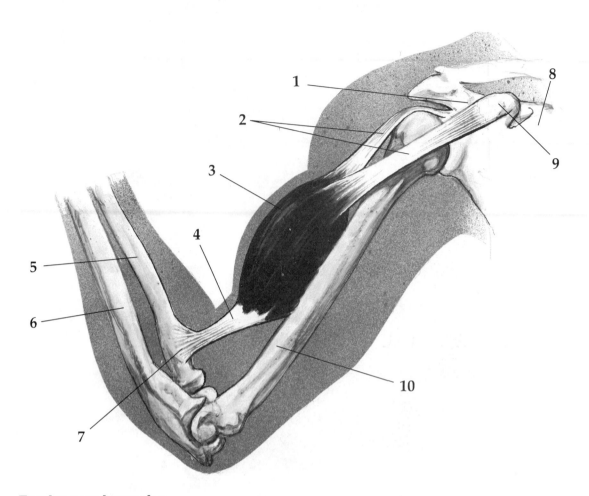

Tendons and muscles

1. origin   6. ulna

2. tendons   7. insertion

3. biceps   8. scapula

4. tendon   9. origin

5. radius   10. humerous

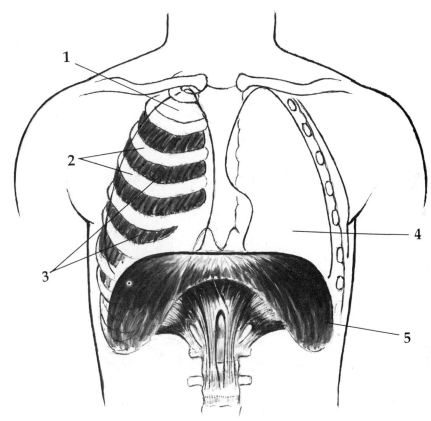

Location of diaphragm

1. right lung

2. ribs

3. inter costal muscles

4. lef lung

5. diaphragm

V.   Completion Exercise

Print the word or phrase that completes each sentence.

1. Normally, muscles are in a partially contracted state, even though they are not in use at the time. This state of mild constant tension is called

   tonus

2. A movement is initiated by a muscle or set of muscles called the

   prinemove

3. The end of a muscle that is attached to a part moved by that muscle is the

   insertion

4. The muscle of the lips is the

   obicularis oris

5. Muscles functioning without enough oxygen fatigue as a result of the accumulation of

   lactic acid

6. The muscle attachment that is usually relatively fixed is called its

origin

7. The movement of a prime mover is opposed by a muscle or set of muscles called the

antagonist

8. A group of muscles that covers the front and sides of the femur and extends the leg is the

quadricep femoris

9. There are four pairs of muscles for chewing. The muscle located at the angle of the jaw is called the

masseter

10. A superficial muscle of the neck and upper back acts on the shoulder. This muscle is the

trapezious

11. The muscle on the front of the leg that raises the sole of the foot (dorsiflexion) is the

tibialis is

12. The largest forearm extensor is the

bicep tricep

13. The muscular partition between the thoracic and abdominal cavities is the

diapragm

14. The large fleshy muscle of the buttocks which extends the hip is the

gluteuou max.

15. The chief muscle of the calf is the toe dancer's muscle, named the

gastrocenimus

16. The band of connective tissue that attaches the gastrocnemius muscle to the heel is the

achilles tendon

17. The muscle that turns the sole of the foot outward (eversion) is the

peroneus

VI. Practical Applications

Study each discussion. Then print the appropriate word or phrase in the space provided.

Group A

Driver J and his three companions tried to race an oncoming train to an intersection. J misjudged the speed of the train, and the train crashed into the car. All four occupants of the car received multiple injuries.

1. Driver J was thrown against the steering wheel, which punctured his chest. This puncture involved the muscles between the ribs, called the

2. Mr. K, the occupant sitting next to the driver, suffered facial injuries, in which the muscle that encircles the eye was cut. This muscle is called the

3. Ms. L was thrown out of the car and received lacerations and fractures of the lower extremities, including the calf of the leg. The largest muscle of the leg is the _____

4. Mr. M received shoulder and upper back lacerations. They involved the muscle that covers the shoulder and abducts the arm, the _____

Group B

In the physical therapy department several patients were receiving physical therapy for muscle injuries.

1. Mrs. K had suffered a stroke that involved the left lower extremity. One of the large muscles used in standing forms most of the buttock, and is named the _____

2. Mr. P had suffered a fracture of the humerus and was receiving treatment for the damage to the large extensor of the elbow, located on the dorsal part of the arm. This muscle is the _____

3. Ms. L had been in a cast for a number of weeks, so she was receiving exercises for the strengthening of many body muscles, including the large muscle that originates from the middle and lower back and inserts on the arm bone (humerus). This strong swimming muscle is the _____

4. Ms. R, age 76, came in for exercises to strengthen some of her extensor muscles to prevent the further development of kyphosis. The large extensor muscle of the back needed particular attention. This is the _____

9

The Nervous System

I. Overview

The nervous system is the body's coordinating system, receiving, sorting out, and responding to both internal and external stimuli. The mechanism by which these activities occur is the **nerve impulse**, an electrical current which spreads along the membrane of the nerve cell or **neuron**. Each neuron is composed of a cell body and nerve fibers which extend from the cell body. **Dendrites** are fibers which carry impulses toward the cell body, and **axons** are fibers which carry impulses away from the cell body. Some axons are covered with a sheath of fatty material called **myelin** which insulates the fiber and speeds conduction along the fiber. Nerve cells make contact at junctions called **synapses**; the nerve impulse travels across the synapse by means of chemicals referred to as **neurotransmitters**. A neuron may be classified as either a sensory (afferent) type, which carries impulses toward the central nervous system, or a motor (efferent) type, which carries impulses away from the central nervous system. There are also connecting neurons within the central nervous system.

The nervous system as a whole is divided into the **central nervous system**, made up of the brain and the spinal cord, and the **peripheral nervous system**, made up of the cranial and spinal nerves. The brain consists of the cerebral hemispheres, diencephalon, brain stem, and cerebellum, each with specific functions. The spinal cord carries impulses to and from the brain. It is also a center for simple reflex activities in which responses are coordinated within the cord without traveling to the brain.

The brain and spinal cord are covered with three layers of fibrous membranes, the **meninges**. Also protecting these central structures is the **cerebrospinal fluid** produced in the ventricles of the brain.

Peripheral nerves, including the 12 pairs of cranial nerves and the 31 pairs of spinal nerves, connect all parts of the body with the central nervous system. Certain nerves within this system are grouped together as the **autonomic nervous system** which controls activities that go on more or less automatically. This system regulates the actions of glands, smooth muscle, and the heart. The autonomic nervous system has two divisions, the **sympathetic** and **parasympathetic** nervous systems, which have opposite effects on given organs.

II. Topics for Review

A. The function of nerve tissue
  1. The nerve cell and its fibers
  2. The nerve impulse
  3. Nerves
B. Divisions of the nervous system
  1. Central nervous system
  2. Peripheral nervous system
  3. Autonomic nervous system
C. Central nervous system
  1. Brain
    a. Cerebral hemispheres
    b. Diencephalon
    c. Brain stem
    d. Cerebellum
  2. Spinal cord
    a. Structure
    b. Function
    c. Lumbar puncture
  3. Coverings of the brain and spinal cord
  4. Cerebrospinal fluid
D. Disorders of the brain and spinal cord
E. Peripheral nervous system
  1. Cranial nerves
  2. Spinal nerves
F. Autonomic nervous system
  1. Structure
  2. Functions

III. Matching Exercises

Matching only within each group, print the answers in the spaces provided

Group A

brain and spinal cord   brain stem   nerve
autonomic nervous system   peripheral nervous system   coordination
stimuli   cerebral hemispheres

1. The main function of the nervous system is   *coordination*

2. The internal and external changes that affect the nervous system   *stimuli*
   are called

3. For study purposes, the entire nervous system has been divided   *brain + spinal*
   into two large systems. One of these, the central nervous system,   *cord*
   is composed of the

4. The cranial and spinal nerves constitute the _peripheral system_

5. The cerebrum is the largest part of the brain. It is divided into right and left parts called the _hemispheres_

6. The midbrain, pons, and medulla oblongata form the _brain stem_

7. The peripheral nerves that regulate activities going on more or less automatically are grouped together as the _autonomic nervous system_

8. Impulses are conducted from one place to another by a bundle of nerve fibers, the _nerve_

Group B

neuron   nerve impulse   mixed
reflex   nerve fibers   autonomic nervous system
neurilemma   dendrite   synapse

1. Most nerves contain both afferent and efferent fibers and are thus described as _mixed_

2. The nerve cell, including the cell body and its projections, is a(n) _neuron_

3. The sympathetic and parasympathetic nervous systems are the two functionally opposing parts of the _autonomic_

4. The threadlike cytoplasmic projections of the nerve cell are the _nerve fibers_

5. An electrical charge which spreads along the membrane of a nerve cell is the _nerve impulse_

6. A nerve fiber that carries impulses toward the cell body is a(n) _dendrite_

7. A nervous response that is coordinated within the spinal cord is termed a(n) _reflex_

8. The point of junction between two neurons is a(n) _synapse_

9. A sheath around some axons that aids in regeneration is the _neurilemma_

Group C

fissure   lobes   afferent
receptor   gyri   motor
cerebral cortex ventricles   neurotransmitter

1. The point at which a stimulus is received is called the _receptor_

2. A chemical that carries the nerve impulse across a synapse is a(n) _neurotransmitter_

3. Impulses must be carried to and away from the brain and spinal cord. Neurons that conduct impulses to the brain and cord are described as _afferent_

fissure *cerebral cortex* *lobes* *gyri* *ventricles* *motor*

4. Nerves that carry impulses away from the brain and cord to muscles and glands are classified as _____

5. All thought, association, and judgment take place in the — cerebral cortex

6. The deep groove that divides the main part of the cerebrum into two hemispheres is the longitudinal — fissure

7. The sulci serve to separate the gray matter into elevated portions known as — gyri

8. Cerebrospinal fluid is produced in spaces within the brain called — ventricles

9. Each hemisphere of the brain is divided into regions, each of which regulates certain types of functions. These areas are called — lobes

Group D

corpus callosum   motor cortex   parietal lobe
occipital lobe   meninges   myelin
temporal lobe   thalamus

1. In the disorder known as multiple sclerosis there is degeneration of the fatlike substance that covers many nerve fibers. This sheath is composed of — myelin

2. The three brain coverings are collectively known as the — meninges

3. In each frontal lobe is an area that controls voluntary muscles. This is the — motor cortex

4. Pain, touch, and temperature are interpreted in the sensory area which is contained in the — parietal lobe

5. Impulses received by the ear are interpreted in the auditory center, which is located in the — temporal

6. Messages from the retina are interpreted in the visual area of the — occipital

7. A band of white matter which acts as a bridge between the cerebral hemispheres is the — corpus callosum

8. Two masses of gray matter which are located in the diencephalon act as relay centers monitoring sensory stimuli. These two masses constitute the — thalamus

Group E

cerebrum   corpora quadrigemina   diencephalon
electroencephalograph   CT scan   medulla oblongata
blood pressure   cerebellum   hypothalamus

1. The part of the brain that contains the thalamus and the hypothalamus is the — diencephalon

2. The portion of the brain that coordinates voluntary muscles and helps to maintain balance is the

Cerebellum

3. The two cerebral hemispheres form much of the largest part of the brain, the

cerebrum

4. The respiratory, cardiac, and vasomotor centers are found in the

5. The vasomotor center affects muscles in the blood vessel walls and thus influences *blood pressure*

medulla oblongata

6. A three-dimensional x-ray of the brain is a

CT Scan

7. The measurable electric currents produced by the activity of the brain cells are recorded by the

electroencephalograph

8. Body temperature, sleep, the heartbeat, and water balance are among the vital body functions regulated by the

hypothalamus

9. The relay centers for eye and ear reflexes are located in the midbrain. They are the four

Group F

epilepsy	cerebral palsy	cerebrovascular accident
aphasia	encephalitis	paraplegia

1. The rupture of a blood vessel, thrombosis, or embolism that causes destruction of brain tissue may be referred to as a stroke, cerebral apoplexy, or a(n)

cer. CVA

2. Abnormalities of brain function without apparent changes in nerve tissues are characteristic of a chronic disorder called

epilepsy

3. A congenital disorder characterized by muscle involvement ranging from weakness to paralysis is known as

cerebral palsy

4. The general term referring to inflammation of the brain is

encephalitis

5. A spinal cord injury in which there is loss of sensation and of motion in the lower part of the body may result in

paraplegia

6. When referring to loss of the power of expression by speech or writing, we use the term

aphasia

Group G

afferent nerves ✓	white matter ✓	efferent nerves ✓
receptor	effector ✓	dorsal root ✓

1. Myelinated fibers make up the regions of the central nervous system described as

white matter

2. The cell bodies of sensory neurons are located in a ganglion on the

dorsal root

3. The spinal cord has several essential functions. One of these is to conduct sensory impulses upward to the brain in tracts within the cord. These impulses are brought to the cord by

afferent

4. The spinal cord also functions as a pathway for conducting motor impulses from the brain downward in descending tracts. These motor impulses leave the cord by way of

efferent

5. The reflex pathway begins with the part of a sensory neuron called a(n)

receptor

6. The sensory neuron conducts an impulse to a central neuron which then transfers it to a motor neuron. This typical reflex pathway terminates in a gland or a muscle termed a(n)

effector

Group H

dura mater	arachnoid membrane	pia mater
meningitis	choroid plexuses	subarachnoid space
arachnoid villi	hydrocephalus	gliomas

1. The innermost layer of the meninges, the delicate connective tissue membrane in which there are many blood vessels, is the

pia mater

2. The weblike middle meningeal layer is the

arachnoid

3. The outermost meningeal layer, which is the thickest and toughest, is also made of connective tissue. It is the

meningitis

4. Inflammation of the brain coverings due to diplococci or other pathogenic bacteria is called

dura mater

5. The majority of brain tumors are derived from the neuroglia and are called

gliomas

6. Normally, the cerebrospinal fluid helps protect the brain and spinal cord against shock. This fluid is formed inside the brain ventricles by the

choroid plexuses

7. Normally, the fluid flows freely from ventricle to ventricle and finally out into the

subarachnoid

8. The fluid is returned to the blood in the venous sinuses through the projections called

arachnoid villi

9. Any obstruction to the normal flow of cerebrospinal fluid may give rise to

hydrocephalus

Group I

visual area	auditory speech center	visual speech center
written speech center	sensory area	left cerebrum

1. Pain, touch, temperature, size, and shape are interpreted in the parietal lobe, in a section called the

sensory area

2. The understanding of words takes place with the development of a temporal lobe area known as the

auditory speech

3. The muscles in the right side of the body are controlled by the

left cerebrum

4. Messages from the retina are interpreted in the region of the occipital lobe known as the

visual area

5. The ability to read with understanding comes with the development of the

visual speech center

6. The ability to write words, which usually is a late phase in a person's total language comprehension, is a function of the

written speech center

Group J

ganglion   plexuses   brachial plexus
cervical plexus   roots   visceral nervous system
somatic nervous system

1. Each spinal nerve is attached to the spinal cord by branches called

plexuses

2. Involuntary control over smooth muscles, glands, and the heart is brought about by the

visceral

3. A collection of nerve cell bodies usually found outside the central nervous system is a(n)

ganglion

4. A short distance away from the spinal cord, each spinal nerve branches into two divisions; the branches of the larger division interlace to form

roots

5. The shoulder, the arm, the wrist, and the hand are supplied by branches from the

brachial plexus

6. Motor impulses to the neck muscles are supplied by the

cervical plexus

7. Skeletal muscles are controlled by the

somatic

Group K

parasympathetic nervous   olfactory nerve   facial nerve
    system   vagus nerve   oculomotor nerve
sympathetic nervous system   vestibulocochlear nerve trigeminal nerve
hypoglossal nerve   optic nerve

1. Recall the functions of the autonomic nervous system. The part that acts to prepare the body for emergency situations is the

sympathetic

2. The part of the autonomic nervous system that aids the digestive process is the

parasym.

3. Impulses controlling tongue muscles are carried by the

hypoglossal

4. General sense impulses from the face and head are carried through the three branches of the _____*trigeminal*_____

5. Sense fibers for hearing are contained within the _____*vestibulocochlear*_____

6. The muscles of facial expression are supplied by branches of the _____*facial*_____

7. The nerve that carries smell impulses to the brain is the _____*olfactory*_____

8. The contraction of most eye muscles is controlled by the _____*oculomotor*_____

9. The sensory nerve that carries visual impulses is the _____*optic*_____

10. Most of the organs in the thoracic and abdominal cavities are supplied by the _____*vagus*_____

IV. Labeling

For each of the following illustrations, print the name or names of each labeled part on the numbered lines.

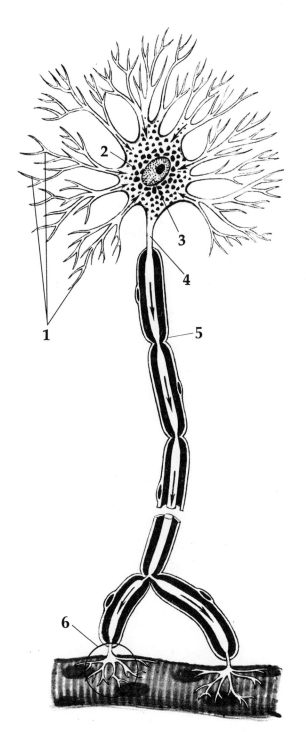

Diagram of a motor neuron

1. dendridtes
2. cell body
3. nucleus
4. nerve fiber (axon)
5. node
6. neuro muscular junction

99

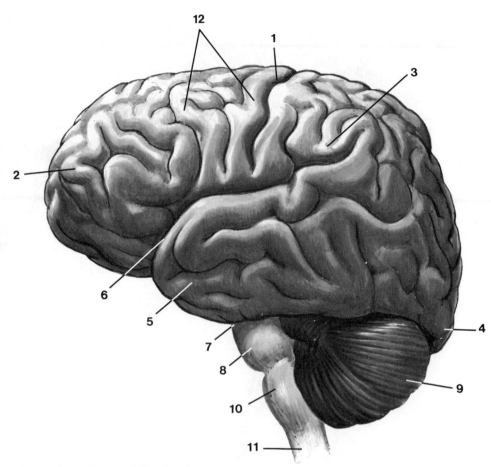

The external surface of the brain

1. _____   7. _____

2. _____   8. _____

3. _____   9. _____

4. _____   10. _____

5. _____   11. _____

6. _____   12. _____

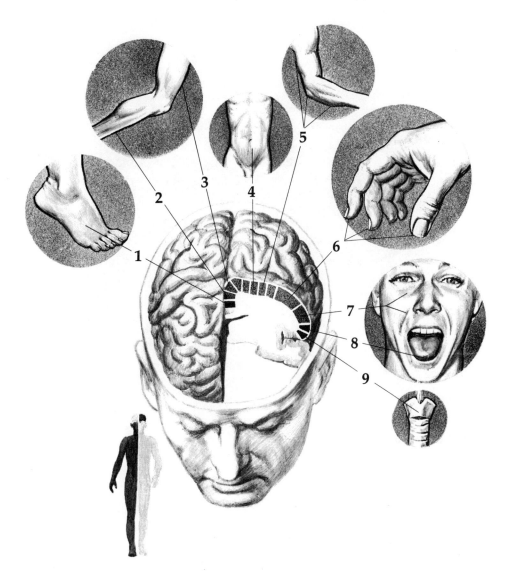

The motor area of the left cerebral hemisphere

1. _____

2. _____

3. _____

4. _____

5. _____

6. _____

7. _____

8. _____

9. _____

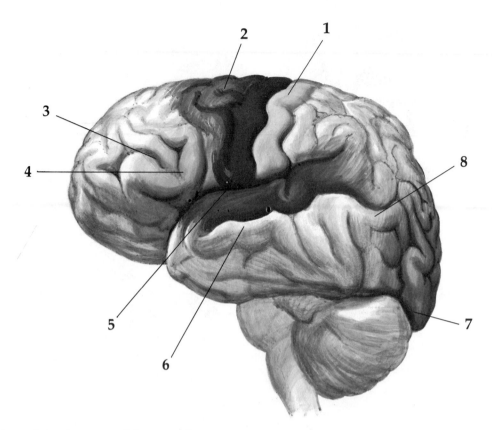

The functional areas of the cerebrum

1. _____

2. _____

3. _____

4. _____

5. _____

6. _____

7. _____

8. _____

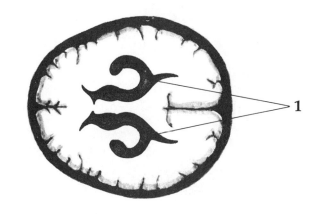

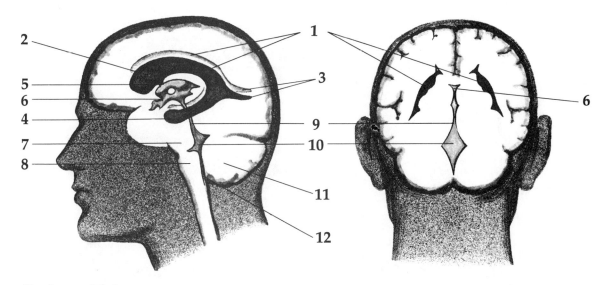

Brain ventricles

1. _____   7. _____

2. _____   8. _____

3. _____   9. _____

4. _____   10. _____

5. _____   11. _____

6. _____   12. _____

1. _____
2. _____
3. _____
4. _____
5. _____
6. _____
7. _____
8. _____

9. _____
10. _____
11. _____
12. _____
13. _____
14. _____
15. _____

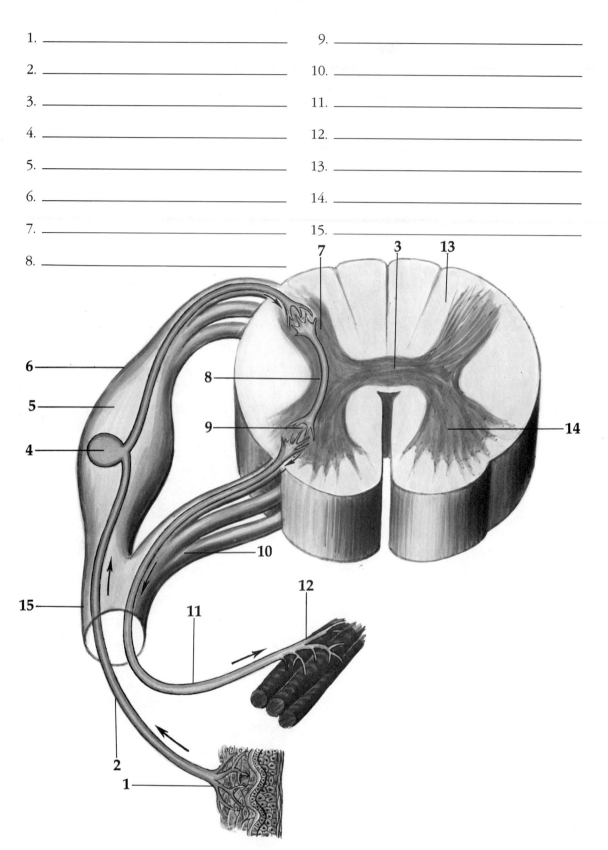

Reflex arc and cross section of spinal cord

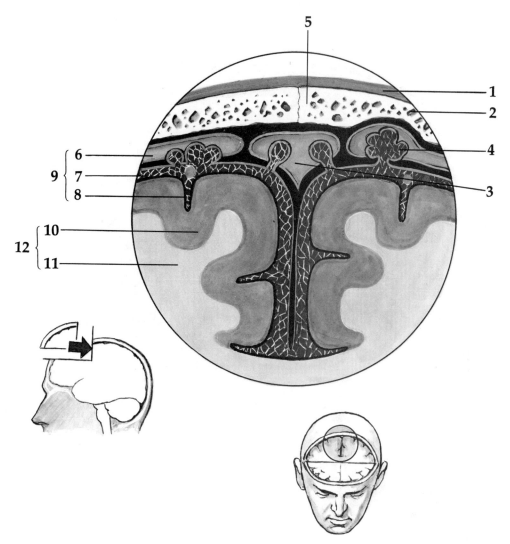

Frontal (coronal) section of top of head to show meninges and related parts

1. _____

2. _____

3. _____

4. _____

5. _____

6. _____

7. _____

8. _____

9. _____

10. _____

11. _____

12. _____

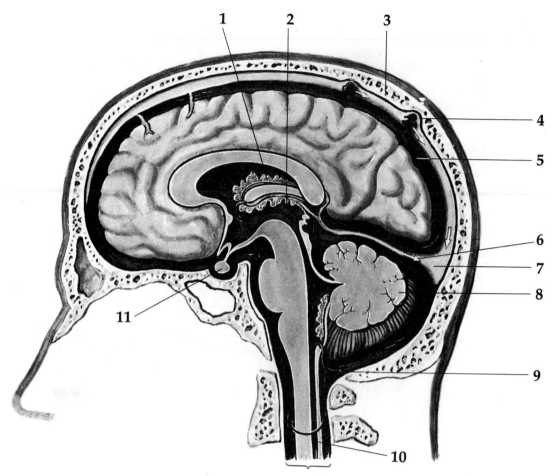

Flow of cerebrospinal fluid

1. _____   7. _____

2. _____   8. _____

3. _____   9. _____

4. _____   10. _____

5. _____   11. _____

6. _____

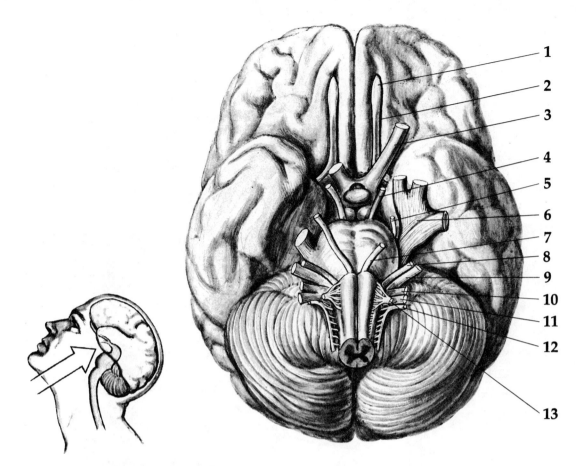

Base of brain, showing cranial nerves

1. _____

2. _____

3. _____

4. _____

5. _____

6. _____

7. _____

8. _____

9. _____

10. _____

11. _____

12. _____

13. _____

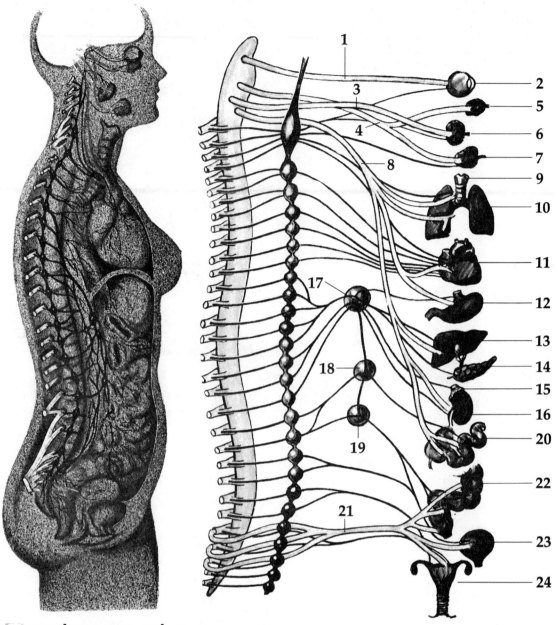

Autonomic nervous system

1. _____

2. _____

3. _____

4. _____

5. _____

6. _____

7. _____

8. _____

9. _____

10. _____

11. _____

12. _____

13. _____

14. _____

15. _____

16. _____

17. _____

18. _____

| 19. _____ | 21. _____ | 23. _____ |
| 20. _____ | 22. _____ | 24. _____ |

V. Completion Exercise

Print the word or phrase that correctly completes each sentence.

1. The brain and spinal cord together are usually referred to as the   _____

2. The cranial and spinal nerves together form the part of the nervous system described as the   _____

3. Activities of the body that go on automatically are under control of the   _____

4. A nerve cell is also called a(n)   _____

5. A nerve fiber that conducts impulses away from the cell body is a(n)   _____

6. A specialized nerve ending that can detect a stimulus is a(n)   _____

7. When referring to inflammation of a nerve, we often use the term   _____

8. The largest branch of the lumbrosacral plexus is the   _____

9. The slightly curved groove or depression along the side of the brain which separates the temporal lobe from the rest of the cerebral hemisphere is the   _____

10. The fluid-filled spaces within the cerebral hemispheres are the   _____

11. Through a large opening in the base of the skull, the spinal cord connects with a part of the brain called the   _____

12. Collections of cell bodies within the central nervous system are called   _____

13. Unmyelinated fibers and cell bodies make up the portions of the central nervous system described as the   _____

VI. Practical Applications

Study each discussion. Then print the appropriate word or phrase in the space provided.

1. Eight-year-old K was brought to the clinic because he had fallen during an epileptic seizure. There was bleeding from a scalp wound and some evidence of a subarachnoid hemorrhage. To aid in making a diagnosis the physician ordered a study of the boy's cerebrospinal fluid. This fluid is obtained by doing a   _____

2. Mrs. M's son found his mother lying unconscious on the floor. Mrs. M was 67 years old and had a history of high blood pressure. She was admitted to the intensive care unit. She was unable to speak or write, or to understand written or spoken language, so she was said to be suffering from   _____

3. Mr. H, age 42, had been suffering for several weeks from persistent, intractable headaches. An x-ray study of the brain was ordered. Such an x-ray film is called an   _____

4. Some of the fluid was removed from the ventricles in Mr. H's brain and replaced with air, as part of the diagnostic study. This fluid is the   _____

5. As a result of the various studies done in Mr. H's case, it was determined that a tumor was present in the left lateral ventricle. Surrounding the left ventricle is the   _____

6. Ms. S's symptoms included paralysis and various motor disturbances. The diagnosis of myelitis, or inflammation of the spinal cord, was made. This nerve cord is located in a space called the   _____

7. Mrs. J, age 60, was brought to the hospital with a diagnosis of stroke. In order to determine the location and extent of the hemorrhage, a test that uses high-frequency sound impulses (echoencephalography) was done. It was found that there was damage on the left side of the brain which accounted for the paralysis of the opposite side of the body, a condition called   _____

8. Young A, age 10, was brought to the emergency clinic following a bicycle accident in which he received trauma to his head. Diagnostic studies included a CT (computed tomography) scan of the head. The purpose of this study was to detect any tears in the brain coverings such that blood could collect in the space between the brain and the skull. The tough outer covering of the brain and cord is called the   _____

10

The Sensory System

I. Overview

Through the functioning of the **sensory receptors**, we are made aware of changes taking place both internally (within the body) and externally (outside the body). Any change that produces a response in the nervous system is termed a **stimulus**.

The **special senses**, so-called because the receptors are limited to a relatively small area of the body, include the vision sense, the hearing sense, and the senses of taste and smell. The receptors of the eye are the **rods and cones** located in the retina. The hearing receptors are found in a portion of the inner ear called the **cochlea**. Receptors for the chemical senses of taste and smell are located on the tongue and in the upper part of the nose respectively.

The **general senses** are scattered throughout the body; they have to do with pressure, temperature, pain, touch, and position. Receptors for the sense of position, known as **proprioceptors**, are found in muscles, tendons, and joints.

The nerve impulses generated in a receptor cell by a stimulus must be carried to the central nervous system by way of a sensory (afferent) neuron. Here the information is processed and a suitable response is made.

II. Topics for Review

A. The eye
   1. Protective structures of eyeball
   2. Coats of eyeball
   3. Pathway of light rays
   4. Sensory receptors
   5. Extrinsic eyeball muscles
   6. Intrinsic eyeball muscles
   7. Nerve supply to the eye

8. Lacrimal apparatus
9. Disorders and defects of the eye
B. The ear
   1. External ear; pinna and auditory canal
   2. Middle ear
   3. Internal ear
   4. Disorders of the ear
C. Other organs of special sense
   1. Taste receptors
   2. Smell receptors
D. General senses
   1. Pressure
   2. Temperature
   3. Touch
   4. Pain
   5. Position

III. Matching Exercises

Matching only within each group, print the answers in the spaces provided. The same answer may be used more than once.

Group A

| cornea | retina | rods and cones | choroid coat |
| accommodation | aqueous humor | vitreous body | color |

1. The innermost coat of the eyeball, the nerve tissue layer, includes the receptors for the sense of vision. This structure is the   retina

2. The pigmented middle tunic of the eyeball is the vascular   choroid c.

3. Light rays pass through a series of transparent eye parts. The outermost of these is the   cornea

4. The watery fluid that fills much of the eyeball in front of the crystalline lens and also helps to maintain the slight curve in the cornea is the   aqueous

5. The spherical shape of the eyeball is maintained by a jellylike material located behind the crystalline lens. This is the   vitreous

6. The receptors for the sense of vision are called the   rods & cones

7. There are three types of cones, each of which is sensitive to a different   color

8. The elasticity of the lens enables it to become thicker and bend the light rays as necessary for near vision. This process is   accomodation

Group B

| iris | optic disk | sclera | ciliary body |
| media | pupil | conjunctiva | receptors |

112

1. The opaque outermost layer of the eyeball is made of firm, tough connective tissue. This coat is the

sclera

2. The central opening in the iris contracts or dilates according to need. This opening is the

pupil

3. The crystalline lens is one of the transparent refracting parts of the eye. Collectively they are called

media

4. The rods and cones of the retina are the visual

receptors

5. The membrane that lines the eyelids is the

conjunctiva

6. The region of connection between the optic nerve and the eyeball is lacking in rods and cones and is commonly called the blind spot. Another term for this is

optic disk

7. The shape of the lens is altered by the muscle of the

ciliary body

8. The pupil is the central opening in the colored part of the eye, the

iris

Group C

fovea centralis	iris	refraction	ophthalmia neonatorum
sphincter	lacrimal gland	intrinsic	trachoma
extrinsic			

1. The muscles that are attached to bones of the orbit and to the sclera are located outside the eyeball and are described as

extrinsic

2. When a light is flashed in the eye the pupil is reduced in size owing to the contraction of a circular iris muscle which forms a(n)

sphincter

3. The amount of light entering the eye is controlled by the

iris

4. The process of bending which makes it possible for light from a large area to be focused on a small surface is known as

refraction

5. Tears serve an important protective function for the eye. They are produced by the

lacrimal gland

6. The clearest point of vision is a depressed area in the retina, the

fovea centralis

7. An eye disease prevalent in poor and underdeveloped countries is characterized by the presence of granules on the lids. This serious disease is called

trachoma

8. A suitable antiseptic prevents a serious eye infection of the newborn called

ophthalmia neonatorum

9. The muscles of the iris and ciliary body are located entirely within the eyeball and so are described as

intrinsic

Group D

astigmatism
myopia
opacity

glaucoma
strabismus
hyperopia

cataract
lacrimation
crystalline lens

1. The eyes do not work together because the muscles do not coordinate in _____ strabismus

2. Blurred vision and eyestrain is characteristic of the visual defect _____ astamatism

3. The light rays are not bent sharply enough to focus on the retina, so that they cannot focus properly on close objects in farsightedness, or _____ hyperopia

4. The focal point is in front of the retina and distant objects appear blurred in nearsightedness, or _____ myopia

5. The lens loses its transparency and blindness ensues as a result of the formation of a(n) _____ cataract

6. Continued high pressure of the aqueous humor may cause destruction of the optic nerve fibers. This cause of blindness is known as _____ glaucoma

7. Removal of a cataract may restore useful vision. This involves removal of the _____ crystalline lens

8. Injury or infection of the cornea may cause scar formation. Light rays cannot pass through the scar because there is now an area of _____ opacity

9. The secretion of tears is called _____ lacrimation

Group E

oval window
ossicles
perilymph

external auditory canal
endolymph
pinna

eustachian tube
tympanic membrane
mastoid air cells

1. Located at the end of the auditory canal is the eardrum, or _____ tympanicm,

2. The three small bones within the middle ear cavity are the _____ ossicles

3. The spaces within the temporal bone which connect with the middle ear cavity through an opening are called the _____ mastoid process

4. Sound waves are conducted to the fluid of the internal ear by vibrations of the membrane that covers the _____ oval window

5. Air is brought to the middle ear cavity by means of the auditory tube which is also called the _____ estauchian

6. The fluid of the inner ear contained within the bony labyrinth and surrounding the membranous labyrinth is called _____ perilymph

7. The fluid contained within the membranous labyrinth is called _endolymph_

8. Sound waves enter the _ext. aud. canal_

9. Another name for the projecting part, or auricle, of the ear is the _pinna_

Group F

optic nerve   vestibule   ophthalmic nerve
oculomotor nerve   cochlear duct   cochlear nerve
rods   equilibrium

1. The organ of hearing is made up of receptors located in the _cochlear duct_

2. The branch of the vestibulocochlear nerve that carries hearing impulses is the _cochlear nerve_

3. The entrance area that communicates with the cochlea and that is next to the oval window is the _vestibule_

4. Visual impulses received by the rods and cones of the retina are carried to the brain by the _optic nerve_

5. Impulses of pain, touch, and temperature are carried to the brain by a branch of the fifth cranial nerve, the _opthalmic nerve_

6. The largest cranial nerve carrying motor fibers to the eyeball muscles is the _oculomotor nerve_

7. The retinal receptors that function in dim light are the _rods_

8. The semicircular canals and the vestibule contain receptors for the sense of _equilibrium_

Group G

analgesic   proprioceptors   olfactory
taste buds   ceruminous   pressure
adaptation   vitamin A

1. The sense of taste involves two cranial nerves as well as receptors known as _taste buds_

2. Night blindness may result from a deficiency of _vitamin A_

3. Among the general senses is that concerned with deep sensibility, commonly called the sense of _pressure_

4. In the case of many sensory receptors, including those for temperature, the receptors adjust themselves so that one does not feel the sensation so acutely if the original stimulus is continued. Such an adjustment to the environment is called _adaptation_

5. Several methods, including use of drugs, are available for relief of pain. Aspirin is an example of the type of drug classified as _analgesic_

6. The wax glands located in the external auditory canal are described as _ceremonus_

7. The pathway for impulses from smell receptors is the first cranial nerve, the _olfactory_

8. Receptors that transmit information on the position of body parts are called _proptiocuators_

IV. Labeling

For each of the following illustrations print the name or names of each labeled part on the numbered lines.

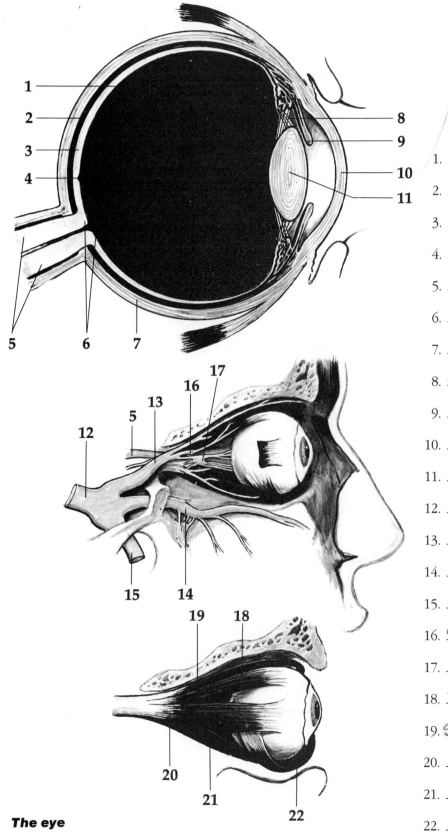

The eye

1. vitreous body
2. choroid
3. retina
4. fovea
5. optic nerve
6. blind spot
7. sclera
8. suspensory lig.
9. iris
10. cornea
11. lens
12. trigeminal
13. opthalmatic
14. maxillary
15. mandibula
16. oculomotor
17. ciliary ganglia
18. sup. oblique
19. sup. rectus
20. lateral rectus
21. inf. rectus
22. inf. oblique

1. _____   5. _____   9. _____
2. _____   6. _____   10. _____
3. _____   7. _____   11. _____
4. _____   8. _____   12. _____

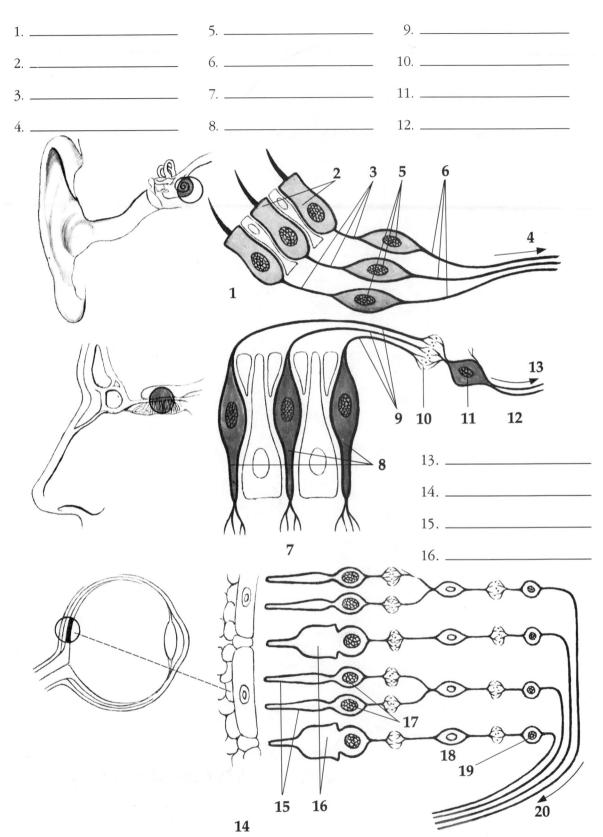

13. _____
14. _____
15. _____
16. _____

Diagram of neurons for receiving special senses

13. _____   16. _____   19. _____

14. _____   17. _____   20. _____

15. _____   18. _____

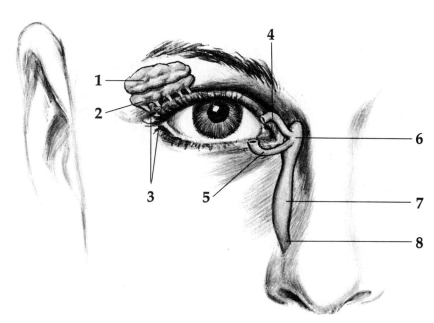

Lacrimal apparatus

1. Sup

2. inf.

3. ducts

4. upper

5. lower d.

6. lacrimal sac

7. nasolacrimal d.

8. mouth of N

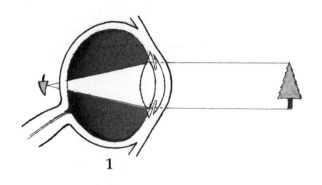

1

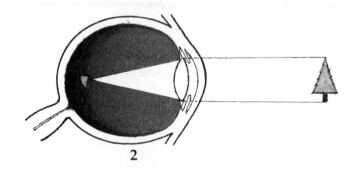

2

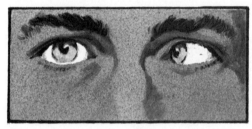

3

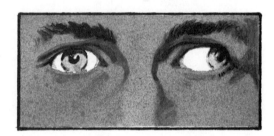

4

Disorders of the eye

1. _hyperopia_   3. _convergent_

2. _myopia_   4. _divergent_

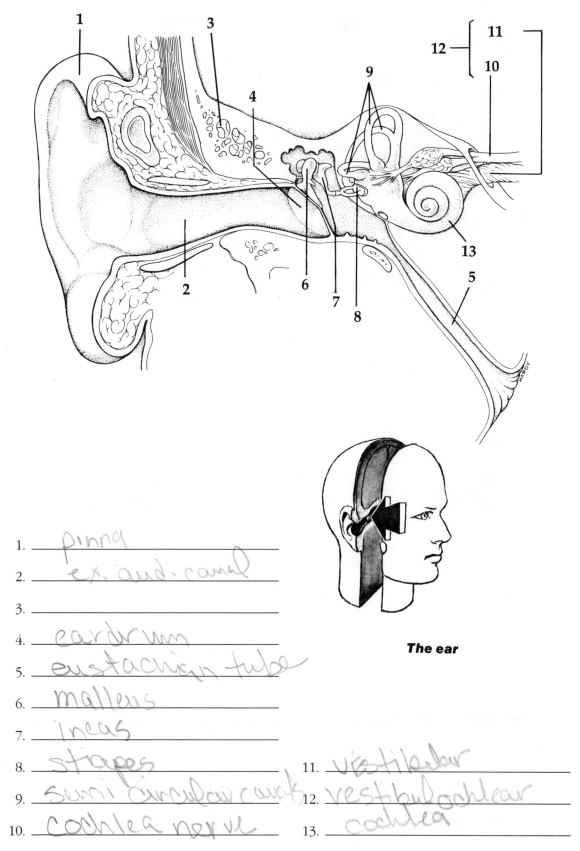

The ear

1. _pinna_
2. _ex. aud. canal_
3. _____
4. _eardrum_
5. _eustachian tube_
6. _malleus_
7. _incus_
8. _stapes_
9. _semi circular canal_
10. _cochlea nerve_
11. _vestibular_
12. _vestibulocochlear_
13. _cochlea_

121

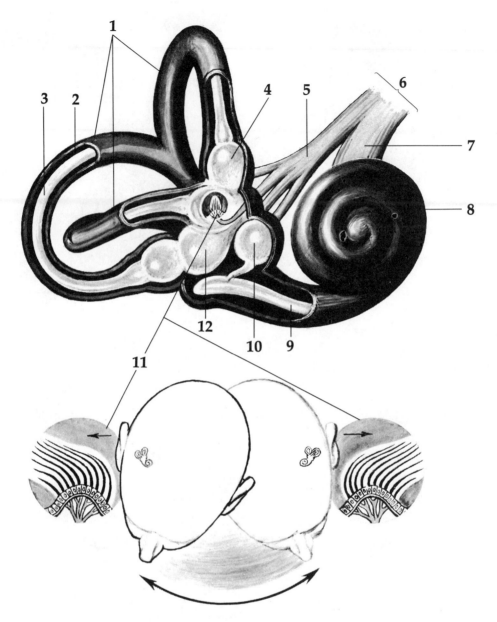

The internal ear

1. Semi circular
2. perilymphatic
3. endolymph
4. membranous ampulla
5. vestibular
6. vestibulocochlear

7. cochlear
8. cochlea
9. lil duct
10. saccule
11. crista ampularis
12. utricle

V. Completion Exercise

Print the word or phrase that correctly completes each sentence.

1. The nerve fibers of the vestibular and cochlear nerves join to form the nerve called the

   vestibulocochlear

2. The inner ear spaces contain fluids involved in the transmission of sound waves. The one that is inside the membranous cochlea and that stimulates the receptors is the

   endolymph

   perilymph

3. The taste receptors of the tongue are located along the edges of small depressed areas, or

   fissures

4. The nerves involved in the sense of taste are the facial and the

   glossopharyngeal

5. Pain that is felt in an outer part of the body such as the skin, yet that originates internally near the area where it is felt, is called

   referred pain

6. The very widely distributed free nerve endings are the receptors for the most important protective sense, namely that for

   pain

7. The tactile corpuscles are the receptors for the sense of

   touch

8. The nerve endings that relay impulses which aid in judging position and changes in location of parts with respect to each other are the

   proprioceptors

9. The sense of position is partially governed by several structures in the internal ear, including two small sacs and the three membranous

   simicircular canals

10. When you enter a darkened room, it takes a while for the rods to begin to function. This interval is known as the period of

    dark adaptation

VI. Practical Applications

Study each discussion. Then print the appropriate word or phrase in the space provided.

Group A

While observing in the emergency ward the student nurse noted the following cases.

1. Ten-year-old K had been riding his bicycle while he threw glass bottles to the sidewalk. A fragment of glass flew into one eye. Examination at the hospital showed that there was a cut in the transparent window of the eye, the

   _____

2. On further examination of K, the colored part of the eye was seen to protrude from the wound. This part is the

   _____

3. K's treatment included antiseptics, anesthetics, and suturing of the wound. Medication was instilled in the saclike structure at

the front of the eyeball. This sac is lined with a thin epithelial
membrane, the _____

4. A construction worker, Mr. J, was admitted because of an accident
   in which a piece of steel penetrated his eyeball and caused such
   an extensive wound that material from the inside of the eyeball
   oozed out. Mr. J tried to relieve the pain by forcing the jellylike
   material out through the wound at the front and side of his eyeball. This matter, which maintains the shape of the eyeball, is
   called the _____

5. Because so much damage had been done, Mr. J was taken to
   surgery for removal of the eyeball. This operation is called _____

6. Mr. N, age 86, had a weakness of the muscle that lifts the eyeball,
   the levator palpebrae. He complained of difficulty in seeing because of his drooping eyelids, a condition called _____

Group B

An ear, nose, and throat specialist treated the following patients one morning.

1. Mrs. B complained of some deafness and a sense of fullness in
   her outer ear. Examination revealed that the wax in her ear canal
   had hardened and formed a plug of (*scientific name*) _____

2. Mr. J, age 72, complained of gradually increasing deafness
   although he had no symptoms of pain or other problems related
   to the ears. Examination revealed that his deafness was the type
   called nerve deafness. The cranial nerve that carries impulses
   related to hearing to the brain is called the _____

3. Mrs. C complained of deafness that resembled the type from
   which her aunt and her mother suffered. She asked whether she
   could undergo surgery since she had heard that this surgical
   treatment was often successful. This disorder, in which bony
   changes prevent the stapes from vibrating normally, is called _____

4. Baby L was brought in by his mother because he awakened
   crying, and was holding the right side of his head. He had been
   suffering from a cold but now he seemed to be in pain. Examination revealed a bulging red eardrum. The eardrum is also
   called the _____

5. The cause of baby L's painful bulging eardrum was an infection
   of the middle ear, called _____

6. Antibiotic treatment of baby L's middle ear infection was begun,
   since this early treatment usually prevents complications.
   However, in this case it was necessary to cut the eardrum in
   order to prevent its rupture. Another name for this procedure is _____

7. Elderly Mr. N had a hearing loss (presbycusis) due to atrophy of
   the nerve endings located in the spiral-shaped part of the internal
   ear, the _____

11

The Endocrine System and Hormones

I. Overview

The endocrine glands are ductless glands that release their secretions directly into the bloodstream. These secretions, called **hormones**, are chemical messengers that regulate growth, metabolism, sexual development, and behavior. The endocrine system is composed of organs that have the secretion of hormones as a primary function. These include the following glands: pituitary (hypophysis), thyroid, parathyroids, adrenals, pancreas, gonads, thymus, and pineal.

The endocrine system and the nervous system are the main coordinating and controlling systems of the body. Both are activated, for example, in helping the body respond to stress. These two systems meet in the **hypothalamus**, a region of the diencephalon of the brain. The hypothalamus is directly above and connected to the **pituitary**. By means of nerve stimulation and hormones, the hypothalamus controls the two lobes of the pituitary. Hormones released from the pituitary, in turn, control the other endocrine glands. The other main mechanism for controlling hormone secretion is **negative feedback**, in which hormone levels, or substances released as a result of hormone action, serve to regulate the production of that hormone.

Chemically, hormones are either **proteins** or **steroids**. The cells on which hormones act make up the **target tissue**. These cells have **receptors** to which the hormone attaches. Either directly or by means of a second messenger, hormones affect the activity of the DNA within the cell and the manufacture of proteins. In this manner they regulate the activities of the cell.

In addition to the endocrine glands, some other structures, including the kidney, stomach, and small intestine, secrete hormones. **Prostaglandins** are hormone-like substances produced by cells throughout the body. They have a variety of effects and are currently under study.

II. Topics for Review

A. General characteristics of the endocrine system
B. Hormones
   1. Chemical makeup
   2. Method of action
   3. Regulation
C. The endocrine glands and their hormones
   1. Control of the pituitary by the hypothalamus
D. Other hormone-producing organs
E. Medical uses of hormones
F. Hormones and stress

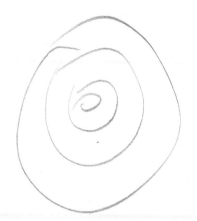

III. Matching Exercises

Matching only within each group, print the answer in the space provided.

Group A

parathyroid glands	thyroid	suprarenal glands
calcitonin	medulla	cretinism
hormones	islets of Langerhans	

1. The substances produced by endocrine glands are known as   _hormones_

2. The adrenal glands are also known as the   _suprarenal_

3. The groups of hormone-secreting cells scattered throughout the pancreas are known as the   _islets of Langerhans_

4. The largest of the endocrine glands is located in the neck. It is the   _thyroid_

5. The inner part of the adrenal gland is called the   _medulla_

6. An individual born without functioning thyroid tissue is said to suffer from   _cretinism_

7. Located behind the thyroid gland and embedded in its capsule are the four   _parathyroid_

8. The hormone produced by the thyroid gland and active in calcium metabolism is   _calcitonin_

Group B

DNA	proteins	hormones
thyroxine	negative feedback	target tissues
hypothalamus	second messenger	

1. The body's "chemical messengers" are the   _hormones_

2. The part of the brain that controls the pituitary gland is the   _hypothalamus_

126

3. All hormones except the sex hormones and the hormones of the adrenal cortex are classified chemically as

proteins

4. Hormones work only on specific tissues known as the

target tissues

5. Production of heat and energy in the body tissues is regulated mainly by the hormone

thyroxine

6. Within the cell, hormones affect the working of the genetic material, the

DNA

7. If a hormone does not enter a cell it acts indirectly by means of a substance within the cell called a(n)

second messenger

8. Most hormones are regulated by a self-controlling mechanism known as

negative feedback

Group C

myxedema	insulin	pituitary
iodine	goiter	receptors
adrenal	parathyroid hormone	

1. A target tissue responds to a given hormone because it has areas to which the hormone attaches. These areas are called

receptors

2. The endocrine gland that is divided into anterior and posterior lobes is the

pituitary

3. The amount of calcium dissolved in the circulating blood is partly regulated by a secretion from small glands on the surface of the thyroid. This secretion is called

parathyroid hormon

4. In order to provide for normal sugar utilization in the tissues, the islets of Langerhans must produce a hormone called

insulin

5. The endocrine gland composed of an external cortex and an internal medulla which act as separate glands with specific functions is the

adrenal

6. In order that thyroxine may be manufactured, the blood must contain an adequate supply of

iodine

7. Enlargement of the thyroid gland results in a swelling of the neck called

goiter

8. Atrophy of the thyroid in the adult causes mental and physical sluggishness; the term used to describe this condition is

myxedema

Group D

steroids	cortisol	calcium
insulin	placenta	anterior lobe
lymphocytes	oxytocin	glucagon

1. A portal system connects the hypothalamus to the region of the pituitary called the ___anterior lobe___

2. In the disorder known as diabetes mellitus, sugar is not "burned" in the tissues to produce energy. This is due to a lack of the hormone ___insulin___

3. The normal development of the embryo is aided by hormones from the ovaries, pituitary, and an organ present only during pregnancy, namely the ___placenta___

4. The sex hormones and the hormones of the adrenal cortex are classified chemically as ___steroids___

5. Hydroxycholecalciferol, a hormone-like substance produced from vitamin D, regulates intestinal absorption of the mineral ___calcium___

6. During stressful situations, such as an injury or surgery, the body is protected somewhat by an adrenal hormone (a glucocorticoid) that acts to reduce inflammation. This hormone is usually called ___cortisol___

7. The hormone produced by the islets of Langerhans that raises blood sugar levels is ___glucagon___

8. The thymus produces hormones that stimulate the production of cells needed in the body's defenses against infection. These cells are the ___lymphocytes___

9. The hormone from the posterior pituitary which causes uterine contraction is called ___oxytocin___

Group E

aldosterone	antidiuretic hormone	ACTH
cortisol	estrogen	progesterone
epinephrine	kidney	

1. Blood pressure is raised and the rate of the heartbeat is increased by the chief hormone of the adrenal medulla, ___epinephrine___

2. Regulation of reabsorption of sodium and secretion of potassium in the kidney tubules is a function of the adrenal cortex hormone ___aldosterone___

3. Testosterone is produced by the male sex glands; the female sex glands produce a hormone that most nearly parallels testosterone in its action. This hormone is called ___estrogen___

4. The hormone produced in the posterior lobe of the pituitary which regulates water reabsorption by the kidney is called ___anti diuretic___

5. A hormone that is necessary for normal development of pregnancy is one produced by the female sex glands. It is called ___progesterone___

6. When the needs of the body are such that amino acids must be changed to sugar instead of protein, the adrenal cortex produces large amounts of the hormone

Cortisol

7. The adrenal cortex is stimulated by the anterior pituitary hormone known as

ACTH

8. The hormone erythropoietin, which stimulates production of red blood cells, is produced in the

Kidney

steroids
insulin
lymphocytes
cortisol
placenta
calcium
anterior lobe
glucagon

IV. Labeling

Print the name or names of each labeled part on the numbered lines.

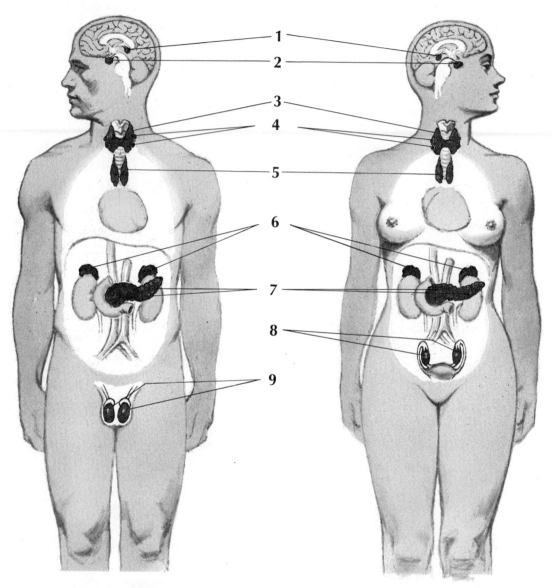

Glands of the endocrine system

1. _____ 6. _____

2. _____ 7. _____

3. _____ 8. _____

4. _____ 9. _____

5. _____

V. Completion Exercise

Print the word or phrase that correctly completes each sentence.

1. The region of the brain that controls the pituitary gland (hypophysis) is the

   hypothalmus

2. Should production of parathyroid hormone decrease, there will be a decrease in the amount of calcium dissolved in the blood. This may be followed by muscle spasms, a condition called

   tetany

3. Growth hormone is produced by the region of the pituitary called the

   ant lobe

4. An abnormal increase in production of the hormone epinephrine may result from a tumor of the

   adrenal medulla

5. The hypothalamus stimulates the anterior pituitary to produce ACTH, which in turn stimulates hormone production by the

   adrenal cortex

6. Hormones secreted by the anterior lobe of the pituitary that control the activity of the sex glands or gonads are described as

   gonadotropic

7. Hormone-like substances that have a variety of effects, including the promotion of inflammation and the production of uterine contractions, are the

   prostaglands

8. When the level of glucose in the blood decreases to less than average, the islet cells of the pancreas release less insulin. The result is an increase in blood glucose. This is an example of the mechanism called

   neg. feedback

VI. Practical Applications

Study each discussion. Then print the appropriate word or phrase in the space provided.

1. Mr. J, age 23, required evaluation of pituitary function. As part of this evaluation, an x-ray examination was planned because of the possibility that a tumor was the cause of his excessive height of 7 feet as well as his abnormal weakness. The tests revealed that a pituitary tumor was present, so his condition was diagnosed as

   giantism

2. Seventeen-year-old Ms. K had never had a menstrual period. The cause could have been a deficiency of the ovarian hormones called

   estrogen

3. Mrs. C, age 56, had been brought to the hospital in coma, that is, she was unconscious and could not be aroused. Tests revealed that her blood sugar was abnormally high. Mrs. C's illness was due to a lack of insulin, and is known as

   diabetis

4. Mrs. K consulted her doctor because she felt weak at times, especially after not eating for a while. She had also noted a darkening of the pigment in her skin. Tests showed low blood pressure and a deficiency of the hormones cortisol and aldosterone produced by the adrenal cortex. Her condition was diagnosed as

addison's

5. Mr. D, a patient in kidney failure, complained of feeling tired and listless. Tests showed that he was extremely anemic. His physician prescribed certain hormones that promote healing and stimulate red blood cell production. These hormones are the

androgens

12

The Blood

I. Overview

The blood maintains the internal environment in a constant state through its functions of transportation, regulation, and protection. Blood is composed of two elements; one, the liquid element or **plasma**, and the other, the **formed elements** consisting of the cells and cellular products. The plasma is 90% water and 10% proteins, carbohydrates, lipids, and mineral salts. The formed elements are composed of the **erythrocytes**, which carry oxygen to the tissues by means of their hemoglobin; the **leukocytes**, which defend the body against invaders; and the **platelets**, which are involved in the process of blood coagulation or clotting.

The forerunners of the blood cells are called **stem cells**. These are formed in the red bone marrow where they then develop into the various types of blood cells.

Blood **coagulation** is a protective mechanism that prevents blood loss when a blood vessel is ruptured by an injury. The first steps in the prevention of blood loss (hemostasis) include constriction of the blood vessels and formation of a platelet plug.

Should the quantity of blood in the body be severely reduced because of hemorrhage or disease, the cells suffer from lack of nourishment. In such instances, a **transfusion** may be given after typing and matching the blood of the recipient and donor. (Red cells with different surface proteins (**antigens**) than the recipient's red cells will react with **antibodies** in the recipient's blood, causing harmful agglutination and destruction of the donated red cells.) Blood can be packaged and stored in blood banks for use when transfusions are needed. Whenever possible, **blood components** such as cells, plasma, plasma fractions, or platelets are used. This practice is more efficient and reduces the chances of incompatibility.

The presence or absence of **Rh factor**, a red blood cell protein, is also important in transfusions. If blood containing the Rh factor (Rh positive) is given to a person whose blood lacks that factor (Rh negative), the recipient may become sensitized to the protein; his blood cells will produce antibodies to counteract the foreign substance. If an Rh

negative mother becomes sensitized by an Rh positive fetus, her antibodies may damage
the red cells of the fetus in a later pregnancy, resulting in **hemolytic disease of the
newborn** (erythroblastosis fetalis).

There are three groups of blood disorders: **anemias, neoplastic diseases**, and **clotting
disorders**. Anemia may result from loss or destruction of red blood cells or from impaired production of red blood cells or hemoglobin.

Numerous **blood studies** have been devised in order to measure the composition of
blood. These include the hematocrit, tests for the amount of hemoglobin, cell counts,
and coagulation studies. Modern laboratories are equipped with automatic counters,
which rapidly and accurately count blood cells, and with automatic analyzers, which
measure enzymes, electrolytes, and other constituents of blood serum.

II. Topics for Review

A. Purposes of blood
B. Blood plasma and its functions
C. The formed elements and their functions
    1. Erythrocytes
       a. Structure
       b. Function
    2. Leukocytes
       a. Types
       b. Functions
    3. Platelets (thrombocytes)
D. Origin of blood cells
E. Blood clotting and hemostasis
F. Blood typing and blood transfusions
    1. Blood groups
    2. Rh factor
    3. Blood banks
    4. Blood components
G. Blood disorders
H. Blood studies

III. Matching Exercises

Matching only within each group, print the answers in the spaces provided.

Group A

1 bone marrow	4 thrombocytes	7 carbon dioxide
2 oxygen	5 plasma	8 erythrocytes
3 hemoglobin	6 leukocytes	9 nucleus

1. The liquid part of the blood is known as   _plasma_

2. The red blood cells are called   _8_

3. There are several types of white blood cells or   _6_

4. Elements that have to do with clotting include platelets, or   _4_

5. An important gas that is transported by the blood from the lungs to all parts of the body is

_____ 2 _____

6. The gaseous waste product carried by the blood to the lungs is the gas named

_____ 7 _____

7. The iron-containing protein in red blood cells is a compound called

_____ 3 _____

8. A connective tissue present in bone is the site of formation of blood cells. The name of this tissue is

_____ 1 _____

9. The mature red blood cell differs from other body cells in that it lacks a(n)

_____ 9 _____

Group B

albumin 4
hemostasis 8
neutrophils 6

cryoprecipitate 2
gamma globulin 9
sickle cell anemia 3

plasmapheresis 1
antigens 7
Rh 5

1. The procedure for removing plasma and returning formed elements to a donor is

_____

2. An individual with hemophilia may receive clotting factors in the form of a fraction obtained from frozen plasma. This fraction is called

_____

3. A hereditary hemolytic disease seen mainly in blacks is

_____

4. The most abundant protein in the blood is

_____

5. The disease erythroblastosis fetalis indicates an incompatibility between a mother and a fetus in the blood factor known as

_____

6. The most numerous leukocytes in the blood are

_____

7. A person who receives blood of a different type than his or her own may have antibodies to proteins on the surface of the red blood cells received. These proteins as a group are called

_____

8. Blood clotting is a step in the prevention of blood loss, a process called

_____

9. The fraction of the blood that contains antibodies is the fraction called

_____

Group C

serum 5
type O 7
megakaryocytes 2

fibrinogen 3
hemoglobin 1
type AB 8

hemolysis 6
pathogens 9
agglutination 4

1. Oxygen, needed by all the tissues, is transported by a substance in red blood cells. This substance is called

    _____

2. The platelets are fragments of large cells known as

    _____

3. As platelets disintegrate they release a chemical that activates a plasma protein called

    _____

4. The process whereby cells become clumped is known as

    _____

5. The watery fluid that remains after a clot is removed is known as

    _____

6. In blood transfusion a dangerous condition that occurs when donor cells are dissolved or go into solution is

    _____

7. Blood that is not clumped by either anti-A or anti-B serum belongs to the group called

    _____

8. If the cells are clumped by both the anti-A and anti-B serums the blood belongs to

    _____

9. The appearance of pus at a body site indicates that the leukocytes are actively involved in the destruction of

    _____

Group D

purpura 9	malaria 7	transfusion 4
leukemia 2	anemia 1	hemorrhage 3
centrifuge 5	bone marrow 8	vitamin B_{12} 6

1. The condition in which the blood is lacking in the number or in the overall quantity of red blood cells is referred to as

    _____

2. An abnormal increase in the number of immature white cells is seen in the neoplastic disease called

    _____

3. Another term for profuse abnormal bleeding is

    _____

4. The transfer of whole blood from one person to another is called a(n)

    _____

5. Separation of blood plasma from the formed elements of blood is accomplished by use of the

    _____

6. In the condition known as pernicious anemia, the body is unable to absorb a substance essential for the formation of red blood cells. This is

    _____

7. Excessive destruction of red blood cells may cause anemia, a symptom often found in the disease

    _____

8. In the condition known as aplastic anemia there is failure of the blood-forming organ, namely the

    _____

9. A disorder in which there are hemorrhages into the skin and mucous membranes is _____

Group E

hyperglycemia 4
leukopenia 9
5000 to 10,000 3

leukocytosis 7
hemocytometer 1
hematocrit 5

4.5 to 5.5 million 2
blood chemistry 6

1. An apparatus made of several parts and used for counting blood cells is called a(n) _____

2. Normally, the number of red blood cells per cubic millimeter is _____

3. Normally, the number of white blood cells per cubic millimeter is _____

4. Blood normally contains some sugar. When the amount is excessive, the condition is referred to as _____

5. The volume percentage of red blood cells in centrifuged whole blood is called the _____

6. Measurements of electrolytes, blood urea nitrogen, enzymes, and glucose are included as part of _____

7. In most infections, as well as in various other types of illness, the white count may be excessive. This finding is referred to as _____

8. An abnormal reduction of the white blood count to below 5000 is called _____

IV. Labeling

For each of the following illustrations, print the name or names of each labeled part on the numbered lines.

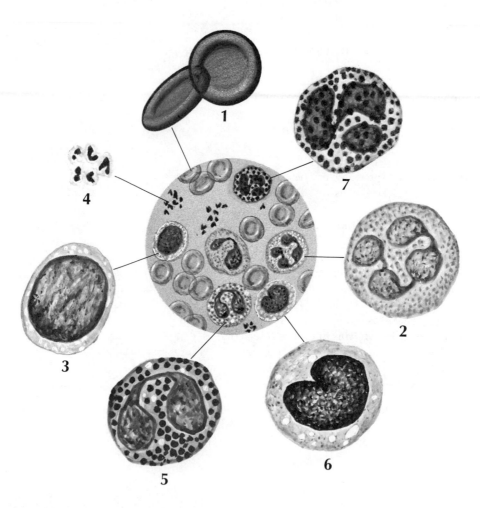

Blood cells

1. _____   5. _____

2. _____   6. _____

3. _____   7. _____

4. _____

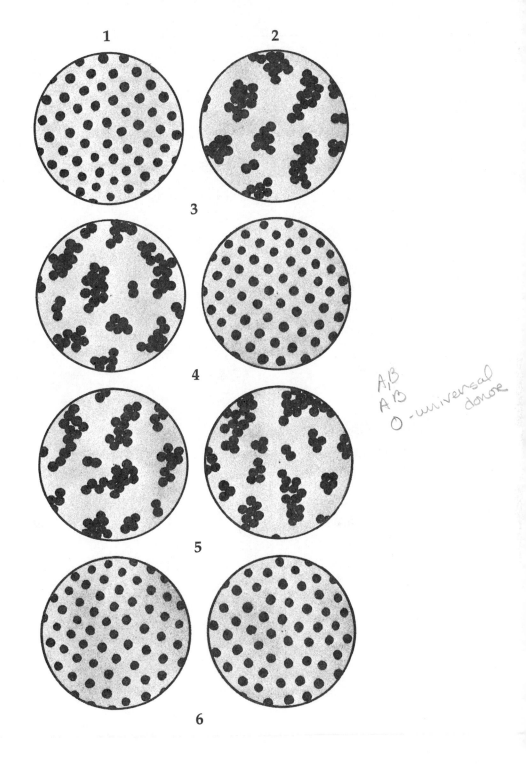

A,B
A,B
O - universal donor

Blood typing

1. _____   4. _____

2. _____   5. _____

3. _____   6. _____

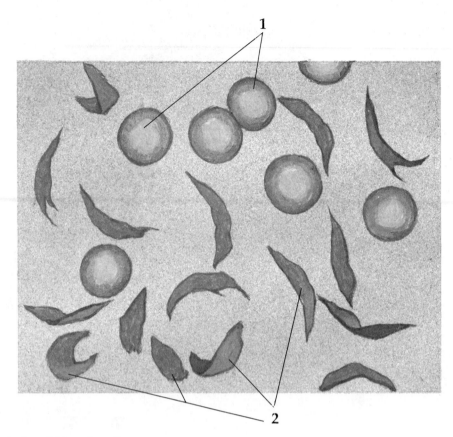

Sickling of red blood cells

1. _____normal_____

2. _____Sickle cell_____ lack of ox. to tissue

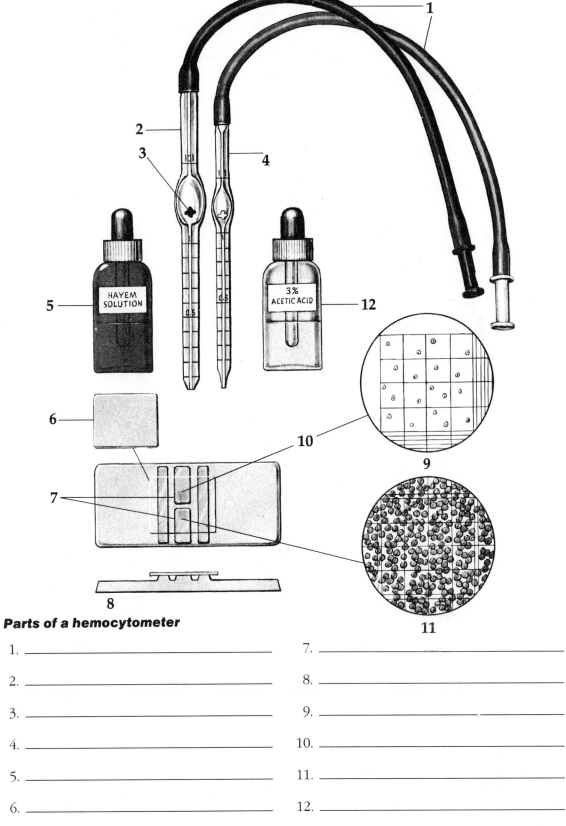

Parts of a hemocytometer

1. _____   7. _____

2. _____   8. _____

3. _____   9. _____

4. _____   10. _____

5. _____   11. _____

6. _____   12. _____

V. Completion Exercise

Print the word or phrase that correctly completes each sentence.

1. The gas that is transported to all parts of the body by the blood and that is necessary for life is called _____

2. One waste product of body metabolism is carried to the lungs to be exhaled. This gas is known as _____

3. Red blood cells are far more numerous than white ones; the proportion is about _____

4. A collection of dead and living white blood cells and bacteria in a region of infection is _____

5. Blood cells are formed in the _____

6. The number of different types of white blood cells is _____

7. Lymphocytes mature and may divide in the thymus and the _____

8. The process whereby cells are clumped together because of an incompatibility between red blood cells and another person's serum is called _____

9. A certain red blood cell protein is present in about 85% of the population. Such individuals are said to be _____

10. The watery fluid that remains after a blood clot is removed is called _____

11. One of the transport functions of the blood is the transmission of a by-product of muscle activity from the muscles to all parts of the body. This by-product is _____

12. The most important function of certain lymphocytes is to engulf disease-producing organisms by the process of _____

13. Digested food proteins are absorbed into the capillaries of the intestinal villi in the form of protein building blocks, or _____

VI. Practical Applications

Study each discussion. Then print the appropriate word or phrase in the space provided.

Group A

1. Ms. G sustained numerous deep gashes when she accidentally broke a glass shower door. One of the cuts bled copiously. In describing this type of bleeding the doctor used the word _____ hemmorage _____

2. While the physician attended to the wound the technician drew blood for typing and other studies. Ms. G's blood was found to agglutinate with both anti-A and anti-B serum. Her blood was classified as group

_____ AB _____

3. Among the available donors were some whose blood was found to be free of both A and B surface antigens. They were classified as having blood type

_____ O _____

4. Further testing of Ms. G's blood revealed that it lacked the Rh factor. She was therefore said to be

_____ RH neg. _____

5. If Ms. G were to be given a transfusion of Rh positive blood, she might become sensitized to the Rh protein. In that event her blood would produce counteracting substances called

_____ Antibodies _____

6. Mr. B had a history of peptic ulcer. On his admission he felt weak and was having severe abdominal pain. He was hospitalized and a series of tests was begun. One of these showed a reduction in the number of red blood cells and a decrease in the hemoglobin percentage. This condition is described by a word that means an insufficiency of blood, namely

_____ anemia _____

7. Mr. R had lost a large quantity of blood when he was injured in an automobile accident. In addition to whole blood, he was given several units of cryoprecipitate to replace lost

clottin
_____ plasma _____

8. Because of Mr. R's extensive injuries, there was a possibility that disseminated intravascular coagulation would develop. If this occurred, it would mean that platelets and clotting factors were being used up too rapidly, and the result would be severe

_____ hemmorging _____

Group B

On the medical ward there were a number of patients who required extensive blood studies.

1. A boy 7 years of age had a history of frequent fevers and a tendency to bleed easily. Physical examination revealed enlarged lymph nodes. A blood smear revealed pronounced cell changes. The number of each kind of white cell was determined by counting the white cells in a sample of blood. This is called a

_____

2. Further study of this patient's blood smear revealed that numerous white blood cells were immature, and that the total number of white cells was tremendously increased. This disorder, a cancer of the blood, is

_____

3. As a further aid in diagnosis, a specimen of his red marrow was obtained from the iliac crest by means of a special needle. This procedure is a

_____

4. Mrs. C's history included rapid weight loss, constant thirst, and episodes of fainting. A blood test showed the presence of excessive sugar, or glucose. This condition is named _____

5. Mr. B, age 28, had a history of heart disease due to bacteria that caused dissolution (dissolving) of red blood cells. This type of disintegration is known as _____

6. Mr. K suffered from a viral infection of the liver. As a protective measure, his young son was given an injection of a protein substance obtained from human plasma. This antibody, which prevents certain viral infections, has the name of _____

7. Mr. Q complained of weakness and difficulty in walking. His red blood cell count was extremely low, and abnormal red cells were found in the blood smear. His stomach hydrochloric acid was reduced. These signs are characteristic of a deficiency disease, a primary anemia called _____

8. A black child was brought in with complaints of swelling and pain in the fingers and toes. Blood studies revealed red cells that were somewhat crescent shaped and inflexible. These are characteristics of a disorder called _____

13

The Heart and Heart Disease

_____

I. Overview

The ceaseless beat of the heart day and night throughout one's entire lifetime is such an obvious key to the presence of life that it is no surprise that this organ has been the subject of wonderment and poetry. When the heart stops pumping, life ceases. The cells must have oxygen, and it is the heart's pumping action that propels oxygenated blood to them.

In size the heart has been compared to a **closed fist.** In location it is thought of as being on the left side, although about one third is to the right of the midline. The muscular apex of the triangular heart is definitely on the left. It rests on the **diaphragm,** the dome-shaped muscle that separates the thoracic cavity from the abdominal space.

In birds and mammals, including humans, the heart has two sides, in which the aerated (higher in oxygen) and the unaerated (lower in oxygen) blood are kept entirely separated. So the heart is really a **double pump** in which the two sides pump in unison. The right side pumps blood to the lungs to be oxygenated, and the left side pumps blood to all other parts of the body.

Each side of the heart is divided into two parts or **chambers** which are in direct communication. The upper chamber or **atrium** on each side opens directly into the lower chamber or **ventricle. Valves** between the chambers keep the blood flowing forward as the heart pumps. The atria are the receiving chambers for blood returning to the heart. The two ventricles pump blood to all parts of the body. Because they pump more forcefully, their walls are thicker than the walls of the atria. The coronary arteries supply blood to the heart muscle or **myocardium.**

The heartbeat originates within the heart at the **sinoatrial node,** often called the pacemaker. Electrical impulses from the pacemaker spread over special fibers in the wall of the heart to produce contractions, first of the two atria and then of the two ventricles. After contraction, the heart relaxes and fills with blood. The relaxation phase is called diastole and the contraction phase is called **systole**. Together these two phases make up one **cardiac cycle**.

Heart diseases may be classified according to the area of the heart affected or according to causes. Causes include congenital abnormalities, rheumatic fever, coronary artery disease, and heart failure due to degeneration of heart tissues.

II. Topics for Review

A. The heart as a pump
B. Structure of the heart wall
   1. Endocardium
   2. Myocardium
   3. Epicardium
C. The pericardium
D. Anatomy of the heart
   1. Septum
   2. Chambers
   3. Valves
E. The cardiac cycle
   1. Diastole
   2. Systole
F. The conduction system of the heart
   1. Sinoatrial node (pacemaker)
   2. Atrioventricular node
   3. Atrioventricular bundle and bundle branches
G. Normal and abnormal heart sounds
H. Heart disease
   1. Classification according to tissue involved
   2. Classification according to causes
I. Abnormal heart rhythms
J. Prevention of heart disease
K. Instruments and drugs
L. Treatment of heart disorders, including surgery

III. Matching Exercises

Matching only within each group, print the answers in the spaces provided.

Group A

tricuspid valve 6	interatrial septum 4	aortic valve 9
endocardium 1	myocardium 2	interventricular septum 5
mitral valve 7	epicardium 3	pulmonary semilunar valve 8

1. The membrane of which the heart valves are formed and which lines the interior of the heart is called _____

2. By far the thickest layer in the heart wall is the muscular one, the _____

3. The outermost layer of the heart is the _____

4. A partition, the septum, separates the two sides of the heart. The thin-walled upper part of this septum is the _____

5. The larger part of the partition between the two sides of the heart is the

_____

6. Between the two right chambers of the heart lies the right atrioventricular valve. It is also called the

_____

7. The left atrioventricular valve is thicker and heavier than the right; it is made of two flaps or cusps. It is called the

_____

8. Situated between the right ventricle and the pulmonary artery is the valve that prevents blood on its way to the lungs from returning to the right ventricle. This is the

_____

9. The valve that prevents blood from returning after the left ventricle has emptied itself is the

_____

Group B

arteries 7
atria 4
atrioventricular node 5

sinoatrial node 3
veins 8
atrioventricular bundle 6

systole 1
diastole 2

1. The contraction phase of the cardiac cycle is called

_____

2. The brief resting period that follows the contraction phase of the cardiac cycle is

_____

3. Impulses in the heart follow a definite sequence, beginning in the pacemaker. The pacemaker is located in the upper right atrial wall and is called the

_____

4. Next, the excitation wave travels throughout the muscles of the upper heart chambers, causing them to contract. These are the

_____

5. Following this, the second mass of conduction tissue (located in the septum) is stimulated. This is the

_____

6. Finally, the ventricular musculature contracts in response to stimulation by branches of the

_____

7. Blood is pumped to the lungs and body tissues through

_____

8. Oxygenated blood from the lungs and deoxygenated blood from the body tissues is carried through the

_____

Group C

stroke volume 7
murmur 6
myocardium 3

tachycardia 1
flutter 8
bradycardia 5

ventricles 2
cardiac output 4

1. A heart rate of greater than 100 beats per minute is described as

_____

2. The pumping chambers of the heart are the

_____

3. The coronary arteries supply blood to the _____

4. The volume of blood pumped by each ventricle in 1 minute
   is the _____

5. A heart rate of less than 60 beats per minute is called _____

6. Abnormal closing of the heart valves may result in a(n) _____

7. The amount of blood ejected from a ventricle with each beat
   is the _____

8. Very rapid coordinated heart contractions of up to 300 beats per
   minute are described as _____

Group D

heart failure 6   thrombus 10   functional murmur 1
congenital heart disease 3 infarct 9   coronary heart disease 7
endocarditis 5   organic murmur 2   ischemic heart disease 8
myocarditis 4

1. The type of murmur that is not associated with abnormalities of
   the heart is called a(n) _____

2. An abnormal heart sound that is evidence of damage to the heart
   or its vessels is a(n) _____

3. A general term that is used to describe abnormalities of the heart
   that have been present since birth is _____

4. Inflammation of heart muscle is referred to as _____

5. The type of heart disease in which the valves are damaged
   is called _____

6. Hypertension is a frequent cause of deterioration of heart tissues
   which leads to a disorder called _____

7. When the walls of the blood vessels that supply the heart muscle
   are damaged, the resulting disorder is called _____

8. A deficiency in blood supply to the heart muscle may destroy the
   muscle cells, a disorder known as _____

9. An area of dead tissue that is formed as a result of a lack of blood
   supply is called a(n) _____

10. The technical term for a blood clot formed within a blood
    vessel is _____

Group E

fluoroscope 4
coronary thrombosis 8
artificial pacemaker 5

digitalis 2
mitral stenosis 9
stethoscope 6

hypertension 7
anticoagulant 1
electrocardiograph 3

1. In order to prevent the formation of a thrombus in a blood
   vessel, the physician may prescribe a(n)   _____

2. A valuable drug that aids in regulating the heartbeat is derived
   from the foxglove plant. This drug is   _____

3. An instrument for recording the electrical activity of the heart
   is the   _____

4. An instrument that uses x-rays in examining deep structures
   is the   _____

5. An instrument that supplies impulses to regulate the heartbeat
   may be implanted under the skin. It is a(n)   _____

6. The simple instrument used by the physician for listening to
   sounds from within the patient's body is the   _____

7. A frequent cause of enlargement of the heart is high blood
   pressure, or   _____

8. Formation of a thrombus within a heart artery may result in complete obstruction of blood flow, a condition called   _____

9. If the left atrioventricular valve becomes narrowed due to rheumatic fever, the resulting condition is   _____

Group F

angina pectoris 6
fibrillations 2
septum 1

echocardiography 4
pericarditis 5

occlusion 7
smoking 3

1. The most common defect in congenital heart disease involves the
   partition between the two sides of the heart, known as the   _____

2. Ineffective contractions of groups of muscle cells in the heart
   are called   _____

3. Numerous studies indicate that the incidence of coronary heart
   disease is increased as much as ten times by   _____

4. A rapid, painless, and harmless test for the presence of lesions of
   the heart uses sound impulses that are reflected and recorded.
   This is   _____

5. Inflammation of the serous membrane on the heart surface and the surface lining the pericardial sac is called _____

6. A severe pain that is felt in the region of the heart, the left arm, and the shoulder may be _____

7. Complete closure of an artery is called _____

IV. Labeling

For each of the following illustrations print the name or names of each labeled part on the numbered lines.

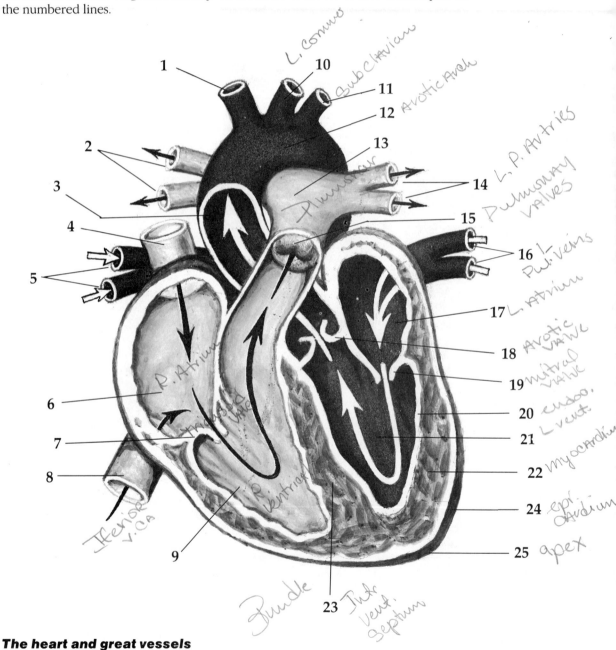

The heart and great vessels

1. _____
2. _____
3. _____
4. _____
5. _____
6. _____
7. _____
8. _____
9. _____
10. _____
11. _____
12. _____
13. _____
14. _____
15. _____
16. _____
17. _____
18. _____
19. _____
20. _____
21. _____
22. _____
23. _____
24. _____
25. _____

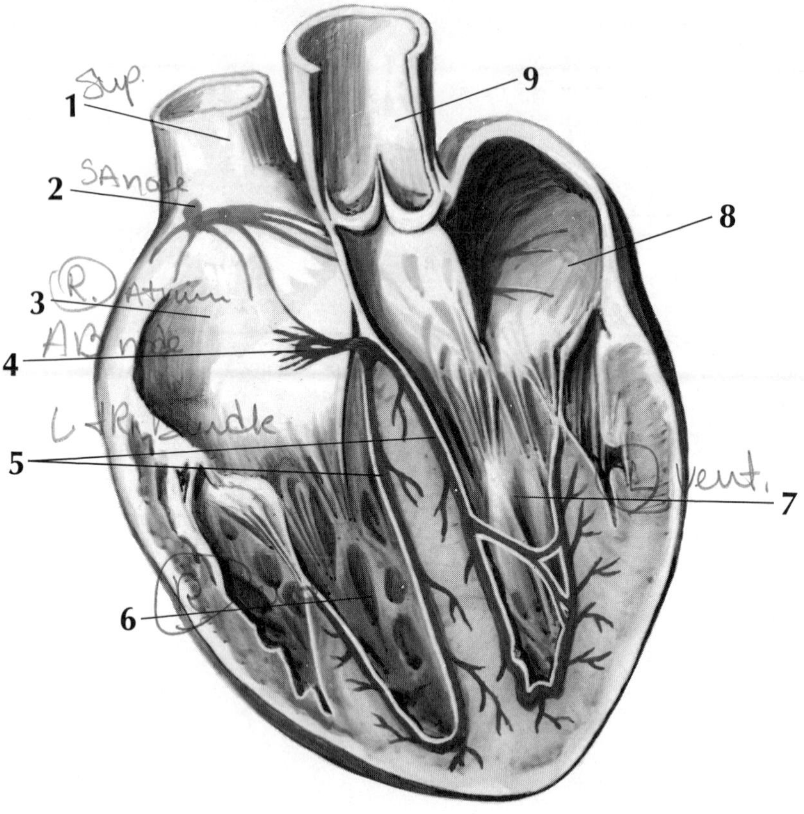

Conduction system of the heart

1. ______________________

2. ______________________

3. ______________________

4. ______________________

5. ______________________

6. ______________________

7. ______________________

8. ______________________

9. ______________________

V. Completion Exercise

Print the word or phrase that correctly completes each sentence.

1. The continuous one-way movement of the blood is known as the _circulation_

2. Each minute the heart contracts on an average of about _72_

3. The fibrous sac that surrounds the heart is the _pericardi_

4. After supplying nutrients to the heart muscle, blood is drained into the right atrium by way of the _coronary sinus_

5. The partition between the two thick-walled lower chambers of the heart is the _entra vent_

6. Because each of the three parts of the two exit valves is half-moon shaped, these valves are described as _semi lunar_

7. The right atrioventricular valve is the _tricuspid_

8. One complete sequence of relaxation and contraction of the heart is called a(n) _cardiac cycle_

9. The stroke volume and heart rate determine the volume of blood pumped by each ventricle in 1 minute, the _cardiac output_

10. The main influence over the heart rate outside of the heart itself is the _nNS_

VI. Practical Applications

Study each discussion. Then print the appropriate word or phrase in the space provided.

1. Mrs. K had rheumatic fever several times during her teenage years. Now at the age of 34 she was often short of breath and complained of some spitting-up of blood. It was found that the left atrioventricular valve had become so scarred that blood could not flow adequately from the left atrium to the left ventricle. This disorder is called _____

2. Using the stethoscope to listen to Mrs. K's heart sounds, the physician detected a(n) _____

3. Mr. L was 42 years of age and overweight. During a game of handball he felt severe heart pains; he collapsed in shock. Examination indicated that a clot had formed in a blood vessel supplying the heart, with complete obstruction of blood flow. The scientific name for this disorder is _____

4. Mr. C, age 74, had not felt well for several months. He had a long history of hypertension. Now he said that he felt weak, and seemed to be out of breath after slight exertion. Considering his history, his heart condition would probably be classified as _____

5. One of the first tests that was done on all these patients was a recording of electric currents produced by heart muscle. The apparatus that records this information is the _____

6. Additional studies on Mrs. K included the introduction of a small tube into the veins of her right arm and then into the right side of her heart. This procedure is called _____

7. Mr. A, age 61, had a history of myocardial infarction and ischemic heart disease. He now complained of dizziness, and his pulse rate was found to be 40, an abnormality called _____

8. Further testing indicated that there was damage to the conduction system of Mr. A's heart. He was scheduled to have surgery in which a device would be inserted to help regulate the heartbeat. This device is called a(n) _____

9. Mrs. P had undergone several tests that showed coronary artery disease to be the cause of her shortness of breath and attacks of angina. Her treatment consisted of surgical substitution for the diseased arteries, an operation called _____

14

Blood Vessels and Blood Circulation

I. Overview

The blood vessels are classified, according to function, as **arteries, veins,** or **capillaries**; the arteries and veins are subdivided into pulmonary vessels and systemic vessels.

The two arterial systems, the **systemic** and the **pulmonary**, can be likened to trees: each has a trunk, the aorta in one and the pulmonary artery in the other. Each trunk has subdivisions, large and small branches that carry the blood into the capillaries where exchanges between the blood and the tissue fluid occur. The tissue fluid provides for the transfer of substances required by the cell in exchange for those not needed or those manufactured for use elsewhere. The venous systems consist of tributaries progressing in size from small to large; they return the blood to the heart, which pumps it into the arterial trunks, thus completing the circuit.

The walls of the vessels, especially the small arteries, contain smooth muscle which is under the control of the involuntary nervous system. The diameters of the vessels can be regulated by the nervous system to alter blood pressure and to direct blood to various parts of the body as needed. These changes, termed **vasodilation** and **vasoconstriction**, are centrally controlled by a **vasomotor center** in the medulla of the brainstem.

The walls of the arteries are thicker and more elastic than the walls of the veins, and the arteries contain blood under higher pressure. All vessels are lined with a single layer of simple epithelium called **endothelium**. The smallest vessels, the capillaries, are made only of this single layer of cells. It is through the walls of the capillaries that exchanges take place between the blood and the tissues.

The **pulse rate** and **blood pressure** are manifestations of the circulation; they tell the trained person a great deal about the overall condition of the individual.

II. Topics for Review

A. The blood vessels
    1. Structure and function
B. Pulmonary and systemic circuits
C. Systemic arteries
    1. Branches of the aorta
        a. Ascending
        b. Aortic arch
        c. Thoracic
        d. Abdominal
    2. Branches of the iliac arteries
    3. Other parts of the arterial tree
D. Anastomoses
E. Systemic veins
    1. Superficial
    2. Deep
    3. Superior vena cava
    4. Sinuses
    5. Inferior vena cava
F. The hepatic portal system
G. Capillary exchanges
H. Vasodilation and vasoconstriction
 I. Return of blood to the heart
J. Pulse
K. Blood pressure
L. Disorders of blood vessels
M. Hemorrhage, shock, and circulatory failure

III. Matching Exercises

Matching only within each group, print the answers in the spaces provided.

Group A

systemic 6   endothelium 4   pulmonary 1
arteries 3   celiac 9   carotid 8
aorta 5   capillaries 2   coronary 7

1. The vessels that are related to the lungs, including the arteries
and their branches in the lungs and the veins that drain lung
capillaries are all designated as   _____

2. Exchanges between the blood and the cells take place
through the   _____

3. Since their function is to carry blood from the heart's pumping
chambers, the blood vessels that have the thickest walls are the   _____

4. The innermost tunic of the artery is composed of   _____

5. The largest artery in the body is divided into four regions. This
vessel is the   _____

6. The arteries that carry food and oxygen to the tissues of the body are classified as

     _____

7. The ascending aorta has two branches that supply the heart muscle; they are described by the term

     _____

8. Supplying the head and neck on each side is an artery named the

     _____

9. One of the unpaired arteries that supplies some of the viscera of the upper abdomen is a short trunk, the

     _____

Group B

blood pressure 6	portal 3	anastomosis 5
valves 7	arterioles 1	vasomotor center 4
venules 2		

1. Small arteries are called

     _____

2. The vessels that receive blood from the capillaries are the

     _____

3. A system that carries venous blood to a second capillary bed before it returns to the heart is described by the term

     _____

4. Dilation and constriction of the blood vessels is controlled by an area of the medulla called the

     _____

5. A communication between two arteries is a(n)

     _____

6. A force that drives materials out of the capillaries is

     _____

7. Blood is prevented from moving backward in the veins by the

     _____

Group C

phrenic artery 5	lumbar arteries 10	common iliac arteries 9
brachiocephalic trunk 1	right subclavian artery 7	left common carotid artery 2
renal arteries 8	hepatic artery 3	superior mesenteric artery 4
brachial artery 6		

1. Coming off the aortic arch is a short artery formerly called the innominate artery. This is the

     _____

2. Supplying the left side of the head and neck is the

     _____

3. Oxygenated blood is carried to the liver by the

     _____

4. The largest branch of the abdominal aorta supplies most of the small intestine and the first half of the large intestine. This branch is the

     _____

5. The diaphragm is supplied by a right and a left

     _____

6. The artery supplying the arm is a continuation of the axillary artery, and is called the

     _____

7. Blood supply to the right upper extremity is through the

_____

8. The largest of the paired branches of the abdominal aorta are those that supply the kidneys. These are the

_____

9. The abdominal aorta finally divides into two

_____

10. Supply to the abdominal wall is through the

_____

Group D

brachiocephalic trunk	radial artery 10	unpaired
mesenteric	femoral artery 8	basilar artery
paired	circle of Willis 1	volar arch
celiac trunk		

1. An anastomosis of the two internal carotid arteries and the basilar artery is located immediately under the center of the brain. It is called the

_____

2. The inferior mesenteric is an example of an artery that is

_____

3. The radial and ulnar arteries in the hand anastomose to form the

_____

4. Anastomoses between branches of the vessels supplying blood to the intestinal tract comprise arches named

_____

5. The right subclavian artery and the right common carotid artery are branches of the

_____

6. The left gastric artery and the splenic artery are two of the three branches of the

_____

7. The union of the two vertebral arteries forms the

_____

8. The external iliac arteries extend into the thigh. Here each of them becomes a(n)

_____

9. The popliteal arteries are examples of the many blood vessels that are

_____

10. The branch of the brachial artery that extends down the forearm and wrist of the thumb side is the

_____

Group E

azygos vein	median cubital	saphenous vein 1
inferior vena cava 8	hepatic portal vein 9	superior vena cava 5
jugular veins 3	brachiocephalic veins	venous sinuses

1. The longest vein is the superficial one called the

_____

2. Because of its location near the surface at the front of the elbow, one of the veins frequently used for removing blood for testing is the

_____

3. The areas supplied by the carotid arteries are drained by the

   _____

4. The union of the jugular and subclavian veins forms the

   _____

5. Veins draining the head, the neck, the upper extremities, and the chest all empty into the

   _____

6. Before reaching the superior vena cava (and then the heart), blood from the chest wall drains into the

   _____

7. Large channels that drain deoxygenated blood are called

   _____

8. The blood from the parts of the body below the diaphragm is drained by the large vein called the

   _____

9. Tributaries from the unpaired organs empty into a vein that enters the liver where it subdivides into smaller veins. This unusual vein is called the

   _____

Group F

sinusoids   hepatic veins 3   left testicular vein
coronary sinus   lateral sinuses   cavernous sinuses
common iliac veins /   superior sagittal sinus   gastric veins
superior mesenteric vein

1. The inferior vena cava begins with the union of the two

   _____

2. The only exceptions to the rule that paired veins empty directly into the vena cava are the left ovarian vein and the

   _____

3. Among the paired veins that empty directly into the inferior vena cava are those draining the liver, the

   _____

4. The vein that drains most of the small intestine and the first part of the large intestine is the

   _____

5. The tributaries of the hepatic portal vein include those that drain the stomach, the

   _____

6. Within the liver, exchanges take place through enlarged capillaries called

   _____

7. The veins of the heart drain mainly into the

   _____

8. The ophthalmic veins drain into the

   _____

9. Nearly all the blood from the veins of the brain eventually empties into one or the other of the transverse or

   _____

10. In the midline above the brain and in the fissure between the two cerebral hemispheres is a long blood-containing space called the

    _____

Group G

atherosclerosis 10
slower 9
hypotension 6
arteriosclerosis 11

dorsalis pedis 3
hypertension 7
faster 5
aneurysm 8

radial artery 2
sphygmomanometer 4
pulse 1

1. Beginning at the heart and traveling along the arteries is a wave of increased pressure started by the force of ventricular contractions. This wave is called the

_____

2. The wave is readily felt at the wrist because of the artery that passes over the bone on the thumb side. This is the

_____

3. Sometimes it is necessary to use the artery on the top of the foot for obtaining the pulse. This is the

_____

4. Blood pressure is recorded by an instrument called a(n)

_____

5. It is important to recognize factors that may influence pulse rate. Emotional disturbance, for example, may cause the pulse rate to be

_____

6. An abnormal decrease in blood pressure, as may occur in shock, is called

_____

7. Kidney disease is one cause of abnormally high blood pressure, or

_____

8. Weakness of a blood vessel wall may give rise to a(n)

_____

9. As the child matures, his pulse rate normally becomes

_____

10. A change in the arterial walls in which yellow, fatlike material replaces muscle and elastic connective tissue leads to a diagnosis of

_____

11. The condition in which calcium salts and fibrous connective tissues infiltrate the artery walls and cause hardening of the arteries is called

_____

Group H

shock
cerebral artery
facial artery
albumin

femoral artery
diastolic pressure
brachial artery
coronary artery

hypertension
systolic pressure
saphenous vein

1. Headaches, dizziness, and mental disorders may be the result of sclerosis of a(n)

_____

2. A decrease in the size of artery lumens throughout the body may be a cause of

_____

3. Arteriosclerosis may involve the arteries that supply the kidneys, in which case one important symptom is the appearance in the urine of the protein

    _____

4. Sclerosis may involve a heart vessel, in which case it affects a(n)

    _____

5. A diseased portion of an artery can be bypassed with a blood vessel from the patient's own body. Often a large vessel from the thigh is used, namely the

    _____

6. During ventricular relaxation the sphygmomanometer measures

    _____

7. The most serious immediate problem following an accident usually is hemorrhage. By pressing certain arteries against the underlying bone, it is often possible to stop this hemorrhage. Hemorrhage around the nose and mouth may be stopped by pressing against the lower jaw to compress the

    _____

8. Hemorrhage from the forearm, wrist, and hand may be stopped by pressing along the groove between the two large arm muscles to compress the

    _____

9. Hemorrhage of the lower extremity may be stopped by pressing in the groin to compress the

    _____

10. A sudden failure of the circulation is called

    _____

11. Blood pressure measured during heart muscle contraction is the

    _____

IV. Labeling

For each of the following illustrations print the name or names of each labeled part on the numbered lines.

1. _____

2. _____

3. _____

4. _____

5. _____

6. _____

7. _____

8. _____

9. _____

10. _____

11. _____

12. _____

13. _____

14. _____

15. _____

16. _____

17. _____

18. _____

19. _____

20. _____

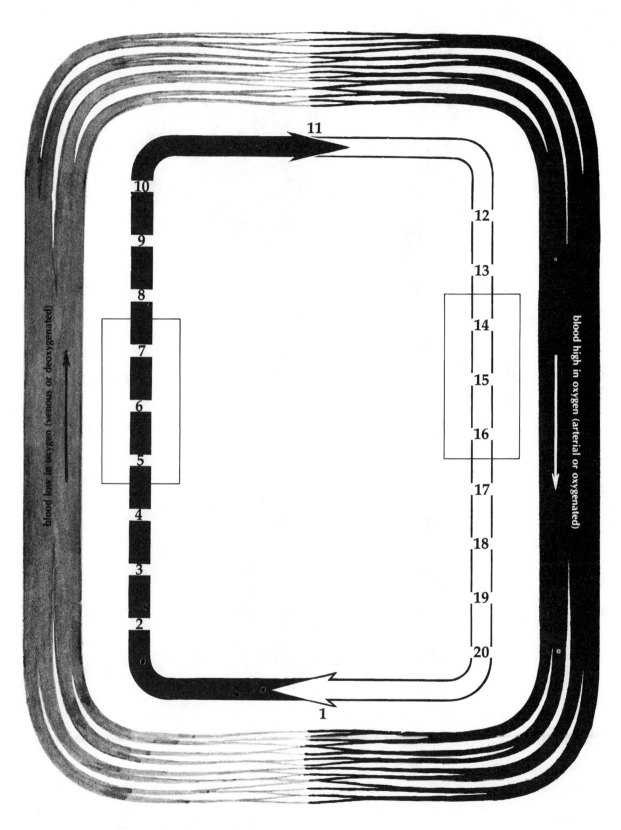

blood low in oxygen (venous or deoxygenated)

blood high in oxygen (arterial or oxygenated)

Diagram to show circuit of blood flow

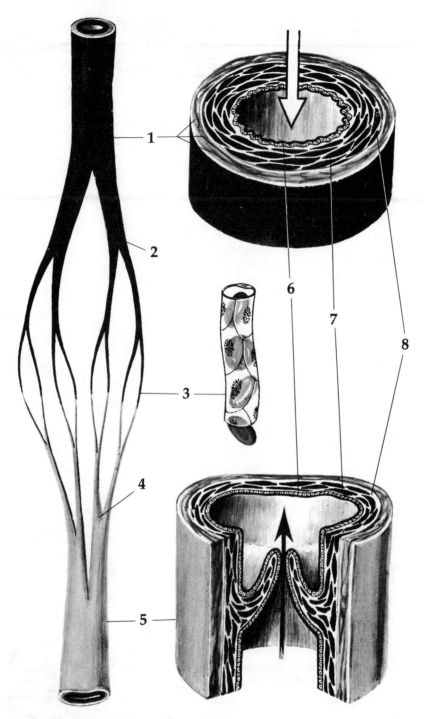

Sections of small blood vessels

1. _____ 4. _____ 7. _____

2. _____ 5. _____ 8. _____

3. _____ 6. _____

1. _____

2. _____

3. _____

4. _____

5. _____

6. _____

7. _____

8. _____

9. _____

10. _____

11. _____

12. _____

13. _____

14. _____

15. _____

16. _____

17. _____

18. _____

19. _____

20. _____

21. _____

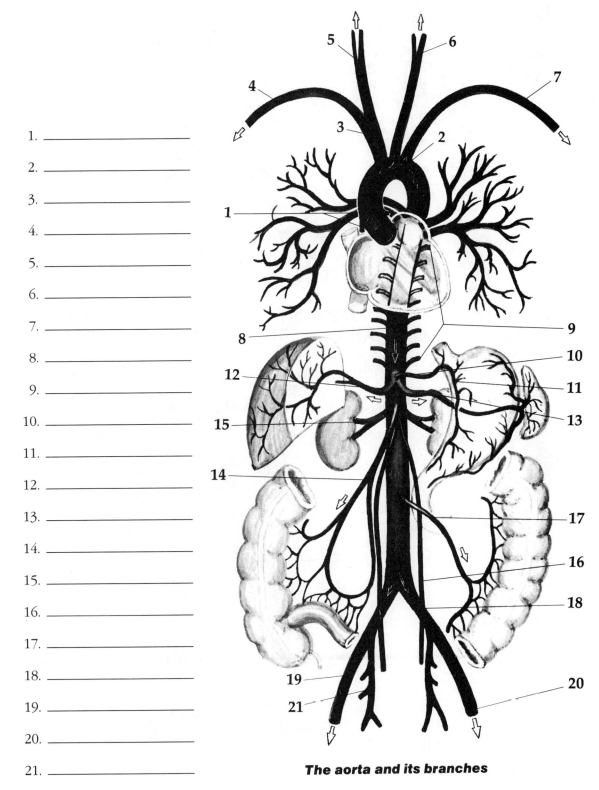

The aorta and its branches

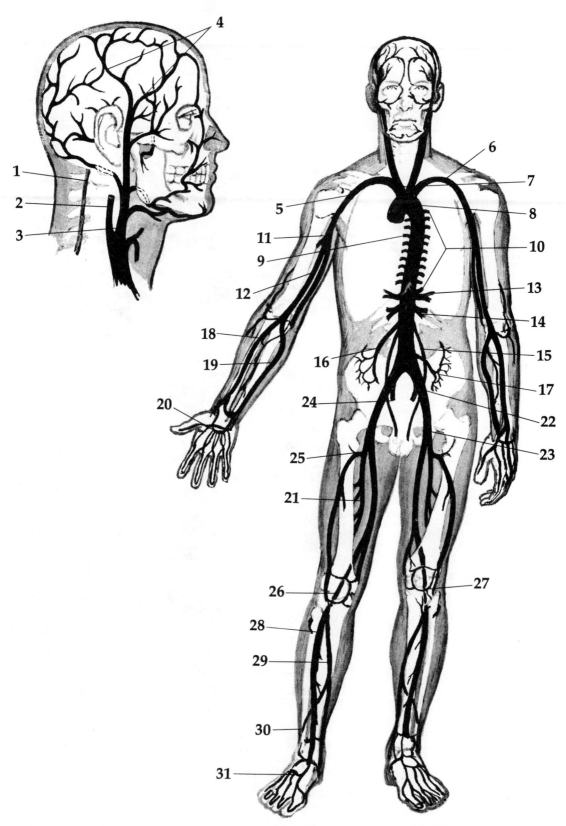

Principal arteries

1. _____
2. _____
3. _____
4. _____
5. _____
6. _____
7. _____
8. _____
9. _____
10. _____
11. _____
12. _____
13. _____
14. _____
15. _____
16. _____
17. _____
18. _____
19. _____
20. _____
21. _____
22. _____
23. _____
24. _____
25. _____
26. _____

27. _____
28. _____
29. _____
30. _____
31. _____

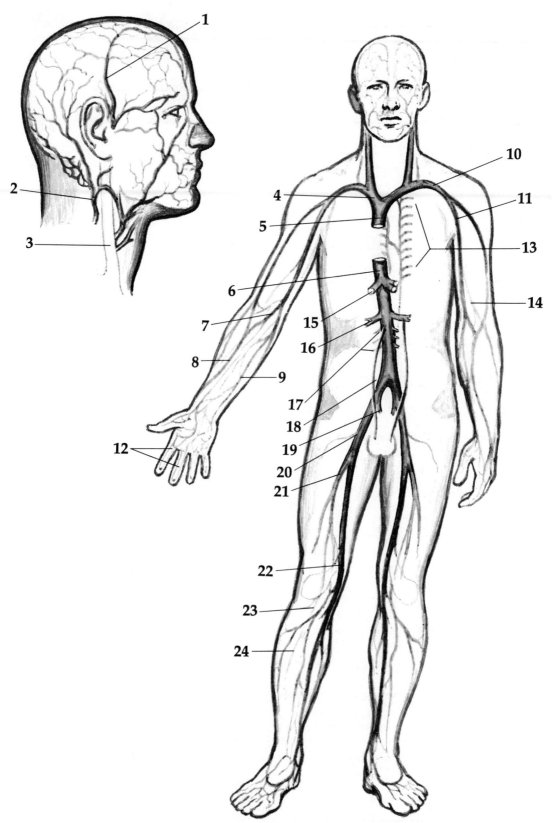

Principal veins

1. _____

2. _____

3. _____

4. _____

5. _____

6. _____

7. _____

8. _____

9. _____

10. _____

11. _____

12. _____

13. _____

14. _____

15. _____

16. _____

17. _____

18. _____

19. _____

20. _____

21. _____

22. _____

23. _____

24. _____

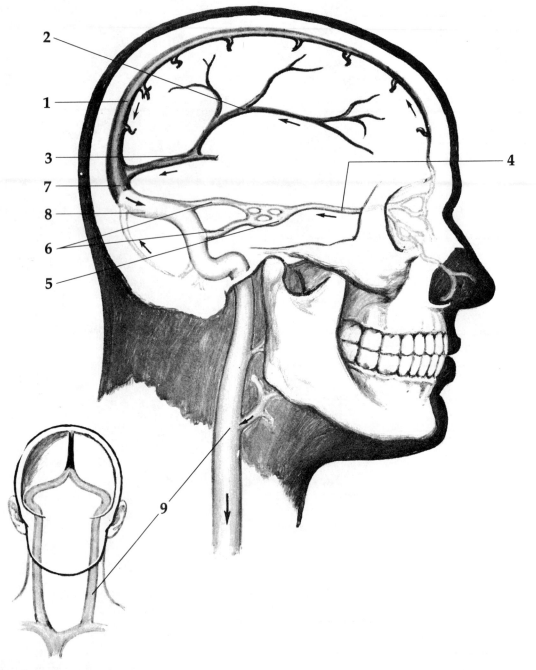

Cranial venous sinuses

1. _____

2. _____

3. _____

4. _____

5. _____

6. _____

7. _____

8. _____

9. _____

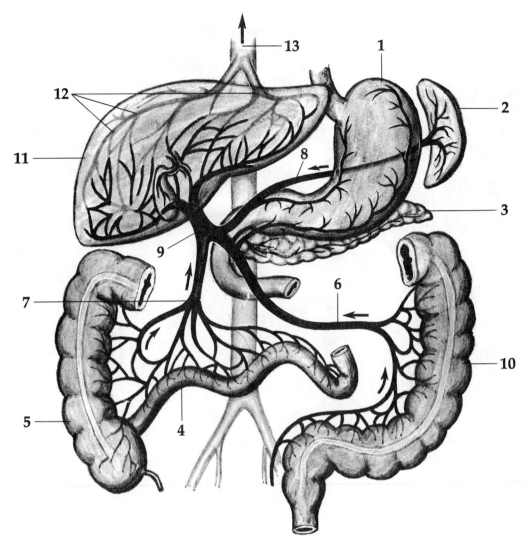

Hepatic portal circulation

1. _____ 8. _____

2. _____ 9. _____

3. _____ 10. _____

4. _____ 11. _____

5. _____ 12. _____

6. _____ 13. _____

7. _____

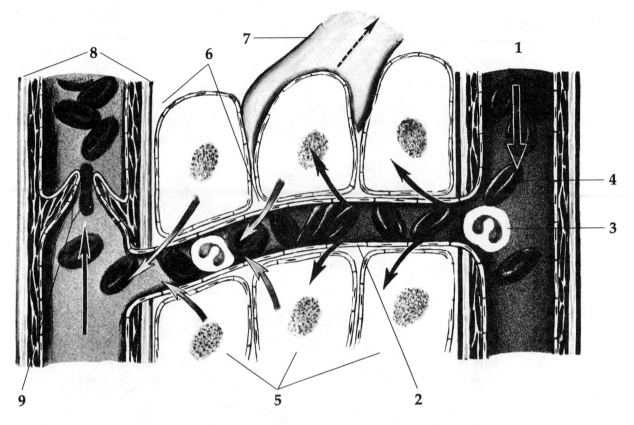

Diagram showing the connection between the small blood vessels through capillaries

1. _____   6. _____

2. _____   7. _____

3. _____   8. _____

4. _____   9. _____

5. _____

V. Completion Exercise

Print the word or phrase that correctly completes each sentence.

1. Deoxygenated blood is carried from the right ventricle by the _____

2. The smallest subdivisions of arteries have thin walls in which there is little connective tissue and relatively more muscle. These vessels are _____

3. Supplying nutrients to body tissues and carrying off waste products from the tissues are functions of the part of the circulation described as _____

4. The middle tunic of the arterial wall is composed of elastic connective tissue plus _____

5. The innermost tunic of the vessels is composed of _____

6. Swollen and ineffective veins are described as _____

7. Hemorrhoids are swollen and tortuous veins located in the _____

8. Persons whose work requires them to stand much of the time frequently suffer from varicosities of the _____

9. The smallest veins are formed by the union of capillaries. These tiny vessels are called _____

10. The circle of Willis is formed by a union of the internal carotid arteries and the basilar artery. Such a union of end arteries is called a(n) _____

11. An increase in the diameter of a blood vessel is termed _____

12. One example of a portal system is the system which carries blood from the abdominal organs to the _____

VI. Practical Applications

Study each discussion. Then print the appropriate word or phrase in the space provided.

1. Mr. S, age 53, complained of shortness of breath, weakness, and pain in the left chest. Examination indicated that the left semilunar valve was not functioning properly. This valve guards the entrance into the largest artery which is the _____

2. Mrs. K, age 69, was admitted to the hospital because she had fainted several times and was unable to recall events before and after these episodes. The physician diagnosed her condition as hardening of the arteries, or _____

3. In such cases as Mrs. K's the gradual narrowing of the arteries in the brain is associated with a reduction in the volume of blood passing through them. This is called

_____

4. When the blood supply to an organ is inadequate, the cells of that organ gradually die. Cell death is called

_____

5. Ms. J, age 78, complained of pain and swelling in the area of her saphenous vein. The term for venous inflammation is

_____

6. Further study of Ms. J's illness indicated that a blood clot had formed in one vein. This condition is called

_____

7. Ms. J was transferred to the intensive care unit because it was feared that the venous clot might become dislodged and be carried in the blood to her lungs. If this should happen, death would be due to

_____

8. Advances in medicine and surgery have made possible the replacement of damaged parts of arteries by using a segment of the saphenous vein from the patient's own body or by use of a synthetic vessel as a

_____

9. Mr. B, age 67, had been diabetic for the past several years. He had neglected his diet and was careless about following his doctor's orders. Now the doctor found it necessary to order amputation of his right foot, because necrosis of the involved tissue eventually resulted in

_____

10. Mr. W was seen in the hospital emergency room. He complained of severe, crushing chest pain. Further observation yielded these objective signs: pulse of 120, weak; blood pressure 76/40; skin cold, clammy, and gray; and rapid, shallow respiration. His symptoms were due to failure of the heart pump, known as

_____

11. Mrs. H, age 72, a clinic patient with a history of varicose veins, was being examined because of the presence of an open sore on her lower leg. The skin surrounding the sore was scaling, inflamed, and cracked—all symptoms of a circulatory deficiency called

_____

15

The Lymphatic System and Lymphoid Tissue

I. Overview

Lymph is the watery fluid that flows within the lymphatic system. It originates from the blood plasma and from the tissue fluid that is found in the minute spaces around and between the body cells. The fluid moves from the **lymphatic capillaries** through the **lymphatic vessels** and then to the **right lymphatic duct** and the **thoracic duct**. The lymphatic vessels are thin-walled and delicate; like some veins, they have valves that prevent backflow of lymph.

The **lymph nodes**, which are the system's filters, are composed of **lymphoid tissue**. These nodes remove impurities and manufacutre **lymphocytes**, cells active in immunity. Chief among them are the cervical nodes in the neck, the axillary nodes in the armpit, the tracheobronchial nodes near the trachea and bronchial tubes, the mesenteric nodes between the peritoneal layers, and the inguinal nodes in the groin area.

In additon to these nodes, there are several organs of lymphoid tissue with somewhat different functions. The **tonsils** filter tissue fluid. The **thymus** is essential for development of the immune system during the early months of life. The **spleen** has numerous functions, among which are the destruction of worn-out red blood cells, serving as a reservoir for blood, and the production of red blood cells before birth.

Another part of the body's protective system is the **mononuclear phagocyte system**, which consists of cells involved in the destruction of bacteria, cancer cells, and other possibly harmful substances.

II. Topics for Review

A. Lymphatic vessels
B. Lymphoid tissue
    1. Lymph nodes
    2. Tonsils
    3. Thymus
    4. Spleen
C. Functions of the mononuclear phagocyte system
D. Disorders of the lymphatic system

III. Matching Exercises

Matching only within each group, print the answers in the spaces provided.

Group A

right lymphatic duct   blood   chyle
lacteals   valves   axillary nodes
endothelium   buboes
cervical nodes   inguinal nodes

1. There is easy passage of soluble materials and water through the walls of lymphatic capillaries, composed of a single layer of cells forming the   _____

2. The lymphatics resemble some veins in that they contain structures that prevent backflow. These are   _____

3. One pathway for fats from digested food to the bloodstream is through specialized lymphatic capillaries of the intestine that are called   _____

4. Lymph is drained from the right side of the head, of the neck, of the thorax, and of the right upper extremity by the   _____

5. The combination of fat globules and lymph gives rise to a milky-appearing fluid called   _____

6. Lymph nodes are named according to location. Those located in the armpits are known as   _____

7. Lymph from the lower extremities and the external genitalia drains through the   _____

8. Abnormally large inguinal nodes, as may be found in certain infections, are called   _____

9. The final destination of filtered lymph is the   _____

10. The lymph nodes located in the neck and draining certain parts of the head and neck are known as   _____

Group B

thymus   pharyngeal tonsils   palatine tonsils
lingual tonsils   lymphangitis
spleen   lymphadenitis

1. The oval lymphoid bodies located at each side of the soft palate are known as   _____

2. The enlarged masses of lymphoid tissue often found on the back wall of the pharynx and commonly called adenoids are correctly called

    _____

3. At the back of the tongue are masses of lymphoid tissue called

    _____

4. The structure that is believed to be essential in the development of immunity very early in life is the

    _____

5. Blood is filtered by an organ located in the upper left quadrant (left hypochondriac region) of the abdomen. This is the

    _____

6. A word that refers to inflammatory disorders of lymph nodes is

    _____

7. Recall that the suffix -itis means inflammation; when referring to lymph vessel inflammation, we use the word

    _____

Group C

lymph nodes   backflow   radial

phagocytosis   drainage   thymus

subclavian vein   antibodies   monocytes

thoracic duct

1. The white blood cells active in the mononuclear phagocyte system are the

    _____

2. Some of the cells in the lymphoid tissue produce substances that aid in combating infection. These are called

    _____

3. The spleen and other lymphoid tissues generate cells that are able to engulf bacteria and other small foreign bodies. This process of ingesting foreign substances is called

    _____

4. T-lymphocytes mature in the

    _____

5. Before the lymph reaches the veins it is passed through organs that act as filters. These are

    _____

6. The lymphatic vessels serve as a system for

    _____

7. Lymph received in the right lymphatic duct drains into the right

    _____

8. Lymph is drained from the body below the diaphragm and on the left side above the diaphragm by the largest lymphatic vessel, the

    _____

9. The valves of the lymphatic vessels prevent lymph

    _____

10. Lymphatic vessels are named according to location; thus, those on the lateral side of the forearm are described as

    _____

Group D

lymphocytes *4*   lacteals *3*   lymph nodes *7*
lymph *6*   superficial *1*   cisterna chyli *2*
veins *8*   plasma *5*

1. Lymphatic vessels located under the skin are described as _____

2. The first part of the thoracic duct is enlarged, forming a temporary storage area. It is called the _____

3. Chyle, the fluid formed by combination of lymph and fat globules, comes from the intestinal _____

4. An important function of lymph nodes is the manufacture of white blood cells known as _____

5. Intercellular fluid originates from the liquid part of the blood. The liquid part of the blood is called _____

6. Tissue fluid passes from the intercellular spaces into the lymphatic vessels; it is then called _____

7. The masses of lymphoid tissue that filter foreign substances from the lymph are known as _____

8. The vessels of the lymphatic system are often located near the _____

Group E

macrophages *2*   spleen *7*   exercise *4*
thoracic duct *6*   chyle *5*   Kupffer's cells *3*
hilum *1*

1. The area of exit for the vessels carrying lymph out of the node is known as the _____

2. When monocytes enter the body tissues and act to destroy foreign matter, they are called _____

3. The phagocytes of the liver are called _____

4. The normal onward flow of lymph is aided by changes in position of various parts of the body and by _____

5. A fluid formed by the combination of fat globules and lymph originates in the intestinal lacteals. The name of the fluid is _____

6. The larger of the terminal vessels of the lymphatic system is called the _____

7. During embryonic and fetal life, red blood cells are produced partly in the _____

IV. Labeling

Print the name or names of each labeled part on the numbered lines.

1. _____

2. _____

3. _____

4. _____

5. _____

6. _____

7. _____

8. _____

9. _____

10. _____

11. _____

12. _____

13. _____

14. _____

15. _____

16. _____

17. _____

The lymphatic system

V. Completion Exercise

Print the word or phrase that correctly completes each sentence.

1. The fluid that moves from blood plasma to the tissue spaces and finally to special collection vessels is called _____

2. Since the prefix *angi-* means blood or lymph vessel, it is to be expected that the term for inflammation of lymph vessels is _____

3. Lymphatic vessels from the left side of the head, neck, and thorax empty into the largest of the lymph vessels, the _____

4. The lymph from the body below the diaphragm and from the left side above the diaphragm is carried into the blood of the _____

5. Between the two layers of peritoneum that form the mesentery are found nodes called _____

6. In city dwellers, nodes may appear black because they become filled with carbon particles. This is true mostly of the nodes that surround the windpipe and its divisions. These are the _____

7. A disease prevalent during the Middle Ages was responsible for the death of hundreds of thousands of people. This disease was characterized by the presence of buboes, inflammatory swellings of the inguinal nodes, so it was called _____

8. The structure popularly known as adenoids is correctly called the _____

9. The spleen and other organs produce cells that can engulf harmful bacteria and other foreign cells, by a process called _____

10. The blockage of lymphatic vessels by filariae may cause tremendous enlargement of the lower extremities, a disorder called _____

11. A tumor that occurs in lymphoid tissue, whether benign or malignant, has the general name of _____

VI. Practical Applications

Study each discussion. Then print the appropriate word or phrase in the space provided.

1. Mrs. B, age 38, underwent biopsy of a small mass in her right breast which was positive for cancer. She now is being admitted in order to have a radical mastectomy. In this operation certain nodes are removed as well as the breast, because cancer cells from the breast often invade them. These are the armpit nodes called the _____

2. Mr. G, age 31, complained of swellings in his neck, his armpits, his groin, and other areas. A diagnosis of Hodgkin's disease was made. The nodes of the neck are designated the _____

3. Mr. K, age 41, had been hunting wild rabbits in the central valley of California. Several days after dressing a number of these rabbits an ulcer developed on his hand. A tentative diagnosis of tularemia, or rabbit fever, was made. The infecting organisms had been carried to the axillary nodes by way of tubes called _____

4. Mrs. M was admitted for study because her spleen was enlarged. This condition is called _____

5. After a number of tests had been done, a diagnosis of splenic anemia was made. Removal of the spleen was carried out. This operation is called a _____

6. Mr. L was admitted for study of pelvic masses. It was feared that his disorder might be a malignancy of lymphoid tissue that is rapidly fatal, called _____

7. Mr. J was 21 years old. His complaint concerned swelling in the groin region. A blood test showed that the young man had contracted syphilis. Infection of the external genitalia is often followed by the appearance of buboes, which are enlarged _____

16

Body Defenses, Immunity, and Vaccines

I. Overview

Although the body is constantly being exposed to pathogenic organisms, infection develops relatively rarely. This is because the body has many "lines of defense" against pathogenic invasion. The intact **skin** and **mucous membranes** serve as mechanical barriers, as do certain **reflexes** such as sneezing and coughing. Next is the process of **inflammation**, by which the body tries to get rid of the irritant or to minimize its harmful effects. Finally, the ultimate defense is **immunity**, the means by which the body resists or overcomes the effects of a particular disease or other harmful agent.

Immune responses are based on reactions between foreign substances or **antigens** and certain white blood cells, the lymphocytes. The **T-lymphocytes** respond to the antigen directly and produce **cell-mediated immunity**. B-lymphocytes, when stimulated by an antigen, multiply and begin to produce specific antibodies which react with the antigen. These circulating antibodies make up the form of immunity termed **humoral immunity**.

There are two basic types of immunity: inborn and acquired. **Inborn immunity** is inherited; it may exist on the basis of **species**, **racial**, or **individual** characteristics. **Acquired immunity** may be of the **natural** type (acquired before birth or by contact with the disease) or of the **artificial** type (provided by a vaccine or an immune serum). Immunity acquired as a result of the transfer of antibodies to an individual from some outside source is described as **passive immunity**; immunity that involves production of antibodies by the individual is termed **active immunity**.

The chemical processes in **allergy** are similar to those in immunity. The **rejection syndrome** that often takes place following organ transplantation might be compared to a greatly increased allergic reaction. Research on the immune system has expanded greatly in the past few decades. Current areas of interest include the study of a virus which causes acquired immune deficiency syndrome (AIDS), study of the role of the immune system in cancer, and study of autoimmune diseases.

II. Topics for Review

A. Nonspecific defenses against invasion
  1. Skin and mucous membranes
  2. Phagocytosis
  3. Inflammation
  4. Interferon
B. Specific defenses: immunity
  1. Inborn
  2. Acquired
    a. Active
    b. Passive
C. Lymphocytes and the immune response
D. Vaccines and immunization
E. Disorders involving the immune system
  1. Allergy
  2. Autoimmunity
  3. Transplants and the rejection syndrome
  4. Immune deficiency

III. Matching Exercises

Matching only within each group, print the answers in the spaces provided.

Group A

nerve tissue   virulence   nonspecific resistance
immunity   infection   portal of entry
toxins   respiratory tract thymus

1. The means by which a pathogenic organism invades the body is called the

    portal of entry

2. The degree to which an organism can cause disease and its power to overcome body defenses are known as its

    virulence

3. The unbroken skin and mucous membranes are elements of the body's defenses against any harmful agent. Such protective devices are part of the body's

    non-specific resistance

4. Some pathogens have an affinity, or preference, for certain tissues. The virus of poliomyelitis, for example, attacks only

    nerve tissue

5. A second example of tissue preference is seen in the common cold and influenza viruses, which invade the

    resp. tract

6. A break in the skin through which pathogenic organisms can easily reach deeper tissues may result in

    infection

7. The poisons produced by pathogens are known as

    toxins

8. The body's ability to defend itself against a certain specific agent is spoken of as its specific resistance, or

    immunity

9. T cells are formed from stem cells that migrate from the bone marrow into the _thymus_

Group B

inborn immunity	inflammatory reaction	antigen
species immunity	racial immunity	attenuation
active immunity	passive immunity	B-lymphocytes

1. The body tries to get rid of (or minimize the effects of) an irritant by a series of nonspecific defensive responses that constitute a(n) _inflm. reaction_

2. Animals are susceptible to diseases that do not affect humans; the reverse is also true. In other words, both possess a(n) _species imm._

3. The greater resistance of black Americans to malaria and yellow fever over white Americans is an example of _racial imm._

4. Any foreign substance introduced into the body by a pathogen provokes a response. The foreign substance is known as a(n) _antigen_

5. An inherited immunity is usually called a(n) _inborn imm._

6. A person who is infected by a pathogen or its toxin produces antibodies that make him immune to that infection for a long period of time, perhaps for life. This type of immunity is called _active_

7. To produce immunity by vaccination, a live weakened pathogen may be administered. The process of reducing the virulence of the pathogen is called _attenuation_

8. The resistance of the newborn infant to contagious diseases is due to antibodies transferred from mother to fetus through the placenta. This type of immunity is classified as _passive_

9. In response to infection, antibodies are produced by the _B-lympho_

Group C

complement	artificially acquired	antigen
plasma cells	memory cells	toxoid
allergy	vaccination	gamma globulin

1. A person who has been bitten by an animal suspected of having rabies is immunized with a killed rabies virus vaccine. Such treatment is a form of _vaccination_

2. Some Rh negative persons may become sensitized to the Rh protein. In such cases the Rh factor is an example of a substance known as a(n) _antigen_

3. The administration of a vaccine results in the type of immunity classified as _artificially acquired_

4. A toxin may be used for a vaccine if it is treated with heat or chemicals to reduce its harmfulness. Such an altered toxin is a(n) _____ *toxoid*

5. The fraction of the blood plasma that contains antibodies is known as _____ *glamma globlin*

6. When B-lymphocytes are stimulated by an antigen, they multiply and become cells capable of producing antibodies. These cells are called _____ *plasma cells*

7. A reaction between an antigen and an antibody that takes place within the cells of sensitized tissue results in _____ *allergy*

8. Booster shots are given to stimulate the activity of _____ *memory cells*

9. A group of blood proteins that may be needed to help an antibody destroy a foreign antigen is called _____ *complement*

Group D

convalescent serum	antivenin	antitoxin
antibodies	allergens	rubella
sensitized	autoimmunity	transplantation

1. Many diseases are now believed to result from the manufacture of antibodies to one's own tissues, a condition termed _____ *autoimmunity*

2. Horses are widely used in the production of immune serums because, when injected with foreign antigens, their tissues produce large quantities of _____ *antibodies*

3. Passive immunity to diphtheria can be provided by giving an immune serum containing diphtheria _____ *antitoxin*

4. The type of serum that is injected to combat the effects of bites of various poisonous snakes is called _____ *antivenin*

5. In susceptible persons, repeated exposure to an allergen will cause tissues to become _____ *Sensitized*

6. Pollens and house dust contain proteins which in susceptible persons act as _____ *allergens*

7. A disorder that may cause serious effects on the developing fetus is _____ *rubella*

8. The serum of a person who is recovering from a certain disease may be administered to another person to provide passive immunity. Serum so used is known as _____ *convalescent serum*

9. The natural tendency for every organism to reject foreign substances has made it difficult to carry out organ or tissue _____ *transplantation*

IV. Completion Exercise

Print the word or phrase that correctly completes each sentence.

1. The mixture of leukocytes and fluid from the blood plasma which is produced as the body tries to defend itself against pathogens is known as the

   immflamatory exudate

2. One aspect of a pathogen's virulence has to do with its ability to overwhelm the host; this may be called its aggressiveness, or

   invasive power

3. The sum of the body's natural defenses against disease is known as its

   resistance

4. The first line of defense against disease includes mechanical methods for removing foreign matter from the respiratory tract. Among these are sneezing and coughing, which are

   reflexes

5. The action of leukocytes in which they engulf and digest invading pathogens is known as

   phagocytosis

6. Circulating antibodies are responsible for the type of immunity termed

   humoral immun.

7. Immunity is a selective process through which a person may be immune to one disease but not to another. This selective characteristic is called

   specificity

8. The word that means the opposite of immunity is

   suceptibility

9. There are two main categories of immunity. One is inborn immunity while the other is

   acquired

10. Heat, redness, swelling, and pain are considered the classic symptoms of the

    Inflammatory reaction

11. An artificially acquired immunity may be provided for a limited time by injecting an immune serum or for longer by using a

    vaccine

12. Antibodies transmitted from the mother's blood to the fetus provide a type of short-term borrowed immunity called

    passive immun.

13. The administration of vaccine, on the other hand, stimulates the body to produce a longer lasting type of immunity called

    active immun.

14. The irritating effects of the allergic response is believed to be an antigen–antibody reaction that results in the liberation of a substance that dilates the blood vessels and is called

    histamine

15. The use of methods to stimulate the immune system in the hopes of combating cancer is a form of treatment called

    immunotherapy

187

V. Practical Applications

Study each discussion. Then print the appropriate word or phrase in the space provided.

1. Mr. O brought his 38-year-old wife to the office for emergency treatment following a bee sting. Since Mrs. O was in a state of near-shock, the physician administered an injection of epinephrine; Mrs. O's condition improved. The physician then made several suggestions to help Mrs. O deal with her sensitivity to bee stings, which he described as a(n) ___allergy___

2. Mrs. R brought her 2-month-old infant to the office for the first of a series of injections to inoculate him against several serious diseases. The vaccine used for this purpose contains the weakened toxins of the organisms causing these diseases. This type of vaccine is known as ___toxoid___

3. Ms. Y was allergic to pollens. In the hope that her tissues would be desensitized, the physician was giving her repeated injections of the ___offending allergens___

4. Mr. N, age 42, had received a kidney transplant. He had appeared well for several months after the operation, when evidences of the rejection syndrome appeared. These reactions are due primarily to the activity of certain white blood cells that defend the body against foreign organisms. They are responsible for cell-mediated immunity and are called ___T-lympho___

5. Mr. T, a construction worker, was careless about cleansing his skin and neglected the abrasions on his fingers. An infection of his right thumb and index finger resulted in painful swelling and prevented him from working. He was treated with hot wet compresses, and in time his natural resistance overcame the infection. To a large extent this resistance was due to the production of quantities of antibodies by the white cells known as ___B-lympho___

6. Mr. K consulted his physician for a generalized weakness and susceptibility to disease. Blood tests showed that he was infected with a virus that weakened his immune system by destroying T-lymphocytes. The name of this disease is abbreviated by the letters ___Aids___

7. Mrs. N was diagnosed as having systemic lupus erythematosus after she consulted her physician for fatigue, skin rashes, and joint pain. Her doctor explained that her disease was caused by a reaction of her immune system to her own body proteins, a condition termed ___autoimmunity___

17

Respiration

I. Overview

Oxygen is supplied to the tissue cells, and carbon dioxide is removed from them by means of the spaces and passageways that make up the **respiratory system**. This system contains the **nasal cavities**, the **pharynx**, the **larynx**, the **trachea**, the **bronchi**, and the **lungs**.

The two phases of breathing are the active phase of **inhalation** and the passive phase of **exhalation**. The movement of air between the outside and the lungs is called **ventilation**. As a result of ventilation, exchanges of oxygen and carbon dioxide occur. The first phase of these exchanges takes place in the lungs and is termed **external respiration**. The second phase, **internal respiration**, involves the exchanges that go on between the blood and the tissue cells.

The exchanges of oxygen and carbon dioxide are based on the physical principle of movement of molecules from areas of higher concentration to those of lower concentration by **diffusion**. Oxygen is transported to the tissues almost entirely by the **hemoglobin** in red blood cells. Some carbon dioxide is transported in the red blood cells as well, but most is carried in the blood plasma as the **bicarbonate ion**. Carbon dioxide is important in regulating the pH of the blood and in regulating the breathing rate.

Breathing is basically controlled by the **respiratory control centers** in the medulla and the pons of the brain stem. These centers are influenced by chemoreceptors located outside the medulla that respond to changes in the acidity of the cerebrospinal fluid. There are also **chemoreceptors** in the large vessels of the chest and neck that regulate respiration in response to changes in the composition of the blood.

Disorders of the respiratory tract include infection, allergy, chronic obstructive pulmonary disease (COPD), and cancer.

II. Topics for Review

A. The respiratory system
B. Pulmonary ventilation
    1. Inhalation
    2. Exhalation

C. Gas exchanges
   1. External respiration
   2. Internal respiration
D. Gas transport
   1. Oxygen
   2. Carbon dioxide
E. Regulation of respiration
   1. Respiratory rates
F. Disorders of the respiratory system

III. Matching Exercises

Matching only within each group, print the answers in the spaces provided.

Group A

diffusion	inhalation	oxygen
exhalation	internal respiration	carbon dioxide
ventilation	external respiration	surfactant

1. The word *respiration* means "to breathe again"; one of its basic purposes is to supply the body cells with the gas _____

2. At the same time that the required gas is being supplied, another gas, a waste product of cell metabolism, is being removed. This waste gas is _____

3. The aspect of respiration involving gas exchanges in the lungs is called _____

4. The second aspect of respiration refers to gas exchanges between the blood and body cells. This is called _____

5. The movement of air into and out of the lungs is termed _____

6. The physiology of respiration involves two phases of breathing. In the first phase air is drawn into the lungs. This is _____

7. In the second phase of breathing air is expelled from the alveoli. This phase is called _____

8. The substance in the fluid lining the alveoli that prevents their collapse is _____

9. Gas exchange depends on the movement of gases from areas where they are in higher concentration to areas where they are in lower concentration. This physical change is named _____

Group B

septum	larynx	trachea
pharynx	conchae	vascular
diaphragm	sinuses	

1. Below the nasal cavities is an area that is common to both the digestive and respiratory systems. This is the _____

2. The cartilaginous structure commonly referred to as the voice box has the scientific name of _____

3. Several parts of the respiratory tract are kept open by a frame-work of cartilage. One of these is the windpipe or _____

4. The partition separating the two nasal cavities is called the nasal _____

5. The surface over which the air moves is increased by three projections located at the lateral walls of each nasal cavity. These are the _____

6. The lining of the nasal cavities contains many blood vessels and is therefore described as _____

7. The small cavities in the bones of the skull lined with mucous membrane are called _____

8. Separating the thoracic cavity from the abdominal cavity is the muscular _____

Group C

hilum (or hilus)	epiglottis	vocal cords
bronchi	esophagus	nasopharynx
ciliated epithelium	oropharynx	

1. The mucous membranes lining the tubes of the respiratory system are mostly made of _____

2. Immediately behind the nasal cavity is the upper portion of the muscular pharynx, the _____

3. The portion of the pharynx located behind the mouth is the _____

4. The lowest part of the pharynx, the laryngeal pharynx, opens into the air passageway of the larynx, located toward the front, and into the food pathway, toward the back. This food pathway is called the _____

5. The production of speech is aided by the flow of air from the lungs to vibrate the _____

6. Food is prevented from entering the trachea by closure of the glottis during swallowing. This is accomplished by a leaf-shaped structure called the _____

7. The two main air passageways to the lungs, formed by division of the trachea, are the _____

8. Each bronchus plus the blood vessels and nerves that accompany it enter the lung at a notch or depression called the

_____

Group D

diaphragm	pleura	bronchiole
glottis	mediastinum	squamous epithelium
alveoli	hemoglobin	carbon dioxide

1. The space between the two vocal cords is the

_____

2. The smallest division of a bronchus is called a(n)

_____

3. The air tubes of the lungs finally end in small air sacs called

_____

4. The walls of the air sacs in the lungs are very thin to allow for easy passage of gases. These walls are composed of a single layer of

_____

5. The heart is located in the space between the lungs called the

_____

6. Most of the work of inhalation is done during quiet breathing by the

_____

7. The serous membrane around each lung is the

_____

8. Most of the oxygen in the blood is carried by

_____

9. Bicarbonate ions are formed when a certain gas goes into solution in the blood. This gas is

_____

Group E

cardiopulmonary resuscitation	tracheotomy	pneumonectomy
bronchoscope	asthma	suction apparatus
tracheostomy	emphysema	phrenic nerve

1. The physician inspects the bronchi and their branches using an instrument called a(n)

_____

2. In order to remove mucus and other substances from the respiratory tract, one may use various types of

_____

3. A useful technique taught in first-aid classes is CPR or

_____

4. An incision into the trachea for the purpose of removing a foreign object or a growth is called a(n)

_____

5. A metal or plastic tube is inserted into the trachea to serve as an intake for air as well as an exhaust duct for carbon dioxide in an operation called a(n)

_____

6. Severe allergies may result in spasms of the bronchi and breathing difficulties, a disorder called

_____

7. The lungs may become immobilized by damage to the nerve that supplies the diaphragm. The name of this nerve is the _____

8. A lifetime of heavy smoking may result in destruction of the alveoli of the lungs, a disorder called _____

9. The operation employed to remove a lung in a patient with cancer is called a(n) _____

Group F

hypoventilation	chemoreceptors	hyperventilation
elasticity	acid	orthopnea
dyspnea	atelectasis	cyanosis

1. In exhalation the lung and chest wall have the capacity to recoil because they have the quality of _____

2. Difficulty in breathing that is relieved by an upright position is called _____

3. Excessive breathing may result in symptoms caused by elimination of too much carbon dioxide. This condition is termed _____

4. Areas in the major arteries of the chest and neck that regulate breathing according to changes in the composition of the blood are called _____

5. Incomplete expansion of a lung or part of a lung is known as _____

6. As bicarbonate ions form in the blood from carbon dioxide, hydrogen ions are also produced. These hydrogen ions tend to make the blood more _____

7. Disease or obstruction of the respiratory tract may limit the amount of air reaching the alveoli, a condition termed _____

8. The symptom of difficult or labored breathing is called _____

9. If there is not enough oxygen in the blood, the skin may take on a bluish color, a condition termed _____

IV. Labeling

For each of the following illustrations, print the name or names of each labeled part on the numbered lines.

1. _____ 6. _____ 11. _____

2. _____ 7. _____ 12. _____

3. _____ 8. _____ 13. _____

4. _____ 9. _____ 14. _____

5. _____ 10. _____ 15. _____

16. _____

17. _____

18. _____

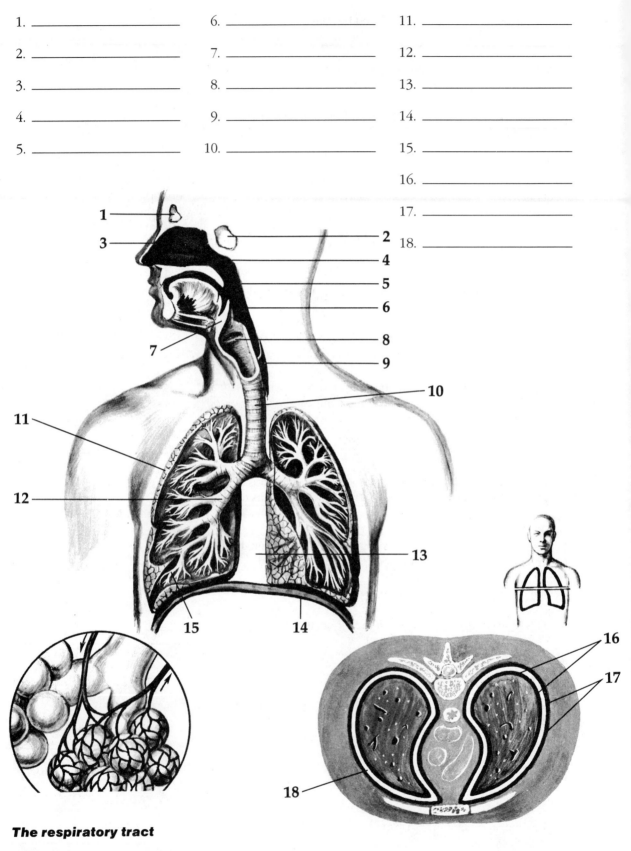

The respiratory tract

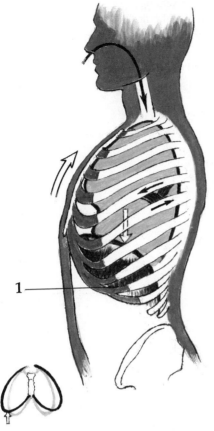

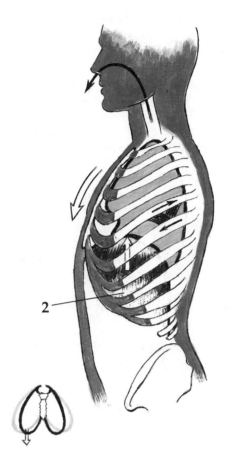

Action of the diaphragm in ventilation

1. _____   2. _____

V. Completion Exercise

Print the word or phrase that correctly completes each sentence.

1. A lack of oxygen is especially harmful to the brain. The word that means "lack of oxygen" is

    _____

2. Suffocation can result from mechanical blockage of the respiratory passages, causing a lack of oxygen available to the lungs, called

    _____

3. Heart disease and other disorders may cause the bluish color of the skin and visible mucous membranes characteristic of a condition called

    _____

4. Very often the partition between the two nasal cavities is structurally defective; this defect is called

    _____

5. An injury or a blow to the nose is a frequent cause of nosebleed, or

    _____

6. In COPD there is damage to the small airways and poor exchange of gases. The first symptom of this disorder frequently is difficult respiration or

_____

7. Overbreathing in which there is an increase in both the rate and depth of respirations is called

_____

8. The respiratory control centers are located in the parts of the brainstem called the pons and the

_____

9. The greatest frequency of tuberculosis occurs in conditions of overcrowding and lack of attention to hygienic measures. The tuberculosis bacillus withstands exposure to many disinfectants, but it is especially vulnerable to

_____

10. Certain diplococci, staphylococci, chlamydias, and viruses may cause an inflammation of the alveoli. The disease is

_____

11. The term for a temporary cessation of breathing is

_____

VI. Practical Applications

Study each discussion. Then print the appropriate word or phrase in the space provided.

Group A

1. Mr. C complained of a severe headache and facial pain. The physician diagnosed the problem as an infection of the air spaces within the cranial bones which are located near the nasal cavities. This infection is called

_____

2. G, age 14, complained of a sore throat and difficulty in swallowing. The physician described the disorder as

_____

3. Ms. F, age 24, complained of hoarseness and said that it was causing her difficulty in speaking to her students. This type of inflammation is called

_____

4. Mrs. D had been suffering from a cold for several days. The physician explained that no entirely effective method of prevention is known as yet. The etiologic agent is a very contagious

_____

5. Because of Mrs. D's lowered disease resistance, she was also suffering from inflammation of the bronchi and their subdivisions. This infection is called

_____

6. The physician warned Mrs. D that if she did not stop working temporarily, and get sufficient rest in order to increase her disease resistance, her illness might extend into the lung with a resulting inflammation of the alveoli, or

_____

7. Mr. G, age 47, was advised to see his doctor because a routine x-ray examination performed at his place of work revealed a lung lesion. Mr. G was a chain smoker. The possibility of a malignancy of the type that originates in the lung was being considered. This most common form of lung cancer is _____

Group B

1. Teenage Jim was brought to the hospital following an automobile accident. There were signs of chest injury, and he was having great difficulty breathing. It was probable that there was air in the pleural space, a condition called _____

2. Ms. J, age 15, had had many episodes of coughing and had expectorated blood-tinged sputum. This is evidence of cavity formation in the lung. Laboratory tests may be used to identify the organism that causes tuberculosis, a bacillus named _____

3. Mr. B had neglected his health following a bout with pneumonia. There was evidence of a tuberculous infection, and fluid that accumulated in the pleural sacs. Such a collection of fluid is called a(n) _____

4. A problem that frequently develops during treatment of tuberculosis with drugs is that new strains of bacteria may cause a form of the disease that cannot be treated effectively with these particular medications. Such bacterial strains are said to be _____

5. Mrs. S, age 67, suffered from the painful condition of pleurisy, which was associated with tuberculosis in her case. The pain was caused by the rubbing together of the pleurae of the lung and the chest wall. As these surfaces stick together there is the development of _____

6. Mrs. S's complaints included shortness of breath, a chronic cough productive of thick mucus, and a "chest cold" of two months' duration. She was advised to quit smoking, a major cause of lung irritation in a group of chronic lung diseases known as _____

7. Symptoms in Mrs. S's case were due in part to the obstruction of groups of alveoli by mucus plugs. A chest film showed patches of collapsed alveoli, a condition which the radiologist identified as _____

8. Student Alice felt nervous and anxious about dancing before a group. It was observed that she had alternating episodes of apnea and rapid breathing, a common response of the respiratory center to abnormal oxygen and carbon dioxide levels produced by _____

18

Digestion

I. Overview

The food we eat is made available to cells throughout the body by the complex processes of **digestion** and **absorption**. These are the functions of the **digestive system**; its components are the **digestive tract** and the **accessory organs**.

The digestive tract, consisting of the **mouth**, the **pharynx**, the **esophagus**, the **stomach**, and the large and small **intestine**, forms a continuous passageway in which ingested food is prepared for utilization by the body and waste products are collected to be expelled from the body. The **liver**, the **gallbladder**, and the **pancreas**, the accessory organs, manufacture various enzymes and other substances needed in digestion. They also serve as storage areas for substances that are released as needed.

Digestion begins in the mouth with the digestion of starch. It continues in the stomach where proteins are digested, and is completed in the small intestine. Most absorption of digested food also occurs in the small intestine through small projections of the lining called **villi**.

The process of digestion is controlled by both nervous and hormonal mechanisms which regulate the activity of the digestive organs and the rate at which food moves through the digestive tract.

II. Topics for Review

A. Components of the digestive tract and the functions of each
B. Accessory organs and their functions
C. The peritoneum
D. The process of digestion
    1. Enzymes involved in digestion
    2. Other substances needed for digestion
E. Absorption
F. Control of the digestive process
    1. Nervous
    2. Hormonal
G. Disorders of the digestive system

III. Matching Exercises

Group A

ingestion	digestive tract	deciduous
tongue	absorption	molars
incisors	digestion	premolars
accessory organs		

1. The process by which food is converted into substances that may be taken into the cells is known as

     _____

2. The transfer of digested food to the bloodstream is called

     _____

3. The structures and organs through which food or its breakdown products pass make up the

     _____

4. The organs that are needed for digestion but are not part of the digestive tract are the

     _____

5. The intake of food into the digestive tract is the process of

     _____

6. Taste sensations can be differentiated by means of special organs of the

     _____

7. The baby molars are replaced by permanent teeth called bicuspids or

     _____

8. The grinding teeth located in the back part of the oral cavity are called

     _____

9. The baby teeth are lost and are therefore described as

     _____

10. The first baby teeth to appear are the eight cutting teeth or

     _____

Group B

6-year molars	canines	mastication
incisors	third molars	32 teeth
caries	20 teeth	parotids

1. Decay and infection of baby molar teeth may easily spread to the first permanent teeth, the

     _____

2. The so-called eye teeth are the

     _____

3. The teeth located in the front part of the oral cavity are the

     _____

4. It sometimes happens that the jaw is not large enough to accommodate the last teeth to erupt. These teeth are identified as the wisdom teeth or

     _____

5. By the time the baby is 2 years old he or she should have all the deciduous teeth, which number

     _____

6. An adult who has a full set of permanent teeth has _____

7. The process of chewing is called _____

8. Loss of teeth is often the result of tooth decay or dental _____

9. The largest of the salivary glands are the _____

Group C

parotitis	esophagus	deglutition
amylase	gingivitis	pharynx
peristalsis	periodontitis	

1. Infection of the gums is known as _____

2. A major cause of tooth loss is infection of the gums and the bones supporting the teeth, a condition termed _____

3. The act of swallowing is known as _____

4. The starch-digesting enzyme in saliva is named salivary _____

5. The common disorder, mumps, is referred to medically as _____

6. Food is propelled along the digestive tract by the rhythmic motion known as _____

7. In swallowing, the tongue pushes food into the _____

8. The tube that carries food into the stomach is the _____

Group D

sphincter	omentum	peritoneum
rugae	villi	mesocolon
parietal	submucosa	mesentery

1. The serous membrane that lines the abdominal cavity and folds over the abdominal organs is the _____

2. A term that describes the layer of a serous membrane that lines a body cavity is _____

3. Extending downward from the stomach is an apron-like double membrane called the greater _____

4. Nerves, arteries, and other structures supplying the small intestine are found between the two layers of peritoneum called the _____

5. A circular layer of muscle that acts as a valve is a(n) _____

6. The layer of connective tissue beneath the mucous membrane in the wall of the digestive tract is the _____

7. The section of the mesentery around the large intestine is the

_____

8. When the stomach is empty, there are many folds in the lining. These folds are called

_____

9. The absorbing surface of the small intestine is greatly increased by numerous projections called

_____

Group E

pyloric sphincter	flatulence	cardiac sphincter
pharynx	soft palate	epiglottis
chyme	vomiting	enzymes

1. The uvula hangs from the back of the roof of the oral cavity. This part of the oral cavity roof is the

_____

2. During deglutition there is contraction of the muscles of the

_____

3. With the muscular contraction that occurs during deglutition, the openings into the air spaces above and below the mouth are closed off by the soft palate and by the

_____

4. The structure that guards the entrance into the stomach is called the

_____

5. The valve between the distal end of the stomach and the small intestine is the

_____

6. In the stomach food is mixed with gastric juice to form

_____

7. The active ingredients in gastric juice are hydrochloric acid and

_____

8. The feeling of illness known as nausea may be followed by reverse peristalsis, resulting in

_____

9. Excessive air (gas) in the stomach or intestine may cause considerable discomfort and a condition referred to as

_____

Group F

adenocarcinoma	peptic ulcer	ileocecal
pyloric stenosis	ileum	sugars
jejunum	proteins	fats
duodenum		

1. Persistent indigestion is an important warning of possible cancer of the stomach. The most frequent type, which originates in the stomach lining, is called

_____

2. The first part of the small intestine is the

_____

3. An abnormally small opening out of the stomach may be due to a constriction of the sphincter in this region. This condition is called

_____

4. Disintegration of tissue associated with loss of membrane substance may occur in many areas of the body; when occurring on the mucous membrane of the esophagus, the stomach, or the duodenum it is called

_____

5. Lying just beyond the duodenum is the second part of the small intestine, the

_____

6. Although bile contains no enzymes, it aids in the digestion of

_____

7. The final, and longest, section of the small intestine is the

_____

8. Because of its location, the valve between the small and large intestine is described as

_____

9. Gastric juice acts mainly to digest

_____

10. Among the classes of nutrients that are essential to cell life are carbohydrates, which include

_____

Group G

glycogen   ascites   hepatitis
urea   hepat   lipase
albumin   trypsin   amylase

1. The accumulation of fluid in the peritoneal cavity, as may occur in certain serious illnesses, is a condition called

_____

2. A word root that refers to the liver is

_____

3. Inflammation of the liver is called

_____

4. The liver has many essential functions. One of these is the manufacture of a waste product later eliminated by the kidneys. This substance is

_____

5. Sugar is stored by the liver and released as simple sugar (glucose) as needed. The form in which sugar is stored is

_____

6. One of the many functions of the liver includes the production of plasma proteins such as

_____

7. Pancreatic juice contains enzymes that act in various ways on the chyme in the small intestine. Starch is changed to sugar by the pancreatic enzyme

_____

8. Fats must be broken down into simpler compounds in order to be absorbed. An enzyme responsible for this breakdown is

_____

9. Proteins enter the bloodstream in the form of amino acids. A pancreatic enzyme that splits proteins is called

_____

Group H

liver	lacteals	feces
cecum	vermiform appendix	small intestine
hydrolysis	pepsin	colon

1. The important function of absorption is carried out through the numerous villi projecting from the mucosa of the

   _____

2. Following their absorption into the bloodstream through the capillary walls of the villi, food materials may be stored and released as needed by the

   _____

3. The enzyme that digests proteins in the stomach is

   _____

4. Much of fat absorption occurs through the lymphatic capillaries of the villi; they are called

   _____

5. Food molecules are split in digestion by the addition of water. The chemical name for this process is

   _____

6. Material to be eliminated moves through the ileocecal valve into the beginning of the large intestine. Here it enters a small pouch called the

   _____

7. The small blind tube attached to the proximal part of the large intestine is called the

   _____

8. In the large intestine layers of involuntary muscle move the solid waste products toward the rectum. This waste material is called

   _____

9. The large intestine is commonly called the

   _____

Group I

diverticula	cirrhosis	flaccid constipation
gastroenteritis	jaundice	spastic constipation
sigmoidoscope	rectum	

1. The lower colon is examined with an instrument called a(n)

   _____

2. Abnormal saclike bulges in the intestinal wall are called

   _____

3. A lazy atonic intestinal muscle is characteristic of

   _____

4. An overstimulated intestinal muscle with a narrowed lumen is found in

   _____

5. Inflammation of the stomach and intestine is known as

   _____

6. The sigmoid colon empties into the

   _____

7. Abuse of alcohol may lead to a type of liver damage called

   _____

8. Liver damage may cause bile pigments to accumulate in the blood. The result is a yellow coloration of the skin called

   _____

IV. Labeling

For each of the following illustrations print the name or names of each labeled part on the numbered lines.

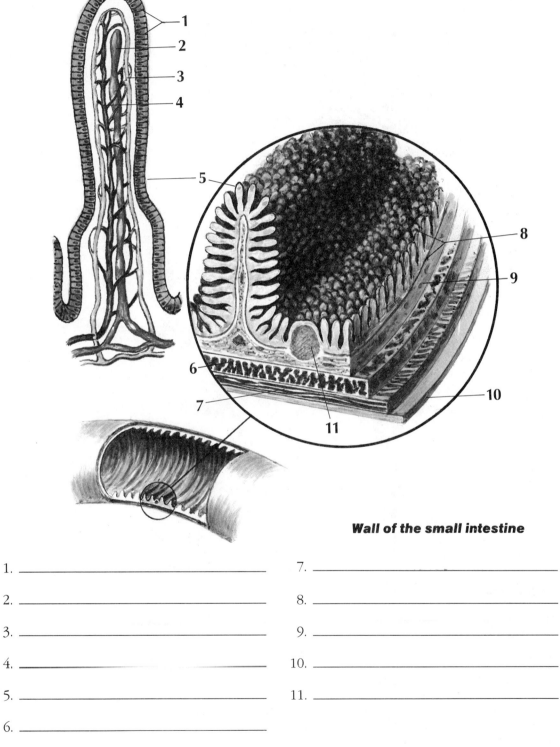

Wall of the small intestine

1. _____   7. _____

2. _____   8. _____

3. _____   9. _____

4. _____   10. _____

5. _____   11. _____

6. _____

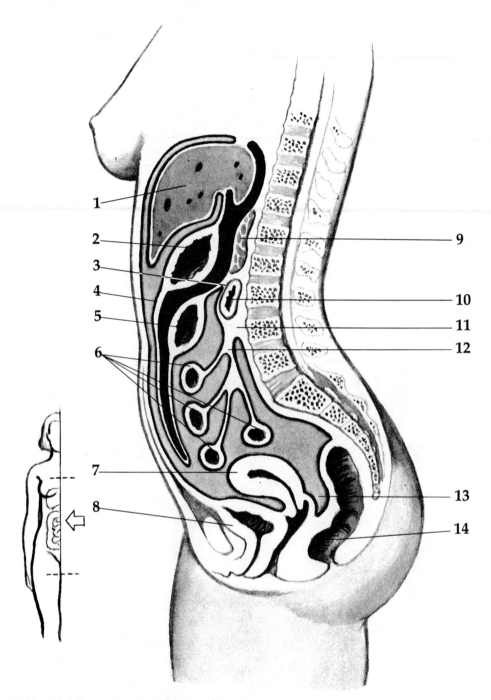

Abdominal cavity showing peritoneum

1. _____

2. _____

3. _____

4. _____

5. _____

6. _____

7. _____

8. _____

9. _____

10. _____

11. _____

12. _____

13. _____

14. _____

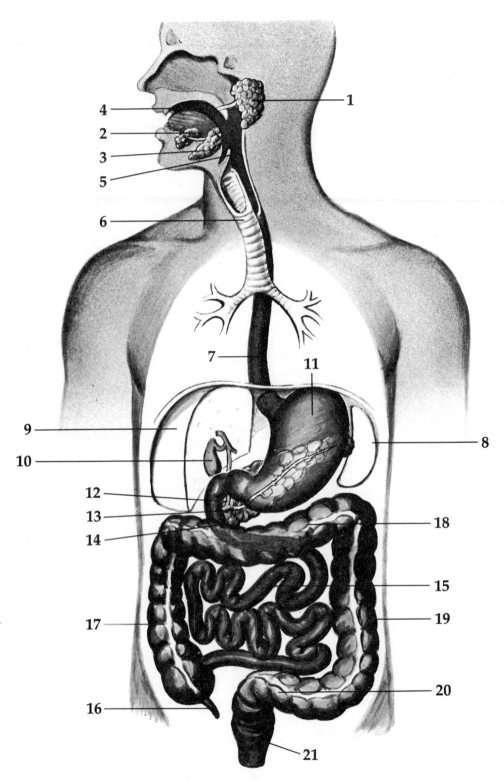

The digestive system

1. _____

2. _____

3. _____

4. _____

5. _____

6. _____

7. _____

8. _____

9. _____

10. _____

11. _____

12. _____

13. _____

14. _____

15. _____

16. _____

17. _____

18. _____

19. _____

20. _____

21. _____

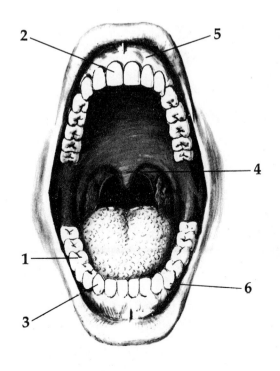

1. _____

2. _____

3. _____

4. _____

5. _____

6. _____

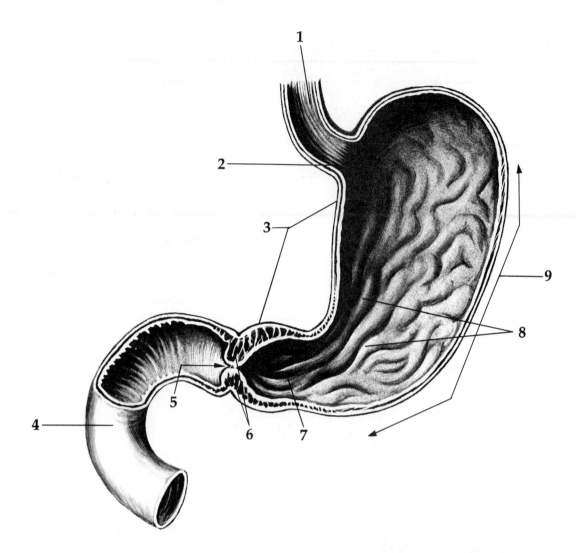

Longitudinal section of the stomach

1. _____ 6. _____

2. _____ 7. _____

3. _____ 8. _____

4. _____ 9. _____

5. _____

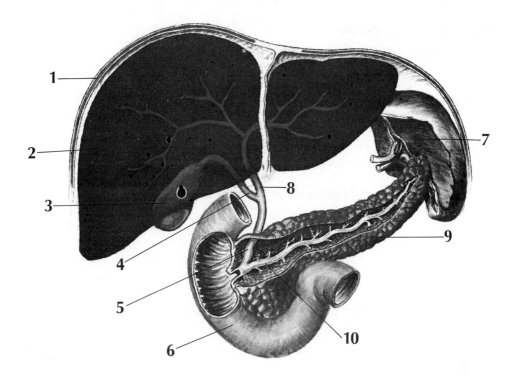

Accessory digestive organs and ducts

1. _____
2. _____
3. _____
4. _____
5. _____

6. _____
7. _____
8. _____
9. _____
10. _____

V. Completion Exercise

Print the word or phrase that correctly completes each sentence.

1. The type of gingivitis that is due to a spirochete and is marked by ulceration of the mucous membrane of the mouth and gums is called _____

2. A common cause of tooth loss is infection of the gums and bone around the teeth, a condition called _____

3. Saliva is produced by three pairs of glands, of which the largest are the ones located near the angles of the jaw, called the _____

4. Such symptoms as nausea, vomiting, diarrhea, and severe abdominal pain are characteristic of an inflammation that involves the stomach and bowels called _____

5. The salivary glands located under the tongue are the _____

6. One component of gastric juice kills bacteria and thus helps defend the body against disease. This substance is _____

7. Most of the digestive juices contain substances that cause the chemical breakdown of foods without entering into the reaction themselves. These catalytic agents are _____

8. Starches and sugars are classified as _____

9. One inflammatory condition in which the pancreas is actually destroyed by the juice it produces is called _____

10. The lower part of the colon bends into an S-shape, so this part is called the _____

11. A temporary storage section for indigestible and unabsorbable waste products of digestion is a tube called the _____

12. The portion of the distal part of the large intestine called the anal canal leads to the outside through an opening called the _____

13. When the intestinal musculature is overstimulated, as by nervous tension, the intestinal lumen may become too small to permit passage of fecal material. This condition is called _____

14. The muscular sac in which bile is stored to be released as needed is called the _____

VI. Practical Applications

Study each discussion. Then print the appropriate word or phrase in the space provided.

1. Mr. C, age 36, complained of pain in the "pit of the stomach." Ingestion of food seemed to provide some relief. The physician ordered x-ray studies to be done. These studies indicated that the first part of the small intestine was involved. This short section is called the

   _____

2. Mr. C was a tense man who felt it was important to do well in his business: he worked long hours. Because of this constant stress, his physician suspected that excessive hydrochloric acid was being produced. The x-ray films confirmed the presence of tissue destruction which is characteristic of

   _____

3. Three-month-old John was brought to the clinic by his mother because he had suffered several bouts of vomiting and could not retain food. The tentative diagnosis was a constricted or spastic pyloric sphincter, a condition called

   _____

4. Mrs. K, age 24, complained that since returning from a brief trip out of the United States she was suffering from frequent watery stools. This symptom is called

   _____

5. Mrs. D, age 47, complained of "indigestion" associated with pain under the ribs of her right side. Tests revealed the presence of stones in the gallbladder. The scientific name for this disorder is

   _____

6. Mr. B had suffered acute abdominal pain and other symptoms of appendicitis. Because of his delay in seeking treatment, his appendix ruptured. He required exacting care following surgery because of a serious infection of the abdominal serosa. This disorder is called

   _____

19

Metabolism, Nutrition, and Body Temperature

I. Overview

The food products that reach the cells following digestion and absorption are used to maintain life. All the physical and chemical reactions that occur within the cells make up **metabolism**, which has two phases: a breakdown phase or **catabolism**, and a building phase or **anabolism**. In catabolism food is oxidized to yield energy for the cells in the form of ATP. This process, termed **cellular respiration**, occurs in two steps: the first is anaerobic (does not require oxygen) and produces a small amount of energy; the second is aerobic (requires oxygen). This second step occurs within the mitochondria of the cells. It yields a large amount of the energy contained in the food plus carbon dioxide and water.

By the various pathways of metabolism, the breakdown products of food can be built into substances needed by the body. The **essential** amino acids and fatty acids cannot be manufactured internally and must be taken in with the diet. Minerals and vitamins are also needed in the diet for health. Since ingested food is the source of all nourishment for the body, a balanced diet should be followed and "food fads" should be avoided.

The rate at which energy is released from food is termed the **metabolic rate**. It is affected by many factors including age, size, sex, activity, and hormones. Some of the energy in food is released in the form of heat, which serves to maintain body temperature. A steady temperature of about 37°C (98.6°F) is maintained by several mechanisms.

Heat production is greatly increased during periods of increased muscular or glandular activity. Most heat loss occurs through the skin, with a smaller loss by way of the respiratory system and the urine and feces. The **hypothalamus** of the brain maintains the normal temperature in response to the temperature of the blood and information received from temperature receptors in the skin. Regulation occurs through vasodilation and vasoconstriction of the surface blood vessels, activity of the sweat glands, and muscle activity.

Abnormalities of body temperature are a valuable diagnostic tool. The presence of **fever**—an abnormally high body temperature—indicates infection most often, but may also indicate a toxic reaction, a brain injury, and other disorders. The opposite of fever is **hypothermia**—an exceedingly low body temperature—which most often comes about when the body is exposed to very low outside temperature and which can cause serious damage to the body tissues.

II. Topics for Review

A. Metabolism
    1. Catabolism
    2. Anabolism
B. Nutrition
    1. Minerals and vitamins
    2. Essential amino acids and fatty acids
    3. Balanced diet
C. Metabolic rate
D. Body temperature
    1. Heat production
    2. Heat loss
    3. Temperature regulation
       a. Role of the hypothalamus
    4. Normal and abnormal body temperature

III. Matching Exercises

Matching only within each group, print the answers in the spaces provided.

Group A

glycogen	BMR	ATP
anaerobic	kilocalorie	catabolism
glycerol	anabolism	mitochondria

1. The breakdown of glucose for energy is an example of _____

2. The first phase of cellular respiration does not require oxygen and so is described as _____

3. A compound that stores energy in the cell is _____

4. The aerobic steps of metabolism occur within the cell organelles called _____

5. The unit used to measure the energy in foods is the _____

6. The storage form of glucose is _____

7. The manufacture of proteins from amino acids within the cell is an example of _____

8. A component of fats is _____

9. The amount of energy needed to maintain life functions while the body is at rest is the _____

Group B

aerobic	minerals	allergy
oxidation	glucose	essential
saturated	legumes	enzymes

1. The main energy food for the cells is _____

2. An amino acid that must be taken in as part of the diet is described as _____

3. The steps of metabolism that release most of the energy from food require oxygen and are termed _____

4. The breakdown of food for energy involves the chemical process of _____

5. The catalysts of metabolic reactions are the _____

6. In addition to fats, proteins, and carbohydrates, the body requires vitamins and _____

7. Fats that are solid at room temperature and are mostly from animal sources are termed _____

8. In some people certain foods cause an adverse reaction that is called a(n) _____

9. Peas and beans are classified as _____

Group C

calciferol	niacin	calcium
B_1	A	B_{12}
C	iron	potassium

1. Beriberi can be prevented by the intake of adequate amounts of thiamine, also known as vitamin _____

2. A constituent of the oxygen-carrying compound hemoglobin is the element _____

3. The vitamin that prevents dry, scaly skin and night blindness is _____

4. The vitamin required for normal bone formation is called vitamin D or _____

5. An element required for normal nerve and muscle activity is found in certain foods in the form of a mineral salt. It is _____

6. Another name for ascorbic acid is vitamin _____

7. A strict vegetarian who eats no eggs or dairy products must be careful to avoid anemia due to a lack of vitamin

   _____

8. Pellagra may result from a lack of

   _____

9. A mineral needed for proper bone development and that is found in dairy products and vegetables is

   _____

Group D

oxygen	hypothermia	blood
homeostasis	fever	hypothalamus
glands	skin	insulation

1. Body heat is produced by combination of food products with

   _____

2. The largest amount of heat is produced in the body by muscles and

   _____

3. Prolonged exposure to cold may result in an abnormally low temperature, a condition indicated by the term

   _____

4. The tendency of body processes to maintain a constant state is called

   _____

5. Heat is distributed throughout the body by way of the

   _____

6. The body possesses several means of ridding itself of heat; the largest part of this loss occurs through the

   _____

7. Clothing and subcutaneous fat represent types of

   _____

8. The chief heat-regulating center, located in the brain, is the

   _____

9. The term *febrile* is used to describe a person who has a(n)

   _____

Group E

pyrogens	evaporation	lysis
crisis	heat stroke	phagocytosis
constrict	infection	heat exhaustion

1. If heat cramps cannot be treated adequately, the next stage of heat disorder may follow. This stage is

   _____

2. Central nervous system symptoms are characteristic of the final stages of excessive exposure to heat. This stage is called

   _____

3. Fever is most often due to

   _____

4. Sometimes fever is beneficial because it steps up the process by which leukocytes destroy pathogens. This process is

   _____

5. A sudden drop in temperature at the end of a period of fever is referred to as _____

6. A gradual fall in temperature at the end of a period of fever is referred to as _____

7. If too much heat is being lost from the body, the blood vessels in the skin are caused to _____

8. The amount of humidity in the air has an effect on the rate of heat loss by _____

9. Bacterial products that produce fever are classified as _____

IV. Completion Exercise

Print the word or phrase that correctly completes each sentence.

1. All the physical and chemical reactions that sustain life together make up _____

2. The process of oxidizing food within the cell for energy is termed _____

3. Organic substances needed in small amounts in the diet are the _____

4. A gland important in the control of the metabolic rate is the _____

5. While most heat loss occurs through the skin, an appreciable amount is also lost in the urine and feces and by way of the _____

6. The most important heat-regulating center is a section of the brain called the _____

7. Shivering is a way of increasing body heat by increasing the activity of the _____

8. During a fever there may be considerable destruction of body tissues. Therefore, the diet should include foods that contain the nitrogenous compounds classified as _____

9. Tissue damage caused by exposure to cold is termed _____

10. The normal range of body temperature in degrees Celsius is _____

11. The formula for converting Fahrenheit temperatures to Celsius is _____

12. Practice changing Fahrenheit to Celsius. Show the figures for changing 50° and 70°F to Celsius. _____

13. Practice changing Celsius to Fahrenheit. Show the figures for changing 10° and 25°C to Fahrenheit. _____

V. Practical Applications

Study each discussion. Then print the appropriate word or phrase in the space provided.

Group A

1. Mrs. S, age 76, was hospitalized for a fracture of the femur caused by a fall. Her physician suspected that the break had resulted from a general weakening of the bones due to osteoporosis. This disorder, common in elderly women, is caused by a number of factors, including the dietary lack of a mineral found in dairy products. This mineral is _____

2. Mr. C, age 78, was accompanied by his daughter to visit his family physician. His daughter was concerned about his general state of health and marked weight loss within several months after the death of his wife. The doctor asked that Mr. C keep a record of his food intake for 2 weeks. Review of this record suggested that he was not eating properly and was suffering from a general lack of proper nutrients in his diet. The doctor described his condition as one of borderline _____

3. Young Mr. N, age 17, had placed himself on a strict vegetarian diet that included no animal products. He was not careful in planning his meals, however, and his family soon began to notice his loss of appetite, irritability, and susceptibility to disease. The school dietitian, when questioned by his mother, suggested that he was not getting the right balance of proteins, especially the building blocks of proteins that must be taken in with the diet, the _____

4. When Ms. R, age 15, went for her regular dental examination, the dentist noticed that her gums bled easily and that she had small cracks at the corners of her mouth. Brief questioning suggested that because of a lack of fruits and vegetables in her diet she was suffering from a lack of vitamins, especially vitamin C and a group of vitamins that includes thiamine and riboflavin, the _____

Group B

A physician working in a desert area of southeastern California saw a variety of cases during the course of a day.

1. A 6-year-old patient appeared apathetic and tired. His face was flushed and hot. On taking his temperature the nurse found it to be 105°F. The physician took the child's history and examined him, then instructed his mother to give the child cool sponge baths and administer the prescribed medication. The cool water sponging would aid in reducing the temperature by the process of _____

2. Men working on a construction project complained of tiredness and nausea. They felt better after resting in the shade and drinking water and fruit juices. Their symptoms were due to a disorder of body temperature called _____

3. Mr. K, age 69, had been working in his garden. The day was sunny and hot, but Mr. K neglected to protect his bald head by wearing a hat. He began to feel dizzy and faint. His wife noted that his face was very flushed and his skin appeared dry. His symptoms were typical of a loss of fluid and an increase in body temperature called _____

4. On a cool fall day, Mr. J spent several hours walking with friends in the canyons of some nearby mountains. He was clad in shorts and a lightweight shirt. Now he was stumbling, his speech was hard to understand, and he complained of being sleepy. He probably had a disorder of body temperature called _____

20

The Urinary System and Body Fluids

I. Overview

The urinary system comprises two **kidneys**, two **ureters**, one **urinary bladder**, and one **urethra**. This system is thought of as the body's main excretory mechanism; it is, in fact, often called the **excretory system**. The kidney, however, performs other essential functions; it aids in maintaining water and electrolyte balance and in regulating the acid–base balance (pH) of body fluids. The kidneys also secrete a hormone that stimulates red blood cell production and another hormone that acts to increase blood pressure.

The functional unit of the kidney is the **nephron**. It is the nephron that produces **urine** from substances filtered out of the blood through a cluster of capillaries, the **glomerulus**. Oxygenated blood is brought to the kidney by the **renal artery**. The arterial system subdivides as it branches through the kidney until the smallest vessel, the **afferent arteriole**, carries blood into the glomerulus. Blood leaves the glomerulus by means of the **efferent arteriole** and eventually leaves the kidney by means of the **renal vein**. Before blood enters the venous network of the kidney, exchanges occur between the filtrate and the blood through the **peritubular capillaries** that surround each nephron.

Prolonged or serious diseases of the kidney have devastating effects on overall body function and health. Renal dialysis and kidney transplants are effective methods for saving lives of persons who otherwise would die of kidney failure and uremia.

The composition of intracellular and extracellular fluids is an important factor in homeostasis. These fluids must have the proper levels of electrolytes and must be kept at a constant pH.

Other mechanisms, in addition to kidney function, that help to regulate the composition of body fluids are the thirst mechanism, hormones, buffers, and respiration. The normal pH of body fluids is a slightly alkaline 7.4. When regulating mechanisms fail to control shifts in pH, either **acidosis** or **alkalosis** results.

Normally, the amount of fluid taken in with food and beverages equals the amount of fluid lost through the skin, and the respiratory, digestive, and urinary tracts. When there is an imbalance between fluid intake and fluid output, serious disorders such as edema, water intoxication, and dehydration may develop.

II. Topics for Review

A. The urinary system
   1. Kidneys
   2. Ureters
   3. Bladder
   4. Urethra
B. Renal function
   1. Glomerular filtration
   2. Tubular reabsorption
   3. Tubular secretion
   4. Concentration of the urine
      a. Role of ADH
C. Disorders of the urinary system
D. Urine
   1. Normal constituents
   2. Abnormal constituents
E. Regulation of body fluids
   1. Electrolytes
      a. Role of hormones
   2. Concentration
      a. Loss and gain of water
      b. The thirst mechanism
   3. Acid–base balance (pH)
      a. Buffers
      b. Kidney function
      c. Respiration
F. Disorders involving body fluids

III. Matching Exercises

Matching only within each group, print the answers in the spaces provided.

Group A

digestive system	nephrons	elimination
respiratory system	adipose capsule	excretion
retroperitoneal space	urine	fibrous capsule

1. Removal of waste products from the body is called _____

2. By contrast, the actual emptying of the hollow organs in which waste substances have been stored is referred to as _____

3. Other systems besides the urinary system perform excretory functions. To mention one example, bile is excreted by the _____

4. The system regulating excretion of carbon dioxide and water is the _____

5. The urinary system excretes water, nitrogenous waste products, and salts, all of which are contained in the _____

6. The functional units of the kidney are the microscopic _____

7. The membranous connective tissue structure that is normally loosely adherent to the kidney itself is called the _____

8. The area behind the peritoneum that contains the pancreas, the duodenum, and the two kidneys is referred to as the _____

9. The circle of fat that helps to support the kidney is called the _____

Group B

collecting tubules	epithelium	filtration
renal pelvis	Bowman's capsule	urea
cortex	convoluted tubules	reabsorption
glomerulus		

1. The cluster of capillaries located at the proximal end of the nephron is the _____

2. Materials that have passed through the capillary walls enter the first part of the nephron, the _____

3. The longest sections of the nephrons are the _____

4. Useful substances that have entered the nephron are sent back to the bloodstream by a process of _____

5. The glandular kidneys are made up mainly of _____

6. The process by which substances leave the glomerulus and enter Bowman's capsule is _____

7. The outer region of the kidney is the _____

8. Within the medulla the distal convoluted tubules of the nephrons come together and empty into the _____

9. The upper end of the ureter is a funnel-shaped basin that receives urine. It is called the _____

10. As body cells use protein, nitrogenous waste products are produced; the chief such product is _____

Group C

electrolytes	internal sphincter	peristalsis
glucose	urethra	hilus
calyces	organic	hydrogen ions

1. Urine is moved along the ureter from the kidneys to the bladder by the rhythmic contraction known as _____

2. Near the bladder outlet are circular muscle fibers that contract to prevent emptying. They form what is known as the _____

3. The tube that carries urine from the bladder to the outside is the   _____

4. Because nitrogen waste products originate from living organisms, they are said to be   _____

5. Mineral salts contained in urine are classified as   _____

6. Diabetes mellitus may be suspected if a test of the urine shows the presence of the simple sugar   _____

7. The area where the artery, the vein, and the ureter connect with the kidney is known as the   _____

8. Tubelike extensions that project from the renal pelvis into the kidney tissue serve to increase the area for collection of urine. These extensions are called   _____

9. The kidney helps prevent conditions of excessive alkalinity or acidity by regulating the body fluid concentration of   _____

Group D

edema	acidity	buffers
diffusion	nephritis	uremia
cystitis	pyelitis	calculi

1. The term that means inflammation of kidney tissue is   _____

2. Kidney failure is one cause of an excessive accumulation of fluid in the body tissues. This condition is called   _____

3. When the kidneys are unable to remove poisonous substances from the blood, these substances accumulate and may cause the serious condition called   _____

4. When uric acid or calcium salts precipitate out of the urine instead of remaining in solution, stones are formed. These are called   _____

5. Inflammation of the urinary bladder is called   _____

6. Stagnation of urine due to interference with its normal flow may cause inflammation of the kidney pelvis, or   _____

7. In order to remove nitrogen waste products from the blood, dialysis utilizes the principle of   _____

8. Exhalation of carbon dioxide is one means of reducing the blood's   _____

9. Body fluids are maintained at a constant pH partly by the action of   _____

Group E

erythropoietin
juxtaglomerular cells
colon bacillus
reabsorption

dilute
polyuria
nocturia
renin

secretion
concentrated
nitrogen
specific gravity

1. The amount of dissolved substances in the urine is indicated by its

_____

2. The kidney releases a hormone-like substance that acts to produce a stimulator of the red bone marrow. This stimulator is called

_____

3. Renin and other hormones are produced in the kidney by the

_____

4. Certain cells in the kidney produce a hormone that activates a blood protein, which in turn induces an increase in blood pressure. This hormone is called

_____

5. Elimination of very large amounts of urine is called

_____

6. Elimination of urine during the night is called

_____

7. A specific gravity of 1.002 would indicate that the urine is very

_____

8. The organism that is most often responsible for urinary bladder infection is the

_____

9. Urea, uric acid, and creatinine are waste products that are derived from proteins; all contain the element

_____

10. The term for the process by which useful substances are returned to the tissue fluid and the blood is

_____

11. If the specific gravity of urine is approximately 1.040, it contains considerable amounts of solutes, and is said to be

_____

12. Urine is more acid than blood because the renal tubule actively moves hydrogen ions from the blood into the tubule to be excreted. This active process is called tubular

_____

Group F

negative
extracellular
intracellular
dehydration

interstitial
cation
parathyroid hormone

ascites
aldosterone
alkalosis

1. Sodium carries a positive electric charge, and therefore is a(n)

_____

2. Phosphate carries electric charges that are

_____

3. Fluid within the body cells is designated   _____

4. Plasma is in the compartment classified as   _____

5. The water located in the microscopic spaces between cells is designated   _____

6. The term used to describe a serious fluid deficit is   _____

7. A collection of fluid within the abdominal cavity is called   _____

8. An increase in the pH of body fluids, such as may result from hyperventilation, is termed   _____

9. A hormone produced by the adrenal cortex that promotes the reabsorption of sodium is   _____

10. A hormone that causes the kidneys to reabsorb calcium is   _____

IV. Labeling

For each of the following illustrations print the name or names of each labeled part on the numbered lines.

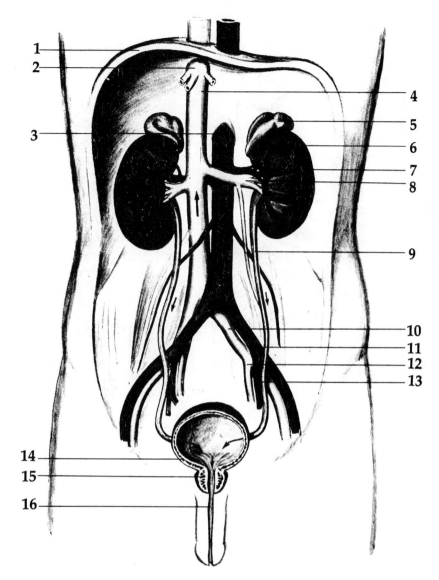

Urinary system with blood vessels

1. _____	7. _____	13. _____
2. _____	8. _____	14. _____
3. _____	9. _____	15. _____
4. _____	10. _____	16. _____
5. _____	11. _____	
6. _____	12. _____	

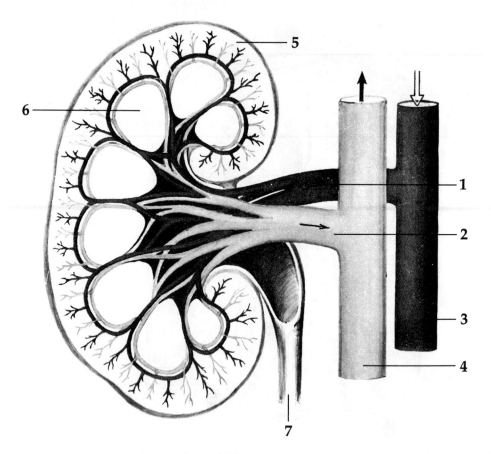

Blood supply and circulation of kidney

1. _____   5. _____

2. _____   6. _____

3. _____   7. _____

4. _____

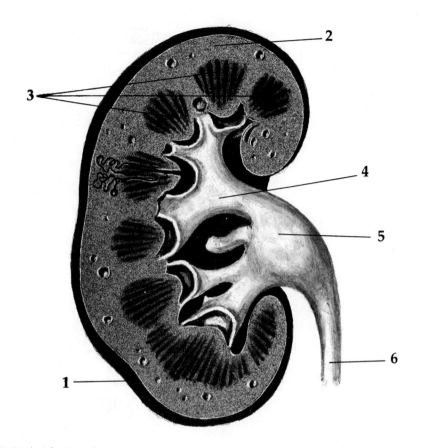

Kidney's internal structure

1. _____   4. _____

2. _____   5. _____

3. _____   6. _____

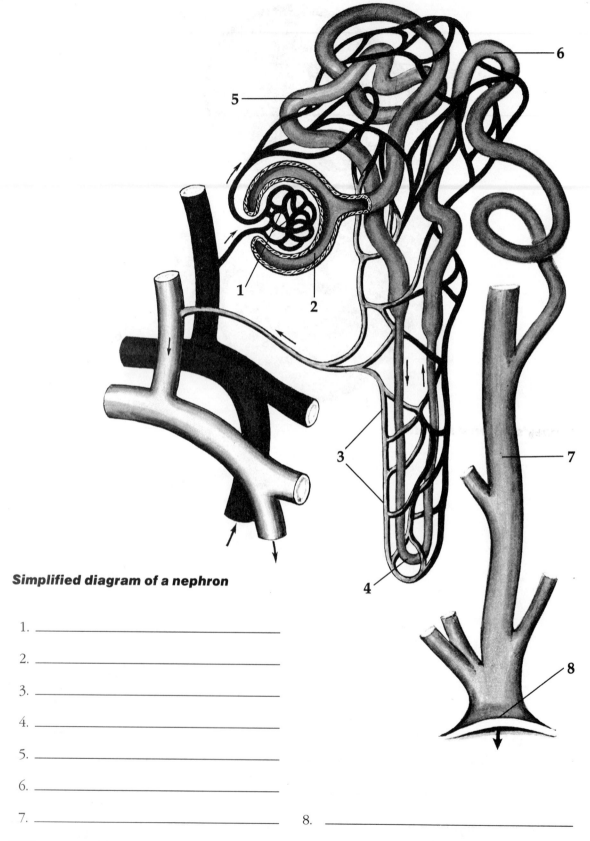

Simplified diagram of a nephron

1. _____

2. _____

3. _____

4. _____

5. _____

6. _____

7. _____   8. _____

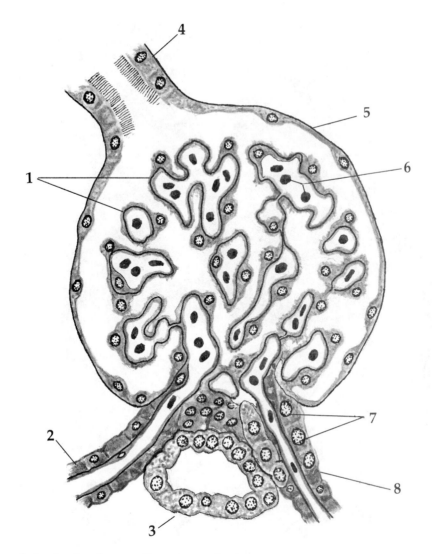

Structure of the juxtaglomerular apparatus

1. _____   5. _____

2. _____   6. _____

3. _____   7. _____

4. _____   8. _____

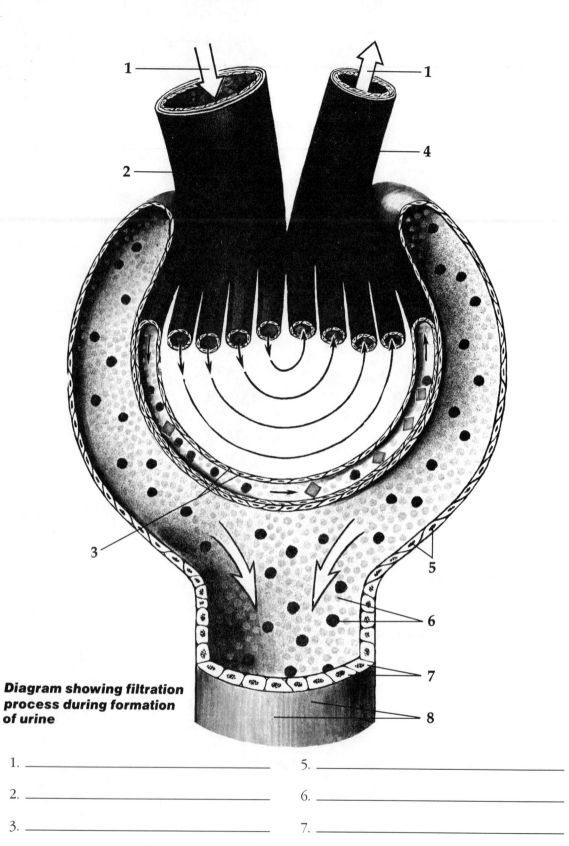

Diagram showing filtration process during formation of urine

1. _____   5. _____
2. _____   6. _____
3. _____   7. _____
4. _____   8. _____

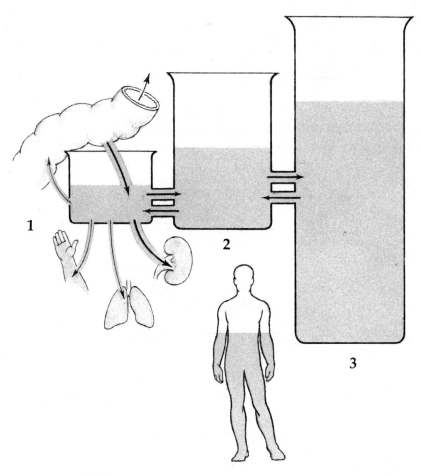

Distribution of body fluids

1. _____   3. _____

2. _____

V. Completion Exercise

Print the word or phrase that correctly completes each sentence.

1. Kidney stones that are large enough to fill the kidney pelvis and extend into the calyces are called _____

2. Because of the oblique direction of the last part of each ureter through the lower bladder wall, compression of the ureters by the full bladder prevents _____

3. There are many causes of ureteral obstruction. One of these is a kinking of the ureter that is due to a dropping of the kidney, or _____

4. When the bladder is empty, its lining is thrown into the folds known as _____

5. The vessel that carries oxygenated blood to the kidney is the _____

6. In the male, two ducts that carry sex cells join the first part of the urethra as it passes through the _____

7. Urine consists mainly of _____

8. The congenital anomaly in which the urethra opens on the under surface of the penis is known as _____

9. The straddle type of injury occurs when, for example, a man is walking along a raised beam and slips so that the beam is between his legs. Such an accident may rupture the _____

10. An important sign of urinary tract disease or injury is blood in the urine, a condition that is called _____

11. In diabetes, starvation, and other conditions, fats are not completely oxidized. A test of the urine may reveal the presence of _____

12. One indication of nephritis is the presence in the urine of molds that have been formed in the kidney tubules. They are called _____

13. Water balance is partly regulated by a thirst center located in a region of the brain called the _____

14. Diabetes insipidus is marked by great thirst and the elimination of large amounts of very dilute urine. The disease is caused by a lack of a hormone from the pituitary that regulates water reabsorption in the kidney. This hormone is _____

VI. Practical Applications

Study each discussion. Then print the appropriate word or phrase in the space provided.

Group A

1. K, age 7, was brought to the clinic because his mother had noted that his urine had a red hue. He had been quite ill with a "strep throat" a few weeks earlier. Tests indicated that K was suffering from the most common disease of the kidneys, namely _____

2. Mrs. L, age 31, K's mother, was concerned because she had had several similar episodes during her childhood. She was assured that her son would recover with appropriate treatment, and was advised to have her urine tested. The tests demonstrated protein in her urine, indicating continuing damage to the kidney tubules. This condition is called _____

3. Mr. R had been exposed to poisonous arsenic compounds in the chemical manufacturing plant where he was employed. He was suffering from an acute renal failure. In order to remove the accumulated nitrogen waste products from his blood, Mr. R was treated by a diffusion process called _____

4. The x-ray examination of Ms. G's urinary tract revealed a structural abnormality of the ureter in the form of extreme narrowing, or _____

5. Mrs. K was suffering from cystitis, a bladder infection. Studies indicated that there was relaxation of the pelvic floor, causing stagnation of urine in the bladder, and corrective surgery was planned. In preparation for this, a catheter was inserted into the external opening, the _____

6. Mr. K, age 61, required several studies to determine the cause of obstruction of his urinary tract. Pus cells were found in his urine specimen. This is an important sign of _____

7. One of the studies done in Mr. K's case revealed that there was an obstruction at the bladder neck, a disorder that is fairly common in men of his age. The obstruction was caused by enlargement of the gland through which the first part of the urethra passes. This is the _____

Group B

1. Mrs. C, age 38, was hospitalized because she was seriously ill and required intensive study. She had suffered from several streptococcal and staphylococcal infections. Now there was such extensive kidney damage that consideration was being given to a recently developed operation in which the kidney of a healthy person replaces the diseased kidney in the sick person. This procedure is called _____

2. Mr. G, age 58, had not consulted a physician for many years. Now he came into the hospital seriously ill. Physical examination revealed enlarged kidneys and ureters. Laboratory studies showed that there was a severe uremia. Despite all measures, Mr. G died within a few days. Autopsy disclosed the presence of greatly distended pelves and calyces on both sides. This condition is known as _____

3. Mr. B, age 38, had been traveling in parts of Asia. He became ill with diarrhea, vomiting, and other symptoms of cholera. Upon admission to a hospital in the United States he was found to be suffering from severe fluid deficit, a condition called _____

4. Mrs. G, age 62, complained of swelling of her lower extremities. She suffered from kidney failure, which caused an abnormal collection of fluids in the tissues, or _____

5. Mr. K had been an alcoholic for some years. Now he was suffering from liver disease and swelling of the abdomen, due to an accumulation of fluid within the abdominal cavity. This condition is called _____

6. Mr. M was under physician's care for diabetes mellitus. It was important to check his urine regularly for glucose and ketones to be sure that his disease was under control. Accumulation of ketones can cause a harmful decrease in the pH of body fluids, a condition called _____

21

Reproduction

I. Overview

Reproduction is the process by which life continues. Human reproduction is **sexual**, that is, it requires the union of two different **germ cells** or **gametes**. (Some simple forms of life can reproduce without a partner in the process of **asexual** reproduction.) These germ cells, the **spermatozoon** in males and the **ovum** in females, are formed by **meiosis**, a type of cell division in which the chromosome number is reduced to one half. When fertilization occurs and the gametes combine, the original chromosome number is restored.

The reproductive glands or **gonads** manufacture the gametes and also produce hormones. These activities are continuous in the male but cyclic in the female. The male gonad is the **testis**. The remainder of the male reproductive tract consists of passageways for transport of spermatozoa; the male organ of copulation, the **penis**; and several glands that contribute to the production of **semen**. The female gonad is the **ovary**. The ovum released each month at the time of **ovulation** travels through the **oviducts** to the **uterus**, where the egg, if fertilized, develops. If no fertilization occurs, the ovum, along with the built-up lining of the uterus, is eliminated through the **vagina** as the **menstrual flow**.

Reproduction is under the control of hormones from the **anterior pituitary** which, in turn, is controlled by the **hypothalamus** of the brain. These organs respond to **feedback** mechanisms which maintain proper hormone levels.

Pregnancy is the period of about 9 months during which a fertilized ovum develops, first as an **embryo** and then as a **fetus**. During this period the developing offspring is nourished and maintained by the **placenta**, formed from tissues of both the mother and the embryo.

Aging causes changes in both the male and female reproductive systems. A gradual decrease in male hormone production begins as early as age 20 and continues throughout life. In the female a more sudden decrease in activity occurs between ages 45 to 55 and ends in the **menopause**, the cessation of menstruation and of the child-bearing years.

II. Topics for Review

A. Formation of the germ cells
   1. The spermatozoon
   2. The ovum
   3. Meiosis
B. The male reproductive tract
   1. Testes
   2. Ducts
   3. Penis
   4. Glands
      a. Semen
C. The female reproductive tract
   1. Ovaries
   2. Oviducts
   3. Uterus
   4. Vagina
   5. Vulva
D. Hormonal control of reproduction
   1. Pituitary
   2. Hypothalamus
   3. Feedback
E. The menstrual cycle
   1. Menopause
F. Disorders of the reproductive systems
G. Pregnancy
   1. Fertilization
   2. Embryo
   3. Fetus
   4. Placenta
   5. Childbirth
   6. Lactation
   7. Disorders of pregnancy and lactation

III. Matching Exercises

Matching only within each group, print the answers in the spaces provided.

Group A

ovum	ovary	epididymis
gonads	asexual	testosterone
testis	scrotum	sexual
spermatozoa	seminiferous	

1. The specialized sex cells in the male are called _____

2. Since the simplest forms of life require no partner in order to reproduce, they are said to be _____

3. The sex glands are also called the _____

4. The specialized sex cell of the female is the _____

5. The female gonad is also known as the
        _____

6. The male gonad is the
        _____

7. The testes are normally located in a sac that is suspended between the thighs. This sac is the
        _____

8. The bulk of the tissue of the testes is arranged in tubules. These tubules are described by the term
        _____

9. Groups of cells located between the tubules of the testes are responsible for the secretion of the male hormone named
        _____

10. The spermatozoa mature and become motile within a temporary storage area, a 20-foot tube, the
        _____

11. Most animal species are differentiated into males and females; within these groups reproduction is said to be
        _____

Group B

seminal vesicles	ductus deferens	FSH
ejaculatory duct	gametes	urethra
spermatic cord	penis	semen
acrosome		

1. A term used in referring to the male and female sex cells is
        _____

2. The straight upward extension of the epididymis is the
        _____

3. The combination of ductus deferens, nerves, and blood and lymph vessels that extends from the scrotum and testes on each side is named the
        _____

4. Behind the urinary bladder in the male are two tortuous muscular tubes with glandular linings. These are the
        _____

5. The ductus deferens on each side is joined by the duct from the seminal vesicle to form a tube that carries spermatozoa through the prostate. This tube is the
        _____

6. In males, a single tube conveys urine and semen to the outside. This tube is the
        _____

7. The external genitalia of the male include the scrotum and the
        _____

8. In ejaculation, a mixture of spermatozoa and secretions is expelled. It is called
        _____

9. A caplike covering over the head of the spermatozoon that aids in penetration of the ovum is the
        _____

10. Sertoli cells are stimulated by
        _____

Group C

phimosis	ejaculation	gonorrhea
penis	Cowper's glands	prostate
oligospermia	cryptorchidism	hernia
infertility	ductus deferens	

1. In the male, the longest part of the urethra extends through the spongelike _____

2. The bulbourethral glands, which are pea-sized organs found in the pelvic floor tissues below the prostate gland of the male, are also known as _____

3. A weak place in the abdominal wall caused by the descent of the testes through the inguinal canal is a common site for the formation of a(n) _____

4. Normally, the testes descend into the scrotal sac during fetal life; if this does not occur, the resulting condition is known as _____

5. Burning and pain on urination, accompanied by a discharge from the urethra, are symptoms in the male of the most common venereal disease, namely _____

6. In both the male and the female, infection that is not adequately treated may result in a decreased ability to reproduce, or _____

7. Degenerative changes in the tubules of the testes may result in a decrease in the numbers of spermatozoa produced. This is called _____

8. Tightness of the foreskin which prevents it from being drawn back is called _____

9. A procedure for sterilizing a male by preventing spermatozoa from reaching the urethra involves removing a portion of the _____

10. Semen is expelled by a series of muscular contractions called _____

11. Blockage of urine and damage to kidney tissue is a frequent result of tumor or cancer formation in the male reproductive structure called the _____

Group D

vulva	vagina	fallopian tubes
ovaries	ovarian follicles	uterus
ovulation	Bartholin's glands	fimbriae

1. Two structures, made of peritoneum and called the broad ligaments, serve as anchors for the uterus and _____

2. The sacs within which the ova mature are called the _____

3. The rupture of an ovarian follicle permits an ovum to be discharged from the ovary surface. This is called

    _____

4. The mature ovum travels from the region of the ovary into the oviducts or

    _____

5. A current in the peritoneal fluid sweeps the ovum into the oviduct. This current is produced by the fringelike

    _____

6. Before birth the fetus grows in a muscular organ located between the urinary bladder and the rectum. This organ is the

    _____

7. The greater vestibular glands, situated above and to each side of the vaginal opening are also known as

    _____

8. Connecting the uterus with the outside is the lower part of the birth canal, the

    _____

9. The labia, the clitoris, and related structures comprise the external parts of the female reproductive system which are called the

    _____

Group E

carcinoma	corpus	fornices	endometrium
dysmenorrhea	cervix	corpus luteum	salpingitis
myomas	fundus	amenorrhea	

1. Located above the level of the tubal entrances is the small rounded part of the uterus called the

    _____

2. The upper part of the uterus is the largest part; it is called the body, or

    _____

3. The necklike part of the uterus dips into the upper vagina; this necklike part is called the

    _____

4. The specialized tissue that lines the uterus is known as

    _____

5. The cervix dips into the upper vagina so that a circular recess is formed; this gives rise to the spaces known as

    _____

6. Painful or difficult menstruation is called

    _____

7. Absence of the menstrual flow is known as

    _____

8. About half of women who reach the age of 50 have one or more uterine growths known as fibroids, or

    _____

9. Inflammatory infection of the fallopian tubes is described as

    _____

10. A test in which cells from the cervix are examined after being treated with Papanicolaou's stain is done to detect

    _____

11. After ovulation, the ruptured follicle becomes the

    _____

Group F

parturition	umbilicus	embryo
fetus	placenta	cervix
afterbirth	toxemia of pregnancy	progesterone
amniotic sac	vernix caseosa	

1. The endometrium is prepared for the fertilized ovum by a hormone produced by the corpus luteum. This hormone is _____

2. Serving as the organ for nutrition, respiration, and excretion for the embryo is a flat, circular structure called the _____

3. Following fertilization of an ovum and until the end of the third month, the developing organism is called the _____

4. From the end of the third month until birth the developing organism is known as the _____

5. The fetus is protected by a fluid contained in the _____

6. Nature provides various protective mechanisms for the fetus. The cheesy material that protects the skin is known as _____

7. The process of giving birth to a child is described by the term labor or _____

8. A small part of the umbilical cord remains attached to the navel for a few days following birth. The scientific name for the navel is the _____

9. Normally, within half an hour after the child is born, the placenta together with the membranes of the amniotic sac and most of the umbilical cord are expelled as the _____

10. Edema, protein in the urine, and hypertension are all symptoms of a serious disorder of pregnancy known as _____

11. In the first stage of childbirth, the regular contractions of the uterus bring about widening of the opening of the _____

Group G

menstrual flow	posterior fornix	radical mastectomy
estrogen	*Trichomonas vaginalis*	hysterectomy
menopause	external genitalia	ectopic pregnancy

1. Removal of the uterus is called _____

2. A pregnancy that develops outside the uterine cavity is referred to as a(n) _____

3. Two ovarian hormones are involved in preparing the endometrium for pregnancy, and both are carried by the bloodstream to the uterus. Preparation is initiated by hormones produced by the follicle as the ovum matures. These hormones as a group are called _____

4. The peritoneal cavity of the female is deepest behind the upper vaginal canal. This means that there is a thin wall separating the lower abdominal cavity from the upper vaginal canal. This dorsal space in the upper vagina is called the _____

5. Bits of cast-off endometrium are found in the bloody discharge that is known as the _____

6. The vulva is also called the _____

7. A common causative organism of leukorrhea is a protozoan that is called _____

8. Cessation of ovarian activity brings about the period of life known as _____

9. Cancer of the breast is the most frequent malignant disorder in women; one form of treatment is the operation known as a(n) _____

Group H

menstrual flow   follicle stimulating hormone   chorionic gonadotropin
placental lactogen   sterility   umbilical cord
luteinizing hormone   colostrum

1. The sac containing the ovum develops under the influence of a hormone from the pituitary called _____

2. Midway during the menstrual cycle the ovarian follicle ruptures under the effects of a hormone from the pituitary called _____

3. Oxygen and nutrients are brought to the fetus and waste products are removed from the fetus through blood vessels contained in the _____

4. Without hormones to support growth, the thickened endometrium is shed, producing the _____

5. A hormone produced by embryonic cells that maintains the corpus luteum early in pregnancy is _____

6. Several hormones are secreted during pregnancy by the placenta, including estrogen, progesterone, and _____

7. In a female, tubal ligation results in _____

8. The first mammary gland secretion to appear is called _____

IV. Labeling

For each of the following illustrations, print the name or names of each labeled part on the numbered lines.

1. _____

2. _____

3. _____

4. _____

5. _____

6. _____

7. _____

8. _____

9. _____

10. _____

11. _____

12. _____

13. _____

14. _____

15. _____

16. _____

17. _____

18. _____

19. _____

20. _____

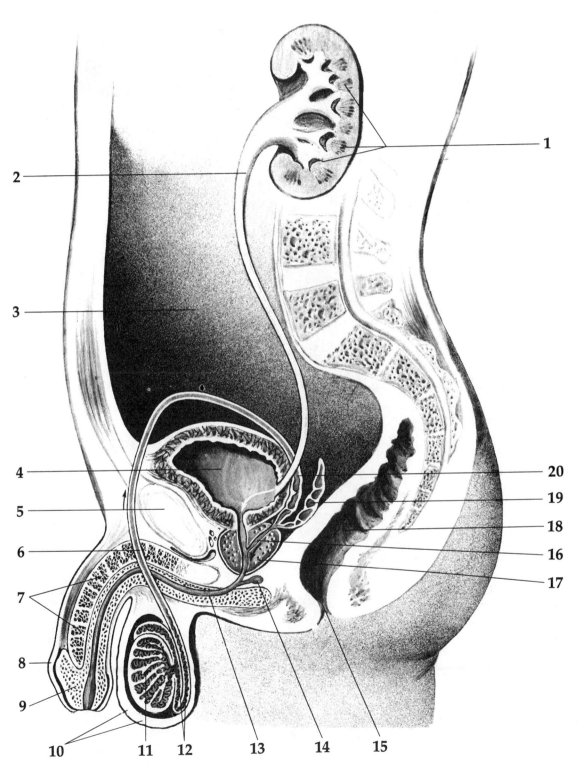

Male genitourinary system

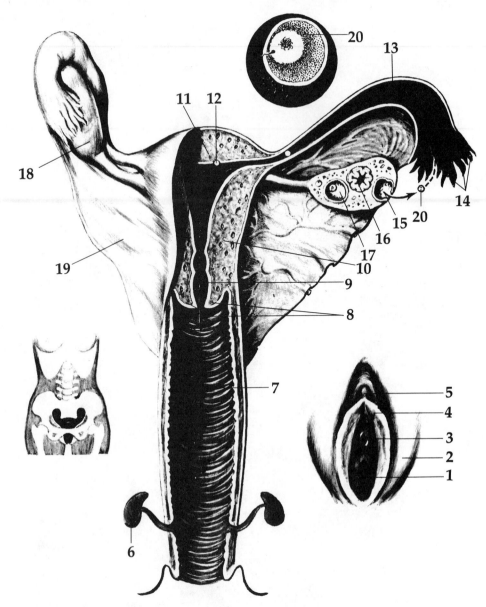

Female reproductive system

1. _____

2. _____

3. _____

4. _____

5. _____

6. _____

7. _____

8. _____

9. _____

10. _____

11. _____

12. _____

13. _____

14. _____

15. _____

16. _____

17. _____

18. _____

19. _____

20. _____

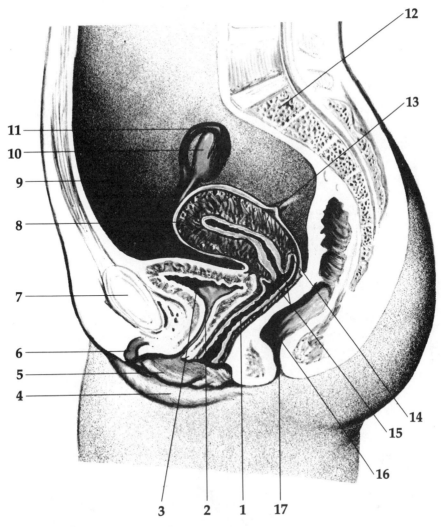

Female reproductive system, sagittal section

1. _____

2. _____

3. _____

4. _____

5. _____

6. _____

7. _____

8. _____

9. _____

10. _____

11. _____

12. _____

13. _____

14. _____

15. _____

16. _____

17. _____

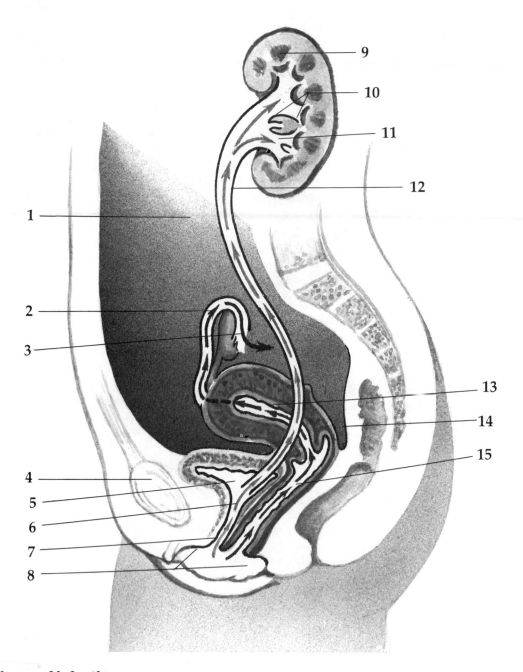

Pathway of infection

1. _____

2. _____

3. _____

4. _____

5. _____

6. _____

7. _____

8. _____

9. _____

10. _____

11. _____

12. _____

13. _____

14. _____

15. _____

Fetal c

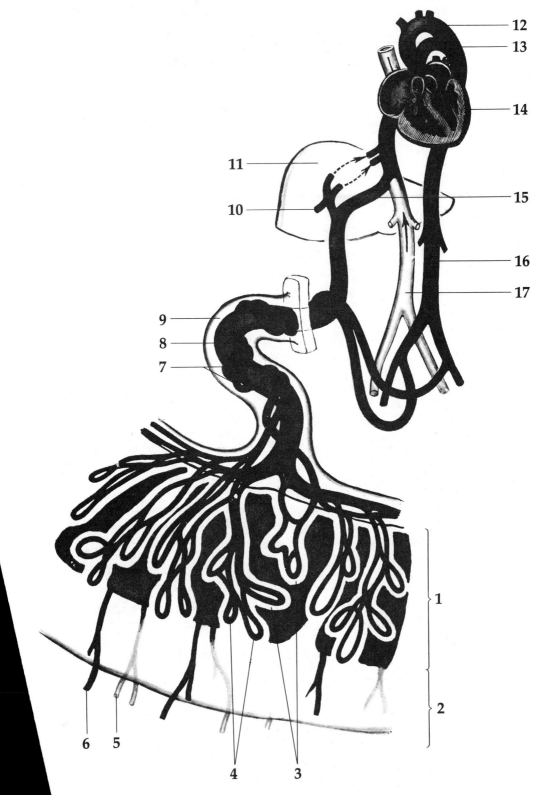

...irculation and the placenta

1. _____

2. _____

3. _____

4. _____

5. _____

6. _____

7. _____

8. _____

9. _____

10. _____

11. _____

12. _____

13. _____

14. _____

15. _____

16. _____

17. _____

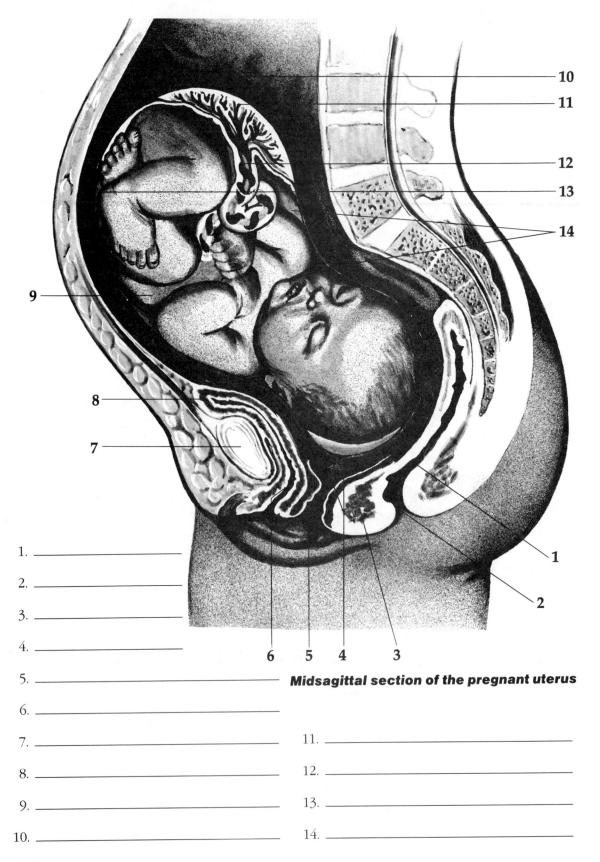

10

11

12

13

14

9

8

7

6   5   4   3

1

2

Midsagittal section of the pregnant uterus

1. _____

2. _____

3. _____

4. _____

5. _____

6. _____

7. _____

8. _____

9. _____

10. _____

11. _____

12. _____

13. _____

14. _____

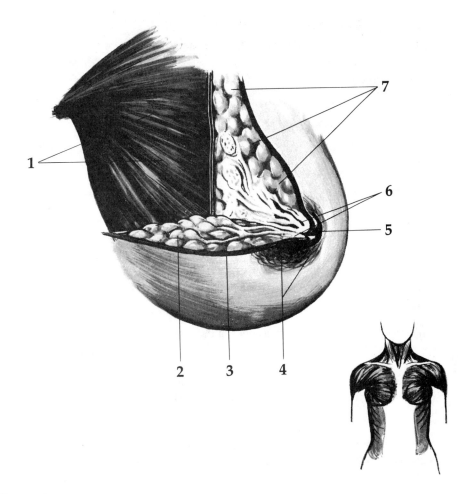

Section of breast

1. _____

2. _____

3. _____

4. _____

5. _____

6. _____

7. _____

V. Completion Exercise

Print the word or phrase that correctly completes each sentence.

1. The process of cell division that reduces the chromosome number by half is

    _____

2. The region of the inguinal canal, being somewhat weak, is frequently involved in the disorder called

    _____

3. The individual spermatozoon is very motile. It is able to move toward the ovum by the action of its

    _____

4. By the end of the first month of embryonic life, the beginnings of the extremities may be seen. These are four small swellings called

    _____

5. The cell formed by the union of a male sex cell and a female sex cell is called a

    _____

6. The science that deals with the development of the embryo is called

    _____

7. The bag of waters is a popular name for the membranous sac that encloses the fetus. The clear liquid that is released during labor is called

    _____

8. About once in every 80 to 90 births twins are born. Some of these twins occur as a result of two different ova being fertilized by two spermatozoa. Such twins are said to be

    _____

9. Some twins develop from a single zygote formed from a single ovum that has been fertilized by a single spermatozoon. The embryonic cells separate during early stages of development. These twins are described as

    _____

10. The medical term for the loss of an embryo or fetus before the 20th week of pregnancy is

    _____

11. The mammary glands of the female provide nourishment for the newborn through the secretion of milk; this is a process called

    _____

12. The hormone that causes ovulation in females is the same hormone that stimulates cells in the testes to produce testosterone. In females this hormone is called luteinizing hormone (LH); in males it is called

    _____

13. An infant born before the 37th week of gestation is considered immature or

    _____

14. The passage of the fetus through the cervical canal and the vagina to the outside takes place during the period of labor termed the

    _____

15. The use of artificial methods to prevent fertilization or implantation of the fertilized ovum is called _____

VI. Practical Applications

Study each discussion. Then print the appropriate word or phrase in the space provided.

Group A

The following patients were among those seen by a physician in a clinic that specialized in women's diseases.

1. Mrs. G complained of soreness and discomfort of the breasts following the birth of her baby. The physician diagnosed her disorder as inflammation of the breast, or _____

2. Mrs. K, age 43, thought that the bleeding she was now experiencing might be associated with early menopause. The physician examined her and found that a firm mass was present in the upper part of the uterus. This might be a myoma, which is commonly called a _____

3. Ms. C, age 16, said that she always felt irritable and depressed the week preceding her menses. A low-salt diet and medication were prescribed to make her more comfortable during this period of _____

4. Because of episodes of hemorrhage during her pregnancy, Mrs. M was hospitalized. There was a possibility that in Mrs. M's case the placenta was attached to the lower part of the uterus instead of the upper part. This condition is known as _____

5. Because of the seriousness of Mrs. M's condition, an operation was considered; this would provide for delivery through an incision made in the abdominal wall and the wall of the uterus. This operation is called a _____

6. Mrs. J, age 47, came to the clinic with complaints of hot flashes and irregular bleeding. Her history included infrequent ovulation as evidenced by her irregular menstrual cycles. The physician did a biopsy of the uterus as an aid in determining whether the bleeding was due to cancer of the lining, the _____

Group B

The following patients were seen by a physician in a urology clinic for men.

1. Mr. T, age 32, complained of the presence of a lump on one testis. He had discovered it during his regular self-examination which he did while showering. His physician ordered that further tests be done so he could determine whether the lump was malignant. The testes are contained in the external genital structure called the _____

2. Mr. C, age 37, requested that a surgical procedure be performed that would render him sterile. This procedure, in which a segment of the ductus (vas) deferens is removed, is called a(n) _____

3. Mr. K, age 28, showed the doctor a number of fluid-filled vesicles (blisters) on his external genitals, and asked what they were. The doctor made a diagnosis of the second most common venereal disease, one that is caused by a virus. It is called _____

4. Because Mr. K had not seen a physician for several years, a more complete examination was performed. Included was a blood test to determine whether the patient could be suffering from a systemic venereal disease caused by a spirochete. This disorder occurs in three stages and is called _____

22

Heredity and Hereditary Diseases

I. Overview

The scientific study of heredity is less than 2 centuries old. During the last few decades there have been brilliant and illuminating findings particularly related to the chromosomes and DNA; nevertheless, many mysteries remain and there is much more to be studied. Gregor Mendel was the first person to put the study of heredity on a scientific footing. He called attention to the independent units of hereditary influence, which he called *factors* and which we now call **genes**.

There are many thousands of genes in each cell nucleus. Each chromosome in the nucleus is composed of a complex molecule, DNA, and the genes are parts of this molecule. The chromosomes containing the genes are passed on to offspring through the **germ cells** formed in each parent by the process of **meiosis**. Genes direct the formation of **enzymes**, which in turn make possible the chemical reactions of metabolism. Defective genes, produced by **mutation**, may disrupt normal enzyme activity and result in **hereditary disorders** such as sickle cell anemia, albinism, and phenylketonuria. Some human traits are determined by a single pair of genes (one gene from each parent), but most are controlled by multiple pairs of genes acting together.

Genes may be classified as **dominant** or **recessive**. If one parent contributes a dominant gene, then all those offspring who receive that gene will show the trait, for example, certain types of dwarfism (achondroplasia), extra fingers (polydactyly), and drooping eyelids (ptosis). Traits carried by recessive genes may remain hidden for generations and be revealed only if they are contributed by both parents, for example, albinism, deaf-mutism (deafness from birth), microcephaly (abnormally small head), and sickle cell anemia. In some cases, treatment begun early may be helpful in preventing problems associated with the disorder. Genetic counseling should be sought by all potential parents whose relatives are known to have an inheritable disorder.

II. Topics for Review

A. Chromosomes
    1. Distribution of chromosomes to offspring
B. Genes and their functions
    1. Dominant and recessive genes
    2. Sex determination
    3. Sex-linked traits
    4. Multifactorial inheritance
    5. Factors influencing gene expression
C. Mutation
D. Genetic diseases
    1. Congenital vs. hereditary
E. Prevention and treatment
    1. Genetic counseling
    2. Fetal diagnoses
      a. Karyotype

III. Matching Exercises

Matching only within each group, print the answers in the spaces provided.

Group A

genes	congenital	DNA
chromosomes	life span	Mendel
dominant	carrier	

1. Among the traits influenced by heredity is a person's   _____

2. A condition that exists from birth is said to be   _____

3. Independent units of heredity are called   _____

4. A gene that is always expressed if present is described as   _____

5. The person who is credited with the first scientific investigation of heredity was an Austrian monk named   _____

6. A combination of thousands of genes is found in each of the nuclear structures known as   _____

7. The complex molecule that comprises the chemical compound of each chromosome is   _____

8. A person who has a recessive gene that is not expressed is called a(n)   _____

Group B

DNA	enzymes	hereditary
RNA	male	female
mutation	sex-linked	

1. Within the nucleus of each cell there is a genetic chemical that controls all the activities of the cell. This chemical is called   _____

2. Proteins are manufactured in the cytoplasm of the cell under the control of a genetic substance called _____

3. Traits transmitted by genes are _____

4. Proteins that promote chemical reactions within cells are _____

5. If a sperm cell carrying a Y chromosome fertilizes an ovum, the sex of the offspring is _____

6. Hemophilia is an example of a trait carried on the X chromosome and described as _____

7. A spontaneous chromosomal change is called a(n) _____

8. A person with two X chromosomes in each cell is a(n) _____

Group C

phenylketonuria   multifactorial   amniocentesis
karyotype   pedigree   mutagenic
albinism

1. A complete family history is a family tree or _____

2. Fetal samples removed by a chorionic villus biopsy are tested for genetic abnormalities. These tests include a study of the chromosomes by means of a(n) _____

3. Removal of fluid from the sac surrounding the fetus is a(n) _____

4. One inherited disorder of metabolism that involves an amino acid is _____

5. Persons who lack skin and hair pigment are especially susceptible to skin cancer. They have inherited the condition called _____

6. Most human traits are determined by two or more pairs of genes acting together in a form of inheritance described as _____

7. A chemical known to produce changes in the genetic material of cells is described as _____

IV. Completion Exercise

Print the word or phrase that most accurately completes each sentence.

1. A spontaneous change in a chromosome is called a(n) _____

2. A picture of the chromosomes arranged according to size and shape for the detection of genetic diseases is a(n) _____

3. In the disorder phenylketonuria, the amino acid phenylalanine cannot be metabolized because a protein is lacking in the cells. This protein functions as a(n) _____

4. The most frequent inherited metabolic disorder of the white race is _____

5. In Down's syndrome the cells have an extra _____

6. Inherited muscular disorders, in which the chief feature is progressively severe muscle weakness, are known as _____

7. The inherited condition in which the skin and hair color is strikingly white is _____

8. The number of chromosomes in each human germ cell is _____

V. Practical Applications

Study each discussion. Then print the appropriate word or phrase in the space provided.

Group A

These patients were seen in a pediatric clinic.

1. A rigid diet had been prescribed for infant M after it had been determined that he had an inherited disorder characterized by a lack of the enzyme required for metabolism of phenylalanine. Infant M's disorder is called _____

2. A black child about 4 years of age was brought to the hospital with a history of swelling and pain in the joints of his hands and feet. Among the studies done was one that revealed crescent-shaped red blood cells. It was determined that his condition was a hereditary one called _____

3. A white child, age 6, had a history of difficulty in breathing, a digestive disorder for which a pancreatic extract was prescribed, and frequent respiratory infections. These problems are typical of a hereditary disorder found mostly in caucasians, namely _____

4. Baby D's face was round; her eyes were close-set and slanted upward at the sides. The infant's condition, commonly called mongolism, is correctly termed _____

5. Young Mrs. D brought her 2-year-old son in so that his response to the prescribed diet and administration of the vitamin thiamine could be studied. In this hereditary disorder, the urine has such a peculiar odor that the disease is often called _____

Group B

In a university clinic studies of several hereditary disorders were under way. Read each discussion and respond in the space provided.

1. Mrs. Y, age 34, was pregnant a second time. Her first child had Down's syndrome, and she was apprehensive lest a second child would be similarly affected. A study of the fluid in the sac surrounding the embryo was ordered. This procedure is called a(n) _____

2. The cells from Mrs. Y's amniotic fluid were grown (cultured) and then stained for special study. A diagnostic indication of Down's syndrome was made, namely the presence of an extra _____

3. Mrs. G and her husband received genetic counseling. They had one normal child and one albino. They wanted to know whether there was a possibility that a third child would be an albino also. Neither parent was an albino, and they knew of no relatives who were. A trait that may be carried from generation to generation without appearing is said to be _____

4. Mr. H, age 25, was scheduled for a check-up and discussion of his diet and medication. He had a hereditary disorder, Wilson's disease, in which there is abnormal accumulation of the metallic ion _____

5. Mr. H was warned by his physician that continued disregard of his dietary prescription and prescribed medication would lead to damage to the largest organ of the abdomen, namely the _____

6. Mrs. G, age 26, had postponed starting a family because her grandfather had polycystic disease. Her mother, age 50, had no evidence of this disease, though an uncle of 40 years' age also had the disorder. To help Mrs. G make a decision about family planning, the genetic counselor prepared a detailed family history, called a _____

23

Medical Terminology

I. Overview

Medical terminology is the special language used worldwide by persons in health occupations. Many terms used today originated from Latin or Greek words, but some have come from more recent languages such as French and German. New words are being added constantly as discoveries are made and the need for words to describe them arises. Because scientific knowledge grows in different places at the same time, there may be two or even more terms in use that mean the same thing. Efforts are always being made, however, to standardize the terminology so that people all over the world will "speak the same language."

Not only does medical terminology have universal application, but there are also other advantages to its use. Often someone will say, "Why not use simple plain English?" The fact is that often there is no English word that is as precise as the scientific term. Moreover, one word or perhaps two can do the work of several sentences in descriptive force and accuracy. Medical terminology is a kind of shorthand; health workers should be so familiar with it that it becomes a "second language" with which they feel completely at ease.

Most medical words are made up of two or more parts. The main part is called the root, or the combining form to which the other parts are attached. These other parts include prefixes, which come before the root, and suffixes, which follow the root. If more than one root or combining form plus one or more other parts form the word, it is a compound word. Take the time to divide each medical word into its parts and then look up the meaning of each part, studying each as you go; you will soon add many words to your vocabulary. Then if you practice saying the word, vocalizing each syllable separately, you will feel at ease with medical terminology. Here are some examples:

1. *hypothermia* (hi″po-therm′me-ah): below-normal body temperature, usually due to excessive exposure to cold weather or icy water
   a. prefix (*hypo* = below normal)
   b. root (*therm* = heat)
   c. suffix (*ia* = condition or state of being)

2. *cardiopulmonary* (kar″de-o-pul′mo-nar-e): related to heart and lungs
   a. combining form (*cardio* = heart)
   b. root (*pulmonary* = related to the lungs)
3. *endometritis* (en″do-me-tri′tis): inflammation of the lining of the uterus
   a. prefix (*endo* = within)
   b. root (*metr* = related to the uterus)
   c. suffix (*itis* = inflammation)
4. *abdominohysterectomy* (ab-dom″i-no-his″ter-ek′to-me): removal of the uterus through the abdominal wall
   a. combining form (*abdomino* = belly or abdomen)
   b. root (*hyster* = uterus or womb)
   c. suffix (*ectomy* = removal of)

II. Topics for Review

1. common word roots and combining forms, such as

abdomin-, abdomino-	cleid-, cleido-	hyster-, hystero-
aden-, adeno-	cost-	idio-
arthr-, arthro-	cyt-, cyto-	lact-, lacto-
bio-	derm-, derma-	leuc- or leuk-, leuko-
carcin-, carcino-	enter-, entero-	neph-, nephro-
cardi-, cardio-	gastr-, gastro-	neuro-
cephal-, cephalo-	gynec-, gyneco-	psych-, psycho-
chole-	hem-, hema-, hemato-, hemo-	somat-, somato-
chondr-, chondro-	hist-, histio-	vas-, vaso-

2. common prefixes (at the beginnings of words), such as

a-, an-	inter-	neo-
ab-	intra-	semi-
circum-	macro-	sub-
contra-	mal-	trans-
di-	meg-, mega-, megalo-	tri-
ex-	met-, meta-	uni-
infra-	micro-	

3. common sufixes (word endings), such as

-algia	-geny	-otomy
-cele	-gram	-penia
-ectasis	-graph	-phagia, -phagy
-ectomy	-itis	-plasty
-esthesia	-logy, -ology	-ptosis
-ferent	-oma	-pnea
-gen	-ostomy	

4. common adjective endings, such as *-ous* and *-al*
5. common noun endings including *-us* and *-um*

III. Matching Exercises

Matching only within each group, print the answers in the spaces provided.

Group A

prefix	suffix	root
-ous, -al	-cele	a-, an-
compound word	combining form	

1. The foundation of a word is its _____

2. When two or more word foundations are used, the result is a(n) _____

3. The part of a word that precedes its foundations and changes its meaning is a(n) _____

4. A word ending used to change the meaning of the word foundation is a(n) _____

5. Examples of endings that indicate the adjective forms are _____

6. The word root followed by a vowel (to make pronunciation easier) is a(n) _____

7. A suffix that means a swelling or an enlarged space is _____

8. To denote absence or deficiency, begin the word with prefixes such as _____

Group B

psych-	abdomin-	-algia
cyt-	hema-	somat-
hist-	aden-	neo-

1. To indicate the belly area, use _____

2. A word root that means gland is _____

3. To show relationship to a cell, use _____

4. A word root for tissue is _____

5. Relationship to mind is shown by _____

6. A word part that means blood is _____

7. A word root that indicates body is _____

8. A prefix that means new is _____

9. A suffix that refers to pain is _____

Group C

arthr-	-itis	carcin-
-esthesia	infra-	-ptosis
meg-	-ectasis	-ectomy

1. A prefix that indicates excessively large is _____

2. A suffix that means downward displacement is _____

3. To indicate inflammation, end the word with _____

4. To show relationship to a joint, use _____

5. Dilation or expansion of a part is indicated by the word ending _____

6. Removal or destruction of a part is shown by the addition of _____

7. To refer to sensation, use the suffix _____

8. To indicate a cancer, use _____

9. To show that a part is located below, use the prefix _____

Group D

-us, -um	-ous, -al	-otomy
leuko-	-genic	-penia
-ostomy	erythr-	ab-
-ia, -ism		

1. To indicate producing, add _____

2. A lack of is shown by the suffix _____

3. A suffix that means incision into a part is _____

4. To indicate the formation of a new opening, use _____

5. To show that something is red, use the word part _____

6. To indicate that something is white, use _____

7. A prefix that means away from is _____

8. Endings that show the adjective form are _____

9. Noun forms of words may end in _____

10. Endings that mean state of are _____

Group E

Combine appropriate word parts from the list below and print the correct words in the blanks.

hemo-, hemat-, or hemato-   aden-   -logy
-costal   arthr-   oste- or osteo-
inter-   -lysis   carcin-
-ectomy   bio-   -cellular
-itis   -oma   intra-
cyto-

1. The study of living things is called   _____

2. Inflammation of a joint is known as   _____

3. Removal of a gland is called   _____

4. The scientific study of cells is known as   _____

5. The removal of a joint is called   _____

6. The space between the ribs is   _____

7. A cancerous tumor is called a(n)   _____

8. The study of blood and its constituents is _____

9. A tumor filled with blood is a(n)   _____

10. The word that means between cells is   _____

11. The word that means inside of or within a cell is   _____

12. A tumor made of glandular kinds of tissue is a(n)   _____

13. The dissolution or disintegration of blood cells (especially red blood cells) is called   _____

14. Destruction or dissolution of body cells may be called   _____

15. A firm tumor made of bone or bonelike tissue is known as a(n)   _____

Group F

Combine two or three word parts selected from the list below in order to correctly complete the following sentences. Print the appropriate words in the spaces provided.

electro-   micro-   trans-
cardio-   encephalo-   an-
-graph   -gram   -cyte
-emia   -orbital   -esthesia

1. A lack of red blood cells or hemoglobin is called   _____

2. An abnormally small red blood cell is a(n)   _____

3. A procedure performed through the bony eye socket is described by the word

_____

4. An x-ray film of the head (including the brain) is called a(n)

_____

5. The instrument that is used for producing a graphic tracing of electrical current in the heart muscle is a(n)

_____

6. A graphic record of electrical currents in the brain (brain waves) is called a(n)

_____

7. The instrument used for producing a graphic record of brain waves is the

_____

8. The tracing of electrical current in the heart muscle is called a(n)

_____

9. A lack of or loss of sensation (especially of pain) is designated

_____

IV. Completion Exercise

Print the word or phrase that correctly completes each sentence.

1. A prefix that indicates very small size is

_____

2. Words that refer to an instrument for recording end with

_____

3. The visible record produced by a recording instrument is indicated by a word ending in

_____

4. A prefix that denotes below or under is

_____

5. To show that something is outside or is sent outside, use the prefix

_____

6. To indicate that there are three parts to an organ, begin the word with the prefix

_____

7. A prefix that means across, through, or beyond is

_____

8. To indicate surgical molding, use the suffix

_____

9. The prefix that shows something is within the structure is

_____

10. The noun form of the adjective mucous is

_____

11. Suffixes that indicate the process of eating or swallowing include

_____

12. The suffix that means bladder or sac is

_____

13. The prefix that means away from is

_____

14. The suffix that means painful is _____

15. A suffix that means removal by surgery or other means is _____

16. A two-letter prefix that means absence or lack of is _____

17. A suffix that means dilation or expansion of a part is _____

18. An agent that produces or originates is indicated by the suffix _____

19. The word root for tissue is _____

20. Prefixes that mean excessively large include _____

V. Practical Applications

Study each discussion. Then print the appropriate word or phrase in the space provided.

1. Mr. A, age 74, was admitted because of weakness and inability to care for himself. The physician noted that Mr. A suffered from malnutrition. Later studies showed there was evidence of mal-union of a fracture of the right thigh bone. The prefix mal- means _____

2. Baby John was brought to the clinic by his observant mother because one of his eyes did not seem normal. The doctor noted that there was unilateral enlargement of the right pupil and that this uniocular condition would require laboratory investigation. The prefix uni- means _____

3. Mrs. B was admitted for treatment of an injured hand. The admitting intern noted that examination of the metacarpal bones showed possible fractures. The prefix meta- means _____

4. Ms. C was examined in the outpatient department. It was noted that she had circumoral pallor and that this pallor was circum-scribed. The prefix circum- means _____

5. Later examination of Ms. C showed ptosis (to'sis) of several abdominal organs, a condition called visceroptosis (vis-er-op-to'sis). The word part ptosis may also be used as a separate word. It means _____

6. Mrs. A was admitted for surgery because of bleeding from the uterus. One word root for uterus is metr-; another is _____

7. A first-aid measure everyone should be able to perform involves the heart and the lungs. This type of resuscitation is described by the compound word for heart and lungs, which is _____